TOURISM, CLIMATE CHANGE AND SUSTAINABILITY

This book addresses many of the key themes that are seen as challenges to achieve sustainability and to mitigate climate change impacts in the near future, as applied to the tourism sector. In particular it focuses on the economic drivers for growth in tourism as they relate to sustainable development, low-carbon travel and climate change impacts. A major feature is the integration of climate change and sustainability challenges, rather than treating them separately or with sustainability as an add-on. The first group of chapters addresses conceptual issues concerning the relationships between sustainability, climate change and tourism. The second section considers regional, national and international responses and initiatives, including those of agencies such as UNESCO World Network of Biosphere Reserves, and the UK's South West Tourism. The third part provides a range of investigative research, including topics such as air travel and coral reef tourism, and case studies from locations such as southern Africa, Scandinavia and the Pacific islands. Other research dimensions discussed in the book are drawn from Brazil, Hawaii, England, Australia and New Zealand. Overall, the book focuses on some of the most crucial challenges facing tourism in developed and developing countries.

Maharaj Vijay Reddy is senior lecturer in tourism at Bournemouth University, UK.

Keith Wilkes is Dean of the School of Services Management, Bournemouth University, UK.

TOURISM, CLIMATE CHANGE AND SUSTAINABILITY

Edited by Maharaj Vijay Reddy and Keith Wilkes

Routledge
Taylor & Francis Group

LONDON AND NEW YORK

First published 2013
by Routledge
2 Park Square, Milton Park, Abingdon, Oxon OX14 4RN

Simultaneously published in the USA and Canada
by Routledge
711 Third Avenue, New York, NY 10017

Routledge is an imprint of the Taylor & Francis Group, an informa business

British Library Cataloguing in Publication Data
A catalogue record for this book is available from the British Library

Library of Congress Cataloging-in-Publication Data
Tourism, climate change and sustainability / edited by Maharaj Vijay Reddy and Keith Wilkes.
p. cm.
Includes bibliographical references and index.
1. Tourism--Environmental aspects. 2. Sustainable tourism. 3. Climatic changes. I. Reddy, Maharaj Vijay, 1977- II. Wilkes, Keith, 1951–
G156.5.E58T678 2012
338.4'791--dc23
2012015128

ISBN13: 978-1-84971-422-8 (hbk)
ISBN13: 978-0-203-12895-4 (ebk)

Typeset in Bembo by Saxon Graphics Ltd, Derby

Printed and bound by CPI Group (UK) Ltd, Croydon, CR0 4YY

CONTENTS

List of figures and tables   ix
Foreword by Luigi Cabrini, UN World Tourism Organization   xiii
List of contributors   xv

PART I
Sustainability, climate change and tourism:
conceptual issues   1

1 Tourism and sustainability: transition to a green economy   3
   Maharaj Vijay Reddy and Keith Wilkes

2 Social representations of climate change: exploring the
   perceived links between climate change, the drive for
   sustainability and tourism   24
   Gianna Moscardo

3 Facilitating sustainable innovations for SMEs in the tourism
   industry: identifying factors of success and barriers to
   adoption in Australia   42
   Robyn Bushell and Bruce Simmons

4 Tourism industry responses to climate change in Hawaii:
   an exploratory analysis of knowledge and responses   58
   Shelly Rowell and Harold Richins

PART II
Responses and initiatives of regional, national and international agencies 79

5 Sustainable tourism development and climate change: opportunities in UNESCO biosphere reserves 81
Natarajan Ishwaran

6 Interpreting climate projections for tourism planning in South-West England 96
Emma Whittlesea and Bas Amelung

7 Climate change policy responses of Australian and New Zealand national governments: implications for sustainable tourism 117
Nadine Elizabeth White and Jeremy Buultjens

8 Key players in the environmental performance of tourism enterprises 134
David Leslie

PART III
Emerging techniques and research implications 153

9 Tourism sensitivity to climate change mitigation policies: lessons from recent surveys 155
Ghislain Dubois, Jean-Paul Ceron and Paul Peeters

10 The importance of visitor perceptions in estimating how climate change will affect future tourist flows to the Great Barrier Reef 173
Marine Ramis and Bruce Prideaux

11 Tourism adaptation to climate change in the South Pacific 189
Min Jiang, Terry DeLacy, Louise Munk Klint and Emma Wong

12 Scenarios of climate change and impacts on Brazilian tourism: a case study of the Brazilian north coast tourism region 209
Gilson Zehetmeyer Borda, Elimar Pinheiro do Nascimento, Helena Araújo Costa, João Paulo Faria Tasso and Leticia Ramos

13 The role of climate change in tourism development strategies: a sustainability perspective in tourism strategies in the Nordic countries 227
Kaarina Tervo-Kankare and Jarkko Saarinen

14 Tourism and climate change in southern Africa: sustainability and perceived impacts and adaptation strategies of the tourism industry to changing climate and environment in Botswana 243
Jarkko Saarinen, Wame Hambira, Julius Atlhopheng and Haretsebe Manwa

15 Contradictions in climate concern: performances at home and away 257
Scott A. Cohen and James E. S. Higham

Index 271

FIGURES AND TABLES

Figures

1.1   Sustainable development: shifts in the focus based on
global priorities   6

1.2   'Business as usual' projection of future carbon dioxide
emissions from tourism   10

1.3   Future carbon dioxide emissions from global tourism:
scenarios of mitigation potential in 2035   12

2.1   Overview of the Sustainability SR Research Programme   30

2.2   An abstract image of sustainability   31

2.3   The nature idyll image of sustainability   32

2.4   The contrasting or negative image of sustainability   33

3.1   Business engagement in the Gumnut program   44

3.2   Results and conclusions from non-Gumnut-participating
parks   45

5.1   Lanzarote Biosphere Reserve   87

6.1   10,000 TCI scores for one of the grid cells (1466), for the
month of July for the 2020s   101

6.2   Disaggregation of TCI scores in their five components for
Bournemouth (grid square 1700), in the baseline period of
the 1970s; a), 2020s; b) and 2050s; c), 50% probability level   103

6.3   a) Grid 1690, TCI score 2020s; b) Grid 1690, TCI
score 2050s   104

6.4   Grid 1690, TCI score variation   105

6.5   a) TCI 90%, July 2050; b) TCI 90%, August 2050   106

6.6   a) Cumulative probability values (10%, 50%, 90%) of the
      Beach Climate Index (BCI) for Bournemouth in the baseline
      (black), 2020s (light green) and 2050s (dark green);
      b) Cumulative probability values (10%, 50%, 90%) of the
      Beach Climate Index (BCI) for Penzance in the baseline
      (black), 2020s (light green) and 2050s (dark green)   108
6.7   a) Threshold Detector results for a heatwave in
      Bournemouth; b) Threshold Detector results for a heatwave
      in Penzance   109
6.8   a) Threshold Detector results for a heavy rainfall event in
      Bournemouth; b) Threshold Detector results for a heavy
      rainfall event in Penzance   110
9.1   Climate mitigation policies cause very long-haul trips to
      shift to the whole range of short to long haul ('weak' climate
      policy) up to a shift from medium to very long haul towards
      short haul only ('very strong' policy)   164
9.2   Climate policy scenarios   167
9.3   Evolution of emissions according to scenarios and economic
      context (overall Mediterranean basin)   168
10.1 Climate change impact model applied to the GBR   177
10.2 Respondents' comparison between the GBR and
      previously visited reefs   180
10.3 Comparison of satisfaction with Michaelmas Cay in the
      morning and afternoon surveys   182
10.4 Comparison between three reefs   184
10.5 Comparison between respondents with previous reef
      experience and first-time reef visitors   185
12.1 Map of Northeast Brazil   210
12.2 The impacts of climate change in the north-east of Brazil   214
12.3 Federal conservation unities and the main attractions of the
      north coast   215
12.4 Average monthly rainfall and approximate tourism
      seasonality   216
14.1 The case study places in Botswana. The study sites are
      located in two ecologically distinct places: Tshabong,
      situated in southwestern Botswana in Kgalagadi South
      District, and Maun, located in Ngamiland District in
      northern Botswana.   248

Tables

2.1	The twelve most frequently mentioned guidelines for sustainable living	36
3.1	SeaChange for Sustainable Tourism program model	48
3.2	Methods to overcome barriers to the adoption of environmental management systems by small to medium businesses	53
4.1	Categories of businesses' responses to sustainability	61
4.2	Respondents in the study by tourism sector	63
4.3	Responsibilities expected of government by participants	72
5.1	Sierra Gorda: carbon transactions	91
6.1	TCI scores for Grid Square 1690 for the 1970s and 50% probability level for 2020s and 2050s	102
6.2	Standard deviation in monthly TCI scores for the South-West in the 2020s and 2050s	107
8.1	Proportion of respondents with a written environmental policy	138
8.2	Membership of a range of organizations	140
8.3	Perceptions of the sector's impact and related aspects	141
8.4	Selection of indicative attitudes of owners/managers	141
8.5	Awareness of selected green initiatives	142
8.6	Involvement in selected green initiatives	142
8.7	Factors discouraging local produce purchasing	143
8.8	Sale of local products	144
8.9	Factors potentially influential to the introduction of environmentally friendly practices	145
8.10	Progress of enterprises towards sustainability	146
8.11	What is of importance to the owners?	147
9.1	Tourism eco-efficiency by destination	165
9.2	Scenarios for arrivals in La Reunion island: 2003, 2020 official strategy, and alternative vision for 2025	166
10.1	Analysed parameters	181
11.1	A snapshot of the policy analysis framework	194
11.2	The PT-CAP pacific tourism and climate change policy analysis framework	197
11.3	Sample of primary data collection in Fiji, Samoa and Vanuatu	198
11.4	Key regional climate-change policies in the Pacific	200
11.5	Policies and the corresponding adaptation types addressed in Fiji, Samoa and Vanuatu	202
11.6	Policies and the corresponding SIDS characteristics addressed in Fiji, Samoa and Vanuatu	202

11.7 Policies identified in PNG, Solomon Islands and Tonga 204
11.8 Policies and the corresponding adaptation types addressed
in PNG, Solomon Islands and Tonga 204
11.9 Policies and the corresponding SIDS characteristics addressed
in PNG, Solomon Islands and Tonga 205
12.1 Estimates on climate change impacts by geographic region
in Brazil 212
13.1 The consideration of climate change in the national tourism
strategies of Finland, Norway and Sweden 231
13.2 The consideration of climate change in regional tourism
strategies in Finland 233
13.3 A summary of climate-change-related opinions among
tourism stakeholders in Kittilä and Jämsä 235
15.1 Summary profile of interview programme participants 262

FOREWORD

Luigi Cabrini

DIRECTOR, SUSTAINABLE DEVELOPMENT OF TOURISM PROGRAMME

The tourism sector is especially sensitive to climate variability and change. Tourism in many regions relies on climate, which defines the length and quality of tourism seasons. Extreme events, such as heat waves, tropical cyclones, heavy precipitations or droughts, are likely to become more frequent and intense, and can play an important role in destination choice. Climate change also has a direct impact on the tourist resources at destinations. Tourism destinations are therefore faced with the necessity to develop adaptation strategies in order to maintain their economic viability and competitiveness. At the same time, activities related to tourism contribute to the emission of greenhouse gases (GHG), and tourism stakeholders should therefore participate in the global mitigation efforts.

To achieve an efficient and coordinated response to climate change requires a close cooperation between international organizations and all the stakeholders involved in tourism. Responding to this need and building on the outcomes of the 2003 Djerba conference, the Second International Conference on Climate Change and Tourism held in Davos, Switzerland, in October 2007, was a milestone event. The Davos Declaration acknowledges the reality of climate change as well as its strong connection with tourism. It recognizes the importance of tourism in the global challenge of climate change, and encourages the sector to progressively reduce its GHG emissions contribution through a long-term strategy within the UN framework. The importance for the tourism sector to identify consensus measures to address climate change without losing sight of all other priorities, especially poverty alleviation and tourism's contribution to the Millennium Development Goals, was also stressed by United Nations World Tourism Organization (UNWTO).

Within the so-called 'Davos Process' the initiatives conducted by the academic world to take actions to mitigate climate change and promote sustainability are of great importance. I wish therefore to commend the initiative taken by the

International Centre for Tourism and Hospitality Research (ICTHR), Bournemouth University, to organize the forthcoming conference under the theme 'Tourism, Climate Change and Sustainability', to be held in September 2012. This event will further elaborate and advance on the outcomes of the previous conference on the same topic held in 2009, where experts and attendees had an opportunity to exchange their knowledge. This publication addresses the main issues relating to climate change, tourism sustainability and green economy, and is therefore an important input for tourism and environment stakeholders.

United Nations World Tourism Organisation
Madrid

CONTRIBUTORS

Bas Amelung is an assistant professor of environmental systems analysis at Wageningen University, the Netherlands. His research focuses on the interrelationships between tourism and the environment. He has published around 20 papers on related issues in international journals. Between 1999 and 2008, Bas worked at the International Centre for Integrated Assessment and Sustainable Development (ICIS) at Maastricht University. In 2006 he received a PhD for his thesis on climate change and tourism.

Julius Atlhopheng is a senior lecturer in the Department of Environmental Sciences, at the University of Botswana. He has a keen interest in the areas of applied geomorphology, water resources, climate change and desertification. Additionally, areas of environmental sustainability, piloting of technologies appropriate for sustainable land management (SLM) and indigenous knowledge systems in resources management have been the focus of his service areas.

Gilson Zehetmeyer Borda is a professor and coordinator of research lines on climate change, sustainability and tourism at the Centre for Excellence in Tourism (CET), University of Brasília, Brazil. He holds a PhD in economic sociology, was a researcher at the Laboratory for Tourism and Sustainability Studies (LETS/CDS) and is currently a postdoctoral researcher at the Centre for Sustainable Development (CDS – University of Brasília). He has led and participated in Brazilian and international sustainable tourism development projects.

Robyn Bushell is a professor in the Institute for Culture and Society, University of Western Sydney, Australia, and researches values-based planning and the relationship between community well-being, tourism and visitor planning, and heritage management. She works with a range of national and international tourism and heritage bodies.

Jeremy Buultjens teaches economics in the Business School at Southern Cross University. In the past he has taught a range of units from industrial relations through to tourism planning and indigenous tourism. His research interests include indigenous entrepreneurship, regional development, tourism in protected areas, and employment relations. He is also the managing editor of the *Journal of Economic and Social Policy*.

Scott A. Cohen is a senior lecturer in tourism management at the University of Surrey. His research takes an interdisciplinary approach to understanding lifestyle, identity and mobility across contexts of tourism and leisure and mitigating tourism's climate impacts through behaviour change. He has published in a range of academic journals, including *Annals of Tourism Research*, *Tourism Management*, *Leisure Studies*, *Tourist Studies* and *Current Issues in Tourism*.

Helena Araújo Costa is a professor and researcher at the School of Business, University of Brasília, Brazil. She holds a PhD in sustainable development and a Master's degree in tourism and hospitality. Currently she coordinates the Laboratory for Tourism and Sustainability Studies (LETS) at the Centre for Sustainable Development (CDS – University of Brasília). She has also published in the major academic tourism journals in Brazil and has experience in tourism development projects.

Jean-Paul Ceron is a social scientist (with initially a business school training) who has been working for three decades on environmental issues (mainly in the French context). He now works at the University of Limoges. The relationship between tourism and the environment, tourism and sustainable development, and more specifically tourism and climate change are now his main fields of interest.

Terry DeLacy is a professor in sustainable tourism and environmental policy at Victoria University. He was previously CEO of the Australian government established, national Sustainable Tourism Co-operative Research Centre, and dean of the Agricultural and Natural Resources faculty at the University of Queensland. His research area is in environmental policy, specializing in natural resources, sustainable tourism, climate change and most recently destinations in the emerging green economy.

Ghislain Dubois is associate professor at the University of Versailles (France) and director of Tourism Environment Consultants (TEC www.tec-conseil.com). He was part of UNEP-UNWTO-WMO on tourism and climate change, and a contributing author to the IPCC's *Fourth Assessment Report*. His field of expertise lies in climate policies, on the mitigation of adaptation side, with a special interest in climate services, low-carbon consumption, sustainable tourism and transport, and regional adaptation strategies.

Wame Hambira is an environmental economist and a lecturer in the Department of Environmental Science at the University of Botswana. Currently she is a PhD student at the University of Oulu, Finland, and she holds an MSc in environmental economics from the University of York, UK. Her main research interests include resource valuation, environmental impact assessment, the economics of water resources management, climate change, and sustainable tourism and policy.

James E. S. Higham is head of the Department of Tourism, School of Business, University of Otago (New Zealand). His current research explores perceptions of climate change and tourist behaviour change in New Zealand's key European markets. Specifically this programme of research addresses evolving attitudes towards tourist aeromobility, particularly air travel to extreme long-haul destinations such as New Zealand.

Natarajan Ishwaran is the director of UNESCO Division of Ecological and Earth Sciences, Paris, and secretary of the Man and the Biosphere (MAB) Programme. He has negotiated UN treaties on heritage and the environment with many governments. Since 1986, he has held several key posts within UNESCO, including chief of the Natural section for UNESCO's World Heritage Centre. He gained undergraduate and Master's degrees from Peradeniya University, Sri Lanka, and a PhD from Michigan State University, USA. He is currently a visiting professor at the University of Queensland, Australia.

Min Jiang is a research fellow at the Centre for Tourism and Services Research, Victoria University. Holding a PhD in environmental law from Macquarie University, Australia, she has extensive research, policy, project and educational experience in environmental law and sustainable tourism in the Asia Pacific. Her main research interests include tourism adaptation to climate change, tourism and the green economy, sustainable use of natural resources, and water governance.

Louise Munk Klint is a PhD candidate and research associate at the Centre for Tourism and Services Research, Victoria University. She holds a Bachelor of Tourism with Distinction and a Master of Social Science with Distinction from University of Western Sydney. With a focus on dive tourism in Vanuatu, her current research explores the factors that make tourism vulnerable and/or resilient to climate change impacts, further proposing adaptation strategies to build the resilience.

David Leslie has just retired from his long-standing position as reader in tourism at Glasgow Caledonian University, UK, where he was instrumental in the development of tourism studies following on from the introduction of the tourism degree at Leeds Metropolitan University, UK. The recurrent theme in his scholarly activity and research has been tourism and the environment, which is manifest in a diverse range of his publications spanning two decades.

Haretsebe Manwa is an associate professor and programme leader of tourism at North West University in South Africa. Previously she worked at the University of Botswana where she was a senior lecturer, head of the Department of Tourism and Hospitality Management and the internal programme leader in the International Tourism Research Centre. Her research interests include service quality, pro-poor tourism, tourist behaviour, cultural tourism, and tourism and climate change.

Gianna Moscardo is a professor in the School of Business at James Cook University. She joined the university academic staff in 2002 and was the associate dean of research for the Faculty of Law, Business and Creative Arts from 2008 to 2011. She is currently a senior fellow in residence at the Cairns Institute at JCU. She has published extensively on tourism and related areas, with more than 150 refereed papers or book chapters, and based on this profile was elected to the World Tourism Organization's International Academy for the Study of Tourism Scholars in 2005.

Elimar Pinheiro do Nascimento is a sociologist, political scientist, associate professor and ex-director of the Centre for Sustainable Development at the University of Brasília, Brazil. She is a coordinator of research lines on sustainability and tourism, and economy, environment and business. She has a degree in sociology from the Ecole Praticque des Hautes Etudes, a PhD in sociology from the Université of Paris V (René Descartes), and a postdoctoral qualification in social sciences from EHESS – the Ecole des Hautes Etudes en Sciences Sociales of Paris.

Paul Peeters is an associate professor specializing in the impacts of tourism on the environment and specifically on climate change. His publications cover a wide range of topics like global and regional tourism and climate scenarios, system dynamic approaches to tourism, tourism transport mode choice and modal shift, policy making and transport technological developments. He is responsible for the NHTV Centre for Sustainable Tourism and Transport and a group of six researchers.

Bruce Prideaux is professor of marketing and tourism management at James Cook University, Australia. He heads a team of eight PhD researchers and a number of visiting scholars, and is actively engaged in climatic change research with a particular interest in its impacts on coral reef systems and rainforests. He has authored over 200 journal articles, book chapters and conference papers on a range of issues related to tourism.

Marine Ramis is an environmental engineer, and graduated from the National Institute of Applied Sciences, France in 2010. She undertook a six-month internship at James Cook University with Professor Bruce Prideaux, studying the impacts of climate change on tourism on the Great Barrier Reef. She specializes in marine and coastal environmental management, dealing with issues such as climate change, port dredging and treated water disposal. She currently works for COPRAMEX, a French engineering consulting firm.

Leticia Ramos works as a researcher in psychodynamics at the psychodynamic and clinical laboratory (LPCT-IP), Brazil. She is currently attending the University of Brasília's Master's program on social, work and organizational psychology and she has a postgraduate qualification in executive coaching from the Integrated Coaching Institute, Brazil. Her professional life has been dedicated to human development and teaching and learning processes in binational centres, multinationals and national organizations.

Maharaj Vijay Reddy is senior lecturer at the School of Tourism, Bournemouth University, UK. He completed his Master's at the Pondicherry Central University in India and his PhD in human geography at the University of Exeter, UK. His research interests include sustainable development, climate change, green economy, small island developing states, heritage and natural disasters. He has published widely and has carried out several projects in the interlinked aspects of tourism commissioned by organizations including UNESCO Paris. He has also been associated with projects and events supported by the European Commission and the British Academy.

Harold Richins is professor and dean of the Faculty of Adventure, Culinary Arts and Tourism at Thompson Rivers University in British Columbia, Canada. He holds a PhD from James Cook University in Australia and BS and MS degrees from University of Oregon. He has recently served as chair of the graduate program in the School of Travel Industry Management at the University of Hawaii. He has served on numerous community, environmental and tourism boards, particularly with a focus on regional tourism destinations, and has published widely on the subject.

Shelly Rowell is the sustainability manager for Sydney Opera House, Australia. She is a sustainability practitioner in the arts and tourism sectors, specializing in strategy, design and stakeholder engagement. She has also held senior management and strategy positions in the tourism sector. Her article in this book is the result of a major research project for a Master's program which she undertook with the support from the East West Centre, University of Hawaii Manoa, and University of Technology, Sydney.

Jarkko Saarinen is Professor of Human Geography at the University of Oulu, Finland, and research affiliate, School of Tourism and Hospitality, Faculty of Management, University of Johannesburg. He is also external program leader in the International Tourism Research Centre (ITRC), University of Botswana. His research interests include tourism development and sustainability, tourism and climate change, indigenous tourism, and the construction of the ideas of nature and local culture in tourism.

Bruce Simmons is an adjunct professor in the School of Natural Sciences, University of Western Sydney. He has many years of experience working in state government environmental management and regulation, with particular emphasis on ecological and social issues relating to water use. In recent years he has worked with the tourism industry to develop educational models for sustainable practices.

João Paulo Faria Tasso is a PhD student and has a Master's degree in sustainable development from the Centre for Sustainable Development (CDS – University of Brasília). He works as researcher in the Laboratory for Tourism and Sustainability Studies (LETS). He has experience in tourism development projects and has coordinated projects on community-based production associated with tourism for the Brazilian Ministry of Tourism, in Jericoacoara National Park (Ceará) and in Delta do Parnaíba (Piauí). He is also a consultant at the Sustainable Brazil Environmental Institute (IABS).

Kaarina Tervo-Kankare is a PhD student in the Department of Geography at the University of Oulu, Finland. Her research focuses on human–environment relations and tourism geographies, especially on the relation of tourism and climate change and the adaptation strategies of the industry.

Nadine Elizabeth White has a travel industry and wine industry background and is now a researcher at Southern Cross University in New South Wales, Australia. She is currently completing her PhD investigating local government climate change adaptation planning and tourism planning in New South Wales. Her research interests are the interrelationship between tourism and climate change, adaptive planning for climate change, ecotourism, indigenous tourism, sustainable tourism and destination management.

Emma Whittlesea is a PhD student at the University of Plymouth. Emma has thirteen years of experience working on sustainable development initiatives. In the last five years she has focused on tourism and climate change, working as a sustainability strategist for South West Tourism. She has developed climate change mitigation and adaptation tools for tourism, working with businesses and destination managers at a regional and local level. She chaired the Climate South West Tourism Sector Group and is undertaking applied research in this area.

Keith Wilkes is Dean of the School of Tourism at Bournemouth University. He has been very actively involved in the development of tourism education in the UK over the past twenty-five years. He is a fellow of both the Royal Geographical Society and the Tourism Society. His research focuses on tourism development, visitor attractions, heritage management and tourism education.

Emma Wong is a lecturer in tourism and event management at University of Surrey, UK. She has more than ten years of experience in teaching and conducting research in tourism in Asia Pacific and Europe. Her main research interests are destination development, tourism adaptation to climate change, and tourism policy. She received her PhD from the School of Marketing, University of New South Wales, Australia.

PART I

Sustainability, climate change and tourism

Conceptual issues

1

TOURISM AND SUSTAINABILITY
Transition to a green economy

Maharaj Vijay Reddy and Keith Wilkes

Introduction

Sustainability in the context of tourism has been of interest to researchers for several decades whereas climate change in relation to tourism has been debated largely only since the late 1990s (although some sources prior to this period exist). Generally, sustainability issues are given relatively less focus when the two most recent decades are compared, and the need for clearer and stronger inclusion within the current climate change discussion has been highlighted. Climate change issues have been largely given focus in the tourism literature since 2000, though more adaptation and mitigation measures are needed to reduce the contribution of the tourism industry to emissions, estimated to be from 5 to 14 per cent of emissions if measured as radioactive forcing (Simpson et al. 2008). Increased coverage of climate change topics is evident not only in tourism but also in research related to mainstream environment and natural resources. For example, out of the 1,961 World Bank projects with an 'environment and natural resources management' theme, the percentage of projects with a pollution and environmental health theme has remained flat or declined, whereas the percentage of projects with sub-themes of biodiversity and/or climate change have recorded a threefold increase (10 per cent to almost 30 per cent) between 1983 and 2008 (Tallis et al. 2008). Several of the recent international conferences encourage researchers, planners and policy makers to approach and tackle sustainability and climate change aspects together.

The First International Forum on 'Sustainability, Climate Change and Tourism', organized at the Bournemouth University in 2009 emphasized the need to approach climate change and sustainability aspects for the long-term viability of the tourism industry. Scott (2011: 28) also stressed 'how tourism responds to climate change is absolutely critical to sustainability of tourism and should the sector retreat from engagement in climate change, it would be to its substantial detriment'. In the light of the green economy debate, it has become essential to look at these issues as two sides of the same coin.

This edited book endeavours to link some of the current research, upcoming methods and research directions in these fields. This chapter aims to review the key international conferences and global agreements that have been shaping our ideas in this direction whilst analysing the transition of sustainability concept since Stockholm 1972 to the forthcoming Rio+20 (June 2012), leading to the green economy approach of low carbon and poverty reduction measures. The final sections of this chapter outline the content of the book that has been arranged to publish some of the recent conceptual debates, responses of organizations at all levels and the emerging techniques and research implications.

Sustainable development: shifts in the focus based on global priorities and our understanding of the concept

From 1972 to 2012, the focus of the sustainability paradigm has shifted based on the global necessities (see Figure 1.1). As debated by many, the concept of sustainable development evolved through the convergence of economic development theory and environmentalism. Environmentalism emerged in the late 19th century when a change in perception saw people valuing the spiritual properties of the landscape over the material, and the national parks began to be established in Australia and North America (Hardy and Beeton 2001; Hardy, Beeton and Pearson 2001). The nascent environmentalism of the 1960s and 1970s was reflected in specific concerns about the environmental consequences of tourism development at that time (Dowling 1992). Authors such as the contributors to Butler and Jenkins, (1998), Hall and Lew (1998), Miller and Twining-Ward (2005), Lane (2009) and Weaver (2006, 2009) have highlighted the evolution of sustainability concept and its application in tourism.

In many destinations worldwide, tourism was found to be in conflict with the environment, along with detrimental social impacts. The concepts of ecological limits, resource use and management and carrying capacities have been found to be appropriate to apply in tourism (Sharpley and Telfer, 2002), before tourism's inclination towards sustainability. Research into the impacts of tourism (well documented by Mathieson and Wall 1989, 2006 and Mason 2003, while Lea 1988, Harrison 1992, 2001, and Mowforth and Munt 1998, 2003 explored them with reference to less-developed countries) has embraced the well-established academic pursuit of examining, defining and assessing the applicability of mainstream concepts of sustainable development to the specifications of tourism and recreation (Sharpley and Telfer 2002). 'As with many other forms of economic activity, tourism has become inextricably linked with the concept of sustainable tourism and much attention has been paid to "sustainable tourism"' (Hall and Lew, 1998: 7). At the same time, as Hardy and Beeton (2001: 169) commented on the global economy scenario of the 1960s and 1970s, 'the failure of economic models to stimulate growth in developing countries and alleviate poverty highlighted the need for alternative economic development models, which would take into account the ecological consequences of economic expansion'. Although there were improvements in finding new economic and environmental development methodologies, there was a growing concern for a new approach, which finally emerged as the 'sustainable development' concept. The first UN Conference on Human Environment 1972 in Stockholm had first discussed the fundamental pillars of sustainability (Figure 1.1).

The 1972 Stockholm Conference

The Stockholm Conference proclaimed the need for the protection and improvement of the human environment on which the well-being of peoples and economic development throughout the world is centred. It first raised awareness that social well-being, economic development and environmental conservation are the three pillars of sustainability (UNEP 2012). *The Limits to Growth* report (Meadows et al. 1972) for the Club of Rome (a global think tank established in 1968) explored a number of scenarios, and stressed the choices open to society to reconcile sustainable progress with environmental constraints. With its focus on long-term vision and provocative scenarios, the report sold more than 12 million copies in some 30 languages worldwide, creating a high global impact at several levels, according to the Club of Rome website (www.clubofrome.org). The later setting-up of the International Union for the Conservation of Nature and the publication of its *World Conservation Strategy* in 1982 increased global attention to biodiversity conservation. In view of the ever-growing threat to environmental health and the lack of progress towards sustainability, the IUCN works towards achieving biodiversity conservation and to initiate programmes of action.

The 1987 Brundtland Commission

By the late 1980s sustainable development was affirmed as the solution to global challenges, and the concept gained real meaning and definition after the publication of a report on *Our Common Future* in 1987 by the World Commission on Environment and Development (also widely known as Brundtland Commission since it was headed by Gro Harlem Brundtland, then Norwegian prime minister) (United Nations 1987). It firmly defined sustainable development as development that meets the needs of the present without compromising the ability of future generations to meet their own needs (Aronsson 2000). The Brundtland Commission report submitted to the General Assembly of the United Nations addressed most common concerns, including symptoms and causes of a threatened future; the links between environment, development, population and human resources; the signs of food security crisis and challenges; extinction patterns and trends of species and ecosystems; the dilemma and upcoming problems of energy choices (fossil, wood, nuclear and renewable) and conservation measures; sustaining industrial growth – producing more with less; growth of cities and challenges; managing the commons (oceans, space and Antarctica) and global cooperation: peace, security, institutional and legal challenges.

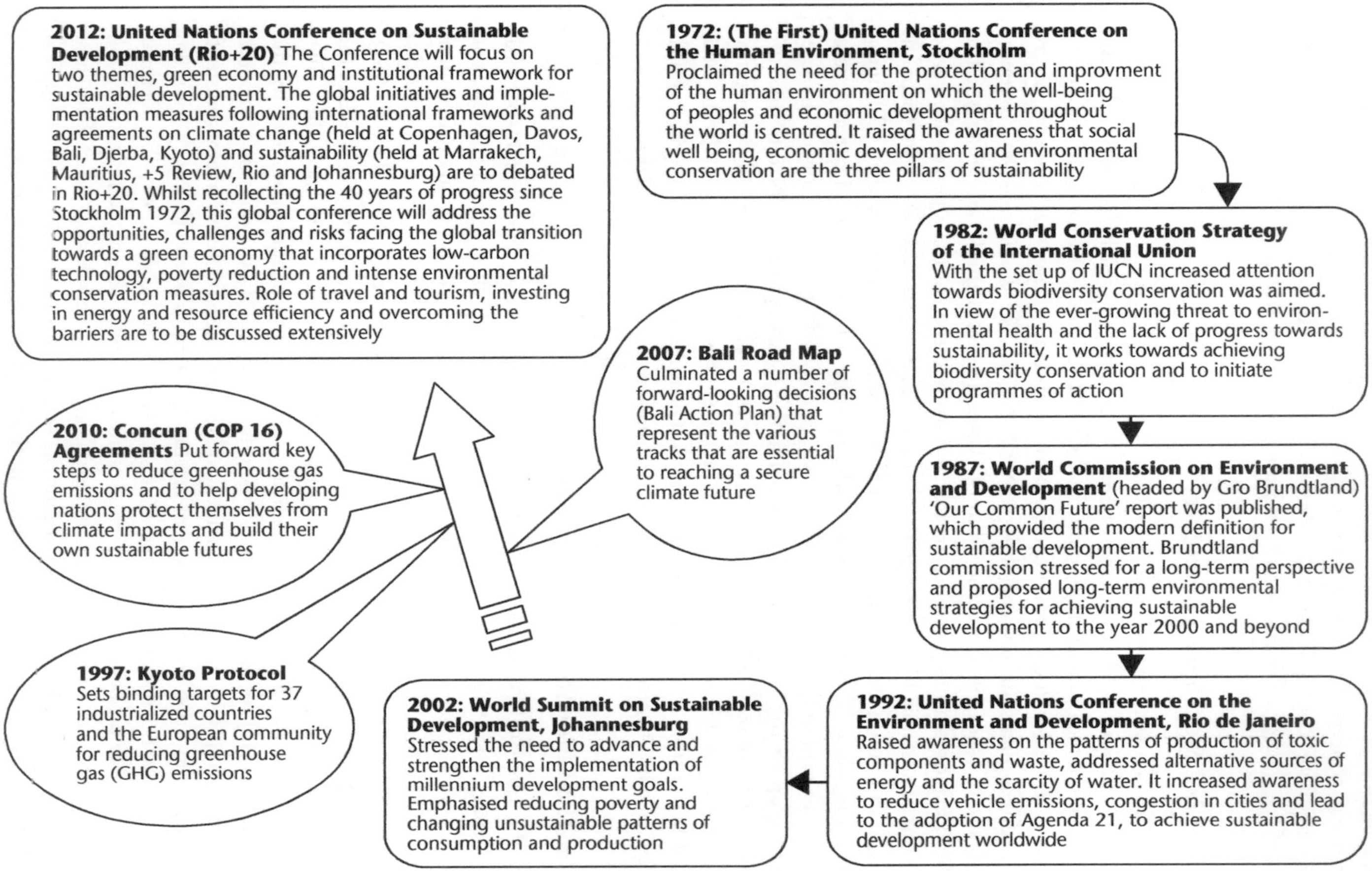

2012: United Nations Conference on Sustainable Development (Rio+20) The Conference will focus on two themes, green economy and institutional framework for sustainable development. The global initiatives and implementation measures following international frameworks and agreements on climate change (held at Copenhagen, Davos, Bali, Djerba, Kyoto) and sustainability (held at Marrakech, Mauritius, +5 Review, Rio and Johannesburg) are to debated in Rio+20. Whilst recollecting the 40 years of progress since Stockholm 1972, this global conference will address the opportunities, challenges and risks facing the global transition towards a green economy that incorporates low-carbon technology, poverty reduction and intense environmental conservation measures. Role of travel and tourism, investing in energy and resource efficiency and overcoming the barriers are to be discussed extensively

1972: (The First) United Nations Conference on the Human Environment, Stockholm
Proclaimed the need for the protection and improvement of the human environment on which the well-being of peoples and economic development throughout the world is centred. It raised the awareness that social well being, economic development and environmental conservation are the three pillars of sustainability

1982: World Conservation Strategy of the International Union
With the set up of IUCN increased attention towards biodiversity conservation was aimed. In view of the ever-growing threat to environmental health and the lack of progress towards sustainability, it works towards achieving biodiversity conservation and to initiate programmes of action

1987: World Commission on Environment and Development (headed by Gro Brundtland) 'Our Common Future' report was published, which provided the modern definition for sustainable development. Brundtland commission stressed for a long-term perspective and proposed long-term environmental strategies for achieving sustainable development to the year 2000 and beyond

1992: United Nations Conference on the Environment and Development, Rio de Janeiro
Raised awareness on the patterns of production of toxic components and waste, addressed alternative sources of energy and the scarcity of water. It increased awareness to reduce vehicle emissions, congestion in cities and lead to the adoption of Agenda 21, to achieve sustainable development worldwide

2007: Bali Road Map
Culminated a number of forward-looking decisions (Bali Action Plan) that represent the various tracks that are essential to reaching a secure climate future

2002: World Summit on Sustainable Development, Johannesburg
Stressed the need to advance and strengthen the implementation of millennium development goals. Emphasised reducing poverty and changing unsustainable patterns of consumption and production

2010: Concun (COP 16) Agreements Put forward key steps to reduce greenhouse gas emissions and to help developing nations protect themselves from climate impacts and build their own sustainable futures

1997: Kyoto Protocol
Sets binding targets for 37 industrialized countries and the European community for reducing greenhouse gas (GHG) emissions

FIGURE 1.1 Sustainable development: shifts in the focus based on global priorities

The 1992 Earth Summit

The 1992 United Nations Conference on the Environment and Development was the next major event, organized in Rio de Janeiro following the Brundtland Commission recommendations. The Earth Summit webpage (United Nations 1997) summarizes that the Rio summit adopted three major agreements aimed at changing the traditional approach to sustainable development:

- Agenda 21 — a comprehensive programme of action for global action in all areas of sustainable development
- the Rio Declaration on Environment and Development — a series of principles defining the rights and responsibilities of states
- the Statement of Forest Principles — a set of principles to underlie the sustainable management of forests worldwide.

In addition, two legally binding conventions aimed at preventing global climate change and the eradication of the diversity of biological species: the UN Framework Convention on Climate Change and the Convention on Biological Diversity (United Nations 1997).

The role of tourism for sustainable development was realized more after the 1992 Rio summit, with recommendations for the tourism industry to adopt the Agenda 21 principles. Bosselman, Peterson and McCarthy (1999: 113) stated that although the sustainable development concept 'grew, out of research, concerning the rapidly escalating world population, industrial expansion, and the related growth in pollution', attention towards its specific implications for tourism were discussed only in 1995. Soon after the 1992 Rio summit, the 1995 Lanzarote Conference (held in the Canary Islands, and attended by a large group of delegates from various governments, decision makers and tourism experts) drafted two documents 'The sustainable tourism plan of action' and 'Charter for sustainable tourism', that outlined 'how tourism should be controlled so that it can be included in the global strategy for sustainable development with special strategies and proposals for action' (Aronsson 2000). Subsequently sustainable tourism was pursued by a wide range of researchers at all levels in many countries, and is often disseminated in the *Journal of Sustainable Tourism*. According to Weaver (2006), the 1996 Bellagio Conference also discussed issues associated with tourism sustainability, specifically as its principles stressed the need to have a 'clear performance for comprehensive model in advocating a holistic, systems-based approach of sustainability that takes an adequate spatial and temporal scope into account' (p. 31), something that was examined by several researchers.

The 2002 Earth Summit 2

These global summits also imparted varied opinions about the changing perspectives of sustainable development based on global priorities. For instance, the 2002 World

Summit on Sustainable Development in Johannesburg (dubbed the Earth Summit 2) had broad objectives to reach to a range of goals on poverty eradication, health issues, preserving the environment and achieving a political declaration aimed at reinvigorating political commitment to sustainable development. The summit also assessed the global situation and progress in implementing the international agreements adopted at Rio in 1992 and Stockholm in 1972. The summit brought together tens of thousands of participants, including heads of state and government, national delegates and leaders from non-governmental organizations (NGOs), businesses and other major groups to focus the world's attention and direct action toward meeting difficult challenges, including improving people's lives and conserving our natural resources in a world that is growing in population, with ever-increasing demands for food, water, shelter, sanitation, energy, health services and economic security (United Nations 2006). Without doubt the summit gave more emphasis to the Millennium Development Goals. From the tourism point of view, the summit emphasized that sustainability of tourism should be a priority due to its potential contribution to poverty alleviation and environmental protection in critically endangered ecosystems (Fennell 2003).

Sustainable tourism – application by scholars

Besides the growing synergy between sustainable development and sustainable tourism, the debates on contemporary tourism planning approaches by various authors (e.g. Cooper et al. 1998, Butler et al. 1998, Butler and Boyd 2000, Hall 2000) started to incorporate sustainability principles more strongly. Resource management techniques and tourism planning approaches are now expected to incorporate the objectives of 'equity, sustainability, efficiency, and resilience' (Bosselman et al. 1999: 17), in order to manage tourism growth and the viability of destinations. According to Holden (2000: 172), 'Coccossis and Parpairis (1996) and Hunter (1996), identify four forms of sustainable tourism, oriented towards the viability of the tourism industry' based on the primary concerns: tourism imperative, product-led tourism, environment-led tourism and neotenous tourism. Many authors, including Pigram (1992), Bramwell et al. (1996), Mowforth and Munt (1998) and Weaver (2006) also discussed the different elements and perspectives of sustainability in the context of tourism. Hall (2000) put forward five approaches of tourism planning, with the final spectrum specifically focusing on sustainability. Besides these, introducing the concept of 'social democracy' in sustainable tourism planning (Burns 2004) are some of the debates in the last decade that gave enhanced dimensions to sustainability. In terms of measuring the diversified impacts of tourism, the 1996 publication of the 'core indicators' by the World Tourism Organization (UNWTO 1996, see also Manning et al. 1996) led to many projects worldwide developing, assessing and monitoring the impact of tourism with the use of sustainability indicators (e.g. Dymond 1997, Miller 2001, Twining-Ward and Butler 2002, Dubois 2005, Choi and Sirakaya 2006, Reddy 2008, Roberts and Tribe 2008). Recently there has been widespread acknowledgement (e.g. Miller et al. 2010) that improving consumer and public understanding of tourism impacts and behavioural changes is very much the next step in achieving sustainable tourism.

Climate change and sustainability: distinct but complex, contested and interrelated concepts

The establishment of the Intergovernmental Panel on Climate Change (IPCC) in 1988, the UN Framework Convention on Climate Change (UNFCCC) international treaty that followed the 1992 Rio Summit and the Kyoto Protocol adopted in 1997 led to with several negotiations and useful measures to reduce greenhouse gases, fight global warming and prevent dangerous anthropogenic interference with the climate system. The implications of climate change have increasingly been addressed in tourism literature since the 2000s as global warming poses severe challenges for developed and developing nations. These in turn will affect destinations and the tourism industry as a whole, as has been established by a wide range of sources. For instance, Gossling and Hall (2006), Peeters (2007), UNWTO (2008), and Simpson et al. (2008, 2010) discussed the impacts of climate change on many destinations, provided climate scenarios and estimated vulnerable hotspots. These challenges will have very significant implications for the small island developing states (Simpson et al. 2009, Kelman and Gaillard 2010). However, the global initiatives of UN organizations since IPCC somewhat moved the climate change debates and our immediate attention out of the mainstream sustainability sphere.

International conferences starting from the First International Conference on Climate Change and Tourism held in Djerba (2003) and a second conference organized in Davos (2007) specifically addressed climate change issues in relation to tourism. Some of the UNWTO reports on this topic (e.g. UNWTO 2008, collated by researchers including Daniel Scott, Murray Simpson, Bas Amelung, Paul Peeters and Susanne Becken) reveal the carbon contribution from tourism, including accommodation, car and air transport and other activities (see Figure 1.2). As a result of the shifts in focus and understanding of these concepts, experts during recent climate conferences increasingly comment that both climate change and sustainability must be approached as a common challenge since both have several commonalities.

Though there are several such discussions linking these two concepts, there has only been limited attention in the tourism academy, which still needs to emphasize ways of tackling these issues together. In contrast, the implementation of the principles of sustainable development in tourism is considered as one of the key challenges, and still there is a need to emphasize sustainable management in the planning and policy measures of many countries with reference to the need to reduce mass tourism forms as well as maintaining economic development and natural resources of host countries. Low-carbon travel patterns (such as slow tourism – see Dickinson and Lumsdon 2010) to mitigate the impacts of climate

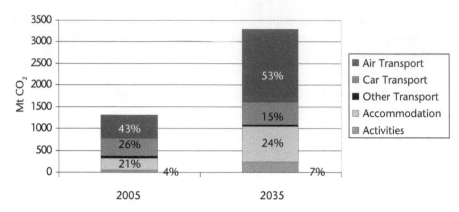

FIGURE 1.2 'Business as usual' projection of future carbon dioxide emissions from tourism★

Source: World Tourism Organization
★Excluding same-day visitors

change might affect the larger number of tourists travelling in future. UNWTO projections of future carbon dioxide emissions from global tourism clearly indicate that tackling climate change and managing sustainable tourism growth together will be huge tasks, and these concerns were highlighted in several UN summits and the subsequent press conferences.

The UN under-secretary general for economic and social affairs has stated that 'climate change is fundamentally a sustainable development challenge' (*Guardian* 2008a). In addition the UN secretary-general, Ban Ki-moon, has warned that 'climate change is a serious threat to development everywhere. Indeed, the adverse impacts of climate change could undo much of the investment made to achieve the Millennium Development Goals'(*Guardian* 2008a). The Copenhagen Accord finalized in December 2009 and involving all the leading member countries of the United Nations claimed that:

> we should cooperate in achieving the peaking of global and national emissions as soon as possible, recognizing that the time frame for peaking will be longer in developing countries and bearing in mind that social and economic development and poverty eradication are the first and overriding priorities of developing countries and that a low-emission development strategy is indispensable to sustainable development.
>
> *(UNFCCC 2010: 5–6)*

There were concerns that the economic slow-down since 2008 was causing added challenges in the momentum of achieving the Millennium Development Goals by 2015.

Obviously there are difficulties in maintaining the flow of investments and funding from some of the richer nations to meet the targets. For instance, the Food and Agriculture Organization's life-saving food assistance operations came under threat in Bangladesh, Chad, Haiti, Kenya, Uganda and the Democratic Republic of the Congo in 2009 as a result of the shortfall of funds from the donor governments across the globe when they slash their aid budgets (*Guardian* 2008b). The UN initiatives in many countries to tackle HIV-AIDS were also affected. Using data collected in March 2009 from 71 countries, the World Bank–UNAIDS analysis pointed out how the crisis could affect the nearly 4 million people living with HIV on treatment, and the 7 million who need treatment but do not have access to it (UNAIDS 2009). Poverty, hunger and health issues are directly related to the Millennium Development Goals and caused a setback in work to achieve the 2015 targets. The UN International Conference on Financing for Development held in Doha 2008, with participants from over 160 countries, stressed the need to meet existing aid commitments to poor nations, even amid the current economic slowdown. The Doha Declaration affirmed, in particular, that the commitment made in the 2002 Monterrey Consensus for developed countries to devote 0.7 per cent of their gross national product to Official Development Assistance must be maintained, despite the current financial crisis (United Nations 2008). The conference pointed out that the economic crisis jeopardizes the ability of countries to provide the necessary financing to meet globally agreed development targets, including the Millennium Development Goals – pledges to slash poverty, hunger, disease and other socio-economic ills by 2015 – and the meeting agreed to consider the need to hold another follow-up conference on development financing in five years (2013) (United Nations 2008).

The increasing role of tourism

Since the publication of the Millennium Ecosystem Assessment (MAweb, 2005), which clearly listed recreation and ecotourism under cultural ecosystem services, there has been more global recognition of the role that tourism could play. Considering the overall tourism demand and forecast figures, researchers and planners warn that achieving sustainability in destinations may be unrealistic in the near future as a result of the existing gaps in climate change policies and their implementation. Scott, Gossling and Hall (2012: 1) argue that :

> while notable progress has been made in the last decade, a number of important knowledge gaps in each of the major impact areas, key regional knowledge gaps, and both tourist and tourism operator perceptions of climate change risks and adaptive capacity indicate that the tourism sector is not currently well prepared for the challenges of climate change.

However, transformation of tourism into one of the leading industries of the world does increase the chances for the tourism and travel sector, as a leading industry, to enhance its contribution as a substitute to meet the Millennium Development Goals when there is not much progress to meet these goals through other industries. Authors such as Weaver (2012) argue that the contemporary tourism is converging towards sustainable mass tourism. The potential of the tourism industry to reduce poverty through pro-poor and responsible approaches (see Ashley, Roe and Goodwin 2001, Ashley 2005, Ashley and Goodwin 2007) and by engaging more tourism and hospitality businesses with fair trade guidelines to improve and maintain decent wages, financing education and clean water programmes in many poor countries, is increasingly recognized. In 2000, the UNWTO Vision 2020 report forecasted that international tourist arrival figures are expected to reach 1.5 billion in 2020. International tourist arrivals recorded a total of 980 million in 2011, and are expected to reach 1 billion by the end of 2012 (UNWTO 2012). This confirms a strong impression that tourism is rapidly growing and by 2020 the arrival figures could go well beyond the estimated 1.5 billion.

The *World Economic Impact Report 2012* from the World Travel and Tourism Council (WTTC 2012) highlighted that travel and tourism's total economic contribution, taking account of its direct, indirect and induced impacts in 2011, was US$6.3 trillion in GDP, 255 million jobs, US$743 billion in investment and US$1.2 trillion in exports. This contribution represented 9 per cent of GDP, 1 in 12 jobs, 5 per cent of investment and 5 per cent of exports, It is anticipated to account for 328 million jobs, or 1 in every 10 jobs on the planet by 2022, which is an encouraging estimation. Now that the tourism industry has shown a remarkable recovery after the global economic crisis, major political changes in the Middle East and natural disasters (such as the Tohoku Pacific earthquake and tsunami), more attention needs to be paid to reach the 2035 carbon mitigation assumptions, with combined scenarios with technical efficiency, transport modal shift and increased length of stay (UNWTO 2012) (see Figure 1.3). It is extremely important to identify methods and pursue appropriate strategies that will reduce the huddles facing the Millennium Development Goals and to work in future for the green economy transition.

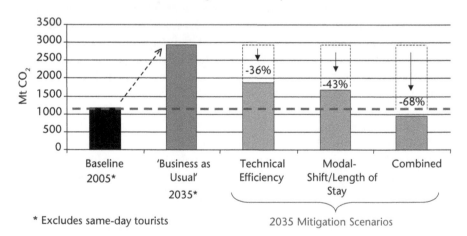

FIGURE 1.3 Future carbon dioxide emissions from global tourism: scenarios of mitigation potential in 2035*

Source: World Tourism Organization.
*Excludes same-day tourists

Rio+20 and transition to a green economy

The green economy concept is not a new one, and in fact is very much framed by several of the recent global initiatives related to sustainable well-being and tackling the threats of climate change. For instance, the Millennium Ecosystem Assessment released in 2005 assessed the consequences of ecosystem change for human well-being and provided a state-of-the-art scientific appraisal of the condition and trends in the world's ecosystems and the services they provide (such as clean water, food, forest products, flood control and natural resources) and the options to restore, conserve or enhance the sustainable use of ecosystems (MAweb 2005). It emphasized the need for unified global action to protect the planet and its resources. Likewise, the international agreements related to climate change, from the Kyoto Protocol and Bali Road Map to Cancun COP16 agreements, and international sustainability frameworks from the Barbados Programme of Action and Mauritius Declaration of the SIDS to the Marrakech Process of Sustainable Production and Consumption (following the Johannesburg 2002 Word Summit) have all very much shaped and led to the green economy approach so far.

The UNEP *Green Economy* report (2011: 16) defines 'green economy as one that results in improved human well-being and social equity, while significantly reducing environmental risks and ecological scarcities'. The report explains further that in a green economy, growth in income and employment should be driven by public and private investments that reduce carbon emissions and pollution, enhance energy and resource efficiency, and prevent the loss of biodiversity and ecosystem services (2011: 16). For the last few years, the green economy has been considered as a potential approach to reduce poverty and achieve low-carbon sustainable growth that also brings a ray of hope to meet the 2035 combined (technical efficiency scenario and transport modal and length of stay shift scenario) mitigation scenarios of the tourism sector. (These call for a 68 per cent reduction in impact over business as usual: see Figure 1.3.) The green economy approach is expected to gain more attention in the near future from researchers, planners, and policy makers after the 2012 UN Conference on Sustainable Development (Rio+20).

The Rio+20 preparatory conferences organized around the world by various UN organizations including UNESCO, UNEP, the UN Development Programme (UNDP), the UN Economic and Social Commission for Asia and the Pacific (ESCAP), the UN Research Institute for Social Development (UNRISD), the UN Conference on Trade and Development (UNCTAD) and the World Bank underline that a green economy approach will reduce our ongoing levels of carbon emissions, enhance environmental conservation measures and reduce poverty in less developed countries. But significant hurdles exist during any transition to a green economy, not only in tourism but also in other industries. For instance, agriculture is the main economic activity of many countries and there is a need to improve food production measures in light of the growing population. However, it will be a key challenge to move developing countries towards more greener ways of agricultural production as agriculture, forestry and land use change currently account for around 30 per cent of total greenhouse gases (GHGs) (Alarcon and Bodouroglou 2011) and the use of pesticides and fertilizers with nitrogen content is three times harmful than carbon.

Key issues that are also likely to receive attention at Rio+20 are vulnerable groups and countries already facing the impacts of climate change (such as small island developing states), countries with high levels of poverty, the funding and expertise needed to make the green economy technology approaches work for larger populations, the need for inclusive growth will alter the production and consumption/consumer patterns (starting from agriculture to manufacturing) and there may be more criticism on some of the less performing countries as happened at the Copenhagen Summit. The United Nations Geneva Preparatory Conference (UNRISD 2011) (attended by the authors) focused mainly on broader social (and economic) priorities. Interestingly, some of the developing countries have started to show more interest than the developed countries in some of the green economy approaches: for instance, the developing countries are a step ahead in terms of solar energy production and similar aspects, although solar panels also use harmful elements/fuels in manufacturing). However, these developing countries need more technical help and financial aid in terms of widening their initiatives in the context of a larger global population, to help with the green economy transition.

At the UN Geneva Conference, the scarcity of expertise was linked by a few experts from UNESCO with the role of education, which is considered to be important for the transition. Appreciation and making more use of indigenous skills and knowledge also need to be explored and adopted. For example, carbon emissions could be reduced in less expensive ways such as the better use of ecosystem and rain forest conservation measures: what is known as reducing emissions from deforestation and forest degradation, or REDD+. In the road to Rio+20, there was also thoughtful intervention by the UN agencies to bring back the social dimension in sustainable development. which very much coincides with socio-economic development and behavioural change. Much importance has been given to the social dimension of the green economy in light of the transformation going on in many countries when lifestyle changes (system change, not climate change) are needed to avoid serious crises (such as shortages of food, electricity or fuel).

Although the transition to a green economy looks gloomy as of now, it does bring a ray of hope for the future. With specific importance to the tourism industry, the Tourism Chapter of the *Green Economy* report (UNEP 2011: 414–15) put forward key messages that outline several areas requiring initiatives by the private and public sector at all levels in the near future:

- Tourism has significant potential as a driver for growth for the world economy.
- The development of tourism is accompanied by significant challenges.
- Green tourism has the potential to create new jobs and reduce poverty.
- Tourism development can be designed to support the local economy and poverty reduction.

- Investing in the greening of tourism can reduce the cost of energy, water and waste, and enhance the value of biodiversity, ecosystems and cultural heritage.
- Tourists are demanding the greening of tourism, with more than a third of travellers found to favour environmentally friendly tourism.
- The private sector, especially small firms, can and must be mobilized to support green tourism.
- Much of the economic potential for green tourism is found in small and medium-sized enterprises (SMEs), which need better access to financing for investing in green tourism.
- Destination planning and development strategies are the first step towards the greening of tourism.
- Government investments and policies can leverage private-sector actions on green tourism.

The tourism challenges facing the green economy transition, however, will include the reduction of energy use in the travel and accommodation sector, water consumption, waste management, management of cultural heritage and growth of tourism from a global resource perspective. Though there are few recent academic initiatives to realize the potential, opportunities and challenges of green economy transition, courses and research initiatives are yet to be established with specific reference to tourism. There is a need for more publications, to promote more green approaches, train green jobs and up skilling workforce. The social and behavioural challenges were somewhat neglected at the first Rio summit in 1992. There were criticisms raised after 1992 stressing that environmental issues must also be integrated with social aspects. However, in terms of travel and tourism, the issue of social dimensions and behavioural change in several aspects including use of transport and water usage have received the attention of several researchers (see Barr et al. 2010, Miller et al. 2010, Cohen et al. 2011, and Gossling et al. 2012). The forthcoming international conference 'Tourism, Climate Change and Sustainability' (September 2012) organized by the authors of this chapter will engage high-level policy makers from international agencies including UNWTO, UNESCO and UNEP and leading research institutions to improve our understanding of the ways favouring the green economy transition of the tourism sector following the Rio+20 global summit.

Organization of the book

While we prepare for the green economy transition, conceptual debates linking sustainability and climate change issues and case study approaches to disseminate best practice and emerging research techniques are vital. The overall focus of this book is to bring together and highlight research initiatives with interesting case studies worldwide and techniques to facilitate the ongoing discussion in relation to tourism, climate change and sustainability. The chapters are under three categories, linked with sustainable tourism and climate change.

1.   Sustainability, climate change and tourism: conceptual issues

In Chapter 2, **Moscardo** points out that sustainability, climate change and tourism can be seen as three distinct but complex, interrelated and contested constructs. Utilizing the social representations theory, this chapter reports on some of the preliminary results of research examining the social representations of these three constructs, and provides some insights into how sustainability is presented and linked to climate change and tourism. The results inform a discussion of directions for both further research into these social representations and some thoughts on how to better engage with stakeholders about changes for sustainability.

Based on three collaborative research and development projects in Australia, **Bushell and Simmons** focus on some of the improved sustainability outcomes by small businesses in Chapter 3. The first two projects are associated with the tourist industry at the sector and precinct scale, and by contrast, the third, set in an outlying region of Sydney, includes a range of SMEs, several of which are associated with tourism. Each project has been at least partially funded by government, and built around established partnerships between the researchers and either local government authorities or a tourism industry association.

In Chapter 4, **Rowell and Richins** explore the relationships between the level of knowledge of climate change impacts, underlying constraints and the potential for implementation of sustainability strategies within the tourism industry to alleviate and adapt to future effects. Their exploratory research was undertaken within the destination-based tourism industry of Hawaii, using qualitative research methods in order to build an understanding of executives' opinions and behaviours on the factors and/or relationships between knowledge sources related to climate change and strategies to mitigate and adapt. With limited resources and a high economic reliance on tourism, they have concluded that Hawaii is extremely vulnerable to climate change.

2.   Responses and initiatives of regional, national and international agencies

Chapter 5 by UNESCO Man and the Biosphere Programme's Director **Ishwaran** explores the greening opportunities for tourism in the context of sustainable development and climate change in UNESCO biosphere reserves. It provides a brief overview of the relationship between climate change and sustainable development, followed by a review of the biosphere reserve concept and the World Network of Biosphere Reserves. The case studies of Lanzarote Biosphere Reserve (Spain), Jiuzhaigou Valley Biosphere Reserve (China) and Sierra Gorda (Mexico) illustrate the use of biosphere reserves as learning laboratories for sustainable tourism development, analysing various information and UNESCO's Seville Strategy for biosphere reserves.

Using the UK Climate Impacts Programme's fifth set of UK climate projections (UKCP09), **Whittlesea and Amelung**, in Chapter 6, explore the impact of climate change on climate suitability and the likelihood of extreme events in the context of regional tourism in the south-west of England. The authors recognize the need to be mindful of longer-term challenges such as adapting to climate change, and suggest that changes in weather and climate could create opportunities for the industry. This chapter introduces the UKCP09 dataset in more detail, and describes the methods used for the assessment of changes in suitability and extreme events; it reports on the results, which are subsequently discussed; and then explores how local and regional stakeholders and decision makers can benefit from the new generation of climate projections and their tourism-specific derivatives.

In Chapter 7, **Buultjens and White** examine the policy approaches of the Australian and New Zealand governments to climate change between 1996 and 2007 and their possible impacts. The authors have selected the period between 1996 and 2007 as it coincides with Howard's Liberal National Party government in Australia. This chapter begins with background on the impacts and interrelationship of climate change and tourism and the political systems of Australia and New Zealand. This is followed by the method used for the study and the results, and the chapter ends with a discussion and concluding comments regarding the impact of the policy approaches on tourism industries and suggestions for improvement.

In Chapter 8, **Leslie** argues it is though not just the impact of energy costs that is of concern, but also the steps being taken in the wider context of sustainability, which is encompassed in the concept of the environmental performance of enterprises. This includes addressing those issues specific to climate change. The majority of small, individual, often owner-managed enterprises do not adopt environmental performance measures. Yet in percentage terms at least, it is arguable that the cost savings on reducing resource consumption would not be dissimilar. Why is this? His chapter aims to address this question, and draws extensively on long-term research into the environmental performance and the adoption of environmental management practices, of predominantly small, independent tourism enterprises.

3. Emerging techniques and research implications

Dubois, Ceron and Peeters, in Chapter 9, argue that mitigation of air transport emissions will unavoidably affect tourism in terms of caps, tradable permits, taxes or legislation, which could reduce the volume and change the pattern of tourism flows. This chapter starts with a presentation of the rationale of the relationship between tourism, air transport and climate policies and of the methods and models to assess it, then critically assesses case studies, and finally presents both methodological and policy recommendations and further research needs. By presenting several case studies (from the Caribbean, the Mediterranean, the Asia Pacific region, the French overseas territories), it evaluates changes in tourism flows within various climate policy scenarios, identifies the impact of changing transport on the (re-)distribution of tourism flows and tourism's contribution to the region's economy.

Outlining the Australian Great Barrier Reef's direct and indirect tourism, **Ramis and Prideaux**, in Chapter 10, argue that there is an urgent need to investigate the extent of the impact that climate change is likely to cause to the Great Barrier Reef, particularly its future ability to attract domestic and international tourists. The aim of the research reported in this chapter was to examine how tourists may respond to the impacts of climate change on the Great Barrier Reef in the future. This chapter provides important data for marine tourism operators who will need to adjust their marketing message as climate change begins to have an impact on the Great Barrier Reef and for the Great Barrier Reef Marine Park Authority.

With specific reference to small island developing states (SIDS) in the Pacific, **Jiang, DeLacy, Klint and Wong** discuss the policy analysis of the Pacific Tourism – Climate Adaptation Project (PT-CAP) research in Chapter 11. It aims to examine the conduciveness of policies in six Pacific SIDS (Fiji Islands, Samoa, Vanuatu, Papua New Guinea, Solomon Islands and Tonga) for the tourism sector to adapt to climate change. Their research activity enables a comprehensive understanding of the existing policy environment in the Pacific SIDS, identifies adaptation issues that still remain as policy gaps, and helps assess the vulnerability of destinations to climate change impacts. The knowledge obtained from this research will inform the future directions of climate change adaptation policies and sustainable strategies for the tourism sector in the Pacific region.

In Chapter 12, **Borda, Nascimento, Costa, Tasso and Ramos** analyse the positive and negative future impacts of climate change on tourism on the north coast of Brazil. The north coast was chosen as a case study for its integrated itinerary under the Brazilian Tourism Development Regionalization Programme with major social and environmental sensitivities. The first part of this chapter examines climate change impact forecasts in Brazil; the second part presents the biotic and abiotic characteristics of the north coast and includes the development scenarios of the itinerary presented before; while the third part analyses the probable impacts that climate change should have on north coast tourism, keeping the focus on the two main tourism destinations.

Tervo-Kankare and Saarinen, in Chapter 13, examine the infiltration of climate change awareness into practical-level tourism development in Finland and its relation to sustainable principles. The foundations of this chapter are with the assumption that national and international policy processes create structures that guide, promote and also aim to limit certain types of tourism development and tourism consumption, while local policy governance networks and tourism developers and entrepreneurs are in the actual position in terms of the implementation of these structures and guidelines. These interpretations were examined in a Finnish context by analysing the occurrence and content of climate change references at national, regional (Lapland and Central Finland) and local scale (two municipalities – Kittilä and Jämsä – with skiing destinations). Their comparison examines whether and how the recognition of climate change in strategy papers also becomes visible in practice in a Finnish context.

Acknowledging the research gaps assessing the estimated impacts of climate change on tourism in African contexts, in Chapter 14 **Saarinen, Hambira, Atlhopheng and Manwa** analyse the impacts of climate change on the tourism industry in southern Africa, especially in Botswana. This chapter provides an overview of the potential impacts of climate change to the industry (and its operational environment) and examines the local tourism operators' perceptions and intended adaptation strategies to the impending impacts and processes. The chapter aims to summarize the perceptions and adaptation strategies of tourism operators on climate change in the arid Kgalagadi (Kalahari) and Okavango Delta wetland environments. This chapter concludes that the tour operators' role, views and level of knowledge are important for the present and future innovation potential of the industry, its sustainability and the construction of an adaptive capacity towards climate change in tourism.

Chapter 15, by **Cohen and Higham**, debates the contradictions in climate concern. It seeks to further understandings of how tourism consumption, and its consequent carbon emissions, are made sense of and justified by consumers in relation to everyday life decisions. Utilizing a set of semi-structured interviews carried out in the United Kingdom and Norway, the chapter illustrates consistencies and inconsistencies in the climate sensitivities consumers show in relation to both everyday domestic (home) and tourism (away) practices. The chapter reveals significant paradoxes in consumer climate sensitivities between the everyday and holidays, and these findings hold important implications for the viability of climate change mitigation strategies and sustainable development goals.

Conclusion

These fifteen chapters set the stage and demonstrate the high-quality research outputs by authors from several countries that improve our understanding of the commonalities and benefits of addressing climate change and sustainability aspects together in light of the Rio+20 conference on green economy and sustainable development. As stated earlier, mobilizing funds for green investments and technology, scarcity of expertise in the green economy topic and the role of education are considered to be important for the transition. Importantly, it is very necessary for closer examination of the day-to-day practices of the larger tour operators, travel companies and hotel chains as well as SMEs and the ways they adapt to green economy practices, while wider agreement on the scientific studies, models and their grassroots adaptation are also necessary. Much importance needs to be given to the social dimension and behavioural change in many countries to make the green economy transition possible, as lifestyle changes in all industries are very much needed to avoid serious of food, electricity and fuel shortages.

This book covered topics on conceptual aspects, responses, emerging techniques and research implications to advance our understanding of the tourism-linked climate change and sustainability aspects. The limitations of this edition, however, include the lack of response by private sector in providing chapters on time, as well as the failure to identify useful responses from fast-developing countries such as India and China.

The forthcoming International Conference (2012) on 'Tourism, Climate Change and Sustainability' topic at Bournemouth University will continue with the initiative of the authors, and is expected to shed more light on the green economy approach, opportunities and challenges for the tourism sector. Our next book will be specifically on tourism in the green economy.

References

Alarcon, D. and Bodouroglou, C. (2011) 'Sustainable agricultural innovation systems (SAIS) for food security and green economies.' International Conference on Green Economy and Sustainable Development. UNRISD, Geneva (10–11 Oct). Available at: www.unrisd.org/80256B42004CCC77/(httpInfoFiles)/CAB6618273F277C0C125792 90041EB16/$file/6-1%20Alarcon%20and%20Bodouroglou%20(pp).pdf (accessed 5 April 2012).

Aronsson, L. (2000) *The Development of Sustainable Tourism.* London: Continuum.

Ashley, C. (2005) 'Lessons learnt from piloting pro-poor tourism in Southern Africa.' ODI Working Paper No. 257. Pro Poor Tourism Paper No. 2, Pro-Poor Tourism Partnership. London: Overseas Development Institute. London.

Ashley, C. and Goodwin, H. (2007) '"Pro poor tourism" – what's gone right and what's gone wrong?' London: Overseas Development Institute.

Ashley, C., Roe, D. and Goodwin, H. (2001) 'Pro-poor tourism strategies: making tourism work for the poor.' Pro-Poor Tourism Report No. 1. London: Overseas Development Institute, International Institute for Environment and Development, and Centre for Responsible Tourism, University of Greenwich.

Barr, S., Shaw, G., Coles, T. and Prillwitz, J. (2010) '"A holiday is a holiday": Practicing sustainability, home and away.' *Journal of Transport Geography* Vol. 18, No. 3, pp. 474–81.

Bosselman, F. P., Peterson, C. A. and McCarthy, C. (1999) *Managing Tourism Growth: Issues and Applications.* Washington DC: Island Press.

Bramwell, B., Henry, I., Jackson, G. and Van der Straaten, J. (1996) *Sustainable Tourism Management: Principles and Practice.* Tilburg: Tilburg University Press.

Burns, P. M. (2004) 'Tourism planning: a third way?' *Annals of Tourism Research* Vol. 31, No. 1, pp. 24–43.

Butler, R. W. and Boyd, S. W. (eds) (2000) *Tourism and National Parks: Issues and Implications.* Chichester: John Wiley.

Butler, R. W., Hall, C. M. and Jenkins, J. (eds) (1998) *Tourism and Recreation in Rural Areas.* Chichester: John Wiley.

Cabrini, L. (2009) 'Tourism, economic crisis and climate change: challenges and opportunities.' Keynote speech, First International Forum on Sustainability, Climate Change and Tourism: Challenges posed by the global economic crisis, 5 November, Bournemouth University. Available at: www.traveldailynews.com/pages/show_ page/33150-Sustainability,-Climate-Change-and-Tourism:-Challenges-posed-by-the-global-economic-crisis (accessed 4 April 2012).

Choi, H. S. and Sirakaya, E. (2006) 'Sustainability indicators for managing community tourism.' *Tourism Management* Vol. 27, No. 6, pp. 1274–89.

Cohen, S. A., Higham, J. and Cavaliere, C. T. (2011) 'Binge flying: behavioural addiction and climate change.' *Annals of Tourism Research* Vol. 38 , No. 3, pp. 1070–89.

Cooper, C., Fletcher, J., Gilbert, D. and Wanhill, S. (1998) *Tourism: Principles and Practice.* Harlow: Addison Wesley Longman.

Dickinson, J. and Lumsdon, L. (2010) *Slow Travel and Tourism.* London: Earthscan.

Dowling, R. (1992) 'Tourism and environmental integration, the journey from idealism to realism.' In Cooper, C. P. and Lockwood, A. (eds), *Progress in Tourism, Recreation and Hospitality Management,* Vol. 4, pp. 33–46. London: Belhaven.

Dubois, G. (2005) 'Indicators for an environmental assessment of tourism at national level.' *Current Issues in Tourism* Vol. 8, Nos 2 & 3, pp. 140–54.

Dymond, S. J. (1997) 'Indicators of sustainable tourism in New Zealand: a local government perspective.' *Journal of Sustainable Tourism* Vol. 5, No. 4, pp. 279–93.

Fennell, D. A. (2003) *Ecotourism: An Introduction,* 2nd edn. London: Routledge.

Gossling, S. and Hall, C. M. (2006) *Tourism and Global Environmental Change.* London: Routledge.

Gossling, S., Peeters, P., Hall. C. M., Ceron, J., Dubois, G., Lehmann, L. and Scott, D. (2012) 'Tourism and water use: supply, demand, and security. An international review.' *Tourism Management* Vol. 33, pp. 1–15.

Guardian (2008a) 'We risk seeing progress reversed: Goal 7: Climate change.' Available at: www.guardian.co.uk/alloutonpoverty/climate.change (accessed 26 August 2009).

Guardian (2008b) 'UN aid agencies facing hunger funding crisis.' Available at: www.guardian.co.uk/world/2008/dec/17/united-nations-zimbabwe (accessed 20 January 2012).

Hall, C. M. (2000) *Tourism Planning: Policies, Processes and Relationships.* Harlow: Prentice Hall.

Hall, C. M. and Lew, A. (eds) (1998) *Sustainable Tourism: A Geographical Perspective.* Harlow: Addison Wesley Longman.

Hardy, A. L. and Beeton, R. J. S. (2001) 'Sustainable tourism or maintainable tourism: managing resources for more than average outcomes.' *Journal of Sustainable Tourism* Vol. 9, No. 3, pp. 168–92.

Hardy, A. L., Beeton, R. J. S. and Pearson, L. (2001) 'Sustainable tourism: an overview of the concept and its position in relation to conceptualisations of tourism.' *Journal of Sustainable Tourism* Vol. 10, No. 6, pp. 475–96.

Harrison, D. (ed.) (1992) *Tourism and the Less Developed Countries.* London: Belhaven.

Harrison, D. (ed.) (2001) *Tourism and the Less Developed World: Issues and Case Studies.* Wallingford: CABI.

Holden, A. (2000) *Environment and Tourism.* London: Routledge.

Kelman, I. and Gaillard., J. C. (2010) 'Embedding climate change adaptation within disaster risk reduction.' In Shaw, R., Pulhin, J. M. and Pereira, J. J. (eds), 'Climate change adaptation and disaster risk reduction: issues and challenges.' *Community, Environment and Disaster Risk Management,* pp. 23–46. Bingley: Emerald.

Lane, B. (2009) 'Thirty years of sustainable tourism drivers, progress, problems – and the future.' In Gossling, S., Hall, C. M. and Weaver, D. (eds), *Sustainable Tourism Futures: Perspectives on Systems, Restructuring and Innovations.* London: Routledge.

Lea, J. (1988) *Tourism and Development in the Third World.* London: Routledge.

Manning, E. W., Clifford, G., Dougherty, D. and Ernst, M. (1996) *What Managers Need to Know: A Practical Guide to the Development and Use of Indicators of Sustainable Tourism.* Madrid: World Tourism Organisation.

Mason, P. (2003) *Tourism Impacts, Planning and Management.* London: Butterworth-Heinemann.

Mathieson, A, and Wall, G. (1989) *Tourism: Economic, Physical and Social Impacts.* London: Longman.

Mathieson, A. and Wall, G. (2006) *Tourism: Change, Impacts and Opportunities*. Harlow: Prentice Hall.

MAweb (2005) *An Overview of Millennium Ecosystem Assessment*. Available at: www.maweb. org/en/About.aspx (accessed 22 January 2012).

Meadows, D. H., Meadows, D. L., Randers, J. and Behrens III., W. W. (1972) *The Limits to Growth: A Report for the Club of Rome's Project on the Predicament of Mankind*. New York: Universe Books.

Miller, G. (2001) 'The development of indicators for sustainable tourism: results of a Delphi survey of tourism researchers.' *Tourism Management* Vol. 22, pp. 351–62.

Miller, G., Rathouse, K., Scarles, C., Holmes, K. and Tribe, J. (2010) 'Public understanding of sustainable tourism.' *Annals of Tourism Research* Vol. 37, No. 3, pp. 627–45.

Miller, G. and Twining-Ward, L. (2005) *Monitoring for a Sustainable Tourism Transition: The Challenge of Developing and Using Indicators*. Wallingford: CABI .

Mowforth, M. and Munt, I. (1998) *Tourism and Sustainability: New Tourism in the Third World*. London: Routledge.

Mowforth, M. and Munt, I. (2003) *Tourism and Sustainability: Development and New Tourism in the Third World*. London: Routledge.

Peeters, P. (ed.) (2007) *Tourism and Climate Change Mitigation: Methods, Greenhouse Gas Reductions and Policies*. Breda: Stichting NHTV.

Pigram, J. (1992) 'Alternative tourism: tourism and sustainable resource management.' In Smith, V. L. and Eadington, W. R. (eds), *Tourism Alternatives: Potentials and Problems in the Development of Tourism*. Philadelphia, Pa.: University of Pennsylvania Press.

Reddy, M. V. (2008) 'Sustainable tourism rapid indicators for less-developed islands: an economic perspective.' *International Journal of Tourism Research* Vol. 10, No. 6, pp. 557–76.

Roberts, S. and Tribe, J. (2008) 'Sustainability indicators for small tourism enterprises – an exploratory perspective.' *Journal of Sustainable Tourism* Vol. 16, No. 5, pp. 575–94.

Scott, D. (2011) 'Why sustainable tourism must address climate change.' *Journal of Sustainable Tourism* Vol. 19, No. 1, pp. 17–34.

Scott, D., Gossling, S. and Hall, C. M. (2012) 'International tourism and climate change.' *Wiley Interdisciplinary Reviews: Climate Change*. Available at: http://onlinelibrary.wiley. com/doi/10.1002/wcc.165/pdf (accessed 6 April 2012).

Sharpley, R. and Telfer, D. J. (eds) (2002) *Tourism and Development: Concepts and Issues*. Clevedon: Channel View.

Simpson, M. C., Gossling, S., Scott, D., Hall, C. M. and Gladin, E. (2008) *Climate Change Adaptation and Mitigation in the Tourism Sector: Frameworks, Tools and Practices*. Paris: UNWTO, University of Oxford, WMO, UNEP. Available at: www.geog.ox.ac.uk/ news/events/ccamts/ccamts.pdf (accessed 3 December 2011).

Simpson, M. C., Scott, D., Harrison, M., Silver, N., O'Keeffe, E., Sim, R., Harrison, S., Taylor, M., Lizcano, G., Rutty, M., Stager, H., Oldham, J., Wilson, M., New, M., Clarke, J., Day, O. J., Fields, N., Georges, J., Waithe, R. and McSharry, P. (2010) *Quantification and Magnitude of Losses and Damages Resulting from the Impacts of Climate Change: Modelling the Transformational Impacts and Costs of Sea Level Rise in the Caribbean* (Summary Document). Barbados: United Nations Development Programme (UNDP). Available at: www.caribsave.org/assets/files/SeaLvlRise-UNDP-CARIBSAVE-SummDoc2010.pdf (accessed 22 December 2011).

Simpson, M. C., Scott, D., New, M., Sim, R., Smith, D., Harrison, M., Eakin, C. M., Warrick, R., Strong, A. E., Kouwenhoven, P., Harrison, S., Wilson, M., Nelson, G. C., Donner, S., Kay, R., Geldhill, D. K., Liu, G., Morgan, J. A., Kleypas, J. A., Mumby, P. J., Palazzo, A., Christensen, T. R. L., Baskett, M. L., Skirving, W. J., Elrick, C., Taylor, M., Magalhaes, M., Bell, J., Burnett, J. B., Rutty, M. K., Overmas, M. and Robertson, R.

(2009) *An Overview of Modelling Climate Change Impacts in the Caribbean Region with contribution from the Pacific Islands*. Barbados: United Nations Development Programme (UNDP). Available at: www.caribsave.org/assets/files/7dec09/Summary%20Document %20Final%20Caribbean%20CC%20UNDP%20Report.pdf (accessed 22 December 2011).

Tallis, H., Kareiva, P., Marvier, M. and Chang, A. (2008) 'An ecosystem services framework to support both practical conservation and economic development.' *Proceedings of the National Academy of Sciences* Vol. 105, No. 28, pp. 9457–64. Available at: www.pnas.org/ content/105/28/9457.full.pdf (accessed 20 January 2012).

Twining-Ward, L. and Butler, R. (2002) 'Implementing STD on a small island: development and use of sustainable tourism development indicators in Samoa.' *Journal of Sustainable Tourism* Vol. 10, No. 5, pp. 363–87.

United Nations (1987) *Report of the World Commission on Environment and Development: Our Common Future*. Available at: http://daccess-dds-ny.un.org/doc/UNDOC/GEN/ N87/184/67/IMG/N8718467.pdf?OpenElement (accessed 20 January 2012).

United Nations (1997) *United Nations Conference on Environment and Development (1992)*. Available at: www.un.org/geninfo/bp/envirp2.html (accessed 20 January 2012).

United Nations (2006) 'United Nations: Johannesburg Summit 2002: Basic Information.' Available at: www.johannesburgsummit.org/html/basic_info/basicinfo.html (accessed 20 January 2012).

United Nations (2008) 'States must meet aid pledges despite financial crisis, Doha forum concludes.' Available at: www.un.org/apps/news/story.asp?NewsID=29164 (accessed 20 January 2012).

UNAIDS (2009) 'Feature story: global economic crisis and HIV.' Available at: www.unaids. org/en/Resources/PressCentre/Featurestories/2009/July/20090706FinancialCrisis/ (accessed 8 April 2012).

UNEP (2011) *Towards a Green Economy: Pathways to Sustainable Development and Poverty Eradication*, pp. 1–626). Advance copy online release. Nairobi: UNEP.

UNEP (2012) 'Declaration of the United Nations Conference on the Human Environment.' Available at: www.unep.org/Documents.Multilingual/Default.asp?documentid=97&art icleid=1503 (accessed 20 January 2012).

UNFCCC (2010) 'Copenhagen Accord.' Advance unedited version. Decision-/CP.15. Available at: http://unfccc.int/files/meetings/cop_15/application/pdf/cop15_cph_auv. pdf (accessed 18 January 2011).

UNRISD (2011) *Green Economy and Sustainable Development: Bringing Back the Social Dimension*, 10–11 October. Geneva: United Nations.

UNWTO (2008) *Climate Change and Tourism – Responding to Global Challenges*. Madrid: World Tourism Organization and UNEP. Available at: http://sdt.unwto.org/sites/all/ files/docpdf/climate2008.pdf (accessed 20 January 2012).

UNWTO (2012) 'International tourism to reach one billion in 2012.' Available at: http:// media.unwto.org/en/press-release/2012-01-16/international-tourism-reach-one- billion-2012 (accessed 11 March 2012).

Weaver, D. (2006) *Sustainable Tourism: Theory and Practice*. Oxford: Butterworth-Heinemann.

Weaver, D. (2009) 'Reflections on sustainable tourism and paradigm change.' In Gossling, S., Hall, C. M. and Weaver, D. (eds), *Sustainable Tourism Futures: Perspectives on Systems, Restructuring and Innovations*. London: Routledge.

Weaver, D. (2012) 'Organic, incremental and induced paths to sustainable mass tourism convergence', opinion piece. *Tourism Management* (in press).

WTTC (2012) 'Travel & Tourism forecast to pass 100m jobs and $2 trillion GDP in 2012.' Available at: www.wttc.org/news-media/news-archive/2012/travel-tourism-forecast- pass-100m-jobs-and-2-trillion-gdp-2012/ (accessed 11 March 2012).

2

SOCIAL REPRESENTATIONS OF CLIMATE CHANGE

Exploring the perceived links between climate change, the drive for sustainability and tourism

Gianna Moscardo

Introduction

Sustainability, climate change and tourism can be seen as three distinct but complex, interrelated and contested constructs. Arguably climate change currently occupies a central place in the public sphere in the media and in politics, and it can be suggested that this high profile has served to highlight and advance sustainability as a construct worthy of public and political attention. But the relationship between these two constructs is a contested one. For some climate change is the central issue driving sustainability, while for others there are concerns that climate change has hijacked the sustainability agenda, possibly to the detriment of other issues. In a similar fashion, albeit with a lower public profile, it could be argued that the relationships between sustainability and tourism and between tourism and climate change are also contested and difficult.

What is not contested in any of these debates is the need to better engage the wider public, including tourism stakeholders, in discussing, understanding and responding to these issues. The first step towards this engagement is to understand what knowledge and theories already exist outside the academic/scientific world about climate change and its relationships to sustainability and tourism. Social representations theory offers a way to develop this understanding, and this chapter will report on some preliminary results of research examining the social representations of these three constructs. More specifically, the chapter will provide some insights into how sustainability is presented and linked to climate change and tourism. These results will inform a discussion of directions for both further research into these social representations and some thoughts on how to better engage with stakeholders about changes for sustainability.

Working definitions of sustainability and climate change

Given the contested nature of these concepts it is important to establish the definitions that the author uses in order to understand points of contrast and comparison made when reviewing other studies and exploring the results of new studies. Sustainability is defined as an approach to production and consumption characterized by principles which include taking a long-term orientation and making a commitment to changing current practices; balancing the needs of current people with those of future generations; recognizing that our activities are part of a complex system in which environmental, social and economic activities are interdependent; being aware of and managing resource use and the social, economic and environmental impacts of our actions; and acknowledging that multiple forms of capital contribute to quality of life and wellbeing and all need to be considered, but understanding that natural capital has a unique position in that it can rarely be substituted with other forms of capital (Moscardo 2011a).

In this approach sustainability is seen as encompassing five main dimensions – environmental, social including justice and human rights, economic, governance and ethics. Other concepts that have been closely connected to sustainability in the academic literature are corporate social responsibility (CSR) and fair trade. CSR can be defined a voluntary commitment by business to behave in a socially responsible fashion, with a strong focus on ethical behaviour, and being proactive in identifying and addressing social and environmental problems at the local, regional and global level (Beltratti 2005, Garriga and Mele 2004, Holme and Watt 2000). Fair trade is a label used by a variety of programmes that seek to ensure that products have been produced under appropriate conditions, including the payment of reasonable wages to production workers and fair prices to producers, minimum workplace standards, adherence to environmentally responsible practices and programmes to support sustainable development in areas of production (Fair Trade Australia 2011).

Climate change is defined using the description given as the basis for the Kyoto Protocol by the United Nations Framework Convention on Climate Change (UNFCCC) (2011). In this description human activity, in particular the burning of fossil fuels, contributes to increased greenhouse gases in the Earth's atmosphere resulting in increased global temperatures. In turn this is changing systems such as cloud cover, rainfall, wind patterns, ocean currents, and the distribution of plant and animal species.

Inherent in these definitions of climate change and sustainability and related concepts is the idea that people need to change the way they live and act. This leads to the idea that there are ways to engage in more sustainable living and to act in more socially and environmentally ways. This idea of responsible behaviour is then linked to particular areas, generating labels such as responsible consumption and responsible tourism. In these cases the use of 'responsible' as an adjective implies that individuals consciously make decisions to improve the sustainability of their actions in this particular area.

Social representations theory

In 1961 a European social psychologist, Serge Moscovici, introduced the concept of social representations (SRs) to explain the interface between individual knowledge and behaviour and collective action and knowledge representation. In his analysis of the phenomenon of psychoanalysis Moscovici explored the way in which scientific theories and information are interpreted and explained in the everyday world and how they become common sense (Jodelet 2008). He distinguished between the reified universe of scientists and the consensual universe of everyday life (Moscovici 1984). SRs were constructs developed to explain how the consensual universe made sense of and responded to ideas and information from the reified universe (Moscovici 1984). SRs are the outcomes of these sense-making activities within social interaction and the collective context (Raudsepp 2005). SRs can be defined as everyday theories that explain the social world, that help individuals and their social groups make sense of the world around them, assist in their communication and guide their responses to various phenomena they encounter (Pearce, Moscardo and Ross 1996).

Social representations theory (SRT) draws from work in cognition in social psychology and the idea of collective representations in sociology, and shares a common philosophical background with more critical and discursive approaches in sociology and psychology (Raudsepp 2005). SRs are created through two complementary processes, anchoring and objectification (Moscovici 1984). In anchoring, groups seek to make sense of new information and/or concepts by locating them within the framework of what is already known. New and unfamiliar concepts are thus connected to existing everyday theories (De Paolis 1990). Objectification then takes the abstract and unfamiliar concept and makes it ordinary and concrete by linking it to a visual image or metaphor (Moscovici 2001). Visual images and metaphors are central elements of SRs. These two processes also take place within an ongoing interaction between individuals within groups, and over time SRs become repeated and refined in this interaction and emerge in the domain of public and social communication (Moscovici 2001). This interaction between the individual and social level and between groups at the social level means that SRs are also linked to ideas of power and social control (Philogene and Deaux 2001).

Within tourism SRT has been used to analyse destination community responses to tourism development (Pearce et al. 1996, Andriotis and Vaughan 2003, Fredline and Faulkner 2000), to explore dominant perspectives on tourism planning processes and governance (Moscardo 2011b), social representations of tourism itself (Moscardo 2009) and social representations of threats to the Great Barrier Reef (Moscardo 2008a). SRT has also been proposed as an important approach to understanding public responses to climate change (Castro 2006, Reser and Swim 2011). It seems likely that a better understanding of the range and features of SRs of sustainability and climate change and their connections to tourism could assist in the analysis of the complex relationships between these three social constructs.

A brief history of sustainability

While the word 'sustainability' has come into widespread use only relatively recently, many of the issues that drive increasing government and public concern have a much longer history (Wells 2011). Weber (2007) traces the origins of sustainability to the rise of mining and manufacturing and the change from an agrarian to a capitalist industrialist economy. In 1758 Francoise Quesnay linked the health of nature to the health of society, in 1776 Adam Smith raised concern about the negative consequences of free markets, in 1798 Thomas Malthus argued for limits to growth, and throughout the 1800s there was considerable debate in Europe amongst the clergy, scholars and politicians about the appropriate tradeoffs between wealth, moral duty and social justice (Lumley and Armstrong 2004). The first seventy years of the 20th century saw the emergence of the environmental movement, driven by concerns about environmental pollution and its consequences for humans and the wider ecosystem (Mebratu 1998). Books such as Rachel Carson's *Silent Spring* (1962) drew attention to the previously unacknowledged environmental costs of the dominant system of consumption and production. This environmental concern became institutionalized at an international level with the establishment in 1972 of the United Nations Environmental Programme (UNEP). This was followed by an international meeting on climate change in 1985, and significant growth in international treaties and agreements focused on environmental issues.

Then in 1987 the Brundtland Report was published by the World Commission on Environment and Development, giving a definition of sustainable development and highlighting the social and economic problems associated with both a deteriorating environment and our current patterns of production and consumption.

Since this report there has been a considerable growth in public, government and business engagement with various aspects of sustainable development or sustainability. A global analysis of major news media over a twenty-year period from 1990 to 2010 shows a marked increase in overall coverage of sustainability and sustainability-related concepts during that time period (Barkemeyer et al. 2010). Within this trend there are some interesting variations and patterns, with a shift from sustainable development to sustainability, and a growth in the second ten years in links between sustainability and CSR, indicating a growing presentation of sustainability as being a central part of CSR. Across the twenty-year period the largest growth in sustainability-related coverage was, however, for climate change, with a general decline in discussions of most other environmental issues. By way of contrast coverage of social issues such a human rights and poverty have shown a slight but steady increase during the same time period with continued low levels of coverage for other issues such as labour rights, child labour and child mortality. None of the social issues have been given the same level of attention as climate change in the last five-year period (Barkemeyer et al. 2010).

This pattern has been noted elsewhere, with a growing debate about the nature of relationship between climate change and public perceptions of sustainability. On the one hand there are those who see climate change as the most urgent global issue and central to sustainability (Leiserowitz 2007). But there are others who argue that sustainability is much broader than climate change and that climate change, along with other environmental issues, has hijacked the sustainability agenda (Victor 2006). It could be argued that too strong a focus on the environmental dimensions of sustainability makes it easier to avoid tackling the core issue of sustainability, which is an economic system where growing consumption by those in the wealthier North is made possible because of production based on low wages and the ability to externalize environmental costs in the poorer countries of the South. There is a second risk associated with aligning sustainability too closely with climate change. There is considerable public debate about all aspects of climate change including its reality, causes and consequences, and it is possible that these concerns could permeate the broader discussion on sustainability, making it harder to gain public acceptance for other sustainability issues and strategies.

Tourism, sustainability and climate change

A cursory examination of the history of sustainability issues in tourism suggests a similar pattern to that outlined in the preceding section. Early anthropological studies of tourist destinations highlighted a number of social, environmental and economic problems associated with tourism, especially in cases where the tourists originated in the wealthier countries of the North and were pursuing holiday options affordable because of their location in the poorer countries of the South (Pearce et al. 1996). Unlike other forms of discretionary spending, tourism is consumed in the location of production and so the negative consequences of that production and consumption system cannot always be hidden from the tourists. Arguably this feature meant an earlier focus in tourism than in many other consumption areas on developing alternatives in an attempt to manage the negative consequences of the activity (Moscardo 2008b), and perhaps an earlier focus on sustainability issues. But like mainstream considerations of sustainability there has been a very strong focus on the environmental dimensions with much less consideration of other dimensions, and there is considerable debate over actual and potential progress in tourism being able to make a significant contribution to the sustainable development of destination regions (Moscardo 2008b, 2008c).

Finally, in recent years there has been a significant increase in academic, government and business attention paid to tourism and climate change, including a number of books such as the present volume. There is insufficient space to engage in a detailed review of this literature, and indeed other chapters in this book will provide much more detail on the relationship between tourism and climate change. But it is important to note that there is a dichotomy in approaches to researching this relationship, between studies focused on the impacts of climate change on tourism where tourism as a victim of climate change (see Hall 2011, and Pham, Simmons and Spur 2010, for reviews and examples of this work), and studies focused on the impacts of tourism on climate change where tourism is a perpetrator of climate change (see Becken and Hay 2007, and Gossling 2009), for details of research in this area). The first approach tends towards the emerging discussion of adaptation strategies (see Nicholls and Amelung 2008 for an example of this approach), while the second tends more towards mitigation and more critical analyses of tourism (Scott, Peeters and Gossling, 2010).

The problem

This brief review of the connections between and history of sustainability and climate change, both generally and specifically for tourism, indicates the complex and contested nature of the relationship between these constructs. But across all these debates there is consensus around the need to change the way we practise business in general and tourism more specifically. Concerns about sustainability and risk assessment of climate change indicate a need to effectively communicate with all stakeholders to change behaviours. At the simplest level effective communication needs to be based on a clear understanding of the consensual universe and how different groups generate and use SRs for sustainability, climate change and sustainable tourism (Castro 2006, Reser and Swim 2011). At a more complex level it is also important to understand the extent to which climate change has become a defining element of SRs of sustainability. Finally, for tourism specifically it is important to understand how tourist behaviour is recognized in SRs of climate change and what implications this might have for changing tourism practice.

Exploring social representations of climate change, sustainability and tourism

The rest of this chapter presents initial results from a programme of research using SRT to analyse and describe the SRs of sustainability, climate change and responsible tourism held by different stakeholder groups. Figure 2.1 provides an overview of the research programme, listing the major stakeholder groups and relationships being explored. The following sections describe three elements of this programme which examine aspects of SRs held by different stakeholder groups, including business managers, government agencies, non-government organizations (NGOs) and the general public, of sustainability, sustainable living, the links between these and climate change and the role of tourism.

Flick and Foster (2008) noted that while there is tendency for SR research to use qualitative methods, especially semiotic analysis and discourse analysis with archival data, SRs can be and have been examined using a wider variety of methodologies, and that multi-method approaches are especially useful for developing detailed pictures of SRs. In keeping with this eclectic approach the studies reported in the following sections use semiotic and content analysis on data collected from semi-structured questionnaires and websites.

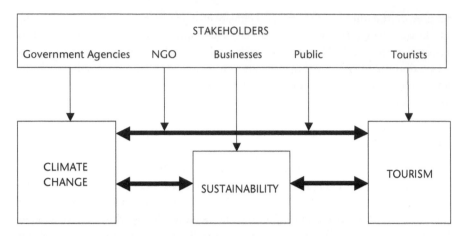

FIGURE 2.1 Overview of the Sustainability SR Research Programme

Managers' images of sustainability and links to climate change

The first study in the research programme was conducted with forty-nine students enrolled in a business and sustainability class within an MBA at a regional Australian university. The students came from India, China, Japan, Brazil, Canada, Germany, the United States and Australia, and the four most common educational backgrounds were undergraduate degrees in accounting, engineering, information technology and medicine. As MBA students all were either currently managers, or had been managers, in government agencies or private business across a number of sectors. The activity was conducted at the start of the class before any lectures or readings had been provided, and involved completion of a semi-structured questionnaire with three elements. First, students were asked to draw a picture to demonstrate what sustainability meant to them. This qualitative approach is consistent with the focus in SRT on visual imagery as a core element of SRs. Second, students were asked to write their definition of sustainability. Finally, they were asked to draw a mind map connecting sustainability to other concepts that they associated with sustainability. Students were free to connect to as few or as many concepts that they associated with sustainability.

The visual images and mind maps were subjected to both a content and semiotic analysis (Mehmetoglu and Dann 2003). This involved three steps – the development of a simple tally of the elements used in the images, an analysis of the co-occurrence of these elements to identify common patterns, and a semiotic analysis of the symbols used and what these and the overall patterns might signify (see Moscardo 2011b, for a description of this analytic approach). The aim of these analyses was to develop some understanding of the existing SRs held by these students.

Three main types of visual image were identified based on the recurring patterns of elements. The first and most common, accounting for nearly half of the images (43 per cent), was called the abstract image of sustainability, with two examples provided in Figure 2.2. These types of images mimicked the sorts of diagram used

FIGURE 2.2 An abstract image of sustainability

in academic textbooks, and used combinations of textboxes and symbols to suggest interactions between different elements of sustainability. The first image in Figure 2.2 includes two very common elements in these types of image – a symbol of balance and the three dimensions of environment, society and economy. The second image in Figure 2.2 contains two other common symbolic elements – the idea of a cycle and a river or stream. Overall these images suggest a social representation of sustainability as being the result of successfully balancing the three dimensions of planet, people and profit.

Symbols suggesting a river or stream were one of the most common elements used, appearing in more than half of all the images. They were particularly common in the second image, the nature idyll image of sustainability, which accounted for nearly 30 per cent of the images (see Figure 2.3). This type of image of sustainability seemed to suggest a desirable end state or goal driving sustainability. Although there were differences in detail, reflecting difference levels of confidence and ability at drawing, as seen in the two images in Figure 2.3, similar elements were

FIGURE 2.3 The nature idyll image of sustainability

included in all. The images all included trees arranged alongside water, and nearly all included simple dwellings and happy people. The suggestion is that sustainability is about achieving a desirable natural environment for human habitation.

The final type of image occurred with the same frequency as the nature idyll, and offered a contrasting or negative view of sustainability. Figure 2.4 provides two examples – the first was an example which contains both a negative and positive situation, while the second is an example of simple negative image. In these images it seemed that the students were defining sustainability as being driven by the need to avoid a bleak future or to move from a currently negative situation to a more harmonious natural state. Both these images and the previous positive versions appear to describe a SR of sustainability that focuses primarily on the environment. Not surprisingly symbols and references to climate change were linked to these images. More than two-thirds of these nature-based images included climate change links. Both of the images in Figure 2.4 provide examples of the sorts of references to climate change that were used.

FIGURE 2.4 The contrasting or negative image of sustainability

The results of the analysis of the mind maps linking sustainability to other relevant concepts were consistent with this focus on climate change, with three-quarters of those who provided a clear definition of sustainability linking climate change to sustainability as a key related concept. Climate change was the concept most commonly linked to sustainability, followed closely by CSR and fair trade. Four types of links were provided between sustainability and climate change, with the most common being the use of a double-ended arrow suggesting interaction such as 'climate change will alter the world and sustainability is how well we'll survive in that world'. The second most common was a link suggesting climate change was a cause or force for sustainability, with comments like 'climate change is a key driver of sustainability'. The opposite link was also suggested, with comments such as 'climate change is the result of behaving without sustainability'. Finally, there were mind maps which had an indirect link between climate change and sustainability through another concept like CSR, explained with statements like 'climate change is the responsibility of every corporation to do something about and this is needed to achieve sustainability'.

Although it was common to link sustainability and climate change there was little evidence of any understanding of what climate change was. None of the students including climate change in their mind maps of sustainability provided a definition close to that used by the United Nations in the Kyoto Protocol (UNFCCC 2011). Half of all the climate change definitions simply suggested that climate change was a change in climate or weather, with no other details provided. Only six offered any discussion of consequences (including bad weather, melting glaciers, destruction of natural and cultural heritage, an endangered environment and affects human lives) or implications for human action (including conserve resources and encourage environmentally friendly actions). The list of causes of climate change in order of frequency of occurrence included pollution (not specified), human actions (not specified), global warming, industry/manufacturing or business, nature/natural forces, resource depletion, ozone layer depletion, vehicles and cars, and fossil fuels.

These findings are consistent with research from surveys of various populations about their understanding of and attitudes towards climate change. Public surveys conducted in a number of countries asking a variety of questions about climate change provide a consistent pattern of results, where most respondents are aware that there is an issue around climate change or global warming, and the majority surveyed in Australia, the United States and various European countries express a level of concern about the issue (Australian Bureau of Statistics 2010, Leiserowitz 2007, Lorenzoni and Pidgeon 2006). But the issue is only seen as a top priority for attention by a small percentage of respondents, typically coming last in ratings of importance compared with other things such the economy, jobs, terrorism and education (Haywood 2011). Concern about climate change is also limited by perceptions that it is unlikely to have negative consequences for respondents or impact where they live in the immediate or even medium-term future (Leiserowitz 2007, Lorenzoni and Pidgeon 2006, Weber and Stern 2011). Few respondents demonstrate an understanding of what climate change is or what causes it, with common misconceptions including that it is related to ozone layer depletion and the use of nuclear power, and there is an almost even balance between those who believe it to be mainly a natural process and those who see human activities as the primary contributing factor (Leiserowitz 2007, Lorenzoni and Pidgeon 2006, Weber and Stern, 2011).

In short, both public opinion surveys and the analysis of visual images and mind maps suggest that few people in the consensual universe have a clear SR for climate change. Climate change is poorly understood, not clearly connected to human activities, given a low priority and is generally seen as most likely to have an impact on other people in other places at some distant future time. This is not surprising given that it is a complex and abstract concept that is difficult to communicate quickly and simply (Moser 2010, Scannell and Grouzet 2010). The remoteness of climate change from the everyday experience of most people makes it a very unfamiliar concept, and the existing evidence suggest that SRs of climate change in the consensual universe are in the early stages of developing, with initial anchoring linking it to sustainability. This initial evidence suggests that climate change and sustainability are very closely related in the everyday world or consensual universe, and while people in this universe are concerned about sustainability, the existing SRs are too vague to alter either individual behaviour or collective action.

Public presentations of sustainable living

This anchoring process is likely to be influenced by the way climate change has been presented in the news and popular media. Boykoff and Mansfield (2008) concluded from their analysis of the representation of climate change in the UK tabloid press that the coverage was generally inaccurate, and there was significant divergence 'from the scientific consensus that humans contribute to climate change' (p. 1). Similar conclusions are offered by Boykoff (2007) from an analysis of the US mass media, which demonstrated a significant focus given to the idea of scientific conflict and uncertainty about climate change.

It could be argued though that newspapers and other traditional mass media have a decreasing importance in the communication of knowledge and construction of SRs compared with the rise of the internet and its related social media. Pan et al. (2011) provide recent internet usage statistics suggesting that a significant number of people worldwide are regularly users of the internet and social media for knowledge and information. The internet is an increasingly important forum for various groups to present their world views on a variety of topics, and it has been suggested that the internet offers a potentially valuable resource for the study of SRs (Flick and Foster 2008). This next section reports on such a study using the internet to explore SRs of sustainable living and sustainable tourism and the links made between these and climate change action.

According to Spink and Jansen (2004), a consistent finding in studies of internet search use is that approximately 70 per cent of people do not go beyond the first two pages of results when using an internet search engine. Using this measure the present study examined the first two pages of results, excluding advertisements and electronic newspapers and magazines, provided by Webcrawler, which combines the three dominant engines of Google, Yahoo and Bing, for a search on sustainable living. The aim of this analysis was to determine the extent to which information on how to live sustainably included discussions of climate change actions and guidance for tourist behaviour. More than half of the websites connected sustainability and climate change, with several moving from the title of sustainable living into a discussion of climate change. This further reinforces the conclusion that climate change has come to dominate public discussion and SRs of sustainability. Most of the sites that linked sustainability to climate change appeared, however, to assume that the reader understood the concept, with almost no explanation in any place of what the concept meant. This is consistent with the low levels of public understanding of the concept.

TABLE 2.1 Twelve Most Frequently Mentioned Guidelines for Sustainable Living

Grow household food in gardens
Recycle/reduce waste
Use car less, carpool, use public transport, bicycle or walk more
Install energy efficient appliances in house
Change to renewable household energy sources
Compost food scraps
Install energy efficient lighting,
Use non-toxic household materials and chemicals
Reduce meat consumption/become a vegetarian
Simplify life
Turn off electricity/electrical appliances
Design houses to use less heat/air conditioning

Table 2.1 contains the twelve most frequently mentioned guidelines for sustainable living, taken from blogs, NGO, government agency and educational outreach websites, presented in order of frequency from most to least mentioned. Twenty-two other suggestions were also provided but none of these were noted in more than one or two places. Four important points can be noted from this table. First, the environmental dimension of sustainability, is dominant with almost all the guidelines focused on reducing environmental impacts. Within these, there is also a dominance of action designed to decrease carbon footprints, and this is was a commonly cited reason for many of the guidelines associated with energy reduction and changes to transport modes and diets. The third point to note is the low priority and lack of detail given to cutting consumption overall, mentioned in only three sites, fair trade options, selecting businesses with sustainability accreditations or good CSR records, or issues related to poverty, justice or human rights. Finally, changes to holiday or business travel or actions related to being a sustainable tourist do not appear on the list, as only two sites mentioned these options. One site only referred to the transport involved in holiday travel, suggesting that people should fly less and use alternative forms of transport where possible in order to cut carbon emissions. The other site offered a more comprehensive approach, talking about conservation of energy while on holidays, use of alternative transport and picking tourism businesses with a good environmental record.

This low priority is consistent with research conducted on ecotourists and their awareness of and commitment to engaging in sustainable travel behaviours (see Lee and Moscardo 2005, and Powell and Ham 2008, for examples) and research more broadly into understanding tourist attitudes towards responsible (Kang and Moscardo 2006), environmentally friendly (Dolnicar, Crouch and Long 2008) or sustainable actions (Budeanu 2007) while on holidays. It is also consistent with the growing body of literature specifically about tourist awareness of and adoption of travel behaviours to limit their contributions to climate change (Becken 2007; Cohen, Higham and Cavaliere 2011; Hares, Dickinson and Wilkes 2010). Despite this research being conducted in a variety of locations with a range of different tourist populations, there is considerable convergence in the results and conclusions. While it seems that effective interpretation programmes can change tourist behaviour, overall results indicate that 'despite their declared positive attitudes towards sustainable tourism, only a few tourists act accordingly' (Budeanu 2007: 499).

In summary, this component confirms both the strong links between sustainability and climate change in SRs and the weak connections between recognizing climate change as a major sustainability issue and specific changes to individual behaviour or lifestyle. These analyses also highlighted the low profile of tourism in these SRs of sustainability. Not surprisingly public links between tourism and climate change are weak.

Conclusions and implications

The results presented here are the very first from the programme of research, and offer only some initial insights into the relevant SRs. More analysis of these data sets and collection of a wider range of data from more stakeholders through different sources is ongoing. But the results reported are consistent with, and expand upon, the existing research in this area, offering some initial conclusions and implications for thinking about the interactions between sustainability, climate change and tourism.

Overall, the available evidence suggests that within the consensual universe there are not yet detailed SRs for either sustainability or climate change. Climate change, in particular, remains a difficult and unfamiliar concept for many people. As predicted by SRT, climate change is being anchored to sustainability, possibly because the existing SRs of sustainability typically stress the environmental dimensions. This was evident in the visual images of sustainability, where a dominant version was about either avoiding or achieving a desirable natural environmental state. This was also clear in the analysis of the internet guidelines for living sustainably, which gave most prominence to environmental actions.

But sustainability itself is not a clearly defined or detailed SR. This lends weight to concerns raised about the possibility of climate change hijacking the broader sustainability agenda (Victor 2006). This is risky in several ways. As noted earlier, if groups within the consensual universe reject climate change then it may become much harder to persuade the public in general and tourists in particular to pay attention to any sustainability messages. It could also be the case that if tourists perceive sustainability as solely about climate change and if holiday travel is not given a high profile in current discussions of personal actions related to climate change, as suggested by the preliminary analysis presented in this paper, then it might be difficult to promote climate change action to tourists. Barr et al. (2010) have noted that it is already difficult to get tourists to continue to pursue the sustainable practices they engage in at home when they go on holidays.

This initial exploration of the SRs of sustainability, climate change and the role of tourist behaviour indicates that it will be a very difficult journey to change tourist behaviours, and it is only just beginning. One option that has often been argued for ecotourism and that should be extended to tourism in general is to more proactively develop programmes within destinations and tourism businesses that inform visitors about sustainability and climate change in general. For example, it may be equally important for a hotel or an airline to have a general sustainability education programme for its guests or passengers as is it is to have an eco-label for its internal operations. We need more public outreach and extension about these concepts.

Finally, there is an emerging theme in SRs of sustainability about the need to cut consumption. In general existing discussions of sustainable tourism and climate change adaptation tend to focus on changing rather than cutting consumption. This may well be a comfortable position for tourism researchers having to interact with tourism businesses for their teaching and research roles, but without tackling the core problem of sustainability, consumption, it is difficult to see how sustainable tourism can be. One student, who also worked as a manager in a mining company, in the MBA class that contributed to the research reported here responded to questions about the sustainability of mining practices by suggesting to his classmates that 'if you all stop buying stuff we'll stop digging it up and then we'll both be sustainable'.

References

Andriotis, K. and Vaughan, R. (2003) 'Urban residents' attitudes towards tourism development: the case of Crete.' *Journal of Travel Research*, 42, 172–85.

Australian Bureau of Statistics (2010) 'Environmental awareness and action.' *Australian Social Trends* 4102.0. Canberra: Australian Bureau of Statistics.

Barkemeyer, R., Figge, F., Hahn, T., Holt, D., Illge, L. and Russon, J. (2010) 'Trends in sustainability.' Leeds: Sustainability Research Institute. Available from: www.trendsinsustainability.com/downloads/trendsinsustainability.pdf (accessed 14 January 2011).

Barr, S., Shaw, G., Coles, T. and Prillwitz, J. (2010) '"A holiday is a holiday": practicing sustainability, home and away.' *Journal of Transport Geography*, 18, 474–81.

Becken, S. (2007) 'Tourists' perceptions of international air travel's impact on the global climate and potential climate change policies.' *Journal of Sustainable Tourism*, 15(4), 351–68.

Becken, S. and Hay, J. E. (2007) *Tourism and Climate Change: Risks and Opportunities.* Clevedon: Channel View.

Beltratti, A. (2005) 'The complementarity between corporate governance and corporate social responsibility.' *The Geneva Papers*, 30, 373–86.

Boykoff, M.T. (2007) 'From convergence to contention: United States mass media representations of anthropogenic climate change science.' *Transactions of the Institute of British Geographers*, 32, 477–89.

Boykoff, M. T. and Mansfield, M. (2008) '"Ye Olde Hot Aire": Reporting on human contributions to climate change in the UK tabloid press.' *Environmental Research Letters*, 3. Available at http://iopscience.iop.org/1748-9326/3/2/024002 (accessed 14 January 2011).

Brundtland, G. (ed.) (1987) *Our Common Future: The World Commission on Environment and Development.* Oxford: Oxford University Press.

Budeanu, A. (2007) 'Sustainable tourist behaviour: a discussion of opportunities for change.' *International Journal of Consumer Studies*, 31, 499–508.

Carson, R. (1962) *Silent Spring*. Boston, Mass: Houghton Mifflin.

Castro, P. (2006) 'Applying social psychology to the study of environmental concern and environmental worldviews: contributions from the social representations approach.' *Journal of Community and Applied Social Psychology*, 16, 247–66.

Cohen, S. A., Higham, J. E. S. and Cavaliere, C. T. (2011) 'Binge flying: behavioural addiction and climate change.' *Annals of Tourism Research*, 38(3), 1070–89.

De Paolis, P. (1990) 'Prototypes of the psychologist and professionalization: diverging social representations.' In G. Duveen and B. Lloyd (eds), *Social Representations and the Development of Knowledge*. Cambridge: Cambridge University Press, 144–63.

Dolnicar, S., Crouch, G. I. and Long, P. (2008.) 'Environmentally-friendly tourists: what do we really know about them?' *Journal of Sustainable Tourism*, 16(2), 197–210.

Fair Trade Australia (2011) 'About fair trade.' Available at: www.fta.org.au/about (accessed 13 October 2011).

Flick, U and Foster, J. (2008) 'Social representations.' In C. Willig and W. Stainton-Roger (eds), *Sage Handbook of Qualitative Research in Psychology*. London: Sage, 195–214.

Fredline, E. and Faulkner, B. (2000) 'Host community reactions: a cluster analysis.' *Annals of Tourism Research*, 27(3), 763–84.

Garriga, E. and Mele, D. (2004) 'Corporate social responsibility theories: mapping the territory.' *Journal of Business Ethics*, 53, 51–71.

Gossling, S. (2009) 'Carbon neutral destinations: a conceptual analysis.' *Journal of Sustainable Tourism*, 17(1), 17–37.

Hall, C. M. (2011) 'Climate change and its impacts on tourism: regional assessments, knowledge gaps and issues.' In A. Jones and M. Phillips (eds), *Disappearing Destinations: Climate Change and Future Challenges for Coastal Tourism*. Wallingford: CABI, 10–29.

Hares, A., Dickinson, J. and Wilkes, K. (2010) 'Climate change and the air travel decisions of UK tourists.' *Journal of Transport Geography*, 18, 466–73.

Haywood, S. F. (2011) *2011 Almanac of Environmental Trends*. San Francisco: Pacific Research Institute.

Holme, R. and Watts, P. (2000) *Corporate Social Responsibility: Making Good Business Sense*. Geneva: World Business Council for Sustainable Development.

Jodelet, D. (2008) 'Social representations: the beautiful invention.' *Journal for the Theory of Social Behaviour*, 38(4), 411–30.

Kang, M, and Moscardo, G. (2006) 'Exploring cross-cultural differences in attitudes towards responsible tourist behaviour: a comparison of Korean, British and Australian tourists.' *Asia Pacific Journal of Travel Research*, 11(40), 303–20.

Lee, W. and Moscardo, G. (2005) 'Understanding the impact of ecotourism resort experiences on tourists' environmental attitudes and behavioural intentions.' *Journal of Sustainable Tourism*, 13(6), 546–65.

Leiserowitz, A. (2007) 'International public opinion, perception, and understanding of global climate change.' Human Development Report Occasional Paper 31. New York: United Nations Development Programme.

Lorenzoni, I. and Pidgeon, N. F. (2006) 'Public views on climate change: European and USA perspectives.' *Climatic Change*, 77, 73–95.

Lumley, S. and Armstrong, P. (2004) 'Some of the nineteenth century origins of the sustainability concept.' *Environment, Development and Sustainability*, 6, 367–78.

Mebratu, D. (1998) 'Sustainability and sustainable development: historical and conceptual review.' *Environmental Impact and Assessment Review*, 18, 493–520.

Mehmetoglu, M. and Dann, G. M. S. (2003) 'Atlas/ti and content/semiotic analysis in tourism research.' *Tourism Analysis*, 8, 1–13.

Moscardo, G. (2008a) 'Exploring public awareness of threats to the Great Barrier Reef environment.' *Interdisciplinary Environmental Review*, 10(1&2), 45–64.

Moscardo, G. (2008b) 'Sustainable tourism innovation: challenging basic assumptions.' *Tourism Review International*, 8(1), 4–13.

Moscardo, G. (2008c) 'Community capacity building – an emerging challenge for tourism development.' In G. Moscardo (ed.), *Building Community Capacity for Tourism*. Wallingford: CABI, 1–15.

Moscardo, G. (2009) 'Tourism and quality of life: towards a more critical approach.' *Tourism and Hospitality Research*, 9(2), 159–70.

Moscardo, G. (2011a) 'Conflicts and challenges: cultural dimensions of sustainability and tourism.' Paper presented at International Tourism Sustainability Conference, 21–24 September, Mauritius.

Moscardo, G. (2011b) 'Exploring social representations of tourism planning: issues for governance.' *Journal of Sustainable Tourism*, 19(4–5), 423–36.

Moscovici, S. (1961) *La Psychanalyse, son image et son public*. Paris: Presses Universitaires de France. (2nd edn in English, 1976).

Moscovici, S. (1984) 'The phenomenon of social representations.' In R. Farr and S. Moscovici (eds), *Social Representations*. Cambridge: Cambridge University Press, 3–70.

Moscovici, S. (2001) 'Why a theory of social representations?' In K. Deaux and G. Philogene (eds), *Representations*. Oxford: Blackwell Press, 8–35.

Moser, S. C. (2010) 'Communicating climate change: history, challenges, process and future directions.' *Climate Change*, 1, 31–53.

Nicholls, S. and Amelung, B. (2008) 'Climate change and tourism in Northwestern Europe: impacts and adaptation.' *Tourism Analysis*, 13(1), 21–31.

Pan, B., Xiang, Z., Law, R. and Fesenmaier, D. R. (2011) 'The dynamics of search engine marketing for tourist destinations.' *Journal of Travel Research*, 50(4), 365–77.

Pearce, P. L., Moscardo, G. and Ross, G. (1996) *Tourism Community Relationships*. Oxford: Pergamon Press.

Pham, T. D., Simmons, D. G. and Spurr, R. (2010) 'Climate change-induced economic impacts on tourism destinations: the case of Australia.' *Journal of Sustainable Tourism*, 18(3), 449–73.

Philogene, G and Deaux, K. (2001) 'Introduction.' In K. Deaux and G. Philogene, (eds), *Representations*. Oxford: Blackwell Press, 1–7.

Powell, R. B. and Ham, S. (2008) 'Can ecotourism interpretation really lead to pro-conservation knowledge, attitudes and behaviour? Evidence from the Galapagos Islands.' *Journal of Sustainable Tourism*, 16(4), 467–89.

Raudsepp, M. (2005) 'Why is it so difficult to understand the theory of social representations?' *Culture and Psychology*, 11(4), 455–68.

Reser, J. P. and Swim, J. K. (2011) 'Adapting to and coping with the threat and impacts of climate change.' *American Psychologist*, 66(4), 277–89.

Scannell, L. and Grouzet, F. M. E. (2010) 'The metacognitions of climate change.' *New Ideas in Psychology*, 28, 94–103.

Scott, D., Peeters, P. and Gossling, S. (2010) 'Can tourism deliver its "aspirational" greenhouse gas emission reduction targets?' *Journal of Sustainable Tourism*, 18(3), 393–408.

Spink, A. and Jansen, B.J. (2004) *Web Search: Public Searching on the Web*. Dordrecht: Kluwer Academic.

United Nations Framework Convention on Climate Change (UNFCCC) (2011) 'Climate change science.' Available from: http://unfccc.int/essential_background/feeling_the_heat/items/2902.php (accessed 17 May 2011).

Victor, D. G. (2006) 'Recovering sustainable development.' *Foreign Affairs*, Jan./Feb. Available from: www.foreignaffairs.org/20060101faessay85109/david-g-victor/recovering-sustainable-development (accessed 12 May 2011)

Weber, E. U. (2007) 'Experience-based and description-based perceptions of long-term risk: why global warming does not scare us (yet).' *Climatic Change*, 77, 103–20.

Weber, E. U. and Stern, P. C. (2011) 'Public understanding of climate change in the United States.' *American Psychologist*, 66(4), 315–28.

Wells, G. (2011) *Sustainability in Australian Business: Fundamental Principles and Practice.* Brisbane: Wiley.

3

FACILITATING SUSTAINABLE INNOVATIONS FOR SMES IN THE TOURISM INDUSTRY
Identifying factors of success and barriers to adoption in Australia

Robyn Bushell and Bruce Simmons

Introduction

According to many sources, climate change is expected to have a significant impact on tourism (Rosenthal 2009, Gossling 2011, Strasdas 2010). Climate-change-induced effects on weather and coastal topography will affect patterns of travel. The tourism industry is itself a contributor, with some 5 percent of energy-related carbon dioxide and other greenhouse gas emissions worldwide (UNWTO/UNEP 2008) produced as part of transporting and accommodating tourists. Discussion in tourism literature of risks associated with climate change are not new (Wall and Badke 1994), but the impending challenges are only now beginning to be comprehended by the global industry and individual operators. It is imperative not only to understand the complexity of the risks. As with all industry sectors, tourism businesses need to implement shifts in practices in order to reduce outputs. That is, tourism must become part of the solution.

The risks to tourism go beyond climatic changes affecting travel. Tourism Northern Territory (2009) has signalled to operators in a region of Australia that relies heavily on nature-based tourism and faces harsh climatic effects, the likelihood of an additional risk, that of growing consumer awareness, and businesses who fail to respond positively becoming less competitive. They suggest travellers informed by sites advising how to 'travel green' will choose to stay with businesses who are able to demonstrate a clear commitment to environmental stewardship. Also evident is the risk of significant price rises if mitigation measures are not implemented. According to Strasdas (2010), forecasts are for a tripling of emissions from tourism, even with modest energy efficiencies, as well as massive price increases associated with the rising costs of fossil fuels.

Climate change mitigation and sustainability go hand in hand. Businesses that proactively and strategically improve their environmental performance with power, water, fuel, supplies and waste minimization will reduce their greenhouse emissions and are also able save money by lowering operational costs associated (Blanco, Rey-Maquiera and Lozano 2009; Gossling, 2011) and be socially responsible.

This chapter critiques three collaborative research and development projects in Australia, focused on improved sustainability outcomes by small businesses. The approach and processes discussed are intended to assist in any climate change strategies geared toward tourism operators.

Case studies

Caravan and Camping Industry Association Gumnut Awards

Background

The first case study concerns the increasingly important caravan and camping sector of tourism. In 2002 it provided over 50 percent of tourist accommodation in Australia (Baillie 2002) and projections are for a sustained visitation growth rate. These tourist parks have an important economic role, particularly in rural and regional areas of New South Wales (NSW), Australia (Simmons et al. 2006).

There are approximately 1,000 caravanning and camping parks in NSW, of which 463 are members of the Caravan and Camping Industry Association of NSW (CCIA). Such parks are frequently located in areas of high natural appeal with inherent high environmental vulnerability, such as adjacent to national parks, beaches and rivers. These locations may also face greater risks from bush fire and/ or extreme weather events such as floods and storm surges, events considered likely to increase in frequency and intensity with the advance of climatic change.

The program

In response to increasing awareness of the need to be proactive, the CCIA developed an environmental management program for its members. Called Gumnuts, it is a program that encourages operators to reduce the ecological footprint of their tourist parks; to provide benefit to local communities; and to transform socially and environmentally responsible practices into economic advantage. The program has sought to actively promote long-term changes in attitude, culture and practices needed for the adoption and implementation of these concepts involving guided and independently assessed self-audit, planning and application stages.

The program was developed jointly by the CCIA and the University of Western Sydney (UWS) as a three-tiered, integrated environmental management and capacity-building system. An awards structure was devised in conjunction with the program to encourage uptake. The Bronze Award is the first stage, based on a tailored training program designed to engage the operator into the program via a relative simple, standardized self-assessment and desk audit together with constructive feedback. Second stage is the Silver Award, involving training operators designing a business-specific planning process that will lead to improvements in owner-identified socio-environmental goals. Finally, the Gold Award rewards achievement and performance via an ongoing iterative process. This systematically addresses internal and external matters, and monitors progress through the operator-designed environmental management plan. All levels have to be renewed routinely or a higher level sought to maintain the award. Categories that must be addressed in the program are landscape, water and wastewater, solid waste, energy efficiency, air and noise pollution, biodiversity conservation, sustainable economics, staff, community relations, and safety and emergency response planning. Similar to its multiple facets, climate change is addressed in each of these categories in terms of resource efficiency (in particular energy and water), environmentally friendly fuel alternatives such as the use of solar and wind-generated power, waste minimization and recycling, supply chain management, staff training and disaster management. The program and award recipients are regularly publicized in caravan and camping park directories, association newsletters and press releases (Bushell et al. 2004).

Program review

The rate of growth of participation in the Gumnuts program to 2008 is shown in Figure 3.1. This indicates an initial rapid engagement of sixty businesses at the Bronze level in the first year, followed by a slight lag then more rapid growth before levelling with gradual increase to 2008. Each growth spurt resulted from strategies to promote the program and assist adoption rates. Initial adoption occurred after publicity at conferences and to members of the association. Significantly, in June 2004 a full-time extension officer was employed to assist parks engage and develop their audits (Bronze level). This resulted in increased

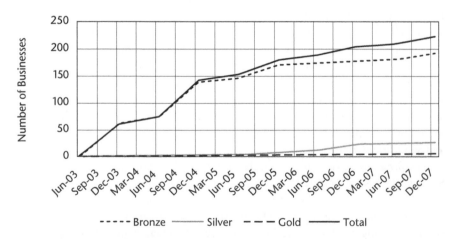

FIGURE 3.1 Business engagement in the Gumnut program

engagement and movement to the higher levels. The progression to the Silver and Gold levels has largely occurred between 2006 and 2008 after members completed two years of Bronze participation. This trajectory has continued with maintenance of the extension officer position providing one-on-one support to those park managers most reluctant to join the program, and providing assistance for those already enrolled to progress through the three stages. The CCIA also support members with a well-resourced website and regular newsletter featuring success stories (see www.gumnutawards.com.au). These strategies have been developed from ongoing evaluation of the program, both its success and the barriers to success.

In early 2005 a mail survey to all CCIA members was undertaken with the aim of identifying reasons some parks had not yet engaged in the program and to understand what support participating members needed for successful involvement (CCIA 2006; Simmons, Bushell and Scott 2010).

Thirty-five parks representing 14.5 percent of the non-participating membership responded to the survey. The findings revealed a high level (90 percent) of awareness in parks not already engaged in the program, and motivation to join was high (>70 percent) (Figure 3.2). Approximately 60 percent believed such a program to be of value to the industry and were already engaged in some type of sustainability activity. However, only 50 percent thought that they would benefit from taking part.

More than 50 percent of respondents claimed that they didn't understand the concept or had no time to implement such a program. Apart from a high 'no response' rate of more than 35 percent, more than 20 percent of respondents appeared to consider the program was inappropriate, would not help their business or was not worth the effort.

Twenty-three (12 percent) of the parks already participating in the Gumnuts program responded to the survey (CCIA 2006). From this limited response, the program appeared to have achieved outcomes on several levels. Awareness raising was a key outcome, with operators commenting that the program highlighted

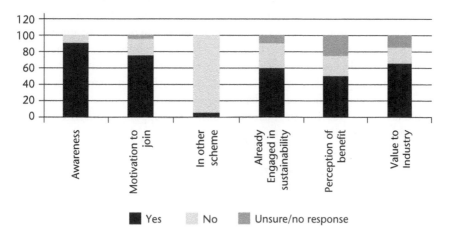

FIGURE 3.2 Results and conclusions from non–Gumnut-participating parks

hidden opportunities and inefficiencies in their operation, such as where to save money, improve environmental performance or develop better relations with the local community and council. This finding has informed the development of the website and regular newsletters to share success stories with non-participating members. The connection between marketing and the environment also appeared strong, and has been another important aspect in the promotion of the program.

Respondents were also asked to nominate aspects of the program that needed to be addressed. These mostly related to lack of awareness, knowledge and experience in regard to their own skills and staff, and relationships with consumers and authorities. Questions also arose as to how best influence the behavior of visitors and/or residents (in those parks with long-stay facilities) in regards to issues such as water and energy use and recycling.

Receptivity of operators to receiving new knowledge was also canvassed. The results suggested that the educational material needed a more user-friendly format, a stronger practical focus, to be easily accessible, and to better demonstrate the benefits of participating in the program. The results strongly suggested more guidance was required, and a flexible format such as web-based was desirable.

A further face-to-face survey was undertaken in 2010 of people attending the CCIA Caravan and Camping Super Show, which asked respondents questions regarding consumer awareness of the Gumnut Award program, as well as general questions aimed at determining attitudes towards eco-certification. This was supplemented with a survey of guests at three Gold Award level parks (Marshall 2010). The aim was to determine whether the program had been successful in establishing a strategic marketing brand, in providing awareness and a point of difference with non-participating operators in relation to a recognizable, environmentally responsible option for the consumer. Whilst the number of respondents was low (212 at the Super Show and 30 at the parks) the results suggest that the marketing potential of the Gumnuts program has not yet been fully realized. Most respondents recognized the program in terms of ecological sustainability but failed to understand the social and economic aspects of sustainability. A good record of environmental management did not appear to be a significant attractant to clients compared with the importance of other factors influencing the decision to stay at a park. The most influential factors were location, price, facilities, cleanliness and friendliness of staff. Environmental accreditation was the least important. Respondents suggested that accommodation discounts would be more motivating than the desire to support the environment or recognition by certification.

SeaChange for Sustainable Tourism

Background

The second case study covers the business precinct in Manly, a coastal urban village located 12 km north-east of the heart of Sydney's business district. Established in the 1850s as Australia's first seaside resort, Manly has a long history of tourism. Today a wide range of tourism-related businesses proliferate in the area, including hotels, motels, bed and breakfast accommodation and backpacker hostels, as well numerous eateries and many attractions, the primary one being a magnificent surfing beach, as well as the Sydney Harbour National Park, a large aquarium and beach-related businesses such as surf schools and boat hire businesses. The area's natural attractions also include the harbour, coastal walks, rugged headlands and natural bush, making it a mecca for tourists all year round. It is estimated that around 6 million people visit Manly each year, with this number expected to continue to increase by up to 6.2 percent per annum (Manly Council 2005).

The program

SeaChange for Sustainable Tourism was developed as a collaborative partnership between businesses (Manly Chamber of Commerce), the community (Manly Council) and an independent third party to guide and moderate the process (UWS). The aim of the SeaChange for Sustainable Tourism program was to foster a high standard of environmental stewardship and sustainability practices within the Manly tourism business sector in order to achieve compatibility between tourism, the environment and local resident amenity. The strategy focused on corporate responsibility and the obligatory role businesses need to assume to ensure that the values of Manly would be protected for both current and future generations. The program model employed education and incentives to support and motivate businesses to adopt triple-bottom-line management practices. This approach aiming to minimize the negative impacts of tourism at the source and generate a sustainable local tourism industry (Bushell et al. 2005).

The program objectives included maintaining and/or improving the physical and biological environment of Manly; demonstrating responsible environmental leadership within the local Manly community; encouraging socially responsible business management; and encouraging continual improvement in sustainable environmental, economic and socially responsible management and recognizing participants' achievements in these areas. The program addressed ten key local issues expressed as categories in the scheme: visual amenity, water and wastewater, solid waste, energy efficiency, air and noise pollution, biodiversity conservation, economics, staff, local community and risk management. The program model incorporated five levels or stages (Table 3.1). Completion of each stage in the program entitled participants to one star in the program's five-star accreditation scheme.

An ongoing promotional campaign was developed to promote business participation and encourage consumers to support businesses engaging in this program. The campaign consisted of advertising and press releases concerning the five-star business accreditation scheme, access to the SeaChange brand for participating businesses and the development of a website for the public and participating businesses. Businesses were recruited into the program via an intensive communications campaign administered by a project officer through mail, email, phone and presentations.

TABLE 3.1 SeaChange for Sustainable Tourism program model

Star Rating	Required Achievement	Assessment Method	Biennial Review Criteria
1-star	• Attend workshop • Complete checklist	Self assessment	Min. 2 stars to remain in scheme
2-star	Complete self audit satisfactorily	Desk audit	Achieve or create 2 benchmarks in each category
3-star	• Attend workshop • Develop 20 EMP goals and indicators (2 per category)	Desk audit	Demonstrate significant engagement with EMP i.e. completion of at least 50% of goals
4-star	Completion of 1 goal per category	Site visit	Renew all expired goals
5-star	Completion of 2 goals per category	Desk audit	Renew all expired goals

Source: (Bushell et al, 2005)

Program review

In the first year twenty-seven businesses of the 150 targeted engaged in the program, attended workshops and completed Stages 1 and 2 (Table 3.1), resulting in a triple-bottom-line audit of their businesses and identification of areas where improvements and changes could be made. Four of these businesses submitted a draft environmental management plan (EMP) (Stage 3: see Table 3.1) incorporating goals for improving environmental, social and economic business performance.

Two surveys were undertaken in a review of the SeaChange program details, the results of which are reported in Simmons, Bushell and Scott (2010). The first of these, a mail-out survey of thirty participating businesses (nine responses) was undertaken to determine the strengths and weaknesses of the program. Strengths of the program appeared to be awareness raising and its practical application and relevance to each business. A weakness however, lay in its low uptake and the need for clear solutions to everyday problems. Challenges lay in the extension of the program into the future. Concerns were also expressed in regards to the five-star system being confused with the 'star' rating system already used in the tourism industry as an indicator of quality, the need to increase awareness and participation rates, the difficulty for small businesses to attend workshops, and the lack of business collaboration in the program design.

The second survey was sent to non-participants to ascertain the level of awareness about the program within the Manly business community. Thirty-two businesses were contacted and fifteen responded. Of these, one-third had heard of the program but had not joined for a variety of reasons. This included shortage of time (the highest response), not considered applicable to the business and lack of knowledge. These reasons were consistent with earlier surveys of small to medium business (Greene 1999 and Rynne 2003, cited in Simmons et al. 2006).

Symmetry

Background

The third case study is in the Macarthur region, covering an area of 3,067 sq.km. in the south-west of Sydney, NSW. It has a population approaching 250,000 and some 17,052 businesses operating in the region. Ideally located on major transport corridors, the region is within half an hour's travel from Sydney. It attracts visitors to the rural atmosphere, colonial architecture, nature and adventure activities and sports. The region has a diversity of business enterprises, including manufacturing, farming, service industries and mining. Small to medium tourism enterprises include accommodation (camping and caravan parks, hotels, motels, bed and breakfast), farm stay, regional food and beverage, nature-based and recreational business operators.

The program

In 2007, the Macarthur Regional Organization of Councils (MACROC) received funding for a mentoring program focused on improving environmental practices of owners and managers of small enterprises employing less than twenty people. The resulting 'Symmetry Sustainable Business Project' was a consortium of partner organizations. UWS provided the conceptual base for the program as well as practical input in the development of the training component. MACROC provided project management skills and managed the proprietary accreditation system. Macarthur Business Enterprise Centre (MBEC) provided mentoring for participating businesses, and Macarthur Centre for Sustainable Living (MCSL) undertook auditing. The project aimed to build the capabilities of small businesses in environmental management skills by training and mentoring 210 small businesses (Bushell et al. 2010).

The Symmetry program was launched in February 2008 with a media campaign and mailout to small businesses in the region. A website space was created on the MACROC website (www.makeitinmacarthur.com.au) to inform and assist businesses.

The triple-bottom-line approach was employed, assessing sustainability across all aspects (environmental, economic and social) of each business's contribution to the local economy and community. The assessments were based on ten categories: site management, water and wastewater, energy efficiency, solid waste management, air and noise pollution, managing environmental impact, work practice, business strategy, local community, and safety and emergency response planning.

Program review

In the first year approximately 620 businesses attended information sessions, around 200 businesses were mentored, 93 small businesses engaged in the program at the Bronze level, and around 30 commenced the Silver level. While the small business mix reflected that of a diverse and growing community, a number of businesses in the program were directly associated with tourism as well several other businesses servicing them. This included accommodation, farm stay, farm gate sales, transport and retail.

At the end of 2009 a survey involving interviews of participating businesses was developed by the partner organizations with the objective to assess satisfaction with the program, motivations and views on how the program might continue once the initial funding ceased. Of the ninety-three Bronze accredited businesses on the Symmetry database in May 2010, 36 percent (thirty-two) completed the survey. However, only two of twenty-nine non-mentored businesses approached were willing to complete the survey.

All of the mentored businesses surveyed were at Bronze level and the majority had learned about the program through business networks such as the Business Enterprise Centre (BEC), indicating the importance of this communication link. Two noteworthy features of the participants were first, that their participation was largely driven by their values in respect to environmental sustainability, and second, their knowledge of sustainability had increased as a result of participating. This indicates that personal beliefs are important in gaining traction. Face-to-face networking, a product champion and knowledge of the local constituency were key elements in the recruitment of these participants to take part in the Symmetry program. It was also made clear that efforts were necessary to build and communicate the business case for participating in Symmetry, such as cost savings and increasing customer base, for the program to remain viable.

Overall participants reported they were very satisfied with the program, having achieved reductions in energy, water use and waste generation within their first year. In general most considered the program also useful from a business sense. While the majority had utilized the logo for branding, they believed the logo was not yet generally recognized by the community and needed more promotion. The level of awareness and knowledge of the existence of government support programs is less than 50 percent within the business community. Over 80 percent of the respondents indicated that they would renew their Bronze level award, and over 90 percent indicated they would recommend the program to other businesses, yet less than half indicated they would go on to Silver or Gold awards. Along with time constraints, cost is a key factor, the majority of respondents indicating that they would only renew their Bronze level if it remained subsidized with no increases in charges for accreditation. If marketing support and workshops were included (including guidance on branding methods and greater exposure of the Symmetry logo) there appeared to be a willingness to pay more (Bushell et al. 2010).

Businesses whose staff went to information sessions but did not enrol in the mentoring and also chose not to take part in the survey expressed lack of time to participate. The two businesses in this category who were willing to provide information cited lack of time to be involved, that they did not consider involvement a good business decision, and lack of belief in environmental issues (such as climate change) as the reasons they did not join the program.

Discussion

A history of engagement by SMEs

It is widely accepted that small to medium business enterprises (SMEs) in general do not significantly engage in environmental or sustainability accreditation systems (Hillary 2004, McKeiver and Gadenne 2005, Simmons et al. 2006). This is in spite of a significant growth of formal and informal accreditation systems within and external to industry. In general business in Australia has been slow to engage in such systems, as shown by surveys conducted up to 2003 (reported in Simmons et al. 2010). At a 2007 NSW Sustainable Development Conference it was reported by the Australian Industry Group that a survey of approximately 800 industries, Australia wide, found that only about 14 percent reported their environmental performance to the community (Australian Industry Group 2007). Earlier studies indicated uptakes of around 10 percent to be average (Simmons et al. 2010). While there has been little data gathered across industries generally, the uptake of sustainability programs conducted and sponsored by government (federal and NSW state) appear to be low. In Australia there are approximately 2 million small businesses (<20 employees), constituting approximately 95 percent of total business numbers, representing 34 percent of private industry value and employing half the country's workforce. Little is known however, of their collective ecological footprint or their engagement in remediation.

It would also appear that little is known about the collective ecological footprint of the tourism industry. Many tourism businesses are considered small to medium in size. But as literature suggests, there has been little engagement in Australia by operators at this level (Simmons et al. 2010). A recent paper on the accommodation sector by Chan (2011) suggests also that there has been little uptake of environmental management systems by small to medium hotels in Hong Kong, which represent the majority of businesses in that destination. In NSW alone there are approximately 2,500 tourist accommodation establishments including hotels and caravan parks, as well as approximately 9,000 holiday flats, units and houses (ABS 2010). The CCIA of NSW represents 463 accommodation operators with access to a well-resourced program, and some large hotels have environmental management programs, but little is known about the remainder.

The poor performance in engagement in environmental/sustainability management programs by SMEs has been consistent for more than ten years (reported in Simmons et al. 2006). Reasons centered on lack of awareness/

knowledge, lack of time, cost and priority. SMEs lacked the appropriate tools to evaluate their performance and the incentive to address directly non-economic factors (Viere et al. 2006). Since that time a significant number of guidelines, tools, calculators and grant systems have been developed to assist small businesses in adopting sustainable practices. For example, in 2010 in NSW there were eighteen programs of assistance from government and non-government agencies. Nonetheless, as suggested by Chan (2011), obstacles still remain. These centered on a lack of urgency, ambiguity of environmental management standards, lack of qualified consultants, conflicting guidance and inconsistent support.

Barriers identified in the programs

In the three programs described above, which share a common model of engagement, capacity building, assessment and monitoring, the surveys undertaken have evaluated performance by those engaged in the programs as well as determining why other businesses did not participate. These surveys were conducted over five years from 2005. Among the reasons given for businesses not participating, there are commonalities across all three programs: lack of knowledge, lack of time and business priorities (Table 3.2). These are consistent with the barriers identified in earlier studies reported in Simmons et al. (2006). It appeared therefore, that in order to be successful, programs need to address these barriers. Educational programs have been designed to achieve this (Table 3.2).

The following discussion relates how successfully these barriers have been addressed in each of the programs and the factors of success.

Anecdotal experience from many sources suggests that relying on grants alone to establish and maintain a program into the future is unlikely to succeed. Whilst engagement rates for the SeaChange program were initially reasonable and for Symmetry program they were high, without ongoing funds being available for management of these programs they are not likely to survive beyond the first few years. Recurrent government funds for ongoing management are not guaranteed. On the other hand the Gumnuts program appears to have a viable future as it has critical mass and members are seen to be gaining from the costs savings and market share that has resulted from the program. This has been the result of a focused and strategic approach. Members therefore support the CCIA Board in maintaining the program from within the association's own budget, contributed to by its member fees. This analysis suggests that such programs are best promoted by supporting associations such as chambers of commerce or individual industry professional associations, which have the knowledge and connections to design programs relevant to their members, and with a membership base with affiliated fees and revenue sources to provide for member-wide communications, development and training activities.

Owing to the rising costs of energy, water, waste management and potential disaster recovery following climate change events, savvy businesses will ultimately move towards savings and preparedness. In a world increasingly aware of environmental and climate change issues, the attitudes of the community and

TABLE 3.2 Methods to Overcome Barriers to the Adoption of Environmental Management Systems by Small to Medium Business (based on Simmons et al 2006 and Simmons, Bushell and Scott, 2010).

Barriers[1]	Addressed by Engagement Model
Lack of knowledge[a, b, c]	Education and training activities as an essential part of the process (workshops, mentoring, resources). Educational design in consultation with the particular industry sector or location.
Lack of time[a, b, c]	Planning by the industry itself and integration into existing activities.
Low priority[a, b, c]	High level of industry and community publicity through association journals and public recognition of achievement. Achievement used as a marketing tool.
Excessive cost[a, b]	Grants. Planning by each business within their budget constraints. Recognition of actions already undertaken. Realization of operational and resource savings.
Lack of credibility	Independent assessment.
Lack of commitment	Investment of time and costs in the program by participating business to foster ownership and longevity of the program.

1 Barriers identified in each of the case studies – a. Gumnuts; b. SeaChange; c. Symmetry

potential customers will become more important for business relevance. The growth of clean technology, green industries and investment protocols is evidence of this. The CCIA has recognized that awareness of environmental issues and their environmental credentials as an industry is the next step to promote engagement by their members in the Gumnuts program. The study undertaken by Marshall (2010) concluded that there is still a generally low awareness of the Gumnuts program (approximately 30 percent) within the community who regularly stay at caravan parks and attend the Association's Caravan Show. This is in spite of growing acceptance of the program by operators in the association. Marketing of such programs has in the past focused largely on the target businesses; however, a new approach is to promote a 'green' industry to the public. The CCIA is moving down this path with a program called 'Travelling Green' which seeks to engage its visitors in environmental awareness. In Marshall's (2010) surveys, respondents suggested that rewards such as discounts for sustainable behaviour (such as for reduced water and energy use) may be effective.

Factors of success

It appears the most important factor in success has been commitment and a sense of ownership by the businesses involved. This involves vision and the commitment of leadership of the business association or organization such as a chamber of commerce in a specific locality. Self-funding and the management of grants appears best in the hands of the associations, with some payment by members enhancing their commitment and ownership. The rewards are the outcomes of good business management and not temporary sponsorship from a government agency, which is generally not well valued. Capacity-building and support services (such as calculator tools and directories) are an integral component to the success of such programs, assisting businesses to develop appropriate sustainability management capabilities. In order to be relevant, a program needs to be co-developed by the businesses involved to ensure they understand the relevance and that skills are tailored to match needs and capability. Good communication between management of the program, businesses and their customers appears important to maintain the momentum of any program, celebrating successes, promoting recognition of achievements and innovations, and adapting to changing needs.

The elements of success listed below (developed from Simmons et al. 2010 and Ali 2010) have been used to varying degrees in of each the case studies. These elements were most achievable where ownership was strongest, in the Gumnuts program. We therefore recommend that such programs be owned and operated by professional business associations, provided committed leadership and program champions exist. The following elements are also integral to success:

- awareness creation
- collaborative development
- sound governance
- relevance to target businesses
- embedded in locality or business sector values
- accessible learning pathways
- triple-bottom-line accountability
- strong communication and marketing strategy
- feedback and examples to the targeted businesses about program advantages
- recognition and strong promotion of achievements
- recognisable trademark, badging and strategic marketing
- user pays, must be self-sustaining even if initiated with seed funds.

Conclusion

The tourism industry needs not only to change the attitudes of operators and increase their awareness of environmental issues associated with climate change, but also to shift practices and modify behaviours in order to achieve essential reductions in consumption and greenhouse gas outputs. These changes are the key challenge in risk reduction.

In a review of tourism and environmental actions, Blanco et al. (2009) found that proactive actions resulted in significant economic advantage while reactive pollution control measures invariably are either cost neutral or an additional expense to a business. Remediation costs can be significant, as are the costs of liability. The message to operators is that being environmentally responsible makes good business sense.

The literature also suggests consumers are increasingly wanting to 'travel green', and this is a trend expected to continue to increase, although our research did not yet show a strong consumer commitment at this time. Nevertheless, other research suggests consumers are beginning to choose to stay with businesses demonstrating a clear commitment to care for the environment (Strasdas 2010). Thus, an additional imperative in the business case to being engaged, environmentally responsible, and protecting the natural resources on which society and tourism is so highly dependent, is to protect one's market share as consumer awareness and demand for ethical business practices rises. Research also suggests a weak positive effect from investors and stock markets toward environmentally responsible firms (Blanco et al. 2009).

Our experience from the studies presented has been that utilizing strategies of engagement, capacity building and tiered reward in recognition of sound management processes as well as good performance are all essential, and are likely to be important to the adoption of any climate change mitigation programs.

Our research into the success and barriers to adoption across the three programs with their different partners and processes, found that for success, any such programs aimed at engaging and capacity-building small business owners into proactive mitigation strategies, need to be owned and operated by the targeted business sector, with a very clear and articulated vision and commitment. They also require a credible and transparent evaluation and accreditation component to provide highly visible recognition for genuine outcomes, backed up by a sound public relations strategy. The marketing of such schemes is a responsibility for both the individual participating business, which should market its achievements directly to its (potential) customers, and the organization running the program, which should market the program as a whole much more widely.

The other aspect we found to be crucial is ongoing monitoring by both the businesses themselves and the program as a whole. The outcomes of such monitoring, provides the incentive to strive for continuous improvement to the program and for participating businesses. Motivation is fuelled by cost savings, as well as the achievement of good environmental outcomes. As businesses become engaged and their awareness increases, so too does the willingness to invest time seeking alternate, improved ways of carrying out everyday operations.

For operators, the most significant barriers appear to be a lack of knowledge in how to engage, a lack of time and a low commitment. However, where they are members of an industry or business association such barriers can be overcome with sound leadership. A significant catalyst and component of this leadership is industry champions who lead others by good example and are willing to share their story and journeys concerning trials and errors, costs and savings, with other operators.

These case studies demonstrate the importance of collaborative partnerships, of context-specific strategies and approaches, and of adaptive and values-based management models in the evaluation of both success and failures of process. Any climate change strategies for small businesses are reliant on each of these elements in order to be successful.

References

Ali, I. (2010) 'Lessons from Symmetry – project manager's reflections.' Unpublished report by Imam Ali, Economic Development Manager, MACROC – Macarthur Regional Organization of Councils, Campbelltown, NSW, Australia.

Australian Bureau of Statistics (ABS) (2009). 'Key Facts – Small Business.' ABS Cat. No. 8165.0. data cube 1 (released December 2010). Australian Government, Canberra.

Australian Industry Group (2007) *Environmental Sustainability and Industry: Road to a sustainable future*. AIG, North Sydney. Available at: http://pdf.aigroup.asn.au/environment/enviro_sustain_indust_report.pdf (accessed 26 April 2012).

Baillie, B. (2002) 'A boom which defies the trend'. *Tourism and Hospitality Review*, Recovery Issue: 8.

Blanco, E., Rey-Maquiera, J. and Lozano, J. (2009) 'Economic incentives for tourism firms to undertake voluntary environmental management'. *Tourism Management*, 30: 112–22.

Bushell, R., Desailly, M., Simmons, B., Scott, J., Baillie, B. and Sinha, C. (2004) 'Environmentally and socially responsible practices in the camping and caravan industry: a case study from Australia'. *Tourism and Recreation Research* 29(3): 39–50.

Bushell, R., Scott, J., Knowd, I. and Simmons, B. (2005) *Sustainable Coastal Tourism for Manly*, Report to Manly Council. Tourism for Healthy Futures, UWS.

Bushell, R., Simmons, B., Robinson, S. and Mesiti, L. (2010) *Symmetry: Sustainable Business Practices for Small Medium Businesses*, Report to MACROC. Centre for Cultural Research, UWS, Sydney.

Caravan and Camping Industry Association of NSW (CCIA) (2006) *Challenging Barriers to Sustainability Practice in the NSW Caravan and Camping Industry Association*. Final Report for Grant No. 2004/ED/0016 to the NSW Environmental Education Trust, Sydney.

Chan, E. (2011) 'Implementing environmental management systems in small- and medium-sized hotels: obstacles'. *Journal of Hospitality and Tourism Research* 35(3): 3–23.

Gossling, S. (2011) *Carbon Management in Tourism: mitigating the impacts on climate change*. Routledge, London.

Hillary, R. (2004) 'Environmental management systems and the smaller enterprise.' *Journal of Cleaner Production 12*: 561–9.

Manly Council (2005) *Manly Visitor Information Centre Business Plan 2005–2007*. Manly, NSW.

Marshall, J. (2010) 'Assessing tourist recognition of the Caravan and Camping Industry Associations Gumnut Award program and its potential as a marketable brand.' Thesis (Bachelor of Social Science Honours), University of Western Sydney.

McKeiver, C. and Gadenne, D. (2005) 'Environmental management systems in small and medium businesses.' *International Small Business Journal* 23(5): 513–36.

Rosenthal, E. (2009) 'Tourism will be affected by climate change.' In R. Espejo (ed.), *What Is the Impact of Tourism?* Greenhaven Press, Farmington Hills, Mich., pp. 64–9.

Simmons, B., Bushell, R. and Scott, J. (2010) 'Fostering responsible tourism business practices through collaborative capacity-building'. In J. Sarkis (ed.), *Facilitating Sustainable Innovation through Collaboration*. Springer, New York, pp. 185–201.

Simmons, B., Scott, J., Bushell, R., Sinha, C., Desailly, M. and Baillie, B. (2006) 'Environmental management partnerships: a research case study from the tourism industry.' In R. Welford, P. Hills and W. Young (eds), *Partnerships for Sustainable Development*. Centre of Urban Planning and Environmental Management, University of Hong Kong.

Strasdas, W. (2010) 'Carbon management in tourism – a smart strategy in response to climate change'. In R. Conrady and M. Buck (eds), *Trends and Issues in Global Tourism*. Springer- Verlag, Berlin, pp. 57–71.

Tourism Northern Territory (2009) 'How will climate change impact tourism?' Available at: www.tourismmnt.com.au/going-green (accessed 20 May 2011).

UNWTO/UNEP (2008) *Climate Change and Tourism – Responding to Global Challenges*. UN World Tourism Organization, Madrid.

Viere, T., Herzig, C., Schaltegger, S. and Leung, R. (2006) 'Partnerships for sustainable business development: capacity building in South East Asia.' In R. Welford, P. Hills and W. Young (eds), *Partnerships for Sustainable Development*. Centre of Urban Planning and Environmental Management, University of Hong Kong.

Wall, G. and Badke, C. (1994) 'Tourism and climate change: an international perspective.' *Journal of Sustainable Tourism* 2(4): 193–203.

4

TOURISM INDUSTRY RESPONSES TO CLIMATE CHANGE IN HAWAII
An exploratory analysis of knowledge and responses

Shelly Rowell and Harold Richins

Introduction

The effects of climate change have the potential to significantly devastate both the natural and built assets of tourism (Agnew and Viner 2001; Becken 2007; Becken, Simmons and Hart 2003; Hall and Higham 2005; Hall 2006; Garnaut 2008; Harrison, Winterbottom and Sheppard 1999; Nurse 2008, 2007). This includes the strong possibility for this key industry sector to not only be affected by, but also have a considerable impact upon global warming and other changes in climate (Hall and Higham 2005, Becken 2007).

Just as climate change as a human-caused phenomena has previously been denied or disputed, so have approaches of sustainability also been marginalized as solutions (Dessler and Parson 2006, Grover 2004, Romm 2006, Singer and Avery 2006). With many years of scientific evidence having more recently been found to be compelling (IPCC 2007; Houghton 2004; McCaffrey 2006; Oreskes 2004; O'Hare, Sweeney and Wilby 2005; Weart 2003), a lack of awareness among the general population in terms of causes and potential effects of climate change within the world's environment has been highly problematic and has in many circumstance not led to substantial action (Dessler and Parson 2006).

As has been acknowledged, climate change will have a major impact on societies, communities and industry and will have important impacts particularly on the diverse tourism industry (Agnew and Viner 2001, Becken 2007, Hall and Higham 2005, Harrison et al. 1999, Pagnan 2003, Wall 1998). With changes in climate having the strong potential to influence tourism flows within various regions throughout the world, this has profound implications on sustainability factors including economic and sociocultural issues in additional to environmental aspects. This may result in redistribution of income, dramatic changes in employment and substantial impacts on the social and cultural aspects of community development. (Berrittella et al. 2006; Gossling 2006; Scott, Jones and Konopek 2007).

With this in mind, important questions may be asked. What response does the tourism industry see in dealing with the issues related to this matter presently and into the future? Are there influences or barriers that are affecting both the knowledge and the actions taken regarding climate change and its impacts? There is great variability in organizations broadly and on an individual basis in their approach to sustainability, particular with relevance to climate change alleviation (Dunphy, Griffiths and Benn 2003). In this regard, understanding opinions and behaviours of leaders within the tourism industry may perhaps provide some definitive knowledge for the development of more relevant and more effective mitigation methods.

The objective of this chapter is to explore the relationships between the level of knowledge of climate change impacts, underlying constraints and the potential for implementation of sustainability strategies within the tourism industry to alleviate and adapt to future effects. The exploratory research was undertaken within the destination-based tourism industry of Hawaii, using qualitative research methods in order to build an understanding of executives' opinions and behaviours on the factors and/or relationships between knowledge sources related to climate change and strategies to mitigate and adapt. With limited resources and a high economic reliance on tourism, Hawaii is extremely vulnerable to climate change. Such consequences may call for determined action by adopting responses with a holistic approach to sustainable tourism (Alber, Tantlinger and Kay 1998; MacKenzie 2006).

Climate change and its issues, constraints and approaches for sustainability

Studies that explore in depth the rationale that leads to decisions to implement or not to implement climate-change-related strategies, particularly with relation to the tourism and hospitality industries, have been modest. However some literature provides possible explanations why such strategies are not implemented. These include misinformation or lack of information and understanding to make decisions (Gelbspan 2004, Hall and Higham 2005), short-sightedness, conflicting long-term and short-term planning horizons, lack of political leadership where short-term economic gains occur at the expense of long-term sustainability (Craig-Smith and Ruhanen 2005), issues of common property and shared resources (Huybers and Bennett, 1997) concerns with immediate issues and priorities (Hall 2006), and the sustainable tourism paradox: that travel is inherently unsustainable and thereby issues are not really being addressed (Gossling and Hall 2006).

These explanations may be considered as potential constraints that prevent organizations from developing responses to climate change. Although the first explanation above explicitly identifies a lack of information and understanding, all five explanations imply varying degrees of ignorance or lack of concern about the magnitude of climate change consequences and/or how to mitigate and adapt.

To develop and implement effective mitigation and adaptation strategies, information and understanding is required to provide a knowledge base to formulate a response. Reports published by the Intergovernmental Panel on Climate Change (IPCC) in 2001 and 2007 identified the impacts for small islands in the Pacific region and implications for tourism. In addition the IPCC indicated that there are also numerous resources providing recommendations for approaches to mitigation and adaptation for both government and the tourism industry. In addition to this there are also authoritative and accessible publications, studies and sources of information on the impacts of climate change of direct relevance to Hawaii (Alber et al. 1998, Shea 2001, MacKenzie 2006). There is clearly no shortage of information available, and we might conclude that it is not probable that lack of information is a true barrier to action.

Given the high level of access to a variety of credible information sources it might be presumed that government, and particularly areas focused on tourism and travel, should have a greater understanding of climate change. However a survey of national tourism organizations highlighted a lack of awareness and understanding of climate change and its potential impact on the tourism industry (Scott, Wall and McBoyle 2005). As research by Hall and Higham (2005) reported, most national tourism organizations have been paying little or no attention to climate change, and those that do have a piecemeal response. However there is some movement in this direction more recently (CEO Challenge, 2008, Lean and Kay 2008).

From an industry perspective, Becken and Hart (2006) conducted individual in-depth interviews with eight members (public and private sector) of a tourism advisory panel. The purpose was to understand their perspectives on climate change in general and responses to fourteen proposed sustainability strategies. It was found that climate change was not a high priority. However, paradoxically the interviewees stressed that sustainability, triple-bottom-line reporting and resource efficiency were important (Becken and Hart 2006). Gossling and Hall (2006) have also reported on such contradictions, noting that the tourism industry often makes official statements about commitment to sustainable tourism, yet does not seem unduly concerned by global environmental change. As they summarize, both government and industry seem unwilling to implement any but nominal solutions at hand.

The industry's lack of will and leadership on this issue may be key constraints, but there are likely to be multiple reasons for this lack of understanding and response, as outlined earlier. One possible issue is the question of responsibility, both to educate and to act (Belle and Bramwell 2005). The question of who should lead this change is pertinent here: Should action be mandated by government or self-regulated by industry (Young and Van der Straaten 2001)?

A perpetual debate ensues in the sustainable tourism literature regarding the responsibility of government intervention versus industry self-regulation, with benefits and costs evaluated on both sides. Although opinions vary on detail, it is generally accepted that sustainability should not be left to industry self-regulation or rely solely on government intervention; it is a joint effort (Hjalager 1996, Young and Van der Straaten 2001).

A number of studies indicate attitudinal barriers to compliance with environmental regulation (Geno and Acutt 2000, EPA 1997) while acknowledging the reluctance of private enterprise to self-regulation (Geno, Dunn and Richins 2003; Kotey and Meredith 1997). Relevant to this is a study conducted by Huybers and Bennett (1997) involving a survey of 208 tourism industry businesses, all members of the Tourism Council of Australia. The respondents were asked to rank the importance of a long list of environmental issues that would affect the demand for tourism. The top-ranking issues were natural resource management, wilderness protection and conservation. Despite this concern only half the respondents perceived that environmental regulation benefited their business; the other half felt that regulation was nothing but a burden.

As mentioned previously, enterprises vary significantly in their approach to sustainability. Dunphy et al. (2003) provided a categorization model for businesses' responses to sustainability and applied these to the climate change issue. Each category is described by typical objectives, strategies and actions. Table 4.1 is a summary of the categories.

TABLE 4.1 Categories of businesses' responses to sustainability

Rejection
Concentrates on short-term profitability
Rejects environmental claims as 'greenwash'
Not concerned about consequences
Seeks exceptions to environmental
    protection legislation
Actively undermines the sustainability
    movement
	Strategic proactivity
	Pursues strategic opportunities for
	    sustainability
	Strong commitment with strategies to
	    become a market leader in sustainability
	Sustainability innovation processes
	Destroys unsustainable product designs
	    and processes

Non-responsiveness
Business as usual, climate change is a
    distraction to be avoided
Avoids costs of change and adaptation
Ignores rising tide of sustainability
    awareness
General ignorance
	Efficiency
	Creates efficiencies through reduction
	    and reorganization
	Strategies in place to reduce resource use
	    (energy and water)
	Designs/redesigns products and processes
	    to reduce ecological footprint

Compliance
Compliant with legislation and regulation
Effective risk management system and
    informed workforce committed to
    compliance
Establishes an organized measurement
    and monitoring system
	The sustaining corporation
	Redefines the business environment for a
	    more sustainable world
	Changes 'rules of the game' to achieve
	    sustainability
	Influences public policy
	Redesigns and reorganizes company's supply
	    chain so whole process is sustainable
	Goes beyond best practice, advances and
	    publicizes best practice and influences
	    the industry.

Source: adapted from Dunphy et al. (2003).

Methodology of the qualitative study

To explore the relationships between the level of knowledge of climate change impacts, underlying constraints and the potential for implementation of strategies within the tourism industry, research was undertaken within the destination-based tourism industry of Hawaii. The research involved exploratory in-depth interviews, which were conducted with the intention to build a theoretical understanding of tourism enterprises in Hawaii regarding their motivation to address climate change in management and development.

Creswell (2003) has indicated that qualitative techniques are best used for this type of research, particularly where the research is seeking the participant's own words and social interactions and knowledge. The study utilized an adapted qualitative method, which has consistency with social constructionism, which emphasizes social interactions and common sense knowledge of reality (Ragin 1994, Taylor and Bogdan 1998, Veal 1997). This approach provided a richness of results for the research, with in-depth interviews (recorded by tape and written notes) in the interview's own words and based on social interactions. Data was then analyzed to form categories and broad patterns to enable the development of a proposed theory and hypothesis.

The in-depth interview technique was used in a similar study conducted by Becken and Hart (2006) in New Zealand. The research explored the level to which tourism stakeholders in New Zealand perceive a need and potential for climate-change related strategies within tourism. Like the study discussed in the present chapter, the Becken and Hart (2006) study involved separate interviews with eight tourism industry stakeholders, with each interview lasting approximately one hour, and it shares many parallel characteristics with the present study such as purpose, context and type of participant.

The method used in the present study is therefore suitable as it seeks to discover and explore tourism stakeholders' attitudes to climate change and mitigation actions. The instrument used in the 45–60 minute in-depth/in-person interviews of this study was a checklist of themes and questions to be raised (Veal 1997). This checklist, which was organized from the conceptual framework and list of data needs, ensured that all relevant topics were covered even though they were in different orders and dealt with in different ways.

In order to acquire a broad range of industry participation, an important objective was to interview at least two companies from each sector of the tourism industry. Though all airlines contacted elected not to participate, interviews were successful with accommodation, transport, attraction, tourist activity and tourism industry associations and government organizations. Of a total of twenty interviews from forty-five major Hawaii enterprises, fifteen were successful as some interviews were not usable either due to lack of sufficient data or, in one case by request of the participant after the interview was conducted. A breakdown of sector and scale is provided in Table 4.2.

TABLE 4.2 Respondents in the study by tourism sector

Sector	No. of respondents	Size/scale
Accommodation	4	2 multinational, 1 medium, 1 small
Transport	3	1 car rental, 1 medium tour, 1 small tour
Attraction	2	1 state-owned, 1 locally owned
Activity	2	1 medium adventure company, 1 small watersports company
Industry association	3	1 cultural tourism, 1 ecotourism, 1 hotel industry
Government	1	1 state-level

Findings

The findings discussed below are represented in terms of the four themes that lead to action and the categories that emerged from within these themes. These themes are knowledge sources, concern, constraints and influence, and responsibility and action.

Knowledge sources

Knowledge sources involve not only where information comes from but also the concept of the trust and credibility of sources and how this influences knowledge creation (Peters 1996). Four distinct categories emerged from participant responses on how they developed their knowledge: science-based reports, media, government and industry information.

Scientific sources

Science-based information sources were only mentioned by four participants, however all those who mentioned them believed these to be the most credible and reliable of all sources. Participants who do not rely on scientific information sources gave reasons such as 'no time to read', 'lack of business relevance', 'overuse of scientific jargon' and 'access to credible articles'. These are discussed later.

One participant felt that the IPCC reports are not credible, perceiving them as political documents with contents changed to meet the desired summary. Two participants were not convinced that climate change is an issue, and needed 'real' evidence rather than computer models and statistics and that there was a high degree of uncertainty in the science. Although a number of regional reports (Shea 2001, MacKenzie 2006) and international reports (IPCC 2001, 2007) are readily available, these appear in some participants' views to lack creditability and instead are considered potentially more political in nature.

Media sources

Mainstream and niche media information sources featured in 87 percent of the participants' responses. Of these participants 85 percent mentioned media as the dominant or only source of information. Print media was the most popular information source, with 69 percent of participants mentioning this source.

The few participants who denied anthropogenic (human-influenced) climate change relied on three or fewer sources of information, and used websites as a primary or only source. Such websites, participants explained, contain downloadable peer-reviewed scientific articles. One article was offered as an example. This article was by non-scientists and published in a medical journal. However the participant had not questioned the doubtful authority of the source. The following quote from one of the participants, for example has little basis in fact:

> In all of the peer-reviewed scientific papers on climate change between 2000 and 2004, over half of them believe it is a natural cycle and so [I] don't believe it is man that is influencing.
>
> *(participant 14)*

Another influence in this situation is credibility and trust. Here the participant displayed a gross mistrust of the mainstream media. This particular participant (participant 14) believes mainstream media are not being truthful and that 80 percent of media have left-leaning philosophies.

A difference was expressed by some participants between mainstream and other media, with a general feeling that it is important to look outside mainstream media. Sensationalist media for some had no credibility, while they gave more trust to public television and radio.

Government sources

Few participants mentioned government sources of information. There was some sentiment, however, that government should play a greater role in educating and promoting alternatives:

> Government's role is education and information about climate change using credible sources.
>
> *(participant 13)*

Four participants did not place much credibility in government as an information source. Of these, two said it depended on who produced the information and who was supporting it. One of the participants felt that climate change is a political viewpoint and not a fact. This participant believed that it is merely a way to alter the economic balance in the world. Again, though numerous government responses have occurred (Mather, Viner and Todd 2005; Craig-Smith and Ruhanen 2005;

Hjalager 1996), there is an apparent lack of credibility with many, due to the perceived political emphasis.

Industry sources

Information from the tourism industry was an important source for approximately half the participants. Five participants mentioned their industry associations as the most influential and credible source of information. The role of industry associations was highlighted by one participant as being important for the dissemination of information and guidance on sustainability issues. Another participant recognized that associations are key influencers in developing a unified strategy on the issue.

Participants from the largest companies, two multinational and one national, mentioned that some of their information was sourced from 'corporate knowledge' and partly stemming from the corporate social responsibility goals of the group or parent company. This was mentioned as an important link in influencing their will to take action. This area of information flow appears to be consistent with a focus on self-regulation through individual and industry associations (Huybers and Bennett 1997).

Information gaps of knowledge sources

Around half participants raised the issue of an apparent information gap. Participants felt that there is a lack of concise, non-sensationalized, scientific jargon free, business-relevant information. The information gap related to the expected impacts, timeframes and their likelihood for the Hawaiian islands. Some particularly identified that there is no real information on how climate change may affect individual businesses and industry, and what should be done to mitigate and adapt to the potential threats of climate change. Even for those who did not identify this specific information gap, it was clear there was a lack of knowledge about possible options for mitigation and adaptation responses:

> Industry needs to be educated on how to do things differently.
>
> *(participant 13)*

Another frequent issue discussed was the gap between the amount of information participants are willing and able to absorb and the amount needed to develop sufficient knowledge and concern to act. This is consistent with Dunphy et al.'s (2003) and Mather et al.'s (2005) indication of information related to strategies and techniques in addressing action areas. As one participant put it:

> We need more than sound bites, but we are too busy to read.
>
> *(participant 7)*

Concern

The concept of past experience seems to be a key differentiator in the level of concern. Those who have past exposure to the extreme fluctuations in tourism demand caused by natural disasters and human-induced events exhibit greater concern about potential climate change implications than do others. Through the in-depth interviews, eight participants gave detailed accounts of past disasters and crises and how they affected business and industry. These events included a fuel crisis, 9/11, hurricanes, earthquakes, floods and storm surges. The effects of these as explained by participants were decreases in visitor numbers, significant economic losses, pay cuts, redundancies, bankruptcy, development ceased, infrastructure damage costs and diminished quality of visitor experience.

The categories of concerns expressed by participants relate to the potential climate change implications for tourism in Hawaii and manifest as supply, demand and other economic issues. These can be categorized further in relation to the nature of the implication:

- change to natural environment
- implications for built environment
- implications on demand
- fuel cost and taxation
- greening markets.

Below is a discussion on the types of concerns over how tourism will be affected.

Change to the natural environment

One concern is that the Hawaii tourism industry is reliant on its natural environment as its major attraction. Five participants felt that changes to the attractiveness of the natural environment will affect the appeal of the destination (participants 10, 9, 3, 15, 6). Sea level rise is seen to have the potential to dramatically alter the natural environment with loss of beaches, issues with water quality and reduction in biodiversity due to diminishing habitat for native wildlife breeding. These strong concerns have also been previously indicated within a context of tropical and island locations (Alber et al.1998, Belle and Bramwell 2005, Craig-Smith and Ruhanen 2005).

Extreme weather patterns were a major concern, with participants recognizing the heightened need for emergency preparedness for natural disasters. There was some optimism in relation to hurricanes, that any fluctuations in arrivals will eventually balance out:

> As we are hit there will be a shift in travel to other destinations while Hawaii is in disaster recovery, then as others are hit tourism will increase to Hawaii and in the end it will all be even.
>
> *(participant 5)*

Implications for built environment

It was recognized by some participants that sea level rise will dramatically alter the built environment. Costs of property and infrastructure, repair and preventive reinforcement were the major concerns here for three participants. Some identified concern over further negative impacts on hotels and issues for properties rebuilding and renovating, as well as damage to access infrastructure such as roads and airports.

Implications on demand

Due to the above implications on supply, concern was frequently raised regarding future demand for Hawaii as a tourist destination. Many expect that climate change issues will result in a decrease in the number of visitors. This is seen as potentially causing market concern about travelling due to storms or perception of storms. It was identified by some that the high level of access to global weather news influences this perception. According to one participant:

> Greater access to information and flexibility in travel plans means that customers can make decisions to quickly change plans based on weather forecasts.
>
> *(participant 3)*

Many fear that changes to the natural and built environments such as loss of beaches will affect demand for the destination. In addition it is expected that there will be far fewer visitors if the environment is damaged as the quality of experience will be diminished.

Fuel cost and taxation

Nine participants believed that additional taxation particularly on fossil fuels would raise the cost of doing business. This is expected to raise not just the direct cost of energy but also the cost of necessary imported goods. The peak oil issue and energy crisis was mentioned by one participant:

> Issues of oil availability are going to have a compounding effect and will exacerbate the issues for tourism.
>
> *(participant 5)*

The economic implications of climate change were a concern for many participants, particularly as Hawaii is heavily reliant on the visitor industry. This however was more connected to a concern of increased regulation as government tries to respond, rather than a concern for economic implications due to physical changes to the environment. These regulation challenges echo previous literature on government intervention (Mather et al. 2005, Craig-Smith and Ruhanen 2005, Hjalager 1996).

Another concern is the long-term economic sustainability of tourism due to access:

> Mass tourism as has been the mainstay of Hawaii tourism is in the long term not suitable due to air transport being the only means of access to these remote islands.
>
> *(participant 12)*

One participant viewed the cruise ship journey (from the mainland United States) of four to five days as taking too long for the ordinary traveller. In addition to this concern, a few expected travel to become more expensive, and this would be devastating for Hawaii's tourism industry.

Greening markets

The increasing environmental ethics of tourists was seen as both a threat and an opportunity. Three believed that there is growing demand from customers wanting to protect the environment. Another perspective on this was that environmental ethics will become mainstream:

> Environmental relations and ethics will drive change for corporate sustainability as businesses take action when visitors ask for better care of the environment.
>
> *(participant 15)*

As one participant also stated:

> Visitors will choose places where government and business are taking care of the environment.
>
> *(participant 13)*

Constraints and influences

Some participants stressed that no business wants to purposely harm the environment; however it is not yet at the forefront of industry leaders' minds that doing nothing is doing harm. As some participants explained, there is a need to act before it is too late, and progress is not fast enough. The broad diversity of constraints impeding action is discussed below, as are the influences to motivate action:

*   short-sightedness
*   reactive culture
*   cost and competition
*   empowerment.

Shortsightedness

Many participants indicated that the lack of urgency is due to the gradual nature of climate change, which in a business world is too slow for comprehension. As the more severe changes are not showing significant effects presently, the industry does not acknowledge urgency. Three participants explained that they had more pressing short-term issues and priorities:

> The further off the impact is then the more likely we are to postpone doing anything about it.
>
> *(participant 6)*

Reactive culture

Even though some recognized that there are solutions at hand, there was a general feeling that the industry is crisis reactive and that on an individual business basis, there is resistance to proactive change. It was explained that organizational behaviour and culture could only change in times of crisis.

Cost and competition

Cost of capital and return on investment were key constraints for several businesses that were knowledgeable about the solutions. Previous bad experiences had informed negative opinions about the economic costs of implementing sustainable solutions. Competition and price were indicated as other factors. These are described in relation to the price competitiveness of tourism on a global scale:

> Costs must be kept to a minimum in order to compete with other destinations on price.
>
> *(participant 13)*

Empowerment

For three participants government policy, bureaucracy and lack of action were perceived as strong constraints against industry taking positive action. Issues of inconsistent legislation and conflicting policies between departments were raised as well as the lack of political will. This is consistent with previous literature indicating the challenges in hindrance of taking action (Becken and Hart 2006, Gossling and Hall 2006).

The situation of offshore owners with centralized management was a constraint for some larger companies; this was not due to not having the will but seen as more to do with the slow progression of initiatives:

> Many hotel and resort companies with properties in Hawaii have ownership and management centralized elsewhere. This makes taking the lead on environmental activities, quite difficult.
>
> *(participant 4)*

Some participants also explained that the lack of shareholder consensus is why many programs do not get funded.

On the opposite side to constraints are influences. Participants from the larger corporate organizations talked about their corporate culture moving toward sustainability. These companies are developing strong corporate social responsibility goals and environmental ethics, which are being embedded in organizational objectives and culture. One participant explained:

> Sustainability is a matter of leadership and will.
>
> *(participant 10)*

There was support from some of the participants for this idea who feel that leadership is needed within industry:

> The greatest influence for the tourism industry will be for other industries to take the lead such as banks, business leaders, insurance companies as well as academics.
>
> *(participant 3)*

However it is possible that the greatest influence for the tourism industry to begin mitigation is the customer. Five participants strongly indicated that climate change mitigation is a marketing advantage with the ability to generate significant positive publicity and to build an attractive competitive brand. This has some consistency to Mather et al. (2005) in their suggestion regarding marketing alternatives influenced by the effects of climate change on tourism.

Three participants commented that change in mitigation would be influenced by three pressures:

- noticeable weather
- market demand
- government enforcement.

Responsibility

An intriguing phenomenon was of the distancing of 'self' from the climate change issue. Participants generally tended to remove themselves and their companies from the issues being talked about by constantly referring loosely to the industry, general business or community. This is discussed below in terms of government, industry collective and individual business.

Government

A common response to the question of responsibility is the expectations and perceptions of the role of government. Several participants view politicians, as not having enough foresight and vision along with a lack of political will to make necessary changes. There also seems to be a deep frustration with an apparent lack of definitive position on the climate change issue and thus lack of clear policy. This frustration manifested with comments such as:

> Government needs to make a decision, they should make it hurt or educate.
>
> *(participant 12)*

Around half the participants saw a need for government to drive the change process with more discussion on solutions. It was suggested that this is because business culture has a short-term planning horizon, therefore it is expected that the government's role is to plan for long-term impacts. However some argued that there is too much planning and not enough action and that the Hawaiian government develops plans that do not get implemented. Concern was expressed regarding a lack of trust in government decision making:

> There is a lack of trust in federal government to make decisions in the best interest of the country's long-term future, due to individual political agendas.
>
> *(participant 8)*

Despite these issues there were numerous responsibilities regarding sustainability and climate change actions, which participants felt were expected of government. These are shown in Table 4.3.

Industry collective

Few saw the climate change issue as solely an industry responsibility. There was however an accepted notion that the industry needs to look at this collectively and that all industry should be responsible for coming up with real solutions. This is supported by Huybers and Bennett (1997) notion of self-regulation. Standardized environmental principles were seen as important:

> Industry should adopt standardized green principles and practice resource and energy conservation.
>
> *(participant 9)*

Most respondents did not believe, however, that industry should take a lead, and there was a clear transference of responsibility to government.

TABLE 4.3 Responsibilities expected of government by participants

Action	Suggested by participant no.
Legislation for zoning of developments	6
Risk management	9
Disaster management	12
Education	13
Introduce alternative sources of energy and renewable fuels	5
Encourage sustainability with incentives, education and promotion of alternatives	5
Ensure access infrastructure (airports, roads etc.) is maintained, repaired and reinforced	12
Publish information on climate change	3
Introduce carbon tax	3
Legislate and mandate for reductions in greenhouse gas emissions	3
Supporting role by introducing tax breaks and other incentives to reward and compensate early adopters	10

Individual enterprises

There was a general consensus that business will only act based on economic need and competition. This is highlighted in terms of the costs associated with taking a personal responsibility. However it was suggested that this could also be a positive influence as corporations can lead through demonstrating how environmental sustainability can be achieved while growing bottom-line profits. Tied to this profit-driven perspective is a common view that business will self-regulate if the market demand exists. Some participants talked about the opportunity to develop a green marketing edge, and this has some consistency with previous literature (Mather et al. 2005, Craig-Smith and Ruhanen 2005):

> A green marketing advantage can be gained through decisive responses to climate change.
>
> *(participant 10)*

Others saw the process of action being a grassroots, bottom-up approach driven by employees, with companies developing a stewardship approach to preserve and sustain resources for future generations. For one participant this manifest in the follow comment:

everything comes for a price and it is time we paid for the environment.

(participant 1)

Another issue relating to individual business responsibility is disaster preparedness. Four participants believed that it is the responsibility of the individual business to ensure they are prepared with plans and contingencies for potential climate change related disasters.

Action

Action for the purposes of this research includes strategy formulation and implementation to mitigate and adapt for climate change. The following section is a description of the responses from participants regarding taking action and some insights on how some of these factors affect decision-making.

Mitigation

Six participants viewed reducing greenhouse gas emissions predominantly as a by-product of saving energy to reduce costs, followed by environmental and social responsibility. All four participants from the accommodation sector mentioned this, and there was a strong belief from some that hotels were leading the tourism industry in terms of environmental initiatives linked to efficiency and cost savings. It was felt that the driving change for the accommodation sector to adopt greener practices was this potential to save money with energy-efficient equipment, and this sentiment is consistent with previous literature (Dunphy et al. 2003) on cost savings as a key driver. It was stressed by a few, however that the industry will not change priorities from seeing efficiency and cost savings as the primary objectives:

> For this industry efficiency will always be number one, environment number two.

(participant 11)

One participant felt that the tourism industry should be a target for a model energy code. However it was noted that although hotels are introducing energy-efficient operations there is very little real cost saving because the cost of energy continues to rise.

Two participants' companies had created special teams to find and implement innovative solutions to achieve both cost savings and emissions reduction. Another participant felt that just planting more trees on their property was a step in the right direction. A few participants talked about the need to educate visitors by doing things to change their behaviour from passive to active in terms of saving energy and water.

Risk, crisis or disaster

There was an overall recognition that Hawaii is crisis-driven because of its vulnerability in physical terms. Hence some participants talked about their crisis plans, disaster preparedness and recovery plans for hurricanes and tsunamis. For all participants, however, risk management as a topic was possibly misunderstood: it was used as a term for crisis management or disaster preparedness for unforeseen natural catastrophic events.

The issue of the need for a financial contingency and having the funds available to both prepare and to cope was raised. This is perceived as a major issue for the industry to address, and may involve lobbying government.

Planning

The issue of planning and its relationship to action was discussed by participants. Perhaps the noticeable lack of action is in part because of lack of planning in the tourism industry. One participant mentioned the Hawaii Tourism Strategic Plan as being a step in the right direction. However this plan does not mention climate change from a risk assessment, mitigation or adaptation perspective (HTA 2008).

Many participants highlighted that their enterprise has a short planning cycle of only one or two years ahead. It was evident that all participants did not consider climate change impacts or implications in their strategic planning process even though they were concerned about them:

> We are aware of the changes that need to be made but the consequences are too far off to start planning for them now.
>
> *(participant 2)*

Some participants raised the issue that they do not have enough information available to assist in effective planning and that more clarification is needed about the known high-probability impacts. It was acknowledged that even with this information, however, there would only ever be slow planned change rather than radical overnight change:

> Destinations as a whole should look at long-term planning in dealing with sustainability and climate issues and what is needed is a coordinated response between government and industry.
>
> *(participant 13)*

Adaptation

Most participants did not understand the concept or need for adaptation, and it required significant probing to get responses. Typically there was some acknowledgement that there was a need to anticipate and prepare for the impacts of climate change.

Four participants took an optimistic view that the tourism industry will survive: it might change and adapt, but it will continue as it is has done in the past. This is typified by the following comment:

> Tourism will recover as everything does, so it is not a question of if tourism will recover from climate change disasters, it is simply a matter of how long it will take.
>
> *(participant 12)*

Conclusion

The purpose of this chapter was to explore the relationships and factors between knowledge of climate change impacts and the development of sustainability strategies to mitigate them and adapt. Several factors were found to have an impact on decision making: knowledge, concern, constraints, influences and responsibility.

It was found that there were four main groups of sources of information apparent in the formation of knowledge. Media was the most prominent source of information followed by industry, science and then government. An information gap was identified in relation to sources of information for industry that are concise, non-sensationalized, scientific jargon-free, accessible and business-relevant.

A factor affecting action was concern. This relates to changes to natural and built environments, demand, fuel cost and taxation and the greening of markets. Concerns centre on either economic or environmental issues, and it was evident that these relate to the level of knowledge. With less knowledge the participants in this study were generally more concerned about economic implications through government intervention than the effects on climate change. Furthermore, past experience was an important element in influencing opinion, and this results in higher levels of concern among participants.

There are several constraints that were seen as clear reasons for participants to resist developing responses despite all other propensities: short-sightedness, reactive culture, cost and competition, and empowerment. These constraints effect different organizations in different ways, with some having one and others several constraints. Several constraints are seen as creating a major resistance to responding to the climate change issue. Influences were few, though it is interesting that a corporate culture with a sustainability ethic and strong leadership are viewed as the main influences. The perception and prospect of an emerging green consciousness within key tourism markets is also seen as creating a propensity to act.

Responsibility appears to play an important role in whether an organization will act or not. Those who believe government should lead and industry should cooperate, generally are seen to transfer responsibility in order to remove themselves from the issue, thereby creating either inaction or a reactive response.

Action itself was discussed in terms of responses of mitigation and adaptation. It is evident that mitigation responses were seen as few and adaptation responses even fewer. There seems to be much confusion about the difference between risk, disaster and crisis, and how each of these should be managed and treated. This poses problems for organizational strategic planning and long-term sustainability.

Leadership in addressing climate change issues is of strategic importance from an industry perspective. Climate change champions within industry sectors may have a significant influence to motivate others within the tourism sector to act. Leaders are required who have the ability to demonstrate and communicate key messages about successful responses to different groups from varying perspectives, such as market-driven, opportunity, corporate social responsibility, sustainability, innovation and disaster preparedness.

Despite the reasons for the slow uptake of mitigation and adaptation strategies, with the preponderance of findings showing both the coming of climate change and the connection of humans to its cause, if the tourism industry does not act quickly and definitively, the consequences are potentially devastating on many levels. As one participant so aptly described the situation and our critical challenges ahead:

> We are all cruising on the *SS Titanic* through the sea of tranquillity and everything seems calm now ... but there is a very big iceberg ahead.
>
> *(participant 10)*

References

Agnew, M. and Viner, D. (2001) 'Potential impact of climate change on international tourism', *Tourism and Hospitality Research*, Vol. 3, pp. 37–60.

Alber, S., Tantlinger, M. and Kaya, M. (1998) 'Hawaii Climate Change Action Plan', State of Hawaii Department of Business, Economic Development and Tourism Energy, Resources, and Technology Division and Department of Health Clean Air Branch.

Becken, S. (2007) *Tourism and Climate Change: Risks and Opportunities* (Climate Change, Economies and Society). Bristol: Channel View.

Becken, S. and Hart, P. (2006) 'Tourism stakeholders' perspectives on climate change policy in New Zealand', Lincoln, New Zealand: Landcare Research.

Becken, S., Simmons, D. and Hart, P. (2003) 'Tourism and climate change – New Zealand Response'. Proceedings of the 1st International Conference on Climate Change and Tourism, 9–11 April, Djerba, Tunisia. Madrid: World Tourism Organization.

Belle, N. and Bramwell, B. (2005) 'Climate change and small island tourism: policy maker and industry perspectives in Barbados,' *Journal of Travel Research*, Vol. 44, No. 1, pp. 32–41.

Berrittella, M., Bigano, A., Roson, R. and Tol, R. S. J. (2006) 'A general equilibrium analysis of climate change impacts on tourism,' *Tourism Management*, Vol. 27, No. 5, pp. 913–24.

CEO Challenge (2008) 'PATA CEO Challenge'. Available at: http://ceochallenge.pata.org/site/A (accessed 22 March 2009).

Craig-Smith, S. and Ruhanen, L. (2005) 'Implications of climate change on tourism in Oceania', *Tourism, Recreation and Climate Change*, Bristol: Channel View.

Creswell, J. (2003) Research Design: Qualitative, quantitative and mixed method approaches, California: Sage.

Dessler, A. E. and Parson, E. A. (2006) *The Science and Politics of Global Climate Change: A guide to the debate*. Cambridge, Cambridge University Press.

Dunphy, D., Griffiths, A. and Benn, S. (2003) *Organizational Change for Corporate Sustainability*. London: Routledge.

Environmental Protection Agency Australia (EPA) (1997) 'Industry and the environment: a benchmark survey of environmental management in NSW industry'. EPA Social Science Research Series, Chatswood, NSW: EPA.

Garnaut, R. (2008) *Garnaut Climate Change Review: Interim Report to the Commonwealth, State and Territory Governments*. Commonwealth of Australia.

Gelbspan, R. (2004) *Boiling Point*. New York: Basic Books.

Geno, B. and Acutt, B. (2000) 'Greening small and medium-sized enterprises in Queensland: challenges for management,' *Proceedings of ANZAM 2000*, Melbourne.

Geno, B., Dunn, J. and Richins, H. (2003) 'Greening small and medium sized tourism enterprises in Queensland: challenges for managers,' *Refereed Proceedings of the Asia Pacific Tourism Association Eighth Annual Conference*, Sydney.

Gossling, S. (2006) *Tourism and Global Environmental Change: Ecological, social, economic and political interrelationships: contemporary geographies of leisure, tourism and mobility*. London: Routledge.

Gossling, S. and Hall, C. (2006) *Tourism and Global Environmental Change*, Oxford: Routledge.

Grover, V. I. (ed.) (2004) *Climate Change: Five years after Kyoto*. Enfield, N.H.. Science Publishers.

Hall, C. (2006) 'New Zealand tourism entrepreneur attitudes and behaviours with respect to climate change adaptation and mitigation,' *International Journal of Innovation and Sustainable Development*, Vol. 1, No. 3, pp. 229–37.

Hall, C. M. and Higham, J. E. (2005) *Tourism, Recreation, and Climate Change*. Bristol: Channel View.

Harrison S., Winterbottom S. and Sheppard, C. (1999) 'The potential effects of climate change on the Scottish Tourist Industry,' *Tourism Management*, Vol. 20, pp. 203–11.

Hawaii Tourism Authority (HTA) (2008) *Hawaii Strategic Plan*. Available at: www.hawaiitourismauthority.org/ (accessed 10 February 2011).

Hjalager, A. (1996) 'Sustainable tourism or sustainable mobility? The Norwegian case,' *Journal of Sustainable Tourism*, Vol. 4, No. 4.

Houghton, J. (2004) *Global Warming: The complete briefing*, 3rd edn. Cambridge: Cambridge University Press.

Huybers, T. and Bennett, J. (1997) 'The environment and Australia's tourism industry,' Canberra: Tourism Council Australia.

Intergovernmental Panel on Climate Change (IPCC) (2001) 'Climate change 2001: the scientific basis,' Contribution of Working Group I to the Third Assessment Report of the IPCC. Cambridge: Cambridge University Press.

IPCC (2007) 'Climate change 2007: the physical science basis – summary for policymakers,' Contribution of Working Group I to the Fourth Assessment Report of the Intergovernmental Panel on Climate Change. Cambridge: Cambridge University Press.

Kotey, B. and Meredith, G. (1997) 'Relationships among owner/manager personal values, business strategies and enterprise performance,' *Journal of Small Business Management*, Vol. 20, pp. 37–64.

Lean, G. and Kay, B. (2008) 'Four nations in race to be first to go carbon neutral,' *Independent*. Available at: www.independent.co.uk/environment/climate-change/four-nations-in-race-to-be-first-to-go-carbon-neutral-802627.html (accessed 22 March 2011).

MacKenzie, F. (2006) *Carbon in the Geobiosphere: Earth's outer shell*, USA: Springer.

Mather, S., Viner, D. and Todd, G. (2005) 'Climate and policy changes: their implications for international tourism flows,' in Hall, C. and Higham, J. (eds), *Tourism, Recreation and Climate Change*, Bristol: Channel View.

McCaffrey, P. (ed.) (2006) *Global Climate Change*. New York: H. W. Wilson.

Nurse, K. (2007) 'Climate change threatens island tourism,' International Centre for Trade and Sustainable Development. Available at: www.policyinnovations.org/ideas/briefings/data/000105 (accessed 28 March 2011).

Nurse, K. (2008) 'Climate change, tourism and services in small island developing economies,' *Bridges Trade Bio Reserve Review*, Vol. 2, No. 4.

O'Hare, G., Sweeney, J. and Wilby, R. (eds) (2005) *Weather, Climate, and Climate Change: Human perspectives*. Pearson Prentice Hall, New York.

Oreskes, N. (2004) 'Essays on science and society beyond the ivory tower: the scientific consensus on climate change,' *Science 3*, Vol. 306, No. 5702.

Pagnan, J. (2003) 'Climate change impacts on Arctic tourism – a preliminary review', *Climate Change and Tourism. Proceedings of the First International Conference on Climate Change and Tourism*, Djerba, Tunisia, April.

Peters, R. (1996) A study of the factors determining perceptions of trust and credibility in environmental risk communication: the importance of overcoming negative stereotypes. International Archives of Occupational and Environmental Health. (68) 6.

Ragin, C. (1994) *Constructing Social Research: The unity and diversity of method*. Thousand Oaks, Calif: Pine Forge Press.

Romm, J. J. (2006) *Hell and High Water: Global Warming: The solution and the politics and what we should do*. New York: William Morrow.

Scott, D., Jones, B., and Konopek, J. (2007) 'Implications of climate and environmental change for nature-based tourism in the Canadian Rocky Mountains: a case study of Waterton Lakes National Park,' *Tourism Management*.

Scott, D., Wall, G. and McBoyle, G. (2005) 'The Evolution of the Climate Change Issue in the Tourism Sector.' In Hall, C. M. and Higham, J. (eds), *Making Tourism Sustainable: The real challenge of climate change in tourism*, Bristol: Channel View.

Shea, E. (2001) *Preparing for a Changing Climate: Pacific Islands*. Honolulu, Hawaii: East West Center.

Singer, S. F. and Avery, D. T. (2006) *Unstoppable Global Warming: Every 1500 years*. Lanham, Md: Rowman & Littlefield.

Taylor, S. and Bogdan, R. (1998) *Introduction to Qualitative Research Methods*. New York: Wiley.

UN World Tourism Organization (UNWTO) (2003) *Climate Change and Tourism*. Madrid: UNWTO.

Veal, A. (1997) *Research Methods for Leisure and Tourism: A practical guide*. Harlow, UK: Pearson Education.

Wall, G. (1998) 'Climate change, tourism and the IPCC', *Tourism Recreation Research*, Vol. 23, No. 2, pp. 65–8.

Weart, S. (2003) *The Discovery of Global Warming*. Cambridge, Mass: Harvard University Press.

Young, S. and Van der Straaten, J. (2001) *The Emergence of Ecological Modernization: Integrating the environment and the economy?* London: Taylor & Francis.

PART II

Responses and initiatives of regional, national and international agencies

5

SUSTAINABLE TOURISM DEVELOPMENT AND CLIMATE CHANGE
Opportunities in UNESCO biosphere reserves

Natarajan Ishwaran

Introduction

In 2012 the United Nations will convene the Rio+20 Summit. In the agenda of that summit deliberations on green economy for poverty eradication in the context of sustainable development and institutional arrangements for sustainable development will figure prominently. Both issues are of critical importance to the future of sustainable development of the travel and tourism sector. This chapter explores the greening opportunities for tourism in the context of sustainable development and climate change in UNESCO biosphere reserves. A brief overview of the relationship between climate change and sustainable development is followed by a description of the biosphere reserve concept and the World Network of Biosphere Reserves (WNBR). Specific characteristics of the biosphere reserve and the World Network which make them important assets for global experimentation with sustainable tourism development in the post-Rio+20 period are emphasized. The chapter illustrates the use of biosphere reserves as 'learning laboratories for sustainable tourism development' using information from selected biosphere reserves.

Sustainable development and climate change

The concept of sustainable development (WCED 1987) rose to prominence at the Earth Summit in 1992. Since then nations have reiterated their commitment to the concept; at the World Summit on Sustainable Development (or Rio+10) in 2002, held in Johannesburg, South Africa, sustainable development was anchored on economic, social and environmental pillars. Rio+20 in 2012 is 'Stockholm+40' for those who trace the origins of the world's intergovernmental environmental agenda to the Stockholm Conference on the Human Environment in 1972

(McCormick 1995). Expectations for the results and outcomes of Rio+20 to lead to focused experimentation with sustainable development practice, and not a mere restatement of principles of and constraints to sustainable development, are running high. Learning from the past and experimenting with new sustainable development initiatives could hence be a timely mission for the travel, tourism and hospitality sector.

The relationship between climate change and sustainable development must be analyzed and understood in the context of the three pillars agreed upon at the Rio+10 Summit in Johannesburg, South Africa: economic, social and environmental. Sustainable development revolves as much around the concept of 'sustainability' as that of 'development'; the origins of the concept may be linked to eco-development which was referred to by the organizers of the Stockholm Conference of the Human Environment in 1972. The eco-development concept, elaborated it in the context of rural economies of the developing world, prefigured but yet was concurrent with the term sustainable development (Vivien 2008).

Deliberations that led to the origins of the global environmental movement and the establishment of the United Nations Environmental Programme (UNEP) in 1972 were marked by growing concerns among the less developed nations that environmental protection might be used as an excuse for curtailing economic growth (McCormick 1995). These concerns continue to prevail even today in the negotiations of the Conference of Parties to the UN Framework Convention on Climate Change (UNFCCC). Part of the reasons for climate change negotiations failing to reach consensus on conditions for the future of the Kyoto Protocol, whose current phase of commitments for reducing greenhouse gas (GHG) emissions by the Parties to the Protocol expires at the end of 2012, is the lack of a tried and tested approach to economic growth different from that effectively used by the industrialized nations to attain their current levels of well-being. Emerging market giants such as China and India, which still have significant parts of their populations in rural and marginal areas below the poverty line, therefore see no alternative to pursuing an economic growth model that will continue to increase their GHG emissions. The post-2008 financial and banking crises and the consequent repercussions on debt, spending and unemployment are testing the resolve of even the industrialized nations, despite their greater technological and human capital, to attempt reduction of GHGs and accelerate the transformation of their economies to various shades of green.

Viewing responses to climate change consequences solely from an urgent need to minimize GHG emissions, though justifiable based on planetary consequences for societal well-being, may significantly impact the economic prospects for less developed parts of the world. The international travel and tourism sector is a good example of this dilemma. Economic returns from tourism are high in countries where visitors come not merely from domestic or regional populations but from far-away industrialized and wealthy nations; international air travel with its high GHG emissions is an unavoidable part of tourism development in less developed parts of the world, including in small island developing states (SIDS) that are most vulnerable to the sea-level rise consequences of climate change. At least in the short to medium term the relationship between climate change and sustainable development will be pursued in pragmatic terms by policy makers, with due attention to the economic and social consequences of changing development pathways that may generate long-term, global environmental benefits. Sustainable development with a balanced emphasis on all three pillars agreed to by Nation States at the Johannesburg Summit in 2002 will therefore be the most likely scenario that will prevail even after Rio+20 in 2012. The UN secretary-general Ban Ki-Moon has said that 'sustainable development will remain his top priority during his second term as the head of the United Nations, saying that key challenges include achieving the global poverty reduction goals and strengthening disaster risk reduction to avert crises caused by climate change' (UN 2011).

Climate change scenarios and their consequences provide greening opportunities, particularly for the economic pillar of sustainable development. Due to its manifold links with travel, hospitality, infrastructure, trade, conservation and other development sectors, tourism can play a significant role in exploring green growth options at global, national and local levels. Sustainable tourism provides a framework that includes eco-, cultural, geo-, adventure and similar niche options; nevertheless, 'mass tourism' irrespective of the pejorative connotations associated with it will continue to be part of the overall equation for improving the sector's sustainability due to its overriding importance for the political economy of tourism development decisions.

The World Network of Biosphere Reserves – an overview

The concept of a biosphere reserve was defined within UNESCO's Man and the Biosphere (MAB) Programme launched in 1971. In the late 1960s and the early 1970s MAB pioneered the imagining within the UN system of a future where human development and ecosystem conservation could spatially converge. Of the fourteen projects that constituted the MAB Programme in the 1970s, project 8 on the conservation of natural areas and the genetic resources they contain resulted in the elaboration of the biosphere reserve concept and the development of the World Network (Ishwaran, Persic and Tri 2008; Ishwaran 2010).

The World Network now counts 580 places in 114 countries. The concept and design of biosphere reserves and their application to specific territories comprising land/seascapes have evolved significantly through reflections at the First (1983; Minsk, Belarus – which was Byelorussia in 1983), Second (1995; Seville, Spain) and Third (2008; Madrid, Spain) World Congresses on Biosphere Reserves (Ishwaran et al. 2008). What originated as an attempt to render the design, development and management of parks and similar reserves community-friendly evolved into an effort to identify and designate land/seascapes dedicated to sustainable development of the region where they are located. The evolution of the concept and its practice over nearly forty years has been influenced by perspectives, constraints and opportunities in the international arena, particularly by the trend for greater integration of environmental and development dimensions of societal and ecosystem change (UNESCO 1984, Batisse 1986). The ten key directions identified by the Seville Strategy are given in Box 5.1.

BOX 5.1 THE SEVILLE STRATEGY

The International Conference on Biosphere Reserves, organized by UNESCO in Seville (Spain), from 20–25 March 1995 identified ten key directions, which formed the foundations of the new Seville Strategy:

1 Strengthen the contribution which biosphere reserves make to the implementation of international agreements promoting conservation and sustainable development, especially to the Convention on Biological Diversity and other agreements, such as those on climate change, desertification and forests.

2 Develop biosphere reserves that include a wide variety of environmental, biological, economic and cultural situations, going from largely undisturbed regions and spreading towards cities. There is a particular potential, and need, to apply the biosphere reserve concept in the coastal and marine environment.

3 Strengthen the emerging regional, inter-regional and thematic networks of biosphere reserves as components within the World Network of Biosphere Reserves.

4 Reinforce scientific research, monitoring, training and education in biosphere reserves, since conservation and rational use of resources in these areas require a sound base in the natural and social sciences as well as the humanities. This need is particularly acute in countries where biosphere reserves lack human and financial resources and should receive priority attention.

5 Ensure that all zones of biosphere reserves contribute appropriately to conservation, sustainable development and scientific understanding.

6 Extend the transition area to embrace large areas suitable for approaches, such as ecosystem management, and use biosphere reserves to explore and demonstrate approaches to sustainable development at the regional scale. For this, more attention should be given to the transition area.

7 Reflect more fully the human dimensions of biosphere reserves. Connections should be made between cultural and biological diversity. Traditional knowledge and genetic resources should be conserved and their role in sustainable development should be recognized and encouraged.

8 Promote the management of each biosphere reserve essentially as a 'pact' between the local community and society as a whole. Management should be open, evolving and adaptive. Such an approach will help

ensure that biosphere reserves – and their local communities – are better placed to respond to external political, economic and social pressures.

9 Bring together all interested groups and sectors in a partnership approach to biosphere reserves both at site and network levels. Information should flow freely among all concerned.

10 Invest in the future. Biosphere reserves should be used to further our understanding of humanity's relationship with the natural world, through programmes of public awareness, information and formal and informal education, based on a long-term, inter-generational perspective.

Today, the essential characteristics of a biosphere reserve (UNESCO 1996, 2008) are:

- A land/seascape of multiple ecosystems, resource use and associated regulatory regimes with resident communities in rural, sub-urban and urban settings.
- Three schematic zones recommended by the Seville Strategy and the Statutory Framework of the World Network, namely core, buffer and transition zones (see Figure 5.1 showing the ideal scheme and its adaptation to the Lanzarote Island Biosphere Reserve in Spain). The three-zone scheme is a spatial arrangement to enable and mix the three functions of the biosphere reserve at the land/seascape level. The three functions are: (i) biodiversity conservation, (ii) improving the socio-economic well-being of people, and (iii) promoting a culture of learning that grows in its awareness and ability to balance economic, social and environmental trajectories of development within the cultural and political context of the biosphere reserve land/seascape.
- Only the core area enjoys legal protection similar to national parks and similar reserves; the buffer and transition zones have resident communities practicing agriculture, forestry, fishing, tourism and many other activities to improve their socio-economic well-being while recognizing and generating opportunities to conserve biodiversity and maintain environmental quality.
- A review of the status of the biosphere reserve must be undertaken at least once every ten years (Price, Park and Bouamrane 2010), and must in particular assess progress in the integration of efforts to ensure biodiversity conservation, enhance the socio-economic well-being of people and promote a culture of learning dedicated to sustainable development.
- Commitment of authorities to involve and consult with all stakeholders in designing, developing and implementing key strategic and policy decisions impacting the entire biosphere reserve.
- Promoting research, education, training, monitoring and pilot projects that can demonstrate the relationship between the biosphere reserve and regional sustainable development options and processes (Jamieson, Francis and Whitelaw 2008).

- Sharing lessons learned, knowledge, experience, data and information on all matters pertaining to the governance and management of biosphere reserves within the World Network.

The Lanzarote Biosphere Reserve (Figure 5.1) is a good example for highlighting some of the major issues currently debated within the World Network, including sustainable tourism development. As it is a whole-island biosphere reserve that is restricted to land there is a natural limit to the transition zone of the biosphere reserve. In mainland biosphere reserves and in island biosphere reserves that include marine ecosystems, the definition of the transition zone boundary is often arbitrary. This outermost zone of the biosphere reserve, however, is where greening socio-economic development could be fully explored, and is unique to the biosphere reserve designation conferred by UNESCO.

Buffer zones are characteristic of even conventional protected areas. World Heritage sites, the more popular UNESCO designation afforded to natural and cultural areas under the 1972 Convention Concerning the Protection of the World Cultural and Natural Heritage (often abbreviated as the World Heritage Convention) requires that a buffer zone be defined to preserve the integrity of the designated area. Definition of additional zones outside of the buffer outside of the buffer is not required for nominating area as a World Heritage site. Furthermore the World Heritage designation, particularly with regard to natural areas, is often restricted to the legally protected part of the nominated area and does not apply to the buffer zone. The biosphere reserve designation however covers the overall territory of core, buffer and transition zones.

The *Independent* (2010) reported that the building craze could end Lanzarote's biosphere status:

> For decades, the island's elegant-and-ecological style of tourism defied the construction craze of its wilder island neighbours, like Gran Canaria. At least so it seemed. Because now Unesco has threatened to strip the island of its prized biosphere status because of a rash of illegal building along the coast. The Canary Island Supreme Court has declared that 24 hotels have been illegally built in coastal resorts such as Playa Blanca, so popular with British tourists that it's easier to order a 'typical English breakfast' than the local potato dish, *papas arrugas*. According to a report in the *Financial Times*, the court retroactively rescinded building permits, but the hotels still stand.

Construction and infrastructure are a frequent concern not only in island, but also in mainland biosphere reserves. But the implication that building would be somehow inimical to the biosphere reserve status is false; in the transition zone of biosphere reserves residential, recreational, industrial and at times even urban/semi-urban infrastructure are common. In biosphere reserve management some of the greening opportunities for economic development are in fact in the transition and buffer zones rather than in the core area.

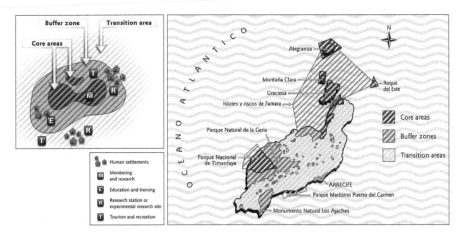

FIGURE 5.1 Lanzarote Biosphere Reserve

In tourism development one of the key factor influencing socio-economic performance as well as environmental quality is infrastructure. Hotels, resorts, restaurants and other business entities that supply 'hospitality' at destinations are often built at inappropriate locations. Their energy, water and waste management systems may not attain economically feasible standards. Where the local transport and travel infrastructure to visitor destinations is not adequately developed, pollution and other impacts on soil, vegetation, water and local communities may be ignored.

A major constraint to the realization of the potential of biosphere reserves as learning laboratories for sustainable development lies in the word 'reserve' itself. The post-Seville (i.e. 1995) biosphere reserves comprise the full territory covered by core, buffer and transition zones, with residential populations in the latter two zones often running into millions of people in countries like Brazil, India and Vietnam. The image of a 'reserve' often conjures up a 'hands-off' approach with regard to development activities in the minds of policy makers. These fears and misunderstandings may have prevented the early use of the biosphere reserve approach for integrating the human dimensions, and particularly tourism, into sustainable development of the Galapagos Islands, which enjoy both the biosphere reserve and the World Heritage designations conferred by UNESCO (Ishwaran 2010, González et al. 2008). The Madrid Action Plan for Biosphere Reserves (2008–13) allows countries to adopt alternative terminology if they choose to do so. The visioning of biosphere reserves as 'regions with a global reputation' and the adoption of the term biosphere regions in place of biosphere reserves in Germany are probably preferred directions for the future (Moller 2007).

Climate change and tourism in the context of sustainable development

Discussions on sustainable tourism development in the context of climate change often tend to get trapped in the need for minimizing the carbon footprint of travel and transport dimensions of the sector. Conscious travellers offset their carbon footprints through contributions to greening projects in destinations they visit in different parts of the world. The airline industry's commitment to improve the energy efficiency of aircraft fuel consumption would also contribute towards minimizing the carbon footprint of international air travel (World Economic Forum 2009).

Sustainability of international travel, however, must not be judged merely based on its negative environmental or climate impacts; it must recognize the significant social and economic benefits that travel makes towards sustainable development at global, national and local levels, including through contributions towards several dimensions of the tourism, events and hospitality sectors. For example, one important measure of tourism growth in many nations is the number of international arrivals; the global number is expected to reach 1.6 billion by 2020 (UNWTO 2001). Such arrivals in a country include not only foreigners visiting the country for business, conventions, leisure and other cultural, sports and artistic events; they also include nationals of that country working abroad and returning to visit family and relatives. Remittances from workers abroad are a significant contributor to growth in their countries of origin. For instance the remittances from Saudi Arabia by foreign workers were estimated at 90 billion Saudi rials for 2010 (Arab News 2011). In many emerging market economies such as Brazil, China and India, incentives to attract the human and financial capital of nationals of the diaspora are common. A combination of these trends is likely to increase contributions of nationals, travelling in and out of their home countries, to poverty eradication and other social and economic indicators of sustainability.

In the Wuyishan Biosphere Reserve of China a recent research study firmly established that Wuyi Lapsang Suchong black tea as the origin of all of the world's black tea, including those varieties sold in markets and malls in the British Isles. It has contributed towards raising the prestige of and income for tea growing in several villages of the Wuyishan Biosphere Reserve (UNESCO-MAB 2010). The fact that many visitors to the Wuyishan are Chinese from overseas territories as well as from the growing number of middle-to-upper class Chinese within the country has enabled the reserve management to sell the tea as a high-end product to visitors. It is also sold as a value-added product in many shops in major cities of China. As the role of diasporas in investments and economic development increases in many countries (*Economist* 2011), new forms of visitor experiences that combine tradition, knowledge and hospitality are likely to become feasible.

The rationale for tourism development policies at national and sub-national levels builds on physical, natural, cultural and other assets to set goals and targets for improving the social, economic and environmental well-being of people. The conservation of those assets on which the tourism industry is dependent is a necessary condition for sustainability; nevertheless, the social and economic performance of the sector is often the principal driver for policy decisions and shifts aimed at improving the sufficiency of the sector's contribution to sustainable development.

The capacity of the tourism sector's contribution to green growth and sustainable development could improve if the sector is able to deliberately associate itself with global, national and regional incentives and opportunities for going green. Growth in the number of arrivals may not be an issue for tourism development planning where nations and destinations have already established, or have the economic flexibility to seek a niche in high-value, low-volume tourism. But in the early stages of tourism development, many nations and regions focus on increasing the number of visitors. Development of hotels and related service providers in urban settings and far-off destinations is often driven by forecasts of an increase in the number of visitors, which if not met could result in widespread social and economic disappointment. Furthermore, throughout the world efforts are being made to attract the millions of middle-class travellers from emerging economies such as China. Opportunities for mixing businesses that promote environmentally sustainable 'mass tourism' with high-value eco- and other niche tourism options at the land/seascape level could be attractive for experimenting with green growth and sustainable development in the post-Rio+20 world.

Biosphere reserves as experimental areas for sustainable tourism development

Biosphere reserves that meet the Seville Strategy and Statutory Framework criteria adopted by UNESCO in 1995 can offer a mix of land/seascapes in natural, rural and periurban/urban settings for experimenting with integrated environmental, social and economic dimensions of sustainable tourism development. Not all the pre-1995 biosphere reserves have the possibility to offer this rich and complex experimental setting. Many of them are dedicated to only one of the three functions considered essential for a biosphere reserve, for instance national parks and similar reserves that are primarily dedicated to conservation of biodiversity; biological and ecological research stations that dedicate themselves to science, data gathering and monitoring environmental problems; or other places with a mix of natural and human-impacted landscapes that focus on employment and revenue generation through tourism or other economic sector activities. Efforts are underway to make all biosphere reserves meet the Seville Strategy and Statutory Framework criteria of 1995 (Ishwaran et al. 2008, Price et al. 2010). More recent adaptations of the biosphere reserve concept to meet new challenges such as urbanization and climate change have been targeted in the Madrid Action Plan for Biosphere Reserves (2008–13) (UNESCO 2008), which when fully implemented will enhance the coherency of the World Network as a global set for sustainable tourism development experimentation.

The Jiuzhaigou Valley Biosphere Reserve (JVBR) provides an interesting illustration of problems and issues that must be considered in sustainable tourism development (Nianyong, Qian and Hong 2008). The JVBR (included in the World Network in 1997), spreading across 106,000 ha, includes the 72,000 ha Jiuzhaigou Valley Scenic Area World Heritage site, which was inscribed on

UNESCO's World Heritage list in 1992. Prior to the establishment of the Jiuzhaigou Nature Reserve in 1984 the surrounding area largely depended on timber for its income. The establishment of the nature reserve in 1984 resulted in tourism becoming the mainstay of the economy. Nianyong et al. (2008) estimate that hotels in the area, almost entirely family-run by local residents, increased their income by almost fifty times between 1983 and 2004. The income of the families in the JVBR and its immediate surroundings was at least ten times that of nearby counties. The gross domestic product (GDP) per capita of Jiuzhaigou County also exceeded the state-level average for the year 1999.

This economic success, with the number of tourists rising by 68 percent between 1998 and 2000, had to be checked as not only was it increasing environmental pressures on water and natural resources, it was also creating serious imbalances in the distribution of the wealth among the residents of the valley. The administration of the reserve took drastic measures such as freezing construction of new family hotels and gradually closing down all hotels inside the reserve. A joint stock company where residents were shareholders was created to eliminate the competition to construct more and more hotels. Many of the owners of the family hotels found employment in the company. New coordinated administrative arrangements covering the entire JVBR were introduced to green the economy of the area. For example income distribution among three villages shifted from 4.3:4.6:1.0 (1993–2001) to 1.9:2.5:1.0 (2004). Visitors were not allowed to enter the reserve in private vehicles but were required to take buses operated by the administration and travel in groups.

The authors identify several measures for the future which the administration may take and which could shift indicators of progress in the sustainability of the tourism from number of visitors to the area towards measures of the quality of the visitor experience. Furthermore, the authors also point out that applying the biosphere reserve concept could help the administration to introduce 'branding' approaches to the management of the area which could simultaneously improve the economic, environmental and social dimensions of tourism development in JVBR. They also recommend that the JVBR Administration share their lessons with other biosphere reserves in the same county as well as within the Chinese Biosphere Reserve Network (CBRN).

As mentioned earlier, tourism infrastructure development – hotels, restaurants and so on – can often go along unsustainable pathways. The wish of local authorities and entrepreneurs for large volumes of visitors may be inevitable in the early stages, but checks and balances need to be built in sooner or later. In biosphere reserves that are essentially multiple-use landscapes it may be best to avoid tourism development becoming the sole source of income for residents. Furthermore, tourism development planning in a biosphere reserve also has the potential for developing a range of visitor interests, products and services. Tourism products in a biosphere reserve need not entirely depend on the attractions of the legally protected core area: product and services development could be distributed across the core, buffer and transition zones. Infrastructure development could also be spatially distributed taking into consideration access and the feasibility to set up clusters and networks of residential facilities, restaurants and other hospitality service providers rather than concentrating their development in a few areas close to popular attractions. With regard to infrastructure development and management, the work of the Institute for Responsible Tourism in Spain to certify 'biosphere hotels' holds the potential for further refinement and experimentation on a broader scale.

Some biosphere reserves, for instance the Sierra Gorda in Mexico, have had access to income generation via carbon offsets from partners and visitors (see Table 5.1).

The tourism sector's responses to mitigation and adaptation to climate change could greatly benefit if infrastructure development emphasizes green pathways with regard to the use of energy, water and natural resources as well as biodiversity. Ecosystem changes as a result of climate change and their impacts on the tourism sector are likely to be more context-specific. Much work has been done on the

TABLE 5.1 Sierra Gorda: carbon transactions

Donor	No. of tons	Donation US$	Date
United Nations Foundation (USA)	5,230	$52,300	2006
United Nations Foundation	88	$880	2007
Utah State University (USA)	203	$3,045	November 2007
TBLI (Holland)	298	$4,470	December 2007
Schwab Foundation (CH)	102	$1,530	February 2008
Live Climate (USA)	200	$3,000	April 2008
World Land Trust (UK)	3,253	$48,795	April 2008
LGT Venture Philanthropy (CH)	350	$5,250	August 2008
Fundación Ecología y Desarrollo (Spain)	8,306	$124,590	October 2008
Acciónatura (Spain)	10,000	$150,000	October 2008 (09 y 10)
TBLI (Holland)	282	$4,230	January 2009
Instituto Internacional de Facilitadores y Cambio S.C. (México)	65	$975	January 2009
Ing. Cuauhtémoc F. Ramírez Arriola (México)	10	$150	December 2009 (10)
Total	28,387	$399,235	

Source: Laura Perez – Arce Burke, Sierra Gorda Biosphere Reserve.

impacts on and vulnerability of coastal ecosystems (for example Moreno 2010), which are often more significant to tourism sector activities than other ecosystems.

In the post-2012 era sustainable tourism development initiatives may also have opportunities to focus more on regional, national and even local levels to combine travel, leisure and hospitality. The tourism sector may aim to build to closer linkages with other social development sectors such as education and health. The Millennium Ecosystem Assessment (MEA 2005) identified among the different categories of services that ecosystems provide a cultural set that is based on recreational, educational, aesthetic and spiritual benefits we derive from ecosystems. The conventional objectives of international travel dedicated to tourism are leisure and fulfilling the curiosity to visit far-off places Not only can these new linkages be emphasized and explored within the cultural set of ecosystem services, the objectives can also include travel related to pilgrimages within one's own country or a neighbouring country, educational travel, artistic and cultural events that attract national and international visitors, and so on.

Educational travel could be of special interest to biosphere reserves, given their role as 'learning laboratories for sustainable development'. An Australian tourism industry expert observed: 'Since 2000, 46 percent of the total growth of Australia's inbound tourism market has been derived from international educational visitors. Over the same period, international holiday makers have delivered just 14 percent of the total growth.' He added that 'Academics are easily stereotyped as being cosseted away from the cut and thrust of the business world, but when everyone else is reeling, it is the education sector providing a guiding light for the tourism industry' (Tourism Futures 2009).

There are possible definitional issues about considering educational visitors as tourists. Students entering a country for graduate studies may stay for a prolonged period and may even remain indefinitely, becoming naturalized citizens. Yet the potential of biosphere reserves for providing platforms for dialogue among a range of stakeholders to discuss a variety of sustainability issues linked to tourism opens up several opportunities for tourism planners to use biosphere reserves in innovative ways:

> Successful innovation equates to a successful marriage of invention and commercialization, and that requires a free flow of information and technology among people and organizations. In particular, it requires three entities with fiercely independent and traditionally non-overlapping cultures – government, universities and the private sector – to engage in meaningful dialogue with each other.
>
> *(Grindlinger, director of scientific programs, quoted in Burke 2011)*

Tourism ministries, academic departments dealing with travel, tourism and hospitality, tourism operators, hotel and resort developers and other business interests of the industry have a significant opportunity to use biosphere reserves to test and develop innovative ways of combining nature, culture, scenic spots, life styles, recreational (including health and wellness) and sport interests and many other assets to launch well-designed sustainable tourism development experiments. The fact that biosphere reserves are networked at global, regional, sub-regional, national and at times even at provincial and local levels provides an untapped research and development potential for innovation. Some individual biosphere reserves like the Mata Atlantica along the eastern coast of Brazil cover millions of hectares and include thousands of municipalities. Sustainable tourism development in such a site could explore a region-wide strategy creating a range of environmental, social and economic benefits.

The Morrill Land-Grant Act of 1862 in the United States created what are today known as land grant colleges. Eligible states were given 30,000 acres (or 121 sq km) of land to create educational institutions that were expected 'to teach such branches of learning as are related to agriculture and mechanic arts ... the liberal and practical education of the industrial classes in the several pursuits and professions in life' (Ohionline nd). The World Network of Biosphere Reserves with its 580 sites in 114 countries covers hundreds of millions of hectares which could be used to experiment and learn practical approaches to sustainability. While that learning opportunity may be usable by any particular field of enterprise, tourism perhaps has a particular responsibility to demonstrate that travel, visitation and associated learning could be a significant contributor to the sustainable development of people and ecosystems in destinations. In the post-Rio+20 years after 2012 an effort to bring government, academia and businesses together to meet this challenge in a selected number of biosphere reserves may well deserve genuine investments in financial and human terms.

Conclusion

In biosphere reserves many examples of tourism's contributions towards economic, employment and other social benefits for local communities can be found. These projects for the most part also improve prospects for biodiversity conservation and environmental quality. In 2011 the International Coordinating Council of the MAB Programme awarded the Michel Batisse Award to an ecotourism case study that brought broad-ranging economic, social and environmental benefits to the Shouf Biosphere Reserve in Lebanon (Hani 2011). Other examples have been referred to in this chapter, though the information is largely secondary, obtained from publications authored by managers and site administrators. Well-designed comparative research studies focusing on some of the sites reported here as well as others would yield more insights into the role of biosphere reserves in promoting sustainable tourism development.

Climate-change-related opportunities for raising finances are being tapped for biosphere reserves management through carbon offsets. Whether the economic benefits generated from some of the studies reported here would fit current views of the green economy is debatable. Nevertheless biosphere land/seascape provides significant opportunities for tourism development based on multiple sets of visitor products and experiences. Sustainability of tourism development may benefit in particular by encouraging the greening of infrastructure and construction dimensions of the industry through improvements in energy efficiency, water and waste management and construction materials. These opportunities, particularly in the transition zone of biosphere reserves, provide hitherto untapped potential for greening the economic component of sustainable tourism development. Exploration and exploitation of those opportunities in the post Rio+20 world would require new levels of cooperation between academics and researchers, site management, and private and business-sector stakeholders.

References

Arab News (2011) 'Local Press: Remittances by expat workers: foreigners working in the Kingdom transferred a total of SR90 billion to their home countries last year.' Available at: http://arabnews.com/saudiarabia/article238349.ece?comments=all (accessed 1 March 2012).

Batisse, M. (1986) 'Developing and focusing the biosphere reserve concept,' *Nature and Resources,* Vol. 22, No. 3, pp. 1–12.

Burke, A. J. (2011) 'How to build an innovation ecosystem – for spurring scientific progress, an interconnected community is key,' *New York Academy of Sciences Magazine,* Spring, pp. 19–20.

González, J. A., Montes, C., Rodríguez, J. and Tapia, W. (2008) 'Rethinking the Galapagos Islands as a complex social ecological system: implications for conservation and management', *Ecology and Society,* Vol. 13, No. 2, article 13. Available at: www.ecologyandsociety.org/vol13/iss2/art13/ (accessed 1 March 2012).

Economist (2011) 'Weaving the world together,' 19–25 November, pp. 68–70.

Hani, N. (2011) 'Creative and innovative approaches to alleviate poverty, stop immigration, improve livelihood and manage sustainably the Shouf Biosphere Reserve. A case study from the Shouf Biosphere Reserve.' UNESCO-MAB Secretariat, Paris.

Independent (2010) 'Building craze threatens to end Lanzarote's biosphere status,' 7 July. Available at: www.independent.co.uk/environment/nature/building-craze-threatens-to-end-lanzarotes-biosphere-status-2020064.html (accessed 2 March 2012).

Ishwaran, N. (2010) 'Biodiversity, people and places,' *Australasian Journal of Environmental Management,* Vol. 17 (December), pp. 215–22.

Ishwaran, N., Persic, A. and Tri, Nguyen Hoang (2008) 'Concept and practice: the case of UNESCO biosphere reserves,' *International Journal of Environment and Sustainable Development,* Vol. 7, No. 2, pp. 118–31.

Jamieson, G., Francis, G. and Whitelaw, G. (2008) 'Canadian biosphere reserve approaches to the achievement of sustainable development,' *International Journal of* Environment *and Sustainable Development,* Vol. 7, No. 2, pp. 132–45.

McCormick, J. 1995. *The Global Environmental Movement.* Hoboken, N.J.: John Wiley & Sons.

Millennium Ecosystem Assessment (MEA) (2005) *Ecosystem Services and Human Well Being: Synthesis.* Washington DC: Island Press.

Moller, L. (2007) 'UNESCO biosphere reserves: model regions with a global reputation,' *UNESCO Today,* issue 2.

Moreno, A. (2010) 'Climate change and tourism: impacts and vulnerability in coastal Europe,' Ph.D. dissertation, University of Maastricht, Netherlands.

Nianyong, H., Qian, Z. and Hong, Z. (2008) 'From experience to institution: the management of Jiuzhaigou Valley Biosphere Reserve faced with institutional transformation and upgrading,' *International Journal of Environment and Sustainable Development*, Vol. 7, No. 2, pp. 145–55.

Ohionline (nd) 'The land grant system of education in the United States,' Ohio *State University News*. Available at: http://ohioline.osu.edu/lines/lgrant.html (accessed 1 March 2012).

Price, M. F., Park, J. J. and Bouamrane, M. (2010) 'Reporting progress on internationally designated sites: the Periodic Review of Biosphere Reserves,' *Environmental Science and Policy*, 13, pp. 549–57.

Tourism Futures (2009) 'Educational travel boosting Australia's tourism industry.' Available at: www.eturbonews.com/10207/educational-travel-boosting-australias-tourism-industry (accessed 1 March 2012).

United Nations (2011) 'UN chief sees sustainable development as top priority in his second term,' UN News Centre. Available at: www.un.org/apps/news/story. asp?NewsID=39288 (accessed 1 March 2012).

UNESCO (1984) 'Action plan for biosphere reserves,' *Nature and Resources,* Vol. 20, No. 4, pp. 1–12.

UNESCO (1996) *Biosphere Reserves. The Seville Strategy and the Statutory Framework of the World Network.* Paris: UNESCO, p.18.

UNESCO (2008) *Madrid Action Plan for Biosphere Reserves (2008–2013).* Paris: MAB Secretariat, UNESCO.

UNESCO-Man and the Biosphere Programme (MAB) (2010) *Building Ecologically Harmonious Civilization: Wuyishan Biosphere Reserve Learning site for Sustainable Development under World Network of Biosphere Reserves.* Beijing: MAB National Committee of China and UNESCO Office.

UN World Tourist Organization (UNWTO) (2001) *Tourism 2020 Vision – Global forecast and profiles of market segments.* Madrid: UNWTO.

Vivien, Franck-Dominique (2008) 'Sustainable development: an overview of economic proposals,' *Surveys and Perspectives Integrating Environment and Society (S.A.P.I.E.N.S)*, Vol. 1, No. 2, pp. 7–14. Paris: Institut Veolia Environment.

World Commission on Environment and Development (WCED) (1987) *Our Common Future.* Oxford: Oxford University Press.

World Economic Forum (WEF) (2009) 'Towards a low carbon travel and tourism sector,' Report prepared with the support of Booz & Company. Geneva, WEF.

6

INTERPRETING CLIMATE PROJECTIONS FOR TOURISM PLANNING IN SOUTH-WEST ENGLAND

Emma Whittlesea and Bas Amelung

Introduction

The latest IPCC reports (IPCC 2007) concluded that the climate is changing. It is highly likely that the climate will continue to change in the future, even though the rate of change cannot be predicted accurately, except perhaps for the immediate future. For a large part this is due to uncertainties in the climate system and in the amount of greenhouse gases that will be emitted in the future. These uncertainties can be interpreted in different ways, which is why climate models produce widely diverging climate projections.

Tourism will be affected by climate change both directly and indirectly (UNWTO, UNEP and WMO 2008). The direct impacts will include changes in the value of the climate as a resource, changes in the likelihood and magnitude of sea level rise and extreme weather events. The latter aspect has hardly been explored for tourism (for an exception, see Bigano et al. 2005), but the former has. One strand of research in this direction explored developments in climate suitability for tourism. The spatial focus of these studies ranges from the world as a whole (Amelung, Nicholls and Viner 2007), Canada (Scott, McBoyle and Schwartzentruber 2004), the Mediterranean (Amelung and Viner 2006) and Europe (Nicholls and Amelung 2008, Ciscar et al. 2011).

The general results of these tourism suitability studies are that conditions in areas around the equator will deteriorate year-round, conditions in higher latitudes will improve year-round, and conditions in middle latitudes such as the Mediterranean will decrease in summer and improve in the shoulder seasons (e.g. Amelung and Viner 2006, Amelung et al. 2007). The study on north-western Europe by Nicholls and Amelung (2008) suggested a significant lengthening of the tourism season (in climatic terms). For example for the South-West of England the average number of months with very good conditions is projected to increase from between zero and two in the 1970s to up to four or five at the end of the century.

While it is useful to identify general patterns, the results from the first-generation suitability studies are not of much practical use for tourism stakeholders and decision makers. They tend to focus on high levels of spatial and temporal aggregation (country, year) and present changes in climate (thirty-year) by monthly or annual means. This limits the results as they do not go down to the local geographies or level of detail required for tourism investment and planning. They are also limited in that they do not make the uncertainties involved explicit, so the estimates do not provide any insight into the probability distributions. These drawbacks can, it is hoped, be reduced now that a new generation of probabilistic and finer resolution climate projections has emerged.

In 2009, the UK Department for Environment, Food and Rural Affairs (DEFRA) through the UK Climate Impacts Programme released its fifth set of UK climate projections, referred to as UKCP09. The projections have been made freely available alongside a suite of tools for individuals and organizations to access the data and utilize it for planning, to help society adapt to a changing climate. The probabilistic projections which go to the end of the century are based on a new methodology developed by the UK National Weather Service (Met Office) which includes information from a range of climate models. Rather than giving point estimates, UKCP09 provides probability distributions of future climate projections. This dataset allows for a more thorough assessment of potential changes in climatic suitability for tourism. Using the UKCP09 projections, this chapter explores the impact of climate change on climate suitability and the likelihood of extreme events in the context of tourism in the South-West of England.

The South-West of England is Britain's foremost holiday destination, with UK residents alone making 19 million trips in 2008 (South West Tourism 2008b). The region's continued success does however rely on the long-term sustainability of the tourism industry, as the regional guidance 'Principles for Success' (South West Tourism Alliance 2011) points out. Continued growth may increase the risks of climate change and it could also lead to highly seasonal and poor-quality jobs, overcrowding of destinations and declining local support for tourism. The regional guidance commits to an overriding principle of 'sustainable low carbon growth'. It recognizes the need to be mindful of longer-term challenges such as adapting to climate change, and suggests that changes in weather and climate could create opportunities for the industry.

The chapter is organized as follows. Section 2 introduces the UKCP09 dataset in more detail, and describes the methods used for the assessment of changes in suitability and extreme events. Section 3 reports on the results, which are subsequently discussed in section 4. Section 5 explores how local and regional stakeholders and decision makers can benefit from the new generation of climate projections and their tourism-specific derivatives.

Data and methods

Making uncertainty explicit is a key aspect of UKCP09, recognizing that no single climate model can project what the future will look like. Instead, UKCP09 provides a range of possible outcomes and attaches a probability to each of these outcomes, based on scientific evidence. In this way, the uncertainty in the modelling of the functioning of the climate system is made explicit and quantified according to the scientific knowledge available. UKCP09 addresses the other major source of uncertainty – the trajectory of future greenhouse gas emissions – by considering three emissions scenarios: low, medium and high.

The climate change projections have been made available for a number of variables: temperature, precipitation, air pressure, cloudiness and humidity. All projections are provided as thirty-year normals of annual, seasonal and monthly averages. Seven thirty-year periods are defined: the '2020s' (2010–2039), the '2030s' (2020–2049) and so on to the '2080s' (2070–2099). The projected changes are relative to the baseline period of 1961–1990 ('1970s') and the spatial resolution of the results is 25 km grid squares. In addition daily projections at 5 km grid square resolution are available through the UKCP09 Weather Generator. Different from earlier datasets, results are not supplied as point estimates, but as probability distributions that the user can sample. The sample size is defined by the user, but has to be between 100 and 10,000 (100–1000 for the Weather Generator).

For the assessment of climate projections for tourism in the South -West, the relevant dataset was defined as follows. To start with, forty-six UKCP09 25 km grid squares were identified that cover the South-West region of England (for details see Whittlesea and Amelung 2010). Next, the time horizon was defined, a trade-off between the climate signal (which gets stronger with time) and practical relevance of the results (which gets weaker with time, given the focus of the tourism industry on short-term developments). Two time slices (thirty-year periods) were singled out as most relevant: the 2020s and the 2050s, the first being of almost immediate relevance, the second sketching a picture of a somewhat more distant future, probably encompassing a greater degree of climate change. Given the relative proximity of the time horizons, the choice of scenario was unlikely to dominate results (see also Cox and Stephenson 2007), and the 'high' scenario was selected for maximum contrast. Sampling uncertainty is a key aspect of the assessment, so that the sample size was set to the maximum of 10,000. All data were downloaded from the UKCP09 site via the user interface.

Two tourism-specific climate indices were used to demonstrate the added value of the new features of the UKCP09 climate projections for climate suitability analysis: the Tourism Climatic Index (TCI) developed by Mieczkowski (1985) and the Beach Climate Index developed by Morgan et al. (2000).

The TCI allows quantitative evaluation of a region's climate for the purpose of general tourism activity. The TCI is based on the notion of 'human comfort' and consists of five sub-indices, each calculated from one or two monthly climate variables: daytime comfort index (maximum daily temperature in °C and minimum daily relative humidity per cent), daily comfort index (mean daily temperature °C and mean daily relative humidity per cent), precipitation (total precipitation, in mm), sunshine (total hours of sunshine) and wind (average wind speed, in km/h).

The TCI can be adapted to fit the climate requirements of specific tourism markets and activities by changing the rating schemes and/or the weights attached to the sub-indices. The TCI that is used in this study is the one for sightseeing, one of the most common tourism activities in the South-West. This TCI instance is weighted and computed as follows:

$$TCI = 8CID + 2CIA + 4R + 4S + 2W$$

where CID = daytime comfort index, CIA = daily comfort index, R = precipitation, S = sunshine and W = wind speed. The rating scheme and weights used in Mieczkowski's TCI are predominantly based on expert knowledge. TCI scores can range from -30 to 100. Mieczkowski (1985) divided this scale into ten categories, ranging from ideal (90 to 100), excellent (80 to 89) and very good (70 to 79) to extremely unfavourable (10 to 19) and impossible (9 to -30). In this study, a TCI value of 70 or higher is considered attractive to the 'typical' tourist.

Morgan et al. (2000) developed a climate index that was specifically tailored to beach tourism: the Beach Climate Index (BCI). In addition, they based the index on the actual preferences of beach visitors in Europe. Similar to Mieczkowski's TCI, the BCI is made up of smaller components (sub-indices) that, after weighting, add up to a maximum score of 100. The weights are based on the importance that the participating beach users attached to each of the four components, expressed on a Likert scale between 1 (not important) and 9 (very important). The Likert scores for each component were added, and these aggregated scores were subsequently scaled so that they added up to 1. The resulting equation is as follows:

$$BCI = 0.18 \cdot TS + 0.29 \cdot P + 0.26 \cdot W + 0.27 \cdot S$$

in which BCI is the Beach Climate Index, and TS, P, W and S are the components of thermal sensation, precipitation, wind and sunshine, respectively. Each of the four components is itself represented by an index with values ranging from 0 to 100. These values are the beach users' evaluation of the underlying weather conditions (for details see Morgan et al. 2000 and Moreno and Amelung 2009). The BCI index itself can also attain values ranging from 0 to 100.

Morgan et al. (2000) calculated BCI scores based on monthly values for climate parameters. This approach, which was also taken by Whittlesea and Amelung (2010), is improved upon in the current chapter by using daily data. Working at a daily resolution provides a valuable insight into the variability of weather conditions in relation to tourism. The South-West's average weather conditions may not be suitable for beach tourism, but conditions on individual days could well be. Daily data were produced using the weather generator that is integrated in the UKCP09 user interface. Results were calculated for two major coastal destinations, Bournemouth and Penzance.

Compared with the TCI, the BCI puts relatively more emphasis on precipitation, wind and sunshine. As a result, BCI analyses should provide insights and supplementary data to the TCI results and are relevant to the South-West because part of the offer is around sun, sea and sand. Naturally, BCI scores are only meaningful for the coastal grid squares.

Two of the climate variables needed for calculating index scores were not available from the UKCP09 projections: minimum relative humidity and hours of sunshine. Minimum relative humidity could be calculated from mean relative humidity and mean temperature, under the assumption that vapour pressure is constant throughout the day (for details see Whittlesea and Amelung 2010). The hours of sunshine could be estimated from day length, which is determined by latitude and time of year and cloudiness, which is a variable in the dataset.

Unfortunately, wind values were not produced by the integrated weather generator. The option of using monthly values to calculate daily BCI values was highly unsatisfactory. Monthly values were typically quite close to the thresholds of 4 and 6 m/s, used in the BCI, so that some areas always had the maximum score on wind, whereas other areas never achieved a positive score. The distribution of wind speeds has been found to closely follow a Rayleigh distribution (Gipe 2004). This distribution is determined by one parameter, the mode, which equals 1.253314 times the known mean. By drawing random numbers between 0 and 1, and feeding these into the inverse cumulative distribution function, daily wind speeds were generated that complied with the observed monthly mean wind speeds.

TCI and BCI scores were calculated for the whole sample of 10,000 data points available for each combination of month, time period and 25 km grid square. Where needed, scores were averaged across months to allow for seasonal analysis. Subsequently, the 10,000 scores obtained were ranked according to magnitude. The median value (the 5,000th score in the ordered list) and the tenth and ninetieth percentiles (i.e. the 1,000th and 9,000th score respectively) were saved for further analysis. As an example, in Figure 6.1 all 10,000 TCI scores are plotted in order of magnitude for one of the grid cells (the most northern one), for the month of July in the time slice of the 2020s. TCI scores range from just over 65 to just under 95. The median (sample 5,000) is 80, the tenth (sample 1,000) and ninetieth (sample 9,000) percentiles are 75 and just over 85.

It is important to investigate and understand the different cumulative probability levels. In general it is 'very likely' that the projection will exceed the 10 per cent cumulative probability level, 'as likely as not' that the projection will exceed the 50 per cent cumulative probability level and 'very unlikely' that the projection will exceed the 90 per cent cumulative probability level, all according to current scientific insight (UKCP 2010).

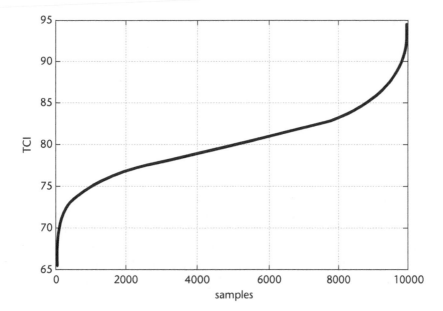

FIGURE 6.1 10,000 TCI scores for one of the grid cells (1466), for the month of July for the 2020s

Incidence of extreme weather

The analysis of changes in the frequency of extreme events was done using UKCP09's Threshold Detector (TD). The TD is a processing tool that uses 100 random sample Weather Generator (WG) runs of daily data, for each month over thirty-year periods as its input. The WG simulation is run for a predefined grid cell or cluster of grid cells, for a user-defined time slice and emissions scenario.

The WG outputs are then run through the TD, where the user defines a weather event (or indices) made up of temperatures or daily rainfall totals greater or lower than a certain threshold. The TD then cycles through the WG outputs and counts the number of occurrences of the prescribed event by month, (January–December), season (winter, spring, summer, autumn) and by year. The TD produces a set of outputs and summary statistics across all of the runs which include the mean, standard deviation, standard error and the minimum and maximum recorded number of events under investigation.

Two types of extreme event were analysed: heatwave and heavy rain. The conditions for a heatwave are predefined in the TD: maximum temperature over 30°C and minimum temperature over 15°C over three consecutive days (or more). The definition for heavy rain was taken from the Met Office: precipitation greater than 25 mm for more than one day (Met Office 2008).

The analysis looked at the 2020s and 2050s for the high emissions scenario. Two 5 km grid squares were identified coinciding with the destinations of the towns of Penzance in Cornwall and Bournemouth in Dorset (see Figures 6.5a and b for locations).

Results

TCI scores in the baseline period vary across the South-West. There is a notable difference between the north-east (top half) which generally receives higher TCI scores and the south-west (bottom half) of the region. In terms of specific destinations (25 km grid squares), Bournemouth and Poole to the east score highest across the region, with the National Parks of Dartmoor and Exmoor positioned in the west scoring the lowest (high altitude). Climate change does not seem to alter this general spatial pattern of TCI scores. TCI scores improve for the whole region for both the 2020s and 2050s; in much of the region gradually moving from 'very good' (baseline) to 'excellent' (2050s) in summer, and from 'marginal' to 'acceptable' in autumn, at the 50 per cent cumulative probability level.

As expected, by far the highest TCI scores are recorded in summer, and according to the projections analysed, this is unlikely to change. Based on the scores at 50 per cent probability, February consistently has the lowest level of improvement with June, August and September having the highest improvement level. As an example, the development of TCI scores for the grid square coinciding with 'Penzance' is shown in Table 6.1.

Changes in TCI scores can have multiple sources; they can stem from any of the five sub-indices of the TCI. As an example, Figure 6.2 shows the monthly distribution of disaggregated TCI scores for Bournemouth in the 1970s, the 2020s

TABLE 6.1 TCI scores for Grid Square 1690 for the 1970s and 50 per cent probability level for 2020s and 2050s

Month	1970s	2020s	2050s	Change, 1970 to 2050
January	29.1	29.6	30.3	1.2
February	33.7	32.7	32.6	–1.1
March	40.7	42.6	42.8	2.1
April	51.2	51.5	53.8	2.6
May	55.3	59.6	63.1	7.8
June	63.2	70.4	78.8	15.6
July	72.2	76.7	81.7	9.5
August	69.7	77.3	82.4	12.7
September	57.3	63.5	71.5	14.2
October	43.4	46.4	48.6	5.2
November	35.7	36	36.4	0.7
December	31.2	32.1	32.2	1

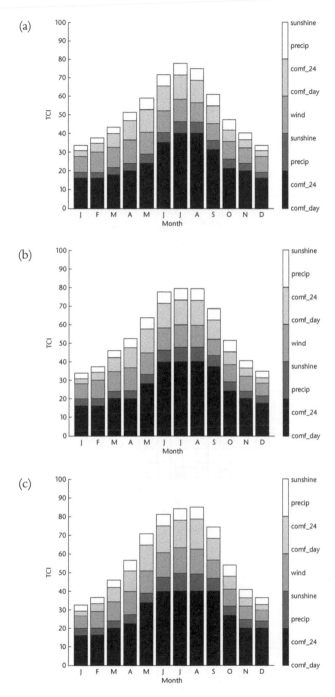

FIGURE 6.2 Disaggregation of TCI scores in their five components for Bournemouth (grid square 1700), in the baseline period of the 1970s (a), 2020s (b) and 2050s (c), 50 % probability level]

and 2050s. TCI scores improve most between April and October. In the shoulder months such as May, most of the increase comes from improvements in daytime comfort (comf_day). In the peak months of July and August, daytime comfort was already at its maximum in the baseline period. In those months, daily comfort (comf_24), sunshine and wind contribute most to the TCI increase. The contribution of wind may be surprising, given that wind speed is assumed constant (because no wind data were available from the projections). The role of wind, however, is not constant, as in Mieczkowski's scheme it depends on temperature. As summer temperature increases, the cooling effect of (modest amounts of) wind is appreciated more. The graphs also reveal improved wind performance in the winter months, caused by reduced wind chill.

The results described above are based on the median values in the projections, with a cumulative probability of 0.5. Taking other cumulative probabilities (CPs) as a starting point yield results that can be very different, as the example of the extreme South-West grid cell ('Penzance') shows (see Figure 6.3a and b). At CP = 0.9 (i.e. 90 % probability), TCI scores well exceed those achieved in the 1970s as well as those projected at CP = 0.5 (and 0.1). At CP = 0.1 (i.e. 10 per cent probability), TCI scores for some months in the 2020s and even the 2050s are lower than in the baseline period of the 1970s.

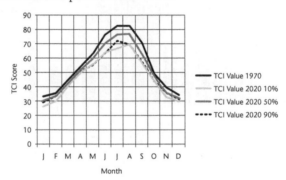

FIGURE 6.3A Grid 1690, TCI score 2020s

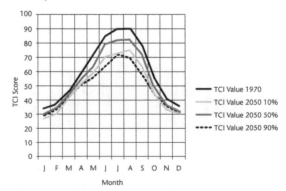

FIGURE 6.3B Grid 1690, TCI score 2050s

Figure 6.4 explores the TCI scores under the 10 per cent cumulative probability further, showing a decline in the scores from the 1970s baseline in both the 2020s and 2050s. In the TCI scores for the 2020s there is a decline for eight months of the year, and surprisingly the largest decline of –5.3 is in July. By the 2050s February and March are still showing a decline, although it is minimal. The increase observed in the remaining months is relatively small in comparison to the scores at 50 per cent and 90 per cent cumulative probability.

Under the 90 per cent cumulative probability, there is no decline in TCI scores for either the 2020s or 2050s and the improvement in scores is also quite significant. For example the 2050s show a large proportion of the region achieving the 'ideal' TCI score (90–100) for the months of July and August (see Figures 6.5a and b), up from 'very good' (70–80) in the baseline period. The months of June, August and September have the greatest degree in improvement from the 1970s baseline (21.5, 19.8 and 20.7 points respectively), amounting to a shift in at least two TCI categories.

To explore the variability and uncertainty in the output, the standard deviation in TCI scores was calculated for each grid cell in each month and each time-slice (see Table 6.2 for the mean values for the South-West). As Table 6.2 shows, the intra-annual variation is largest in the summer and shoulder months, in the 2020s as well as the 2050s. As could be expected, uncertainty increases between the 2020s and the 2050s. Standard deviation increases in all months except for September, with the largest increases in October, May and April.

For the South-West of England the BCI scores are lower than the TCI scores, because for beach tourism wind requirements are more stringent, precipitation is valued more negatively, and preferred temperatures are higher. Figures 6.6a and b

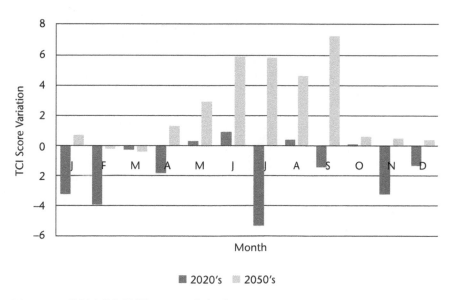

■ 2020's ▨ 2050's

FIGURE 6.4 Grid 1690, TCI score variation]

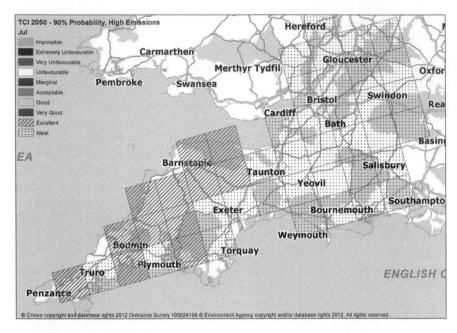

FIGURE 6.5A TCI 90 %, July 2050

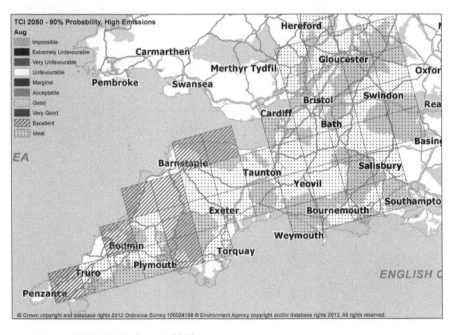

FIGURE 6.5B TCI 90 %, August 2050

TABLE 6.2 Standard deviation in monthly TCI scores for the South-West in the 2020s and 2050s

	2020s	*2050s*	*Change*
January	1.78	2.60	0.82
February	1.78	2.77	0.99
March	1.68	2.11	0.43
April	1.94	3.43	1.49
May	4.06	5.70	1.64
June	4.28	5.19	0.91
July	5.23	6.09	0.86
August	4.91	5.95	1.04
September	5.38	5.17	–0.22
October	2.40	4.48	2.08
November	1.97	2.66	0.68
December	2.01	2.23	0.22

display BCI scores for Bournemouth and Penzance, two major coastal tourist destinations in the South-West, for the baseline period, the 2020s and the 2050s, at cumulative probabilities of 10 per cent, 50 per cent and 90 per cent. In the baseline period at 50 per cent probability, maximum scores are in the mid-50s for Bournemouth and in the high-40s for Penzance. The lower BCI values for Penzance are due to less favourable wind conditions. On the top 10 per cent of the summer days, BCI values reach values in the low 70s or higher in Bournemouth and the high 60s or higher in Penzance. On the bottom 10 per cent of the summer days, scores do not exceed 35 in Bournemouth and 30 in Penzance.

When comparing the baseline situation with the scenario results for the 2020s and 2050s, one of the most striking results is the increase in variability. For both Bournemouth and Penzance, the scores at 90 per cent probability increase, whereas the scores at 10 per cent probability decrease or remain unchanged at best. At 50 per cent probability, BCI scores for Bournemouth deteriorate in winter, while improving in the rest of the year. For Penzance, scores improve from May to September and remain virtually unchanged in the other months of the year. BCI scores for the 2050s are generally higher than for the 2020s, but the degree of change between the 2020s and the 2050s is much smaller than the amount of change between the baseline and the 2020s.

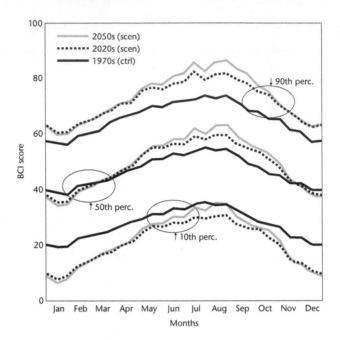

FIGURE 6.6A Cumulative probability values (10 %, 50 %, 90 %) of the Beach Climate Index (BCI) for Bournemouth in the baseline (black), 2020s (light green) and 2050s (dark green)

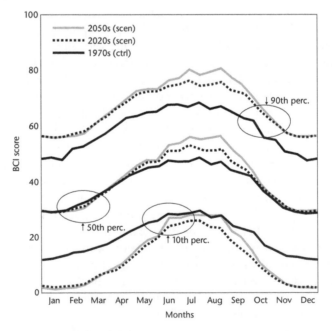

FIGURE 6.6B Cumulative probability values (10 %, 50 %, 90 %) of the Beach Climate Index (BCI) for Penzance in the baseline (black), 2020s (light green) and 2050s (dark green)

Incidence of extreme weather

Two thresholds were run through the TD: one for a predefined heatwave event (similar to that experienced by the South-West in 2003) and the second for a custom-defined heavy rainfall event for two 5 km grid squares coinciding with Bournemouth and Penzance. The baseline statistics show that a heatwave event did not occur in these locations during the baseline thirty-year period from 1961–1990. Figure 6.7a and b illustrate the projected results for the 2020s and 2050s, which show that over time the likelihood of a heatwave event will increase in both locations, mainly affecting the month of July.

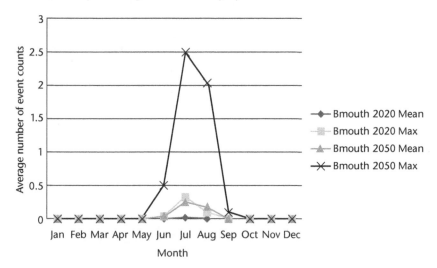

FIGURE 6.7A Threshold Detector results for a heatwave in Bournemouth

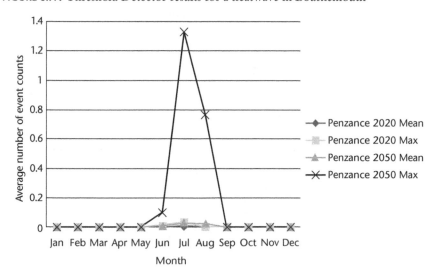

FIGURE 6.7B Threshold Detector results for a heatwave in Penzance

Using Bournemouth as an example and because it appears the most likely of the two destinations to experience a heatwave, the maximum average occurrence of a heatwave for the summer season (June to August) could be up to 0.3 each year in the 2020s and 4.2 each year in the 2050s. The baseline thirty-year period showed zero events of this nature in relation to the projected maximum of up to nine events in the 2020s and 126 events in the 2050s thirty-year periods. The mean average occurrence for the summer season is much lower at 0.03 per year for the 2020s and 0.5 for the 2050s, implying a potential of up to 0.9 and 15 heatwave events respectively for the 2020s and 2050s thirty-year periods.

The results show that some destinations will be more prone to a heatwave event than others, for example the maximum average annual occurrence for a heatwave event is 4.2 in Bournemouth and 1.5 in Penzance in the 2050s.

The second TD run was user-defined looking at the likelihood of heavy rain (similar to the cause of the floods in 2007) occurring using the Met Office definition of 'precipitation greater than 25 mm for more than one day' (Met Office 2008). The summary statistics are presented in Figure 6.8a and b.

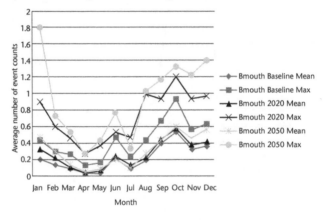

FIGURE 6.8A Threshold Detector results for a heavy rainfall event in Bournemouth

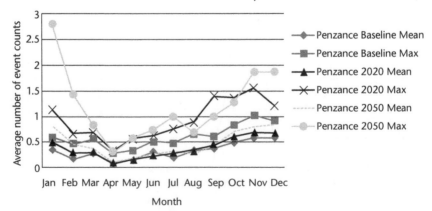

FIGURE 6.8B Threshold Detector results for a heavy rainfall event in Penzance

There is an increase in the mean and maximum number of events from the baseline to the 2020s and 2050s, especially for the winter season (December to February). The overall pattern for the mean number of counts for each time slice is fairly consistent but for the maximum number of counts the results are more sporadic. Penzance appears to be affected most out of the two destinations, with the maximum average number of events per annum being 6.7 in the 2020s and 7.5 in the 2050s, amounting to 201 and 225 total events for the respective thirty-year periods.

The results show that the summer months are also set to experience increased incidences of heavy rainfall from the baseline. The peak summer months of July and August in the 2020s have a similar if not higher number of counts for heavy rainfall than the 2050s.

Discussion

The UKCP09 climate projections for the South-West show that the climate will become warmer with high summer temperatures becoming more frequent, and very cold winters becoming increasingly rare. Winters will become wetter, while summers will become drier. Relative sea level will continue to rise and the frequency and intensity of extreme weather events (such as flooding, heatwaves and drought) will increase (Climate South West 2010).

The TCI and BCI have been used before to explore how the changing climate may affect different destinations and activities, but calculating them with the UKCP09 projection data represents a major step forward. UKCP09's probabilistic projections use a range of models with the production of multiple projections per model, covering not only uncertainties in climate system representation, but also the variability in the system itself. The first index-studies (e.g. Amelung and Viner 2006) were based on central estimates from only one or several climate models, whereas more recent studies (e.g. Perch-Nielsen, Amelung and Knutti 2010) were based on central estimates from multiple models. Probabilistic projections make probability distributions for impact-related indicators (such as TCI and BCI) much easier to produce, and these distributions allow for much better risk assessments.

Probability distributions are of great value to policy makers, because they can act as what-if scenarios against which policy makers can assess their policy options, and they provide a basis for risk assessment. From the perspective of impact research, probabilistic projections also mark a major improvement. The climatologists producing the projections answer a whole range of important questions that require in-depth climatological knowledge (such as what models to use, what weight to give to each model, how to produce a model sample), so that impact researchers, having downloaded one single dataset, can dedicate most of their time to using the data and interpreting results. The weather generator that is integrated in the UKCP09 User Interface allows for probabilistic analyses at the daily level.

The TCI findings show the scores to improve for the whole region and in particular for the summer, with a shift by at least one category (for instance, from 'good' to 'very good'). Some of the highest climate improvement scores are in June and September, providing the potential for tourism that requires 'sightseeing' conditions to increase in the shoulder period. This aligns closely to an ambition set out in the South-West's tourism strategy 'Towards 2015' (South West Tourism 2005) and more recently in its 'Principles for Success' document (South West Tourism Alliance 2011) to work to reduce seasonality of tourism and increase the value of visitor spend in the off-peak periods. Overall the TCI results look promising for tourism planning, especially for the north-east of the region. Future studies should consider using daily data produced by the weather generator, to calculate changes in frequencies of favourable and unfavourable days in terms of TCI.

For the BCI calculations, weather generator data were used to analyse changes in climate suitability for beach tourism in two coastal resorts, Bournemouth and Penzance. In summer, acceptable or better conditions are projected for 50 per cent of the days as early as the 2020s; conditions on the 10 per cent best-scoring summer days are projected to improve from (very) good to excellent. Even these higher scores, however, are no match for the top-scoring beach destinations in Europe, now and in the future (Moreno and Amelung 2009). For planning purposes the prospects of the South-West of England becoming an internationally competitive beach destination within a few decades appear unlikely.

At the national level, however, the South-West seems to be in a good position to strengthen its leading role in (beach) tourism in England. Future studies may perform a comparison between BCI results and calculations with CIT, the second generation Climate Index for Tourism (de Freitas, Scott and McBoyle 2008). CIT, which so far has only been implemented for beach tourism, differs from BCI in several ways, such as the treatment of precipitation and wind as overriding rather than complementary factors. Comparing BCI and CIT results may yield additional insights into the robustness of the results. Once CIT implementations for light outdoor activities (sightseeing) become available as well, robustness testing of suitability scores for this market segment could be performed as well.

The TD results show there is a strong likelihood that heatwaves and heavy rainfall are set to increase and will affect the peak summer season, in particular the month of July. Applying this analysis to two separate 5 km grid squares highlights the need to look at destinations individually and that a regional analysis is not detailed enough.

Relevance for tourism planning

The tourism sector of the South West's economy is one of its largest, with 21.2 million staying visitors and 96.8 million day visitors spending approximately £9.4 billion and supporting around 269,000 jobs (South West Tourism 2008b). This in part is due to the region's southerly location offering warmer climes and also its landscape, beautiful coastline and its wealth of natural and historic features. A large part of the region and its infrastructure satisfies the needs of visitors, and the most popular visitor activities and main reasons for a visit are shopping (75 per cent), walking (69 per cent) and visits to heritage sites (36 per cent) (South West Tourism 2008a).

A significant proportion of tourism infrastructure is located in coastal locations that are vulnerable to storm surges, coastal erosion, rising sea levels and flooding. In addition, businesses are also vulnerable to flooding from heavy rainfall, especially if they are located in riverside locations or on flood plains. The projected increase in heavy rainfall events will pose key challenges for the tourism industry, not only in relation to infrastructure and day-to-day operations, but the visitor decision to take a holiday in or make a repeat visit to the South-West.

One of the most vulnerable areas to changes in the weather is the day visitor market, which attracts around 97 million day visitors to the South-West per annum, contributing £4.4 billion (47 per cent) of the tourist spend in the region (South West Tourism 2008b). In addition, the South-West relies heavily on its domestic tourism market which contributes around 89 per cent of its staying visitors (South West Tourism 2008a), and repeat visits comprise a significant proportion of the market at 82 per cent (South West Tourism 2009a). Weather plays an important role in the visitor experience and can directly influence whether a repeat visit will be made. A recent survey of non-visitor and lapsed visitors to the South West (South West Tourism 2009b) highlighted the 'lack of guaranteed sunshine' as a key reason why they are not travelling to the South-West for their holiday. Poor and unpredictable weather forms part of the value equation and leads to greater entertainment costs.

Today, English consumers prefer to take holidays abroad because of the lack of sunshine and the amount of rain in the United Kingdom, identifying good, hot weather as a key ingredient for a holiday which cannot be guaranteed in the United Kingdom, (Platt and Retallack 2009). In view of the UKCP09 projections showing an improvement in tourism climate conditions for the South-West, this could change, especially when the results are combined with other studies that project a deterioration of climatic conditions in competing destinations around the Mediterranean that are popular with tourists from the United Kingdom (Amelung and Viner 2006).

In addition, transport costs are likely to become an even more important factor in the overall cost of a holiday, in particular for trips involving air travel. This combination of factors could result in more visitors to the South-West, leading to a bigger tourism market, improved economy and more jobs. In turn, destinations will require careful planning and development to prevent increased congestion, insensitive development and pressure on natural resources, local infrastructure, services and supplies. There are destinations and businesses in the South-West that already face management challenges from excessive visitor pressure, inadequate infrastructure and poor service planning.

For example, the heatwave in August 2003 brought high temperatures of 31+ °C, attracting record numbers of visitors to Bournemouth and Poole, and leading to accommodation that was full and beaches that were packed (*Dorset Echo* 2003c). It also pushed local infrastructure, facilities and services to its limits. The weekend attracted 20 per cent more traffic than usual, leading to pollution that was more than double the government health limit (*Dorset Echo* 2003a). There were queues for car parks, around 700 parking tickets were issued, access for emergency vehicles was blocked and the heat caused health issues for many (*Dorset Echo* 2003b).

At the time of writing there are no apparent national government work streams or strategic plans for tourism around climate change adaptation. However, the sector is starting to take the lead, with organizations such as the National Trust spearheading coordinated planning initiatives like Shifting Shores, to plan for and work with a changing coastline and the subsequent impacts on their properties, sites and tourism services. In the South-West, 279 km of National Trust coastline and 852 hectares of coastal sites are at risk of erosion or tidal flooding (National Trust 2008).

In addition, regional climate change adaptation partnerships such as Climate South West are recognizing the importance and potential vulnerability of the tourism sector, realizing that it will be far better to plan and prepare than have a reactive response. Climate South West together with the regional tourism body coordinates a multi-stakeholder 'tourism sector group'. Since the release of the UKCP09 datasets, the group facilitated one of the first national case studies applying the data, which in turn led to advice for destinations and the development of a bespoke tourism website that provides businesses with a range of practical help, case studies and advice (see www.climateprepared.com).

Detailed tourism planning mainly occurs at the local destination and business level, and strategy timeframes tend to be five to fifteen years, so having data for the 2020s is useful to help with short to medium planning horizons. The 2050 data is also useful to consider, ensuring that planning and decisions taken now are resilient into the future.

Conclusion

The UKCP09 probabilistic climate projections are a tool to interpret the latest insights from climate science, and these can be applied to tourism planning. They allow tourism researchers and practitioners to explore the likely (50 per cent probability) impact of climate change on climate suitability and the likelihood of extreme events in the context of tourism, alongside the very likely 10 per cent and not so likely 90 per cent probabilities. For the South-West, results indicate that there is a high probability that conditions for sightseeing tourism and beach tourism will improve in the summer and shoulder seasons. However, this is not absolutely certain and there is a slight probability that conditions will deteriorate.

The benefits of daily data at destination geographies for strategic planning time horizons like the 2020s are what really makes the projections useful, relevant and accessible for tourism practitioners.

The trend towards better conditions in the South- West of England, which has been noted in a number of previous studies, can now be qualified, made much more specific, and linked to probability and risk assessments. Since the UKCP09 projections are relatively easy to use, there is scope and potential for far greater use and application of climate projections. The results indicate that climate change could improve tourism conditions and the subsequent popularity of the South-West of England as a tourism destination, but it could also bring challenges of extreme weather. The detail could help to inform tourism practitioners and planners regarding the future sustainability and development needs of the industry to ensure it is resilient to change.

The biggest and most important challenge will be engaging tourism practitioners and businesses at the local level, and aligning and embedding activity into the broader sustainability agenda. Destination managers and businesses have an important role to play, to aid the interpretation of this data and its subsequent application. Utilizing the outputs and engaging the sector will help to ensure that the industry is informed and prepares itself, especially as extreme weather events look set to increase and can be detrimental. The information can be used to help guide long-term solutions, direct resources, inform policies, and encourage sustainable planning and decisions that will promote tourism resilience and adaptation.

References

Amelung, B., Nicholls, S. and Viner, D. (2007) 'Implications of global climate change for tourism flows and seasonality', *Journal of Travel Research*, vol. 45, no. 3, pp. 285–96.

Amelung, B. and Viner, D. (2006) 'Mediterranean tourism: Exploring the future with the Tourism Climatic Index', *Journal of Sustainable Tourism*, vol. 14, no. 4, pp. 349–66.

Bigano, A., Goria, A., Hamilton, J. and Tol, R. S. J. (2005) 'The effect of climate change and extreme weather events on tourism', in R. Brau and A. Lanza (eds). *Tourism and Sustainable Economic Development: Macroeconomic models and empirical methods*, Edward Elgar, Cheltenham.

Ciscar, J. C., Iglesias, A., Feyen, L., Szabó, L., Van Regemorter, D., Amelung, B., Nicholls, R., Watkiss, P., Christensen, O. B., Dankers, R., Garrote, L., Goodess, C. M., Hunt, A., Moreno, A., Richards, J. and Soria, A. (2011) 'Physical and economic consequences of climate change in Europe', *Proceedings of the US National Academy of Sciences*, vol. 108, no. 7, pp. 2678–83.

Climate South West (2010) *Warming to the Idea: Building resilience to extreme weather and climate change in the South West*, Climate South West, Exeter.

Cox, P. and Stephenson, D. (2007) 'A Changing Climate for Prediction', *Science*, vol. 317, no. 5835, pp. 207–8.

De Freitas, C., Scott, D. and McBoyle, G. (2008) 'A second generation climate index for tourism (CIT): specification and verification', *International Journal of Biometeorology*, vol. 52, no. 5, pp. 399–407.

Dorset Echo (2003a) 'Parking mayhem', 12 August.

Dorset Echo (2003b) 'Resort is now a smog blackspot', 12 August.

Dorset Echo (2003c) 'Resorts packed full as records tumble', 11 August.

Gipe, P. (2004) *Wind Power: Renewable energy for home, farm, and business*, Chelsea Green, White River Junction, Vt.

Intergovernmental Panel on Climate Change (IPCC) (2007) *Climate Change 2007: Synthesis report*, IPCC, Geneva.

Met Office (2008) *Together: Make a difference with a co-ordinated response to emergency management*. Table 2: Threshold criteria for the issue of Flash Warnings, p. 7.

Mieczkowski, Z. (1985) 'The Tourism Climatic Index: a method of evaluating world climates for tourism', *The Canadian Geographer*, vol. 29, no. 3, pp. 220–33.

Moreno, A. and Amelung, B. (2009) 'Climate change and tourist comfort on Europe's beaches in summer: a reassessment', *Coastal Management,* vol. 37, no. 6, pp 550–68.

Morgan, R., Gatell, E., Junyent, R., Micallef, A., Ozhan, E. and Williams, A. T. (2000) 'An improved user based Beach Climate Index', *Journal of Coastal Conservation*, vol. 6, no. 1, pp 41–50.

National Trust (2008) *Shifting Shores in the South West: Living with a changing coastline*, The National Trust Exeter, England

Nicholls, S. and Amelung, B. (2008) 'Climate change and tourism in north-western Europe', *Tourism Analysis*, vol. 13, no. 1, pp. 21–31.

Perch-Nielsen, S. L., Amelung, B. and Knutti, R. (2010) 'Future climate resources for tourism in Europe based on the daily Tourism Climatic Index', *Climatic Change*, vol. 103, no. 3, pp 363–81.

Platt, R. and Retallack, S. (2009) *Consumer Power: How the public thinks lower-carbon behaviour could be made mainstream*, IPPR, London.

Scott, D., McBoyle, G. and Schwartzentruber, M. (2004) 'Climate change and the distribution of climatic resources for tourism in North America', *Climate Research*, vol. 27, no. 2, pp. 105–17.

South West Tourism (2005) *Towards 2015: Shaping tomorrow's tourism*, South West Tourism, Exeter.

South West Tourism (2008a) *South West Visitor Survey*, South West Tourism, Exeter.

South West Tourism (2008b) *Value of Tourism*, South West Tourism, Exeter.

South West Tourism (2009a) *South West Visitor Survey*, South West Tourism, Exeter.

South West Tourism (2009b) *Survey of Non-Visitor and Lapsed Visitors to the South West*, South West Tourism, Exeter.

South West Tourism Alliance (2011) *Principles for Success: Guidance for tourism in South West England*, South West Tourism Alliance, Exeter.

UKClimate Projections (UKCP) (2010) 'Box 3: How are probabilistic projections presented & how should they be interpreted?' 28 May. Available at: http://ukclimateprojections. defra.gov.uk/content/view/1989/689/ (accessed 26 April 2011).

UN World Tourism Organization (UNWTO), UN Environment Programme (UNEP) and World Meteorological Organization (WMO) (2008) *Climate Change and Tourism – Responding to global challenges*, UNWTO and UNEP, Madrid.

Whittlesea, E. and Amelung, B. (2010) 'Cost-a South West: What may tomorrow's weather and climate look like for tourism in the SW of England?' South West Tourism, Exeter.

7

CLIMATE CHANGE POLICY RESPONSES OF AUSTRALIAN AND NEW ZEALAND NATIONAL GOVERNMENTS
Implications for sustainable tourism

Nadine Elizabeth White and Jeremy Buultjens

Introduction

Climate change is a central contemporary issue facing governments across the world (Garnaut 2008, Stern 2006). Governments that, in recent decades, have begun to embrace sustainability principles in their policy and regulation now also need to integrate climate change adaptation and mitigation into policy frameworks. Many governments seem to be grappling with this challenge, despite the commonalities between sustainability and climate change. Getting these policy frameworks right is critical to providing the best possible outcomes for environments, societies and industries.

Government climate-change policies and consumer responses to climate change can have impacts on society and a broad range of industries including tourism industries. The Australian and New Zealand tourism industries are especially vulnerable since they are highly climate dependent (see Australian Business Roundtable on Climate Change – ABRCC 2006), and are two of the most distant long-haul destinations. Climate change impacts and policies on tourism in both countries will be important because of the economic importance of the sector. In Australia, the contribution of tourism to the economy in 2007–08 was approximately A$70.4 billion (6.2 per cent) of GDP (Tourism Research Australia 2009). The total tourism expenditure for New Zealand for the same year was NZ$21.5 billion, contributing 9.2 per cent to GDP (Statistics New Zealand 2009).

This chapter examines the policy approaches of the Australian and New Zealand governments between 1996 and 2007 to climate change, and their possible impacts. This period has been selected as it coincides with Howard's Liberal National Party government in Australia. The chapter begins with background on the impacts and interrelationship of climate change and tourism and the political systems of Australia and New Zealand. This is followed by the method used for the study and the results. The chapter ends with a discussion and concluding comments regarding the impact of the policy approaches on tourism industries and suggestions for improvement.

Background

Impacts and interrelationship of climate change and tourism in Australia and New Zealand

The Intergovernmental Panel on Climate Change (IPCC) anticipate that many of the impacts of climate change will occur within the next forty years in Australia and New Zealand. By 2020, significant loss of biodiversity is projected to occur in some ecologically rich tourism destinations, including the Great Barrier Reef and Queensland wet tropics in Australia. Water availability problems are projected to intensify in eastern and southern Australia, and in Northland and some eastern regions of New Zealand by 2030 (Hennessy et al. 2007). There are expected increases in the intensity and frequency of drought, fire, heavy rains and tropical cyclones. By 2050, continuing human population growth and coastal development in some areas are projected to exacerbate risks from the severity and frequency of storms and coastal flooding as well as sea level (Hennessy et al. 2007). There are 'serious implications for sustainability in both Australia and New Zealand' (Hennessy et al. 2007, p. 528), and while some impacts of climate change may be benign or even beneficial for certain tourism industries or destinations, most are expected to have deleterious effects in Australasia.

Tourism also directly and indirectly impacts on climate change in a number of ways. There is strong international scientific consensus that the accelerated rate of climate change being experienced globally is attributable to human activity: that is increasing anthropogenic greenhouse gas concentrations. Indeed global greenhouse gas emissions (GGE) due to human activities have increased 70 per cent between 1970 and 2004 (IPCC 2007). GGE produced by air travel, road travel, shipping, rail travel, and the activities of hotels are the most obvious contributions to climate change from tourism. This complex interrelationship between tourism and climate change leads to questions regarding the resilience of Australia's and New Zealand's tourism industries. The ability of these industries to withstand and indeed flourish in a changing climate, as well as the market and regulatory responses, will determine their sustainability.

Australia's and New Zealand's political systems

New Zealand's parliament is unicameral as it only has one chamber, the House of Representatives, whereas Australia is bicameral with two chambers: the House of Representatives, and the Upper House, known as the Senate, which has the power to block government legislation. In Australia, John Howard assumed the role of Australian prime minister on 11 March 1996 and lost power in November 2007.

In New Zealand, between 1996 and 2007 there was a succession of MMP (mixed member proportional), National Party and Labour governments. These governments were led by Jim Bolger, Jenny Shipley and then Helen Clark.

Method

This research consists of a desktop study, using the documentary method, of the responses of the New Zealand and Australian national governments to climate change. The documentary method is used to critically analyse secondary data sources including documents and public records (Jennings 2001). The data sources included websites, policy documents, media releases, parliamentary proceedings, and commentary from books, journals and the media. The data sources were studied for references to tourism, climate change policy and general issues surrounding climate change. Due to the need for brevity, not all government publications have been presented. It is therefore important that the policies described in this chapter not be considered comprehensive. Instead the policies selected for inclusion are considered to be the most relevant, and indicate the general climate change platform of the governments.

Results

Major international climate change policies

During the study period there were two substantial international climate change initiatives in place – the 1992 United Nations Framework Convention on Climate Change (UNFCCC) and the 1997 Kyoto Protocol. Both these initiatives, which related to mitigating climate change through reduced greenhouse gases, formed the core of international climate change policy. The response of the Australian and New Zealand governments to these initiatives was indicative of their position on climate change.

The UNFCCC was signed at the UN Conference on Environment and Development (UNCED) in Rio de Janeiro in 1992, and entered into force in March 1994. The objective of the UNFCCC was the stabilisation of greenhouse gas concentrations in the atmosphere at a level that would 'prevent dangerous anthropogenic interference with the climate system' (UNFCCC 1992, p. 4). Australia and New Zealand both ratified the Convention. Despite its being ratified by Parliament, in 1997 Howard stated that Australia should never have signed the UNFCCC (Hamilton 2000a). In contrast, New Zealand has remained relatively supportive of the UNFCCC.

The Kyoto Protocol, formulated in December 1997 as part of the UNFCCC, was considered to be the centrepiece of international policy. Under Kyoto, industrialized countries commit themselves to target GGE ceilings with some flexibility arrangements built in, such as international emissions trading permits. There was an agreement to the specific reductions to be made in emissions of six greenhouse gases over the period 2008 to 2012, as well as a general commitment to a 5 per cent reduction in overall GGE from 1990 levels for each of the agreeing parties. Countries were also allowed to set individual emissions objectives: many set reductions of 7 to 8 per cent.

Australia and the United States did not ratify the Protocol during the period of the study. Both countries were seen as protecting their national interests rather than committing to global efforts to reduce GGE (Davenport 2006; Yu and Taplin 2000); indeed Australia was accused of sabotaging the Kyoto Protocol (Naughten 2006). Australia committed to only slowing its growth in emissions rather than actual reductions (Davenport 2006; Stewart and Hendriks 2008). The Australian target was 108 per cent of its 1990 level, second only to Iceland at 110 per cent (Gillespie 2000). The government argued that Australia should be able to increase its carbon dioxide levels. Other governments were 'shocked by Australia's stance' (Clancy 2007, p. 45).

New Zealand ratified the Protocol in 2002, while successfully exempting itself from the average 5 per cent cut in emissions, with a target of 100 per cent of its 1990 level (Gillespie 2000). It took on a dominant and overt advocacy role for the 'net approach' to emissions reductions rather than the gross approach at the Kyoto Conference. New Zealand also pressed strongly for sinks to be included in the Protocol. This approach was supported by Australia, as well as a number of other countries including the United States and Canada (Gillespie 2000), despite critics arguing the fundamentally different nature of reduction by sinks and complexities around the issue of 'additivity' (Solomon et al. 2007).

Australia and New Zealand were both members of the 'Umbrella Group', a loose coalition of non-EU developed countries that arose to counter EU efforts to constrain the adoption of 'flexibility mechanisms'. This included international emissions trading, where developed countries would be able to purchase emission reductions from other, including developing, countries, as a substitute for domestic action (Kelly 2010).

Australian Government policies

On taking office in March 1996, the Coalition Government began to abolish or wind back several federal programs aimed at reducing emissions (Hamilton 2000a). For example, the National Energy Efficiency Program, the main national program aimed at increasing the efficient use of energy, had its budget cut by 60 per cent in the 1997–98 budget. This led to the abolition of the Enterprise Energy Audit Program, which had subsidized the cost of energy audits for the business sector (Hamilton 2000a). The Energy Research and Development Program (ERDP) was also abolished in the 1997 federal budget as part of its 'tight fiscal discipline' (ALII 2008, p. 1). The ERDP had been created to stimulate investment in effective energy innovation including alternative and renewable energy sources (Hamilton 2000a).

The government's first response in 1997 to the Kyoto Protocol was a $180 million package, Safeguarding the Future (Pearse 2007). Despite acknowledging the science on climate change – 'the world's climate scientists have provided us with a clear message – that the balance of evidence suggests humans are having a discernible influence on global climate' (Howard cited in Pearse 2007, p. 82) – the government only promised to cut Australia's emissions to 118 per cent of 1990 levels (Pearse 2007). In comparison, most other developed nations had agreed to reduce, not increase, their emissions from 1990 baseline levels. However, the package did contain some positive responses, including the establishment of the Mandated Renewable Energy Targets (MRET) for energy suppliers. The MRET required electricity providers to purchase 2 per cent of their power from renewable energy sources by 2010 (Clancy 2007, Stewart and Hendriks 2008). In 1998, a nationally agreed policy on GGE reduction was laid out in the National Greenhouse Strategy, which was followed by the establishment of the Australian Greenhouse Office (AGO), overseen by a Greenhouse Ministerial Council, to lead federal climate change policies (Fowler 2007).

Some critics argued that the government's failure to ratify Kyoto meant that Australia would miss out on opportunities in global clean energy technology and carbon trading markets (Clancy 2007, Muller 2008). Overall, many believed the government displayed a lack of leadership on the issue of emissions reduction legislation (Fowler 2007). The government defended its lack of political will to act on GGE by emphasizing the Australian economy's reliance on energy and greenhouse-gas-intensive industry, and claiming that other major greenhouse-gas-producing countries were also not acting on emissions (Taplin and Yu 2000).

In 1999, Australia's per capita contribution of carbon dioxide equivalents (CO_2-e) was the highest in the world (27.9 tonnes per person per year). This level was almost twice as much as New Zealand, which produced 14.4 tonnes per person per year (Tiffen and Gittins 2004). At this time the government announced the Measures for a Better Environment package. The package focused on paying the polluter to combat emissions through the centrepiece of the package: the Greenhouse Gas Abatement Program (GGAP). This program was valued at $400 million over four years, funding emission reduction programs for the biggest polluters for more than 250,000 tonnes of carbon dioxide annually (Pearse 2007, Stewart and Hendriks 2008). Some argue that the package was designed to induce the Democrats to pass the Goods and Services Tax proposal through the senate (Pearse 2007). In 2008, the Strategic Review of Australian Government Climate Change Programs (Wilkins Review) found GGAP not to be complementary to a carbon price (Wilkins 2008). It was then terminated at the end of the 2008–09 financial year.

A Senate review of Australia's response to climate change conducted in 2000 criticized the Government's inertia and 'called upon it to take a leadership role in international negotiations, with a view to a timely signing of the Kyoto Protocol' (Beresford 2008, p. 79). Despite this pressure, the government did not respond. In 2002, the Australian federal government, in what appeared to be a proactive initiative, established a government–business climate change dialogue. However, a participant in the dialogue, Environment Business Australia chief executive Fiona

Wain, said that it was 'full of people wanting to block any action, who couldn't see how important climate change was' (Wain as cited in Minchin 2006, p. 1).

This resistance by the government to adequately addressing climate change continued in 2003. The MRET program was reviewed, and the independent reviewers recommended a small increase in the proportion of renewable energy from 2 to 4 per cent. However the government 'ignored the recommendation for even this very modest increase, and refused to lift the level of MRETs. The bottom then fell out of the renewable energy sector' (Clancy 2007, p. 44). Clancy (2007) goes on to argue that Australia lost any advantage it could have had in the renewable energy industry in the future.

When the government gained control of both houses of parliament in 2004, pressure for it to seriously address climate change was reduced. After the election, the government released its *Energy White Paper* (*EWP*), in which it committed approximately $700 million to climate change. Much of these funds were directed into 'clean coal' technologies (Stewart and Hendriks 2008). Stewart and Hendriks (2008) argue that this measure was largely symbolic, to assist the government to appear as though it was doing something about climate change without really addressing the issue.

Also in 2004, the Australian National Climate Change Adaptation Programme commenced. A number of activities were funded under the $14 million programme, including the National Biodiversity and Climate Change Action Plan for 2004–2007, developed to coordinate a response to the impacts of climate change on biodiversity (NRMMC 2004) and the Integrated Assessment of Human Settlements sub-program. In 2004 the Department of Industry Tourism and Resources (DITR) also released a *Tourism White Paper* (DITR 2004). This document was designed to be a medium to long-term strategy for tourism, and yet it makes no reference at all to climate change.

In 2005, the Australian Government released the Australian Climate Change Science Program – Strategic Research Agenda (2004–2008) which was intended to support the development of a national climate modelling capacity. At this time, Australia also became one of the six partners, along with the United States, Japan, China, South Korea and India, to the Asia Pacific Partnership on Clean Development and Climate (AP6) (Christoff and Eckersley 2007). AP6 is a voluntary framework for cooperation to support, among other things, new 'clean' technologies to reduce GGE, and at the time the government promoted it as the centrepiece of its commitment to addressing climate change (Christoff and Eckersley 2007). However, AP6 provided no binding GGE reduction targets or timetables, no new carbon markets and no enforcement mechanisms (Christoff and Eckersley 2007, Clancy 2007), and appeared to be a symbolic initiative for the countries to appear to be doing something about climate change (Stewart and Hendriks 2008). Additionally, the AP6 was seen as an attempt to destroy or undermine the Kyoto Protocol (Clancy 2007).

In 2006 the government released its guide for business and government about strategies for public and private sector organizations to manage risk and climate change impacts (AGO 2006). This was effectively the first government document that addressed adaptation other than the aforementioned biodiversity action plan. It has been criticized for its inappropriate focus for the large majority of Australian businesses (O'Donnel 2008). Notably there was just one very brief reference to tourism in the 72-page document.

At this point, the Australian government attitude to climate change appears to take a particularly contentious turn. In 2006, allegations arose that scientists were being gagged from speaking about climate change. One former Commonwealth Scientific and Industrial Research Organisation (CSIRO) senior scientist and internationally recognized climate change expert, Dr Graeme Pearman, was 'reprimanded and encouraged to resign after he spoke out on global warming' (Chandler 2006, p. 1). Dr Barrie Pittock was also 'instructed to remove politically sensitive material from a government publication on climate change' (ABC 2006, p. 1). This did not appear to be a government that was transparent and open about its response to climate change.

However, a rising tide of public opinion appears to have panicked Howard into reshaping his approach at the end of 2006 (Beresford 2008). The apparent shift in policy is reflected in Howard's comment that to 'downplay the seriousness of climate change [was] no longer appropriate' (Stewart and Hendriks 2008, p. 219). The government commissioned a joint taskforce with business on carbon emissions trading in November 2006. This was met with some scepticism as there had been a backlog of reports on emissions trading going back as far as 1999 (Minchin 2006), including the government–business climate change dialogue discussed above. The Prime Ministerial Task Group on Emissions Trading was also found by some to have developed proposals that suggested a deliberate strategy of selecting coal and energy-intensive industry over efficiency and renewable energy industries (Muller 2008).

In 2007, an election year, the government appeared to make climate change a 'first order issue' (Stewart and Hendriks 2008). With opinion polls reflecting a growing concern over global warming and the business community calling for a national emissions trading scheme, the government ramped up its climate change activities. In April 2007, the Council of Australian Governments (COAG), consisting of the prime minister, state premiers, territory chief ministers and the president of the Australian Local Government Association, released the National Climate Change Adaptation Framework. While this is not a federal government policy document as such, it is noteworthy that the framework includes a section on tourism. Potential areas of action that were identified were assessment of the impacts of climate change on tourism and tourism values and the relative impact on different forms of tourism, and developing adaptation strategies for nature-based tourism (COAG 2007). The COAG Framework gave the Tourism Ministers' Council (TMC) responsibility for developing an Action Plan over two years. In August 2007, tourism ministers established the Tourism and Climate Change Taskforce to develop the action plan. This was the only significant step taken towards protecting tourism industries from the negative impacts of climate change, and it was taken by COAG, not the federal government.

By June 2007 the government announced that it was committed to an emissions trading scheme to be established no later than 2012. However, the scheme was criticized by environmental and business groups due to the lack of detail provided (Stewart and Hendriks 2008). In July 2007, the government released *Australia's Climate Change Policy: our economy, our environment, our future*. The policy focused on mitigation, specifically on an aspirational long-term emissions reductions goal, indicating reliance on the COAG Framework to deliver adaptation outcomes. The government did, however, release its policy for local government adaptation in 2007. The document. *Climate Change Adaptation Actions for Local Government* (DEWR and AGO 2007) outlined policy guiding local governments to undertake risk assessments and incorporate potential climate-change actions into strategic planning.

The culmination of Howard's climate-change position occurred in September 2007 when he hosted the annual APEC conference in Sydney. At this event he showcased a major statement on climate change. However by this time the Labor party was perceived to be 'owning' the climate change debate (Stewart and Hendriks 2008). Climate change was seen as an important reason for Howard's loss at the November 2007 federal election, where arguably the electorate held the government accountable for its inaction on climate change (Stewart and Hendriks 2008).

New Zealand government policies

In contrast to Australia, New Zealand governments appear, at first glance, to have been relatively proactive in responding to climate change. An examination of the period immediately prior to the time frame used in this study is instructive as to how this came to be. In 1988, the New Zealand Climate Change Program, convened by the secretary for the environment, created four working groups, and shortly afterwards the government launched a public consultation document on climate change (Hamilton 2000b). The minister for the environment then commissioned a range of research into climate-change issues through the Policy Research Contract Scheme (Basher 2000).

This early policy analysis as well as the subsequent impact of the efforts of the Labour prime minister and environment minister, Geoffrey Palmer, in the development of the Resource Management Act (Basher 2000), and the establishment of the National Science Strategy Committee on Climate Change (NSSCCC), represented steps in the right direction. During the period 1994 to 2002 the NSSCCC developed a comprehensive strategy for climate change research. The committee actively promoted linkages between science providers and end-users, which was a needed outcome for a variety of industries in order to plan for and adapt to climate change.

Simon Upton, who served as environment minister under prime ministers Jim Bolger and Jenny Shipley in the National Party government from 1990 to 1999, was a strong supporter of the IPCC and advocated scientific research into climate change and subsequent science-based policy formation (Basher 2000). He restructured the government science departments to a new market model which, according to Basher (2000, p. 127), largely achieved its objectives to 'make science providers more responsive to society's changing needs'. However there were other problems, including the need for government departments to purchase scientific assessments regarding climate change using their own budgetary resources, and that most of the country's funding for science was locked up in multi-year contracts. The multi-year contracts restricted the ability to quickly undertake a climate assessment without the allocation of extra funding.

Interestingly, the strength of Upton's commitment to addressing climate change issues appears to be somewhat at odds with Bolger, the first prime minister under whom he served. It appears that Bolger had 'little understanding of the nexus of environmental protection and sustainable land use and sustainable industry' (Basher 2000, p. 129). Basher's assessment is supported by referring to a major foreign policy speech made by Bolger on 13 March 1996. In this speech there was no reference at all to climate change. In contrast Shipley, the next prime minister, specifically noted continued support of the IPCC in her 1998 budget speech.

At the end of 1996, the government deferred the issue of a low-level carbon charge, which it had been discussing since 1990 and announced after the Rio Summit in 1992, until after the Kyoto Conference of the Parties (Hamilton 2000b). In 1997 the parliamentary commissioner for the environment produced a report, *Management of the Environmental Effects Associated with the Tourism Sector* (1997). Interestingly there was no mention of climate change in the report. The commissioner refers to air pollution caused by tourism; however there is no link made to climate change.

In 2001, the Ministry of Tourism released its *New Zealand Tourism Strategy 2010*. The strategy highlighted the importance of sustainability; however it did not identify explicit targets to be achieved. Its acknowledgement of climate change was limited to investigating options for carbon neutrality (Parliamentary Commissioner for the Environment 2002). In 2002 the New Zealand Transport Strategy, which included environmental sustainability as one of its objectives, was released. Also in 2002, a national energy-efficiency strategy was implemented, and the then Labour coalition government also announced that a carbon tax would be operational from 2007. In September 2005, an election led to the creation of a new coalition government. Several members in the newly formed coalition had opposed the tax prior to the election (Kelly 2010). There was also strong sectoral opposition to the tax from farmers and major energy users. Subsequently the government reversed its decision on the carbon tax in December 2005.

In 2003, the New Zealand Climate Change Office (NZCCO) was created within the Ministry for the Environment (MfE) to implement a comprehensive climate change policy programme centred on a carbon tax affecting major emitters and a number of supporting policies. In March 2004, amendments were made to the Resource Management Act which required councils to take into account the effects of climate change (MfE 2004). Additionally, in May 2004 the government, through the NZCCO, released a guidance manual for local government on climate change effects and impact assessment (NZCCO 2004). The 153-page document presented a fairly comprehensive overview of available climate information, challenges facing local government, and ways to attempt to overcome these challenges including best practice guidelines. Interestingly it also referred to impacts on or from tourism several times.

In the following year the government conducted a review, commissioned by the Cabinet, of New Zealand's core objectives and policy approach to climate change (MfE 2005). The focus of the review was on climate change mitigation policies: adaptation was specifically not included in the scope of the review. The review found, amongst other things, that the government should formulate an 'alternative climate change goal' and that due to its net emissions position, it ought to purchase some Kyoto-compliant units internationally (MfE 2005, p. 409). In 2006, the government stated that it had 'no specific policies aimed at reducing greenhouse gas emissions of air and maritime transport' (MfE 2006, p. 68).

In 2007 the national energy efficiency strategy was remodelled and in September 2007 the Government proposed the New Zealand Emissions Trading Scheme (NZETS), which was enacted in 2008, beyond the temporal scope of this study. Ultimately when it was implemented in 2008, it had limits on participation for the first five years and as such was severely limited in its impact in the first commitment period of the Kyoto Protocol. With the exception of the NZETS, there were no substantive policy measures implemented to reduce GGE for the First Commitment Period of the Kyoto Protocol (Kelly 2010).

New Zealand's response to reducing GGE came very late in the study period. Most measures were implemented after 2005, and those that did offer concrete reduction actions were limited in terms of potential impact (Kelly 2010). There was no single 'umbrella instrument' to bring together and integrate the range of sectoral initiatives. Interestingly in 2007, the *New Zealand Tourism Strategy 2015* (Ministry of Tourism, Tourism New Zealand, and Tourism Industry Association New Zealand 2007) called for such an instrument.

The *New Zealand Tourism Strategy 2015* made significant advances in the discussion of the relationship between tourism and climate change over the 2010 strategy, which had only briefly mentioned carbon neutrality (Becken and Hart 2004). The 2015 strategy identified the need for a whole-of-New Zealand environmental management plan that encompassed all the work being done across government around climate change including the NZETS. It stated that a 'clear national framework, articulating a national direction and national priorities, will provide certainty and context for the tourism sector' (*New Zealand Tourism Strategy 2015* p. 11). It also discussed other relationships, including the need for the tourism sector to work with local government to manage climate change impacts, climate change concerns affecting international and domestic tourists' decision making, and reducing and mitigating carbon emissions.

Mitigating carbon emissions from the transport sector would prove to be one of the great challenges for the tourism industry in New Zealand. The country's gross

GGE rose by 26 per cent between 1990 and 2006, and net emissions rose by 33 per cent, as the contribution of sinks (land use change and forestry) was limited (Kelly 2010). The largest contribution to GGE was energy use, and the principal user of energy was transport at 46 per cent, of which 63 per cent supported motor car use (Ministry of Economic Development 2007).

Discussion

The IPCC has stated that, under the lowest mitigation scenario category, GGE need to have peaked and be on a downward trend by 2015 in order to avoid dangerous climate change (IPCC 2007). Consequently, government policy that addresses the anthropogenic sources of GGE is pivotal to addressing the issues associated with climate change. However, among the leaders of the developed countries of the world, John Howard, along with George Bush, was seen as the slowest to respond to climate change (Clancy 2007).

In terms of denying climate change, Howard led the way, and the decision not to ratify Kyoto was his (Brett, 2007). As mentioned previously, some argue that the objective of the Howard Government was to sabotage the Kyoto Protocol (Naughten 2006). The Liberal-National coalition appeared to have been immersed in a culture of climate change denial but it was Howard's personal goals and convictions that shaped those of the government (Brett 2007). Interestingly, prior to the period of this study, the Liberal Party in opposition, under Andrew Peacock and then John Hewson, had a policy to reduce GGE by 20 per cent by the year 2000 (Pearse 2008), thus the Howard government's policies can arguably be seen as devolutionary.

In New Zealand, while the government's will to effectively respond to climate change has been debated (see Gillespie 2000, Hamilton 2000b), it appears slightly more positive than Australia's political response, particularly in terms of ratifying the Kyoto Protocol. However, upon closer analysis, New Zealand was able to make little progress in its efforts to mitigate climate change, despite its avowed idealism, 'clean green' branding and imagery (Kelly 2010). The efforts of Upton as minister for the environment in his advocacy for climate change research and his support of the IPCC in the 1990s, and the work of the NSSCCC, are notable exceptions.

The 'back flipping' on policy by both the Australian and New Zealand governments, particularly on the implementation of an ETS and a tax earlier in New Zealand, arguably hampered the efforts of tourism stakeholders to make effective decisions around adaptation and mitigation activities. As mentioned previously, in the Howard government's earliest statements on climate change there seemed to be an acceptance of the scientific consensus that humans were having a discernible impact on global climate (Pearse 2007). This acceptance, and then later non-acceptance, is potentially the most damaging aspect of the Howard government's policy platform. The abolition of existing programs left business and industry floundering in a policy vacuum. The NSSCCC consistently delivered sensible research strategies on both adaptation and mitigation for New Zealand (see for example NSSCCC 2002). However the government's reversal of its decision on a carbon tax was destabilizing.

The aforementioned contribution of transport to New Zealand's GGE has significant implications for the tourism industry, depending on the policy environment. Tourism industries, like most other industries, require clear long-term policy and/or regulation in order to inform their decision making and strategic planning. Certainty is crucial for encouraging continued investment in an industry. In order to mitigate the contribution made by tourism to climate change, Gössling, Hall, Peeters and Scott (2010) argue that consumption-based approaches have to be developed that are based on equity principles and climate justice. However, they identified within the wider global tourism industry what seemed to be a strong reluctance to agree to the idea of a future with less air transport (Gössling et al. 2010).

Interestingly two studies conducted in New Zealand during the temporal scope of this study found that climate change was not a priority of tourism stakeholders and entrepreneurs (see Becken and Hart 2004, Hall 2006). Furthermore, a theme emerging from both the studies was a concern or even direct opposition to 'carbon taxes' imposed on their businesses or customers. In addition, stakeholders from the Becken and Hart (2004) study acknowledged that some legislation would be required but indicated that this ought to be in the form of partnership between government and industry that allowed for industry initiatives such as voluntary certification. Tourism industry representatives in New Zealand admitted that it was 'hard for individual operators to invest in new technologies, products or itineraries, or to engage in voluntary self-regulation, because this results in a competitive disadvantage for the company' (Becken and Hart 2004, p. 202). At that time the Ministry of Tourism had no formal climate change policy. The *New Zealand Tourism and Climate Change Plan* (Ministry of Economic Development 2008) was not implemented until October 2008, well after the scope of this study. Becken and Hart (2004) postulate that this dearth of tourism-specific policy may have resulted in a lack of concern about climate change itself on the part of tourism stakeholders, demonstrating the need for a favourable policy framework. In Australia, the situation was even worse, as evidenced by the *Tourism White Paper*'s complete lack of attention to climate change or the need to address it.

In terms of adaptation to climate change, both countries' policies were lacking. In the beginning of the study period the policy focus of both countries was predominantly on mitigation, with adaptation having a secondary role in terms of effort and funding. This changed somewhat after the IPCC's *Third Assessment Report* (*TAR*) was released, and some concrete steps were taken to 'bolster the pre-conditions for adaptation' (Hennessy et al. 2007, p. 514). The creation of New Zealand's Climate Change Office, the 2004 amendments to the Resource Management Act and release of the manual for local government were positive steps in the right direction for that country. However, the IPCC has asserted that Australia and New Zealand have limited planned adaptation options and 'few integrated regional and sectoral assessments of impacts, adaptation and socio-economic risk' (Hennessy et al. 2007, p. 530). The IPCC also suggested that in both nations tighter planning and regulation was required for coastal development in order to remain sustainable. This is particularly important for tourism industries, as coastal regions support much of the tourism activity in Australia and New Zealand.

The lack of focus on adaptation measures by both governments is unhelpful for an industry that is expected to feel the impacts of climate change before any effects of mitigation are realized. While mitigation is intended to slow global warming, there is 'unlikely to be any noticeable climate effect from reducing GGEs until at least 2040. In contrast the benefits of adaptation can be immediate' (Hennessy et al. 2007, p. 529). Physical risks (namely weather-related risks) are rated by the firm KPMG (2008) as being high risk for tourism. For this reason, it can be concluded that adaptation policies that focus on these physical risks ought to be given the highest priority. Unfortunately, the results of this study show that investment in adaptation has been overshadowed by mitigation in both countries.

In New Zealand, this lack of solid adaptation policy is also at odds with the climate-change response strategies favoured by tourism businesses. In a study of forty-three New Zealand tourism entrepreneurs' attitudes from 2002 to 2005, Hall (2006) found that at both the personal and national level, responses focused on adaptation rather than mitigation. This dearth of tourism-relevant adaptation policy was not conducive in assisting tourism businesses to adapt.

Conclusion

The Australian government's inertia and reluctance to address/accept the issue under Howard has led to a slow policy response to climate change in Australia. As discussed above, many commentators argue that Howard's personal views on climate change arguably created a culture of climate change denial in the Liberal-National coalition government. The slow policy response has been to the detriment of Australian industries including tourism industries.

Similarly, despite the 'clean and green' branding of New Zealand's tourism industry, the government failed to develop effective climate change policies to support the brand. Many of the New Zealand government's measures to address climate change were recent, modest in their effect and lacked coordination. As described by Kelly (2010), despite their stated good intentions, there was a major deficit in policy implementation. New Zealand's climate change policy, argue Chapman and Boston (2007, p. 113), has consisted of 'governmental indecision and prevarication, and a series of significant policy reversals'.

There has been a conspicuous absence of strategic practical action on climate change in the policies of the governments examined in this study. A lack of emphasis on adaptation has been particularly evident. Despite the positive attempts of some government staff and elected representatives, the nature of politics and electoral cycles appears to have led to systemic short-termism, which is unhelpful to the development of good tourism and climate change policy. In conclusion, neither government's policies have been conducive to assisting tourism industries transform and adapt to climate change issues. This is despite being in a privileged position as developed nations, with a wealth of natural resources and substantial tourism industries to protect, so it bodes poorly for the advancement of sustainable tourism in a broader global context. Fortunately however, this chapter reflects upon a single discrete period of Australasian history, and policy iterations and improvements may, in the future, herald a new age for the sustainability of tourism in the era of climate change.

References

Australasian Legal Information Institute (ALII) (2008) *Commonwealth Numbered Regulations – Explanatory Statements: Energy Research and Development Corporation Regulations (Repeal).* 1998 No. 6. Available at: www.austlii.edu.au/au/legis/cth/num_reg_es/eradcr1998n6614.html (accessed 21 August 2008).

Australian Broadcasting Corporation (ABC) (2006) 'The Greenhouse Mafia', Program Transcript, *Four Corners*, Monday 13 February. Available at: www.abc.net.au/4corners/content/2006/s1568867.htm (accessed 14 October 2009).

Australian Business Roundtable on Climate Change (ABRCC) (2006) *The Business Case for Early Action*, April. Available at: www.businessroundtable.com.au/pdf/F078-RT-WS.pdf (accessed 26 February 2009).

Australian Government (AGO) (2006) *Climate Change Impacts and Risk Management: a guide for business and government.* Canberra: Department of Environment and Heritage.

Basher, R. E. (2000) 'The impacts of climate change on New Zealand.' In A. Gillespie and W. C. G. Burns (eds), *Climate Change in the South Pacific: Impacts and responses in Australia, New Zealand, and small island states* (pp. 121–42). Dordrecht, Netherlands: Kluwer Academic.

Becken, S. and Hart, P. (2004) 'Tourism stakeholders' perspectives on climate change policy in New Zealand.' In A. Matzarakis, C. R. de Freitas and D. Scott (eds), *Advances in Tourism Climatology* (Vol. 12, pp. 199–207), Berichte des Meteorologischen Institutes der Universität Freiburg.

Beresford, Q. (2008) 'Climate change: Australia and the Kyoto Protocol.' In A. Cullen and S. Murray (eds), *The Globalization of World Politics: Case studies from Australia, New Zealand and the Asia Pacific* (rev. edn, pp. 77–80). South Melbourne: Oxford University Press.

Brett, J. (2007) 'Exit right: the unravelling of John Howard.' *Quarterly Essay*, 28, 1–96.

Chandler, J. (2006) 'Scientists bitter over interference.' *The Age*, 13 February. Available at: www.theage.com.au/news/national/scientists-bitter-over-interfere nce/2006/02/12/1139679479548.html (accessed 30 June 2009).

Chapman, R. and Boston, J. (2007) 'The social implications of decarbonising the New Zealand economy,' *Social Policy Journal of New Zealand* (31), 104–36.

Christoff, P. and Eckersley, R. (2007) 'Kyoto and the Asia Pacific Partnership on Clean Development and Climate.' In T. Bonyhady and P. Christoff (eds), *Climate Law in Australia* (pp. 32–45). Leichhardt, NSW: Federation Press.

Clancy, M. (2007) *Howard's Seduction of Australia: Where to now?* 2nd edn. Watsons Bay, NSW: Fast Books.

Council of Australian Governments (COAG) (2007) *National Climate Change Adaptation Framework.* Available at: www.coag.gov.au/coag_meeting_outcomes/2007-04-13/docs/national_climate_change_adaption_framework.pdf (accessed 13 July 2009).

Davenport, D. S. (2006) *Global Environmental Negotiations and U.S. Interests.* New York: Palgrave Macmillan.

Department of the Environment and Water Resources (DEWR) and AGO (2007) *Climate Change Adaptation Actions for Local Government.* Canberra: Commonwealth of Australia.

Department of Industry Tourism and Resources (Australia) (DITR) (2004) *Tourism White Paper: A medium to long term strategy for tourism.* Canberra: DITR.

Fowler, R. (2007) 'Emissions reduction targets legislation.' In T. Bonyhady and P. Christoff (eds), *Climate Law in Australia* (pp. 103–23). Leichhardt, NSW: Federation Press.

Garnaut, R. (2008) *The Garnaut Climate Change Review: Final report.* Port Melbourne, Victoria: Cambridge University Press.

Gillespie, A. (2000) 'New Zealand and the climate change debate: 1995–1998.' In A. Gillespie and W. C. G. Burns (eds), *Climate Change in the South Pacific: Impacts and responses in Australia, New Zealand, and small island states* (pp. 165–88). Dordrecht, Netherlands: Kluwer Academic.

Gössling, S., Hall, C. M., Peeters, P. and Scott, D. (2010) 'The future of tourism: can tourism growth and climate policy be reconciled? A climate change mitigation perspective.' *Tourism Recreation Research,* 35(2), 119–30.

Hall, C. M. (2006) 'New Zealand tourism entrepreneur attitudes and behaviours with respect to climate change adaptation and mitigation,' *International Journal of Innovation and Sustainable Development,* 1(3), 229–37.

Hamilton, C. (2000a) 'Climate change policies in Australia.' In A. Gillespie and W. C. G. Burns (eds.), *Climate Change in the South Pacific: Impacts and responses in Australia, New Zealand, and small island states* (pp. 51–77). Dordrecht, Netherlands: Kluwer Academic.

Hamilton, K. (2000b) 'New Zealand climate policy between 1990 and 1996: a Greenpeace perspective.' In A. Gillespie and W. C. G. Burns (eds), *Climate Change in the South Pacific: Impacts and responses in Australia, New Zealand, and small island states* (pp. 143–64). Dordrecht, Netherlands: Kluwer Academic.

Hennessy, K., Fitzharris, B., Bates, B. C., Harvey, N., Howden, S. M., Hughes, L. et al. (2007) 'Australia and New Zealand.' In M. L. Parry, O. F. Canziani, J. P. Palutikof, P. J. v. d. Linden and C. E. Hanson (eds), *Climate Change 2007: Impacts, adaptation and vulnerability: Contribution of Working Group II to the Fourth Assessment Report of the Intergovernmental Panel on Climate Change* (pp. 507–40). Cambridge, UK: Cambridge University Press.

Intergovernmental Panel on Climate Change (IPCC) (2007) *Fourth Assessment Report: Climate change 2007 synthesis report.* Geneva: IPCC.

Jennings, G. (2001) *Tourism Research.* Milton, QLD: John Wiley and Sons Australia.

Kelly, G. D. (2010) 'Climate change policy: actions and barriers in New Zealand,' *International Journal of Climate Change Impacts and Responses,* 2(1), 277–90.

KPMG (2008) 'Climate changes your business: KPMGs review of the business risks and economic impacts at sector level.' Available at: www.kpmg.com/NL/en/Issues-And-Insights/ArticlesPublications/Documents/PDF/Sustainability/Climate_Changes_Your_Business.pdf (accessed 14 January 2011).

Minchin, L. (2006) 'Howard blows hot and cold on emissions.' Available at: http://www.environmentbusiness.com.au/n-ar-howard.asp (accessed 26 February 2009).

Ministry of Economic Development (New Zealand) (2007). *New Zealand Energy Greenhouse Gas Emissions 1990–2006.* Wellington: Ministry of Economic Development.

Ministry of Economic Development (New Zealand) (2008) *New Zealand Tourism and Climate Change Plan.* Available at: www.tourism.govt.nz/Our-Work/Our-Work-Summary-page/Climate-Change/ (accessed 14 January 2011).

Ministry for the Environment (MfE) (New Zealand) (2004) *A Changing Climate*. Available at: www.mfe.govt.nz/publications/climate/a-changing-climate-nov04/a-changing-climate.html (accessed 14 January 2011).

MfE (New Zealand) (2005) *Review of Climate Change Policies*. Wellington: New Zealand Government.

MfE (New Zealand) (2006) *New Zealand's Fourth National Communication under the United Nations Framework Convention on Climate Change*. Wellington: Ministry for the Environment.

Ministry of Tourism, Tourism New Zealand, and Tourism Industry Association New Zealand (2007) *New Zealand Tourism Strategy 2015*. Wellington, New Zealand: Ministry of Tourism.

Muller, F. (2008) 'Australian Science Media Centre: Prime Ministerial Task Group on Emissions Trading Report – Carbon trading experts respond.' Available at:www.aussmc.org/Carbon_trading_emissions_report_RR.php (accessed 4 August 2008).

National Science Strategy Committee on Climate Change (NSSCCC) (2002) *Climate Change Research Strategy 2002*. Wellington: MfE.

Natural Resource Management Ministerial Council (NRMMC) (2004) *National Biodiversity and Climate Change Action Plan 2004–2007*. Canberra: Department of the Environment and Heritage.

Naughten, B. (2006) 'Climate change: Howard holds a monkey wrench.' Available at: http://cpd.org.au/article/climate-change%3A-howard-holds-monkey-wrench (accessed 8 March 2010).

New Zealand Climate Change Office (NZCCO) (2004) *Climate Change Effects and Impact Assessment: A guidance manual for local government in New Zealand*. Wellington: MfE.

O'Donnel, C. (2008) *Submission to the Garnaut Review*. Available at: www.garnautreview.org.au/CA25734E0016A131/WebObj/CarolODonnelCompiledsubmission/$File/Carol%20O%20Donnel%20Compiled%20submission.pdf (accessed 14 January 2011).

Parliamentary Commissioner for the Environment (2002) *Background Paper: Creating Our Future. Sustainable development for New Zealand, government strategies*. Available at: www.pce.parliament.nz/assets/Uploads/Reports/pdf/creating_bkgrd3.pdf (accessed 1 March 2011).

Parliamentary Commissioner for the Environment (1997) *Management of the Environmental Effects Associated with the Tourism Sector*. Available at: http://pce.parliament.nz/assets/Uploads/Reports/pdf/Pre97-reports/Management-of-the-Environmental-Effects-Associated-with-the-Tourism-Sector-Review-of-Literature-on-Environmental-Effects-Nov-1977.pdf (accessed 14 January 2011).

Pearse, G. (2007) *High and Dry: John Howard, climate change and the selling of Australia's future*. Camberwell, Vic.: Penguin.

Pearse, G. (2008) *High and Dry* presentation slides and notes (October 17–27), Guy Pearse/Greenpeace speaking tour. Available at: www.highanddry.com.au (accessed 20 November 2008).

Solomon, S., Qin, D., Manning, M., Chen, Z., Marquis, M., Averyt, K. B. et al. (eds) (2007) *Climate Change 2007: The physical science basis. Contribution of Working Group I to the Fourth Assessment Report of the Intergovernmental Panel on Climate Change*. Cambridge: Cambridge University Press.

Statistics New Zealand (2009) *Tourism Satellite Account: 2009*. Wellington: Statistics New Zealand.

Stern, N. (2006) *Stern Review on the Economics of Climate Change*. Available at: www.hm-treasury.gov.uk/independent_reviews/independent_reviews_index.cfm (accessed 20 March 2007).

Stewart, J. and Hendriks, C. (2008) 'Discovering the environment.' In C. Aulich and R. Wettenhaul (eds), *Howard's Fourth Government* (pp. 206–26). Sydney: University of New South Wales Press.

Taplin, R. and Yu, X. (2000) 'Climate change policy formation in Australia: 1995–1998.' In A. Gillespie and W. C. G. Burns (eds), *Climate Change in the South Pacific: Impacts and responses in Australia, New Zealand, and small island states* (pp. 95–112). Dordrecht, Netherlands: Kluwer Academic.

Tiffen, R. and Gittins, R. (2004) *How Australia Compares.* Cambridge: Cambridge University Press.

Tourism Research Australia (2009) *Tourism's Contribution to the Australian Economy 1997–98 to 2007–08.* Canberra: Tourism Research Australia.

UNFCCC (1992) *United Nations Framework Convention on Climate Change* Available at: http://unfccc.int/resource/docs/convkp/conveng.pdf (accessed 23 March 2008).

Wilkins, R. (2008) *Strategic Review of Australian Government Climate Change Programs.* Canberra: Commonwealth of Australia.

Yu, X. and Taplin, R. (2000) 'The Australian position at the Kyoto conference.' In A. Gillespie and W. C. G. Burns (eds), *Climate Change in the South Pacific: Impacts and responses in Australia, New Zealand, and small island states* (pp. 113–20). Dordrecht, Netherlands: Kluwer Academic.

8

KEY PLAYERS IN THE ENVIRONMENTAL PERFORMANCE OF TOURISM ENTERPRISES

David Leslie

The international political arena in recent years evidences a substantial shift in terms of the environmental agenda, as set out in the early 1990s in Agenda 21 (Dodds 2002), away from sustainability and increasingly on climate change (Leslie 2009a). This emphasis on climate change and thus on greenhouse gas emissions has generated substantial debate and led to the current popularity of terms such as 'carbon footprint', 'carbon offsetting' and 'carbon tax' and the politically driven campaign for renewable energy. At the same time global demand for energy continues to increase, particularly of fossil fuels and hence the emergence of trading schemes and carbon taxes. The inescapable outcome of this is increased (and increasing) energy costs, a fact which all enterprises have to address. Such increased costs are also influencing the prices of consumer goods and services, especially those involving a travel element, which holds substantial implications for the tourism sector (see Hall and Gossling 2009, Gossling and Hall 2006). It is not just the impact of energy costs that is of concern, but what steps are being taken in the wider context of sustainability, which is encompassed in the concept of the environmental performance of enterprise; This includes addressing those issues specific to climate change. This broader area of sustainability is what lies at the heart of this chapter.

In many countries across the globe there are initiatives designed to promote the introduction of environmental management systems on the part of tourism enterprises as one way to address their environmental performance (EP) and thus 'sustainability'. The actual success of these schemes measured in terms of the number of accredited enterprises proportional to the total number of such enterprises in any one area or region is limited. All the more so when examined in further detail, which reveals that a substantial number of accredited enterprises are parts of a national or international company. However, while the latter represent a substantial proportion of provision and revenues they are in the minority, actually accounting for a comparatively small number of the total for tourism enterprises in any area. The question thus arises why this dichotomy has arisen between the large operations and the myriad small/micro enterprises which dominate supply. From a company perspective, the larger organizations arguably recognize the substantive savings in costs they can achieve through environmental management (EM) practices, and the potential value in the marketplace of promoting a 'green image' (Chan 2009, Preigo, Najera and Font. 2011, Leslie 2012a). Thus, all operations within the same company adopt, as appropriate, the same environmental measures (though there are exceptions: see Anon 2009a). In contrast the majority of small, individual, often owner-managed enterprises do not adopt such measures. Yet in percentage terms at least, it is arguable that the cost savings on reducing resource consumption would not be dissimilar. Why is this?

This chapter aims to address this question, and draws extensively on a long-term research into the EP and the adoption of environmental management practices of predominantly small, independent tourism enterprises.

Background

Since the late 1980s we have witnessed a deepening agenda, driven by recognition of the impact of the activities of humankind and related practices (such as industry in general, and tourism) on the environment. This has led to increased pressure on industry and business more generally to address and reduce consumption of resources (energy, water) and pollution (emissions) (Leslie 2009a). Tourism enterprises are no less susceptible than any other business to these forces. Furthermore, 'the industry and tourists individually are being expected and required to shoulder more responsibility for the effects of travel and behaviour on host communities, both physical and human' (Butler 1993: 5). In the 1990s as environmental concerns increased, pressure mounted 'on industry to address the actual and potential contribution of their operations in contributing to environmental degradation and develop systems to assess the environmental performance of individual operations – enterprises' (Welford and Starkey 1996: xi). The issues of climate change, energy consumption and waste 'will require significant behavioural change by businesses and the general public as well as by government. There is still widespread ignorance about the nature of some of these problems and the need for more sustainable solutions' (Department of Environment Transport and the Regions – DETR 2000: 10 cited in Leslie 2007a). Additional vectors are that there is no doubt that energy prices will continue to increase. 'Businesses that delay action on reducing energy consumption and greenhouse gas emissions will be forced to act in the medium term and will be incurring higher bills' (Masero 2009: 19). Government and EU intervention is also exacerbating energy prices: 'government policies are determining national energy strategy, transportation strategy, fuel prices, and other initiatives that are not directed at your products and services, but that have a direct impact on your cost of operation' (Infor 2008: 2).

More directly significant to tourism enterprises and the United Kingdom (given the context of the research) is UK government policy on tourism, which since

1989 and the launch of the Tourism Task Force has been promoting the greening of the tourism throughout the United Kingdom (Leslie 2002a). Most recently, it has been arguing for more sustainable and environmentally friendly ways of working; as the tourism minister said, 'we must take sustainability seriously and not see it just as an add-on luxury.' This approach has been reinforced in Scotland. The Scottish government has been applauded for its stated position on climate change through establishing far-reaching targets for reductions in greenhouse gas emissions by 2050, targets which are in excess of any other country to date. This positioning of Scotland as the leader in this field affirms the Scottish government's commitment to 'greening' Scotland, manifest in the government's stated economic policy (SG 2007), a key strategic objective of which is for a greener Scotland and thus to 'improve Scotland's natural and built environment and the sustainable use and enjoyment of it' (SG 2007: 3) and in the process support Scotland's biodiversity, which is considered to be 'one of our country's most important assets and need to be well looked after, if we are to achieve our objective in delivering sustainable development' (Scottish Enterprise 2003). The importance of the environment/tourism interrelationship is recognized in VisitScotland's Corporate Plan 'We can contribute by promoting Scotland as a green tourism destination, through sustainable tourism to protect Scotland's landscape' and 'To be Europe's most sustainable tourism destination' (VisitScotland 2007a: 2.1)

It is in this context that tourism enterprises are being encouraged to 'go green' – to address their EP and adopt environmental management practices and thus an environmental management system (EMS). The most frequently cited process of assessing the EP of an enterprise is environmental auditing; defined as 'a management tool comprising a systematic, documented, periodic and objective evaluation of the performance of the organization, management system and processes designed to protect the environment' (Goodall 1994: 30); BS 7750, Eco-Management and Audit Scheme (EMAS) and ISO 14001 are the main examples of such tools. However, these methods are not necessarily appropriate to small enterprises, particularly micro-businesses, because of their scope and potential costs (Chan 2011). Recognition of this has led to the launch of a variety of schemes (Leslie 2005a), of which the most popular in the United Kingdom is the Green Tourism Business Scheme (GTBS), launched in the late 1990s in Scotland and now promoted throughout the United Kingdom and potentially in other European countries (Leslie 2012b). In effect, the GTBS is 'A simple environmental auditing process [which] can achieve worthwhile results with clear economic gains' (PTC (Jersey) 1998).

Thus given the policies and practices being promoted in the 1990s, it was opportune at the end of the decade to seek to investigate to what extent tourism enterprises were 'going green'. Encompassed within the project's aims was to identify and evaluate the level of awareness, attitudes and perceptions of green issues, and associated practices, of owners/managers of tourism enterprises.

The first, and most substantive stage, of this research was undertaken in the Lake District National Park and involved over 350 tourism enterprises (Leslie

2001), as well as attractions (Leslie 2005b) and self-catering operations (Leslie 2007b). The methodology derived included a comprehensive survey of tourism enterprises designed to establish the approach and actual practices of owners/ managers of tourism businesses based on an extensive set of sustainability indicators specifically derived for the study. Further, the survey sought to establish key influential factors that either help or hinder the adoption of such practices. Following on from the survey fifty serviced accommodation operations agreed to participate in subsequent more detailed investigations (in effect environmental audits involving extensive personal interviews).

The second stage was based on a survey of predominantly rural tourism enterprises in Scotland (214 enterprises), in effect replicating the methodology of the Lakes study (with minor adjustments of the survey vehicle to allow for geographic variances) but with no follow-up interviews. The third stage, undertaken over the last two years, involved a more diverse range of enterprises. Again a preliminary survey was undertaken, then the owners/managers were invited to participate in the more in-depth audit and personal interview stage (seventy-eight enterprises). Thus three data sets have been established, which are noted as 2001, 2005 and 2011. The first two are both based on rural enterprises, while the final set comprises both rural and urban enterprises and also evidences a more diverse range of businesses as regards ownership and whether the operation is part of a regional company. The 2011 findings are arguably more representative of the hospitality sector as a whole. However, they are all serviced accommodation operations and thus similar to the 2001 set. A second key difference is that the participation of the 2001 group was entirely based on an invitation included in the primary survey. In contrast, the 2011 group was also encouraged by asking for their involvement to aid the studies of final-year students on the tourism management degree at Glasgow Caledonian University. As such, it is arguable that this group are possibly less interested in the 'greening' aspect of the research and potentially less likely to evidence a bias to such matters.

The focus on the outcomes of this longitudinal study in this context is to explore the data that particularly relates to the perceptions and attitudes of the owners/ managers as regards different facets of sustainability. A second focus is to identify what they consider to be the main influential factors in the adoption of EM practices.

Environmental management

Overall the study finds that comparatively few enterprises have developed an environmental policy or introduced an EMS (see below), which is not surprising when other studies suggest that currently only some 3,000 leisure and tourism companies in the United Kingdom participate in an eco-label (i.e. EMS) scheme (Freezar and Font 2010). See Table 8.1.

This does not mean that other companies have not adopted various environmental management practices, but rather that this has not been formalized into a written

TABLE 8.1 Proportion of respondents with a written environmental policy

Data set	2001	2006	2011
Written policy:	12%	25%	19%

policy or developed through seeking accreditation for some form of EMS. To an extent this does reflect Preigo et al.'s (2011) study, which found a lack of integration of EM into mainstream strategic management and objectives. Indeed as both Preigo et al. and Baird (2010) found, such accreditation is not automatically seen as being of competitive advantage. However, as indicators of EM activities, the reuse of paper and recycling is a common practice. Indeed, recycling of paper, glass and cans has increased over the period; a finding that mirrors other studies (IH 2007, Anon 2009b). This is largely due to increased recycling facilities, including requirements on companies collecting waste to segregate it, which is a contribution to reducing the carbon footprint of the enterprise and reducing demand for landfill and associated pollution (see Radwan, Jones and Minoli 2010). Further, more enterprises are willing to be involved but are not because of a lack of space and/or waste collection facilities, a finding evident in other studies (Radwan et al. 2010).

The enterprises with a written policy in 2011, with one exception, are involved in the GTBS. According to Ebeling (2008), in 2000 there were 231 accredited businesses and 842 by 2007, a figure which is supported by the participation of the National Trust in Scotland and also Historic Scotland properties. Thus this figure is not solely representative of the private-sector tourism enterprises in Scotland. Numbers, however, dipped in 2009 to 746, which is probably due to a combination of costs and the finding that the scheme was not actually influencing demand (Baird 2010). Despite the widespread and continuing promotion of this scheme there is little doubt that government and tourist board policy and trade associations are largely ineffective in this area (Leslie 2002a). The noted decrease has also been found in other studies: for example a recent survey found that the number of enterprises with a formalized EMS has decreased, and the main reason given was that such systems are of no use to the business (Anon 2009a). This is contrary to the oft-cited point that these systems are beneficial in terms of marketing and promotion (Freezar and Font 2010). This appears to be true for the major national and international companies, which do consider the adoption of EMS and social responsibility as 'good for business' (see Tari et al. 2010); for example Whitbread plc (with brands including Costa Coffee and Premier Inns) has launched 'Good Together' and is the first hospitality company to gain the Carbon Trust Award, the first international award for reducing carbon footprint. However, this is more reflective of the finding that EMS and corporate social responsibility (CSR) are to be found in the major players in the marketplace rather than amongst the myriad small and micro-businesses that dominate tourism supply (Leslie 2001, 2009a).

Overall, this finding raises an interesting question: how to interpret two other outcomes of the 2011 results. First, 53 per cent of the managers said that the principle and practices involved in EMS and CSR, as identified in the survey and interviews, should be more widely adopted. Second, 62 per cent indicated that they support the introduction of an accredited environmental award scheme. This data suggests that there should be more enterprises with an EP and EMS than the relatively small numbers found. Few researchers would argue that there are differences between what people say, agree to support and what they actually do themselves. Second, awareness and attitudes are also influential factors on choice and in decision making. Thus we now turn attention to the managers and their attitudes.

The managers, their perceptions and attitudes

The study sought to explore a range of personal indicators on the basis that attention to the environmental performance of the business could be influenced by the managers' length of time spent in the sector, by interests (as represented for instance by involvement in environmental organizations) or professional affiliations (such as the Institute of Hospitality or the Tourism Society). The profile of the managers of the enterprises of 2011 compared with 2001 is generally similar in regards to the length of time they have been involved in the tourism sector and qualifications. Membership of 'green' organizations and professional bodies, as shown in Table 8.2, exhibits a number of significant differences. First, 2011 shows a comparatively low figure for membership of the area's Tourist Board; perhaps this reflects a locational bias to urban areas but it might also be influenced by the costs involved in membership. Second, the higher participation in local community groups in 2011 is attributable to such schemes as hotel and neighbourhood watch. Overall and significant in terms of knowledge and awareness of sectoral initiatives relating to sustainability is the notably low membership of the sector-specific professional organizations, the Institute of Hospitality and the Tourism Society. However, it has been argued that the trade associations are more intent on promoting the agenda of the major players in the market (who tend to dominate the agenda) and seek to influence government and national tourist board policy in the direction of demand and support rather than focus on resources and management. Therefore, membership might not reflect an interest in EP or social responsibility (Tyler and Dinan 2001).

Further exploration of the data revealed that there is no substantive correlation between membership of professional or green organizations and becoming involved in a scheme such as GTBS. However, there are correlations between such memberships which affirms, to an extent, that values do have an influence. But it is not a definite correlation and the reverse is not found to be true: that is, adoption of an EMS or similar action is not a definite indicator of environmental interests and behaviour. In effect what people do personally does not necessarily translate into other areas (Barr et al. 2010).

Even so, the introduction of EM practices and development of these into a formalized EMS of one form or another will be influenced by the perceptions and

TABLE 8.2 Membership of a range of organizations

Organization	2001 (%)	2006 (%)	2011 (%)
Cumbria Tourist Board/ VisitScotland	65	84	44
National Trust	32	15	4
Chamber of Commerce	31	15	26
Royal Society for the Protection of Birds	12	10	6
Institute of Hospitality	11	8	4
Local community group	8	15	18
A tourism forum	6	14	9
Tourism Society	5	3	6
World Wide Fund for Nature	7	2	4
Greenpeace	4	1	0
Friends of the Earth	2	1	1

attitudes of the manager with regard to the environment and related matters. This area was explored through a range of statements (see Table 8.3). The first point of note is that there is little change across the decade in the mean responses to the statements presented; the exception being an increase in agreement that claiming to be 'green' is more of a marketing ploy. Partly contrary to this is the finding for 2011 that 20 per cent of the enterprises seek to attract custom through 'green' messages. Evidently, the majority of managers consider the sector has an impact, though notably less so than in the manufacturing sector. Second, there appears a general consensus that adopting EM practices is not counter to profitability.

To further this line of inquiry, the interviews involved further and more direct exploration of the managers' attitudes (see Table 8.4). Certainly attitude is a key factor, but attitude to management practices (such as not changing approach in the way the resources of the business are managed) may well outweigh attitudes to other aspects. Support for 'greening' is not necessarily a behavioural trait (Frey and George 2010). This is reflected in the responses presented in Table 8.4, and further affirmed by the finding of a recent study that 48 per cent of staff noted that they had no interest in environment matters, policy and similar issues at work (wired gov, 2009).

Apparently the environment is held in higher regard by managers in the Lake District than their counterparts in Scotland. However, this may be accounted for by the higher proportion of urban enterprises in 2011 and, quite possibly, by the prevailing economic climate in the United Kingdom over the last few years. There is more comparability in the finding that while interviewees indicate interest, the number of them demonstrating actual commitment is substantially lower.

TABLE 8.3 Perceptions of the sector's impact and related aspects

Statement	Mean		
	2001	2006	2011
The hospitality sector has an impact on the environment	4.02	3.90	3.96
The hospitality sector's impact on the environment is significantly less than the manufacturing sector	3.54	3.50	3.81
Operators who claim to be 'green' are using it as a marketing ploy	3.06	3.40	3.67
Most owners/managers do not have time to worry about the environment	2.92	3.20	3.11
Customers are not interested in whether an operation is environmentally friendly	2.56	2.51	2.37
It is not possible to be profitable and be environmentally friendly	2.06	3.00	2.19

Mean: based on scale of 1 = 'Strongly agree' to 5 = 'Strongly disagree'

TABLE 8.4 Selection of indicative attitudes of owners/managers

Factor	Yes (%)	
	2001	2011
Is the owner/manager interested in the impact on the environment of the business?	98	77
Is the owner/manager interested in the impact on the environment of tourism in the local area?	92	70
Is the owner/manager committed to reducing negative impacts?	58	32
Is the enterprise involved in any local community schemes?	40	26
Is the business involved in local projects at all?	36	24
Does the enterprise provide/facilitate any opportunity to donate to conservation schemes?	18	4

If we then bring into focus the number of managers indicating participation in community schemes, the overall commitment bears witness to the following critique: 'Conventional wisdom has it that small local business will have the greatest regard for the community environment but there is scant evidence to justify that. The opposite seems probable' (EIU 1993: 96).

As indicated in Table 8.4, some managers/enterprises do participate in a variety of schemes. To an extent this will be a function of awareness, and thus the surveys sought to establish the awareness of a range of environmental 'labels' (see Table

8.5) and subsequently, involvement in sustainability initiatives (see Table 8.5). The generally low membership of both professional and green organizations may explain a lack of awareness of policy and related initiatives promoting EM practices as shown, and thus the findings presented in Table 8.5 are not unexpected.

Also of note is the level of similarity across the three data sets, with the main exception being awareness of ISO14001. This may be due to increased reference in the media, particularly in the context of business. However, neither interest nor awareness means participation – as the low participation figures presented in Table 8.6 demonstrate.

TABLE 8.5 Awareness of selected green initiatives

Initiative	Aware (%)		
	2001	*2006*	*2011*
BS 7750	18	23	16
Ecolabelling	18	15	16
ISO14001	10	17	16
Green Audit Kit	8	4	11
Green Globe	8	6	4
British Airways Environment Awards	8	7	4
Green Business Scheme	n/a	27	14
International Hotels Environmental Initiative	3	4	6

TABLE 8.6 Involvement in selected green initiatives

Initiative	YES (%)		
	2001	*2006*	*2011*
Made in Cumbria/ Made in Scotland	7	4	1
Business Environment Network	2	2	6
Green Business Scheme	n/a	11	16
A Tourism Forum	n/a	14	10
Participate in a Conservation Scheme	★	16	6
International Hotels Environmental Initiative	1	2	1

★ Tourism and Conservation Partnership: Survey 12% Audited enterprises: 18%

Social responsibility – the wider context

Within the spectrum of research (limited!) into small tourism enterprises and EM, this is an area that gains no attention. As such, our focus here is all the more germane.

As noted above, some managers do participate in what we may term social responsibility-related activities. Such activity holds social benefits to the enterprises involved. As Nicolau (2008) argued, CSR activity in the community promotes trust and value with consequent ongoing positive benefits to the enterprise in both social terms and financial performance. Second, and arguably the more substantial issue in terms of tourism and sustainability, is the involvement of the enterprise in directly supporting the local economy and community and thus developing the interrelationships that exist between the business, the economy and the community. This is illustrated here by reference to the purchase of local produce and products, which has added value in that buying local, seasonal produce can reduce the environmental costs involved in food purchasing and processing and so contribute to reducing an enterprise's carbon footprint (see Gossling et al. 2011). This view is also affirmed by the launch (in 2010) of the Sustainable Restaurant Association.

Overall, it is identified that many enterprises make little effort to seek to purchase local products and produce. This finding was explored in the interviews through consideration of those factors identified in the first part of the study as most commonly discouraging such activity. As Table 8.7 shows, the data sets evidence little difference with the exception of cost and are similar to other studies (for example, Frey and George 2010).

However, it is not only food produce/products that is applicable here but also locally produced products such as arts and crafts. As noted below, a substantial number of enterprises in the 2001 data display local arts and crafts for sale (often on

TABLE 8.7 Factors discouraging local produce purchasing

Factor	Mean	
	2001	*2011*
Cost (too expensive)	3.26	**4.00**
Portion control e.g. not preportioned	2.35	2.67
Quality control	**4.22**	**4.50**
Availability	3.91	4.11
Time to go and purchase	3.20	3.29
Hygiene/environmental health/regulations	**4.07**	**4.16**
Lack of awareness of what is available	2.89	2.80

Mean based on scale of 1 = not significant to 5 = very significant

TABLE 8.8 Sale of local products

Date set	2001	2011
Arts displayed for sale	30%	15%
Local products in service	18%	10%

a commission basis) and, to a lesser extent, purchase locally produced products for use within the operations (for example, condiments). This is far less found to be practised in the 2011 study. Partly accounting for this might be the comparatively fewer opportunities in available the enterprise's locality to find such products.

As the findings here attest, more effort needs to be made to contribute to the local community – to encourage local enterprise, 'promoting the development of other sectors for example, greater production and utilization of local produce and products, thereby contributing to a stronger economy with more diverse opportunities for employment' (Leslie 2002b: 9) and to a more sustainable society. Instead, the bias is towards direct, measurable gain in the sense of cost savings.

What will influence the introduction of an EMS?

The managers were presented with a range of factors to seek their opinion on how influential they considered such factors are in terms of introducing environmentally friendly practices. As the data presented in Table 8.9 shows, there is a potential trend over the decade suggesting a shift towards cost savings and the influence of competitors, industry standards and legislation. The findings suggest increased competition and likely government action, and as such, further emphasize that the major influence will come from extrinsic factors. The little more than 'average' rating for legislation is arguably understated given that many hoteliers have been found to be unaware of current environmental legislation such as waste disposal regulations (Radwan et al. 2010). The higher mean for cost savings reflects both the current economic climate in the United Kingdom and the rising cost of utilities. But action is not evidently strong given the absence in the majority of cases of an energy policy or the monitoring of water consumption and waste.

The comparatively low level of influence given to customer demand evidences little change over the years, despite the findings of other surveys such as Mintel (see Leslie 2012b). Overall these outcomes correlate with the findings from similar questions in the interviews carried out for 2001 and 2011. Further, they mirror the trend in government, and notably EU action, over the last decade. In other words more widescale adoption of EM practices is likely to arise only when either enterprises are forced through legislation to do so and/or there are tax breaks which encourage such action. In effect, they appear to expect that it is up to others to take (enforce) action rather than take responsibility themselves (see SCRT 2006). The downside of that is the probability of minimal compliance (see Preigo et al. 2011).

TABLE 8.9 Factors potentially influential to the introduction of environmentally friendly practices

Factor	Mean		
	2001	*2006*	*2011*
Customer care	3.96	4.34	4.06
Cost savings	3.74	4.23	4.55
Health and safety	3.48	4.29	3.83
Care for the environment	3.76	4.23	3.64
Customer demand	3.74	3.96	3.57
Personal beliefs	3.64	3.81	3.54
Quality management	3.3	3.85	3.97
Public relations	2.96	3.83	3.74
Potential legislation	2.62	3.19	3.81
Industry standards	2.44	3.13	3.88
Competitors' actions	2.14	2.71	3.89

Mean based on 1 = least likely to influence to 5 = most likely to influence

The final area explored in the interviews was respondents' views on what progress they considered is being made towards sustainability on the part of tourism enterprises (see Table 8.10).

Generally there is little to distinguish between the findings of 2001 and 2011, so it could be argued that no real progress has been made. The responses affirm the view that the easy steps may be taken but there is evident resistance to participation in EMS certification schemes (as also found by Lawton and Weaver 2010 and Preigo et al. 2011). They also support the general rhetoric that cost is a barrier (IH 2007). Furthermore, they are indicative of a lack of faith in the purported market demand for 'green hotels' (or those accredited as eco-labelled) (see Infor 2008, Leslie 2012a). This is also supported by a recent study, which found that being green is more about PR (Greenbiz 2009) and less reflective of demand (Preigo et al. 2011).

Thus, having explored the managers' attitudes and perceptions, it is timely that we turn the attention to what do they consider to be important.

What *is* important to the managers?

As the figures in Table 8.11 attest, not surprisingly, managing customers and profitability and achieving budgetary targets are the primary concerns. Indeed,

TABLE 8.10 Progress of enterprises towards sustainability

Question	Mean	
	2001	*2011*
Commitment to greening the business is being used to gain competitive advantage	2.34	2.59
Apart from a few notable examples, little progress has been made over the last five years	3.26	3.18
Compared with five years ago, owners/managers have a better understanding of how to maintain financial performance while improving environmental and social performance	3.02	2.95
Anyone can introduce some environmentally friendly practices and claim to be green.	3.80	3.56
The 'first steps' practices, such as reducing heating costs and waste, all save on costs.	4.34	4.26
Once the first steps have been taken, there are few – if any – cost savings	2.80	2.47
By and large, the deciding factor for potential customers is the price of the accommodation	3.90	4.10
Operators should support local producers, even if the products cost a little more	3.78	3.14
Environmental problems are threatening the future of the local tourism industry	2.84	2.52
Guests are not really concerned about the environment	2.82	3.14

Mean based on: 1 = Strongly agree to 5 = strongly disagree

aspects of sustainability are comparatively of least concern. In one sense this is correct in that staying in business and thus being a net contributor to the economy and local community (as an employer) is a primary responsibility of any business. The data also evidences little variance in such findings over the last decade with the exception of staff retention. The latter's increased significance may well be due to the economic climate, with managers recognizing that on the one hand it is more cost-effective to retain quality staff but on the other being able to retain staff in a recession may also be an influence on their decision. Conversely, it is harder to obtain staff in the Lake District, thus one might have expected the 2001 figure to be higher.

As regards staff retention, most studies into EMS and more so CSR find that involving staff in the development of these activities invariably has positive outcomes in terms of staff morale and retention (Chan and Hawkins 2010, Bohdanowicz and Zientara 2008). This is evidently not recognized or realized by

TABLE 8.11 What is of importance to the owners?

Factor	Mean	
	2001	2011
Addressing customer complaints.	4.80	4.37
Maintenance/improvement of profitability.	4.46	4.56
Achievement of budget.	4.26	4.47
Staff retention.	3.04	4.14
Achieving environmental targets.	2.42	2.36
Environmental reporting.	2.22	2.38

Based on Likert scale: 1 = most important to 5 = least important

the majority of enterprises! That is not surprisingly perhaps when one considers that 23 per cent of the managers do not think staff are concerned over such matters, and a further 37 per cent 'don't know'. Perhaps they are not, but it is interesting to note that a survey by wiredgov (2009) found that only 5 per cent of the workforce of organizations noted that they were more environment conscious at work than at home, and overall there was a remarkable degree of 'eco-apathy'.

A Greenbiz (2009) survey of business found that those with a real commitment to sustainability performed better than those companies without such a commitment – suggesting that green products and services have a higher resilience to downturns in the market – but also noted that initiatives which may have been introduced more for public relations reasons are more likely to be dropped to save on expense.

However, in terms of promotion, it is notable that advocates of the value of an accredited EMS argue that the 'message' should be more about the positive dimensions such as healthy food, local produce, Fairtrade and CSR activity rather than the EMS accreditation (Han, Hsue and Sheu 2010).

Conclusion

The findings indicate some degree of progress in the adoption of EMS and, albeit to a lesser extent, address the wider aspects of the EP of the enterprise, for example, activities within the scope of social responsibility. These findings are supported by similar studies based on research in the United Kingdom, across Europe (Leslie 2012a) and more globally (Leslie 2009). These outcomes also reflect businesses more generally (see Ethical Corporation 2010). Furthermore, the major players in the hotel sector are considered to be behind many other sectors in terms of progress, albeit some newer 'brands' are placing sustainability more centrally (Anon 2009b). Yet this is despite recent studies that indicate that there are wider benefits to the adoption of EMS and CSR than just the potential cost savings.

Responses suggest that, although many enterprises consider that they are committed to environmental management, this commitment is overshadowed by greater attention to attaining maximum financial returns through the adoption of good housekeeping policies. Findings from the attitudinal questions support this, and evidence a degree of cynicism and a large amount of ambivalence about 'green' ideas, environmental impacts and related initiatives. Although there are signs of progress there is a clear need for more direct encouragement and promotion. Even so, given the extensive promotion of attention and related policies and initiatives to environmental management practices, linkages with the local economy and community, why are not more enterprises taking the appropriate responsive action? Clearly, the values and attitudes of owners/managers are influential. As the findings expose, there appears to be no clear indicator, such as membership of a green organization or professional association, or qualification, that is identifiable as a definitive predictor. Furthermore, just because a person may be interested in green issues does not mean that this translates into environmental business practices. From this study and similar studies, as noted throughout the discussion, more can and should be being done by these enterprises in terms of resource efficiency at the very least.

However there are barriers to taking action, which collectively come within the areas of behavioural, financial and a lack of information (DEFRA 2011, Leslie 2009). From this study, a finding supported by others, there is an evident consistency in factors considered to be hindering further progress. These are:

- lack of interest, inertia or ambivalence on the part of owners/managers
- limited information, awareness and understanding
- lack of time, too busy
- lack of resources, costs involved for instance for 'green products' and/or participation in a formal EMS scheme
- lack of supporting infrastructure
- for local produce/products, a lack of availability and/or awareness coupled with costs and quality.

The noted lack of awareness brings into question the efficacy of government, and the more limited actions of the main professional associations' lead efforts, especially where such effort is neither localized nor takes account of the practical realities of the enterprises involved. In this sense the findings are not unexpected, and effectively demonstrate that the policies presented by the leading bodies involved are often little more than rhetoric. This is not surprising given that such organizations are not part of the actual business sectors they seek to influence. Furthermore, such outcomes should also not be unexpected given the very limited awareness of such policies and related initiatives, a factor that brings into question their value and the approaches to dissemination and implementation.

The objective of 'greener' tourism enterprises demands that companies operate in more sustainable ways, and in the process develop and build on more extensive links with other sectors of the local economy and with the local community more generally. However, it is evident from these findings that there is substantial scope for enhancing this role and developing the environmental performance – the sustainability – of tourism enterprises, and particularly those activities that come within the scope of social responsibility. This is exemplified in the attention given in this survey to purchasing local produce and products. Developing much stronger linkages with other more localized sectors and promoting greater production and utilization of local produce and products will contribute to the sustainability of the local economy and provide more opportunities for employment. However, the fact that individual environmental awareness and practice is limited indicates that there is no collective commitment to cultural and social sustainability. Thus there is a 'requirement for more creative planning in order to maximize the cross-sectoral economic links that can be achieved in the development of tourism. This demands a more comprehensive approach' (Leslie 2002b: 9).

More problematic is how to encourage the myriad tourism enterprises to put environmental issues, and the adoption of environmentally friendly management practices, to the forefront of their business operations and strategic decisions. A factor, which will certainly play a part in the wider adoption of such a process, is the possibility of legislation that directly targets energy consumption and waste. In the meantime, this will only happen through increased awareness of the 'why', 'what' and 'how' involved in addressing environmental performance and a requirement for such messages to be presented in the right way: that is, positively and with the right message. Furthermore, such an approach could pre-empt the question an owner/manager might ask: Why should a tourism enterprise address its environmental performance? What are the reasons, the benefits of adopting such an undertaking? Even then, there is a need for such promotion and action to be manifest and championed at the local level by individual leadership – in effect, the presence of a 'champion' in an influential position (Lawton and Weaver 2010). Appropriate encouragement will be required in order to overcome a primary difficulty (if not a barrier), the 'I will if you will' syndrome (see SCRT 2006). Relevant exemplars illustrating the advantages of the pertinent systems and practices will have to be identified, and presented effectively with facilitating mechanisms if they are to have any real effect.

In the meantime, it is all too evident that those owners/managers who hold intrinsic values that not only steer their own environmental behaviour but which also lead them to applying such behaviours in their businesses will adopt a form of an EMS even if they do not become formally accredited. Also, those who are well focused on the financial performance and ongoing success of the business will seek to adopt those practices that have perceived benefits. However, for the majority of owners/managers engaged in the operation of the plethora of small, independent tourism enterprises, further green steps will only be accomplished through regulation. Until that happens, we will see little improvement in the sustainability of the tourism supply.

The likelihood of such regulation specifically for tourism being introduced is very low indeed, especially given the influence that the major stakeholders in tourism have, particularly through their professional associations. But the ongoing initiatives driven by political will to address climate change will lead to further green taxes, including a carbon tax (in one form or another). This will certainly catalyze the laggards in tourism enterprises to address a range of environmental management practices. Even so, facets of sustainability such as social responsibility and interrelationships with local communities and the local economy will continue to gain lesser consideration, and quite probably even less so in the future.

References

Anon (2009a) 'Hotel Sustainability – could do better.' Available at www.catersearch.com/Atciles/Article.aspx?liArticleID=330200 (accessed 12 October 2009).

Anon (2009b) 'A framework for green success,' *Hospitality*, Issue 16, pp. 38–9.

Baird, J. H. (2010) 'Green tourism accreditation: the impacts of the Green Tourism Business Scheme (GTBS) on Scotland's tourism sector.' BA dissertation, Tourism and International Management, Glasgow Caledonian University.

Barr, S., Shaw, G., Coles, T. and Prillwitz, J. (2010) '"A holiday is a holiday": processing sustainability, home and way,' *Journal of Transport Geography*, Vol. 18, pp. 474–81.

Bohdanowicz, P. and Zientara, P. (2008) 'Hotel companies' contribution to improving the quality of life of local communities and the well-being of their employees,' *Tourism and Hospitality Research*, Vol. 9, No. 2, pp. 147–58.

Butler, R. (1993) in Butler, R. and Pearce, D. (eds), *Change in Tourism: people, places and processes*, London. Routledge, pp. 1–11.

Centre for the Environment and Business in Scotland (CEBIS) (1996) 'Tourism: what does "green" mean?' *Sustainability*, CEBIS and Scottish Education Forum, Issue 9.

Chan, E. S. W. (2011) 'Implementation of environmental management systems in small and medium sized hotels: obstacles,' *Journal of Hospitality and Tourism Research*, Vol. 35, No. 1, pp. 3–23.

Chan, E. S. W. and Hawkins, R. (2010) 'Attitude towards EMSs in an international hotel: an exploratory case study,' *International Journal of Hospitality Management*, Vol. 29, No. 4, pp. 641–51.

Chan, W. W. (2009) 'Environmental measures for hotel's environmental management systems ISO14001,' *International Journal of Contemporary Hospitality Management*, Vol. 21, No. 5, pp. 542–60.

Department of Culture Media and Sport (DCMS) (2009) 'Tourism industry looks to "greener" future,' press release, London, DCMS, 26 March.

Department of Environment, Food and Rural Affairs (DEFRA) (2011) 'Research shows companies can save money by helping the environment,' press release, London, DEFRA, 14 March.

Dodds, F. (2002) *Earth Summit 2002: A new deal*. London, Earthscan.

Ebeling, S. (2008) Personal Communication. Green Tourism Business Scheme, Aberdeen.

EIU (1993) Travel and Tourism Analyst. Economic Intelligence Unit, London, Number 1.

Ethical Corporation (2010) 'Social and economic impacts: measurement, evaluation and reporting,' London. Ethical Corporation, September.

Freezar, J and Font, X. (2010) 'Marketing sustainability for small leisure and tourism firms,' *Countryside Recreation*, Vol. 18, No. 1, pp. 9–11.

Frey, N. and George, R. (2010) 'Responsible tourism management: the missing link between business owners' attitudes and behaviour in the Cape Town tourism industry,' *Tourism Management*, Vol. 31, No. 5, pp. 621–8.

Goodall (1994) 'Environmental auditing: current best practice (with special reference to British tourism firms),' in Seaton, A. (ed.), *Tourism: The state of the art*, London, Wiley, pp. 655–74.

Gossling, S. and Hall, C. M. (2006) 'Conclusion: wake up … this is serious,' in Gossling, S. and Hall, C. M. (eds), *Tourism and Global Environmental Change: Ecological, social, economic and political interrelationships*, New York, Routledge, pp. 305–20.

Gossling, S., Garrod, B., Aall, C., Hille, J. and Peeters, P. (2011) 'Food management in tourism: reducing tourism's carbon "footprint",' *Tourism Management*, Vol. 31, No. 3, pp. 534–43.

Greenbiz (2009) 'Most small biz owners say customers won't pay more for green.' Available at www.greenbiz.com/news/ (accessed 21 June 2009).

Hall, C. M. and Gossling, S. (2009) 'Global environmental change and tourism enterprise,' in Leslie, D. (ed.), *Tourism Enterprises and Sustainable Development: International perspectives on responses to the sustainability agenda*, New York, Routledge, pp. 17–35.

Han, H., Hsue, L.-T. and Sheu, C. (2010) 'Application of the theory of planned behaviour to green hotel choice: testing the effect of environmentally friendly activities,' *Tourism Management*, Vol. 31, pp. 325–34.

Institute of Hospitality (2007) 'Envirowise and Institute of Hospitality "green" survey,' London, Institute of Hospitality.

Infor (2008) *Performance Management Strategies: Creating social and financial value by going green*. Alpharetta, Georgia, Infor, February.

Lawton, L. J. and Weaver, D. B. (2010) 'Normative and innovative resources management at birding festivals,' *Tourism Management,* Vol. 31, No. 4, pp. 527–36.

Leslie, D. (2001) 'Serviced accommodation, environmental performance and benchmarks,' *Journal of Quality Assurance in Hospitality and Tourism*, Vol. 2, No. 3, pp. 127–47.

Leslie, D. (2002a) 'The influence of UK government agencies on the "greening" of tourism,' *Tourism Today*, No. 2 (Summer), pp. 95–110.

Leslie, D. (2002b) 'National parks and the tourism sector,' *Countryside Recreation*, Vol. 10, No. 3/4, (Autumn/Winter), pp. 5–10.

Leslie, D. (2005a) 'Rural tourism businesses and environmental management systems,' in Hall, D., Kirkpatrick, I. and Mitchell, M. (eds), *Rural Tourism: Issues and impacts*, Clevedon, Channel View, pp. 228–49.

Leslie, D. (2005b) 'Cultural tourism attractions and environmental performance,' in Sigala, M. and Leslie, D. (eds), *International Cultural Tourism: Management, implications and cases*, place? Elsevier Butterworth-Heinemann, pp. 66–79.

Leslie, D. (2007a) Scottish rural tourism enterprises and the sustainability of their communities: a local Agenda 21 approach in Augustyn, M. and Thomas, R. (eds) Tourism in the New Europe, Perspectives on SME policies and Practices. Advances in Tourism Research Series. Oxford, Elsevier, pp. 89–108.

Leslie, D. (2007b) 'The missing component in the "greening" of tourism: the environmental performance of the self-catering accommodation sector,' Special issue on self-catering accommodation, *International Journal of Hospitality Management*, Vol. 26, No. 2, pp. 310–22.

Leslie, D. (ed.) (2009) *Tourism Enterprises, Environmental Performance and Sustainable Development: Perspectives on progress from across the globe*, New York, Routledge.

Leslie, D. (2012a) Tourism, Tourists and Sustainability in Leslie, D. (ed.) *Tourism Enterprises and the Sustainability Agenda across Europe. New Directions in Tourism Analysis*. Ashgate, Farnham pp. 15–34.

Leslie, D. (ed.) (2012b) *Tourism Enterprises and the Sustainability across Europe. New Directions in Tourism Analysis*. Ashgate, Farnham.

Masero, S. (2009) 'Why it pays to act now,' *Sustainable Business*, August/September, pp. 18–19.

Nicolau, J. L. (2008) 'Corporate social responsibility: worth-creating activities,' *Annals of Tourism Research,* Vol. 35, no. 4, pp. 990–1006.

Preigo, M. J. B., Najera, J. J. and Font, X. (2011) 'Environmental management decision-making in certified hotels,' *Journal of Sustainable Tourism*, Vol. 19, No. 3, pp. 361–81.

PTC (Jersey) (1998) Jersey in the New Millennium: a sustainable future. Policy and Resources Committee, St. Helier.

Radwan, H. R. I., Jones, E. and Minoli, D. (2010) 'Managing solid waste in small hotels,' *Journal of Sustainable Tourism*, Vol. 18, No. 2, pp. 175–90.

Scottish Enterprise (2003) "Biodiversity Matters": a draft strategy for Scotland's Biodiversity. Scottish Enterprise, Edinburgh.

Scottish Government (SG) (2007) *The Government Economic Strategy*, Edinburgh, SG.

SCRT (2006) I will if you will: Towards Sustainable Consumption. Sustainable Consumption Round Table, London, May.

Sustainable Consumer Round Table (SCRT) (2006) *I Will If You Will: Towards sustainable consumption*, London, SCRT, May.

SG (2009) News release, 1 May, available at wwwscotland.gov.uk (accessed 9 January 2010).

Tari, J. J., Claver-Cortes, E., Periera-Moliner, J. and Molina-Azorin, J. F. (2010) 'Levels of quality and environmental management in the hotel industry: their joint influence on firm performance,' *International Journal of Hospitality Management*, Vol. 28, No. 3, pp. 500–10.

Tyler, D. and Dinan, C. (2001) 'Trade and associated groups in English policy arena,' *International Journal of Tourism Research*, Vol. 3, pp. 459–76.

Tzschentke, Kirk D. and Lynch, P. A. (2004) 'Reasons for going green in serviced accommodation establishments,' *International Journal of Contemporary Hospitality Management*, Vol. 16, No. 2, pp. 116–24.

VisitScotland (2007) *VisitScotland Corporate Plan: 2008–2011,* Edinburgh, VisitScotland.

Welford, R. and Starkey, R. (eds) (1996) *The Earthscan Reader in Business and the Environment*, London, Earthscan Publications.

wiredgov (2009) available at net/wg/wg-content-1.nsf/vLookupIndustryNewsByD/21? (accessed 27 July 2009).

PART III

Emerging techniques and research implications

9

TOURISM SENSITIVITY TO CLIMATE CHANGE MITIGATION POLICIES
Lessons from recent surveys

Ghislain Dubois, Jean-Paul Ceron and Paul Peeters

Introduction

Because of its dependency on air transport, mitigating tourism greenhouse gas (GHG) emissions might become the most important challenge for the sustainability of the sector. Moreover climate change mitigation will be more and more in conflict with other sustainability objectives such as poverty alleviation and biodiversity conservation through tourism. Indeed, tourism increasingly contributes to global GHG emissions. Transport, and in particular air transport, have the largest share in those emissions, with respectively 75 per cent and 40 per cent of the tourism 5 per cent share of global carbon dioxide (CO_2) emissions estimated for 2005 (UNWTO et al. 2008). In terms of the actual contribution to climate change, measured in radiative forcing, the share of air transport is between 54 per cent and 83 per cent of tourism, depending on assumptions made on non-CO_2 effects of aviation (Scott et al. 2010). Projections show a strong growth, with more than a doubling by 2035 (UNWTO et al. 2008). In a context where climate policies try to maintain global warming within the limit of +2 °C, this current tourism growth is apparently at odds with global emission reduction targets (Bows, Anderson and Peeters, 2007; Gössling et al. 2010).

For scientists, the reasons for producing figures on tourism emissions was not self evident. Indeed, GHG emissions have been assessed essentially from a production, sectorial and territorial point of view (e.g. Bastianoni and Pulselli 2004, CGDD 2010, IPCC 1996, Dubois et al 2011).This method was designed to provide base information for international negotiations (in particular the Kyoto Protocol). It had two main shortcomings. First, it did not shed light on the influence of consumption and social practices (Aall and Hille 2009, IFEN 2006, Munasinghe and Dasgupta 2009, Peters and Hertwich 2006); whereas it has been shown that the behaviour of households influences three-quarters of emissions (Edgar et al. 2009, Pasquier 2010).

Second it does not allow taking into account international aspects, in particular the emissions from international shipping and aviation (European Commission 2001, United Nations 2003), which are particularly important regarding tourism, and the emissions embedded in trade (Edgar et al. 2009, Helm and Smale 2007, Lenglart, Lesieur and Pasquier 2010, Munksgaard and Pedersen 2001). Within the International Panel on Climate Change (IPCC), in spite of the willingness to take into account the mitigation potential of socio-economic systems besides pure economic sectors such as energy, agriculture and transport (IPCC 2001), this position was not really taken into account in the *Fourth Assessment Report* and tourism was only dealt with from the 'impacts and adaptation' perspective, within working group II (Wilbanks et al. 2007). The templates of the working group III chapters in the *Fifth Assessment Report* (IPCC 2009) include features such as consumption patterns, behavioural and lifestyle changes in at least seven chapters out of sixteen. Therefore, tourism is now increasingly identified as a driver for emissions growth within the scientific community involved in the IPCC.

On the stakeholders' side, following the first research on the topic, UN institutions (and in particular the UN World Tourism Organization, UNWTO) recognized that the emissions from tourism are a problem (UNWTO 2009; UNWTO, UNEP and WMO 2007). Yet these emissions were not seen as incompatible with a sustainable growth of tourism, which is viewed as indispensable in particular to alleviate poverty in less developed countries (LDCs) (UNWTO 2004). It also became clear that emissions from origin/destination transport form the major part of emissions, with 75 per cent globally, and more for remote destinations (UNWTO et al. 2008), and consequently that good practice at the destination, on which goodwill stakeholders usually dwell, is simply not sufficient to create environmentally sustainable tourism development. Logically, after a phase of denial (Gössling and Peeters 2005), tourism stakeholders gradually admit they are concerned. Similarly to the vision of UNWTO, the issue is not seen as a need to modify the growth prospects of the industry (BALPA and, IATA 2009). In the most recent forward-thinking papers issued by some aviation stakeholders, it is recognized that the industry will have to go further than what the progress in management and technology will yield (UNWTO 2009). Much (and probably excessive) hope is put into carbon-neutral fuels from biomass (Hileman et al. 2009), and as this will not be enough, buying emission rights from other sectors is the adjustment variable that should allow carbon-neutral growth beyond 2020 (IATA 2009).

This growing but still imperfect level of awareness and knowledge from the industry and destinations led to a growing demand of research on the impact of future policies on the tourism system. This research can be purely academic, or commissioned by policy makers. The use of long-term policy scenarios, based on methods of future studies, helps in imagining consistent visions of the tourism and transport system, far beyond the current market and institutional context. They can either assess the impact of ambitious climate policies (such as a high carbon price, or emissions trading with tight emission caps) or prepare some more creative visions of a 'low-carbon' tourism allowing for global growth.

The first part of this chapter outlines the methods presented in recently published studies for assessing the relationship between tourism, air transport and climate policies. The second section critically assesses case studies (covering the entire world, and a sample of developing countries, the Caribbean, Asia Pacific, French Overseas Territories and the Mediterranean), and the final section discusses policy options and presents methodological recommendations.

Methodological options

Reported studies found in the literature use varying methods to assess the relationship between tourism, air transport and climate policies, according to several parameters.

- The objectives can be either to show the potential risks for tourism associated with climate policies, or more proactively to explore alternative options, reducing the carbon intensity of tourism. This influences methods towards a comparison with a baseline using a forecasting perspective in the former case (Mayor and Tol 2010, Tol 2007, Veryard 2009), or towards the development of contrasted scenarios, often with a backcasting perspective in the latter (Ceron, Dubois and de Torcy 2009; Dubois et al. 2011; Peeters and Dubois 2010).
- The modelling approaches differ widely, depending on the project objective, and also on the research team background. They can have a predominant qualitative scope, a quantitative one, or endeavour to combine both (Ceron et al 2009). All the case studies in the sample presented in this chapter include a substantial task of quantification/modelling of future tourism demand. Some models are based on a central parameter, like price/demand elasticity, other on a combination of parameters (prices, elasticity, absolute volume of trips and so on). There are considerable discrepancies in the values given to these parameters, sometimes without clear justification.

In particular we must question the use of constant elasticities to assess the impacts of mitigation policies on demand. Though elasticities are certainly a good way to get a first-order sense of the impact of measures, they are statistical artefacts and their validity is low when large price shocks are assumed (see for a wider discussion e.g. Brons et al. 2002, Seetaram 2010). Another problem most case studies face is to choose a single value from the large range of values published for elasticities. For example air transport elasticities range from -3.2 to +0.3 (Brons et al. 2002). The main problem is that elasticities do not describe a 'physical' property of systems, but just the outcome of statistical properties of a database (of tourism arrivals in relation to generally prices, transport travel times and tourists' income). This however can never catch second-order systemic changes in the tourism system.

For example, very strong mitigation policies may affect tourism to a not too remote island (like Corsica, Ireland or the Isle of Man) in two ways: a strong reduction of air transport and a strong increase of arrivals by ferry in combination with car, bus and/or rail (the so-called slow travel concept). Such a change will immediately cause a reduction of the supply (frequency) of flights, thus reducing the quality (travel time, choice of arrival time) of air travel, further diminishing its share. On a longer term the ferry companies will see their demand increase, invest in a higher frequency and better supply and thus attract even more passengers, which will finally induce more lines to be opened and new harbours to be built. Such dynamic changes in the infrastructure and supply can never be captured by single constant price elasticities as applied in most studies. What many studies do provide is sensitivity to the assumed elasticity, at least covering the impacts of uncertainty in the value of elasticities.

- The main methodological issue we would like to insist on is the choice of boundaries for the studies, which proved to impact drastically on the results. This covers the geographical scope (worldwide, regional, national); the focus on international tourism only or on both international and domestic markets; the inclusion of ground transport modes or not. Indeed, focusing on a too narrow field might hinder the possibility of considering substitutions between markets and transport modes, and therefore opportunities that might arise from climate policies. Indeed, a major problem we found in many studies (e.g. just looking at the international market in Tol 2007, Uyarra et al. 2005, Veryard 2009, or ignoring opportunities of different organization of a large event to reduce the transport cost and impact, as in DEAT 2009) is that the researchers ignored the impact of the choice of system boundaries on the conclusions. Generally the impacts of climate policies are evaluated for international tourism arrivals only, and sometimes they are even further restricted to arrivals by air. This inevitably has serious implications for the results. If you evaluate an emissions tax on aviation and just looks at air transport arrivals for a destination, than you will always find a loss of arrivals and a reduction of the contribution of these arrivals to the destination's GDP. However, such a tax will have a much more complicated impact as it will affect the whole tourism economy of the destination in both negative and positive ways. For example if the study looks at an emission tax on air transport only and evaluates the impacts on whole countries, as in for instance Veryard (2009):
  - air transport arrivals will reduce (reduction of both emissions and GDP)
  - air transport departures (outbound tourism) will reduce (reduction of emissions, but there will be an increase in GDP as people will not spend their money in other places any more)
  - domestic tourism will increase (relatively small increase of emissions and increase of GDP generated by the country's tourism industry)
  - short-haul non-air tourist arrivals from neighbouring countries will increase (relatively small increase in emissions, increase in GDP)

- short haul non-air arrivals to neighbouring countries will increase (relatively small increase in emissions, decrease in GDP).

In most countries, domestic tourism and short-haul tourism between neighbouring countries are up to two orders of magnitudes larger than tourism using medium to long-haul flights. Thus, the impacts of the often ignored parts of the economy can be much larger, and can even reverse the outcome found by just investigating air tourist international arrivals. We will insert some critical methodological notes to all case studies, mainly regarding the issue of ignoring large parts of the tourism system.

Case studies

Global

Tol (2007) uses an existing model – the Hamburg tourism model (Hamilton et al 2005) – to estimate the impact of a carbon tax on demand and emissions. Three values are considered: $10, $100 and $1000 per ton of CO_2. A $1000 tax would reduce demand by 0.8 per cent and emissions by 0.9 per cent.

The results are sensitive to the choice of price/demand elasticity, which is not well known: the option for a very high elasticity would almost double the reduction of emissions. If domestic holidays were allowed to substitute for international travel (which is not the case in the base model) the cut in emissions could rise to -7.59 per cent (still for a $1000 tax). The results are also sensitive to the distance threshold above which the use of aviation is deemed indispensable: if this distance is doubled the baseline emissions are 14 per cent lower, which means that the total share of aviation is smaller and thus the impact of a carbon tax will also be smaller.

The author concludes that 'as travel behaviour is not very responsive to the limited price signals that carbon taxation would bring about, behavioural and technical changes may contribute more to emission reduction' (Tol 2007: 137). However, non-market measures are not part of this paper.

In some cases the paper shows that CO_2 emissions might increase if there is an increase in carbon tax. This is for example the case if all international tourists are assumed to travel by air. There may be two causes for this. First the author assumes the relative impact on price of tickets to be larger for short-haul flights than for long-haul ones, because the author (rightly) assumes higher emission factors for short than for long-haul flights. But this is only true if the ticket cost is more or less proportional to distance flown (as is assumed by the author, who uses only a moderate $30 fixed cost per flight). However, the difference in emission factors between short and long haul is rather small for flights above 1500 km, and the difference in share of fuel cost in total operating cost is much larger than is assumed by this paper (e.g. 13 per cent for a 1000 km flight with a Boeing 737-400 and 19 per cent for a 7000 km flight with a Boeing 747-400: Dings et al. 2000).

A second cause for the increase of the emissions with increased carbon costs is the assumption in the Hamburg model that total number of trips remains equal and that people do not substitute between distance classes. Apparently the Hamburg model first calculates all reductions in trips per distance class and then corrects the total number of trips upward with the same factor, to get the original number of flights. Therefore long-haul destinations will receive more tourists when the cost of carbon is raised and short-haul destinations fewer. The reality will be very different, as people will not just all of a sudden spend much more on tourism: they are more likely to try to compensate for the price rise by for example choosing a nearer destination. This is confirmed by the Hamburg model when domestic tourism is considered to be an alternative for international tourism, causing a much larger reduction of CO_2 emissions for a given CO_2 cost. To summarize, the impacts given on CO_2 emissions are most likely too low because of the lack of substitution to low-carbon travel in the model and probably erroneous assumptions regarding the cost of air tickets.

The Caribbean

Pentelowe and Scott (2009) examined the impact on tourist flows to the Caribbean of the price of carbon combined with different scenarios for oil prices. The study is limited to the main originating markets (Europe and the United States), and the time horizon extends to 2020. The authors built eighteen scenarios combining three carbon prices, two oil prices and three elasticity estimates. The model includes:

- a business as usual (BAU) projection of tourist arrivals and travel emissions
- a calculation of the change in the cost of air travel owing to the introduction of an Emissions Trading Scheme (ETS) in originating markets, and to the change in oil prices, and based on this
- a calculation of the change in arrivals in the Caribbean using elasticities.

Over the range of scenarios, total arrivals decrease between -1.28 per cent and -4.29 per cent relative to a BAU scenario in 2020. This does not impact significantly on the growth in volume over the same time period, which remains around 50 per cent.

The authors also considered the effects on the market of holiday packages through a specific case study on Jamaica. Since flight costs represent approximately a third of the total vacation cost and since 15 per cent of the hotel costs are considered as sensitive to oil price increases, not surprisingly the effect is lower than for flights alone (e.g. -2.6 per cent compared with -3.2 per cent for one scenario). Following this, it could be suggested that in a highly competitive market where tour operators are in a dominating position, they should increase their pressure on the local tourism industry so as to pass part of the cost increase onto them, which would further dampen the impact.

This paper also indirectly draws attention to the differences in results that can stem from the choice between a 'realistic' option which uses foreseeable actions in the medium term (such as a gentle cap on the emissions from aviation, with only 15 per cent of emissions being above the cap) and a more normative view (for example, applying an uplift factor of two to CO_2 emissions to take account of the specificity of aviation, as in Gössling, Peeters and Scott 2008). Quite obviously as no stringent actions are projected by the institutions and stakeholders, the effects on demand will be low.

This study also takes air arrivals as the base for the model used, although in this case, evaluating the impacts on small islands, this assumption is less problematic as international arrivals will represent a relatively large sector of the tourism industry. But even in this case some countries may compensate for part of the disadvantage of losing international air arrivals by reducing international outbound tourism. Also including domestic tourism will dilute the impact on tourists in a country like Surinam by a factor of five or six, and the economic impacts maybe by a factor of two (based on UNWTO tourist statistics and domestic statistics calculated with the method presented in Peeters 2010).

Developing countries

The need to prioritize poverty alleviation in developing countries is often mentioned as an objective that potentially conflicts with climate change mitigation, and could even limit the possibility of implementing a global scheme for air transport emissions. Therefore, even if they are still minor in global tourism, developing countries are a key aspect of the climate change and sustainability debate, and it must be informed with robust and rigorous data, instead of opinions and value judgements.

Gössling et al. (2008) deal with ten small developing island destinations. They analyse the consequences for tourism arrivals and the economy of two sets of hypotheses. The first set corresponds to a rather hard version of a 'realistic' approach. It is based on the inclusion of aviation in carbon trading schemes (using a cost of carbon of \$65/ton in 2020). It takes into account the objectives the European Union currently puts forward without translating them into policy measures. The authors themselves draw from the objectives implications which seem consistent, but which in the current state of things are not accepted by aviation stakeholders. Their EUETS scenario thus represents 'the least favourable scenario for the aviation industry as currently discussed by the EU'. The second scenario, called 'Worldwide serious climate policy' (WSCP), 'assesses the consequences of global climate policy for aviation where costs of 230\$/t CO^2 are introduced by 2020'. Both scenarios present a high and a low variant depending in particular on the choice of a figure for elasticity.

For the EUETS scenario the decline in demand compared with the baseline is comparable to the one found by Pentelowe and Scott (2009). This means that with an elasticity of -0.5 demand will decline by less than 1 per cent (relative to no EUETS); with an elasticity of -1 it could decline by up to 6 per cent in the Seychelles compared with BAU. Growth in volume would globally continue but be slowed. In terms of emissions this scenario is in fact far from complying with the carbon reduction objectives as seen by the European Union. Under the WSCP scenario, growth (using an average of low and high variants) continues for six destinations out of ten, although a decline is clear for the Seychelles and Bonaire. On average the conclusion is that growth in volume would continue to 2020 but would be delayed differently according to the hypotheses adopted and the individual country characteristics. What happens after 2020 is another question.

The paper ends with an analysis of the vulnerability of the different destinations, taking into account the vulnerability of tourism to emissions (depending on the different carbon intensities of earnings) and the dependency of the country's economy on tourism (which ranges from around 5 per cent for Sri Lanka or Madagascar to 80 per cent of GDP for Anguilla).

Methodologically this paper suffers from ignoring non-air arrivals, all outbound tourism and domestic tourism. It proves that for most of the countries assessed, the overall impact of mitigation policies is not unmanageable. However, the paper does not investigate alternative policy options, such as the possibility of introducing a more favourable treatment for vulnerable destinations, for instance through differentiated carbon prices, delay in the introduction of taxes and carbon trading, funding some adaptation of the tourism supply or the substitution of tourism by less carbon-intensive activities. It also ignores the impacts on outbound and domestic tourism, which might alleviate to some extend the impacts on international inbound tourism.

Asia Pacific

Veryard (2009) analyses the potential effects for the coming years of the introduction of a carbon price and of the variation of oil prices on tourism, in Asia Pacific Economic Cooperation (APEC) countries (looking at arrivals, tourism income and GDP). The survey was commissioned by APEC.

The study assumed a carbon price of $50/ton of CO_2 and tested three hypotheses for oil prices corresponding to typical situations in the past decade, to evaluate the impacts on international arrivals by air transport within the region. It concluded that:

> although there is significant variation across the price scenarios, the overall magnitude of the operating cost change is typically less than 10% for most feasible short-term values for both the carbon price and fuel price. This variation can be compared with the 500% increase in fuel prices observed between 2000 and 2008 or the subsequent 50% reduction since the peak in 2008.
>
> *(Veryard 2009: 19)*

The effect on air arrivals is estimated from this study to be around -3 to -5 per cent compared with BAU. The effects are the lower for tourists with the most distant origins, which reflect the lack of alternative transport means and the relatively high income of the tourists, who are less responsive than those of more modest means to price changes. The effect on tourism income should only be slightly lower than on arrivals because the great majority of international tourists in this area come by air. An 'indirect tourism income multiplier' is used to assess the effects on GDP (a twofold multiplication of the direct effect); this results in a reduction of 0.1 per cent to 0.6 per cent in GDP.

A sensitivity analysis is presented in this study which allows for departing from a mid-term 'realistic' point of view. First, whereas up to a price of US\$100/ton for CO_2 the effects of carbon prices appear to be relatively low, 'for much larger carbon prices impacts on aviation arrivals and GDP are proportionally larger, with a carbon price of US\$500/ton CO_2 suggesting a near halving of aviation arrivals and GDP impacts of over -2 per cent for many of the sample economies'. Second, the effects are proportional to the value of the multiplier, which appears to be little known: 'if the indirect impacts are 2 to 5 times the original impact of the carbon price, the overall impact can be pronounced, particularly for Malaysia, Singapore and Thailand' (Veryard 2009: 34).

The results of this study are most likely not correct if they are interpreted as impacts on the whole tourism industry and GDP of the countries studied. This is because the study just refers to international arrivals by air, ignoring several effects that might improve the contribution of tourism to the GDP of the countries. The study ignores the impacts on the local tourism industry from domestic tourism, international arrivals by other modes and international departures by both air and other modes. Therefore the impacts of arrivals and the tourism economy are most likely wrong in magnitude (percentage damage) and even in direction (some countries might benefit from a reduction of long-haul travel, because they will gain from both fewer departures from their own country and increased short-haul arrivals from neighbouring countries. A very tentative result from our ongoing research, using the global tourism database of the Global Tourism and Transport (GTTMadv) model (Peeters and Dubois 2010) and assuming certain levels of mitigation policies which cause a shift from long and medium-haul to medium and short-haul world-wide and start a complex chain of reactions with respect to market development for each country, is given in Figure 9.1.

Figure 9.1 clearly shows that larger countries like Australia and New Zealand might benefit from strong policies, because their strong outbound tourism will reduce as well, compensating for the loss of international arrivals through an increase in domestic arrivals. Very small countries (Singapore) and countries depending heavily on inbound tourism (Thailand) might suffer from mitigation measures. This contrasts with the results of the Asia Pacific study (Veryard 2009), which shows only reductions in the tourism industry and its contributions to the economy.

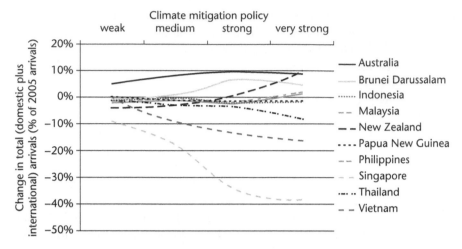

FIGURE 9.1 Climate mitigation policies cause very long-haul trips to shift to the whole range of short to long haul ('weak' climate policy) up to a shift from medium to very long haul towards short haul only ('very strong' policy)

Source: Paul Peeters, ongoing research

French overseas territories

The study by Ceron et al. (2009) was commissioned by the French Development Agency (AFD). It aimed to:

- estimate current GHG emissions caused by tourism in French overseas departments and territories
- measure emissions against tourism activity (calculating the sector's 'eco-efficiency' (Gössling et al. 2005) and compare different originating markets as well as tourism with other economic activities
- draft strategies to deal with the carbon constraint by identifying variables that affect emissions and using them to develop scenarios up to the year 2025.

To examine how the carbon constraint will affect tourism in the regions concerned by this study, scenarios were developed. Variables were modified to analyse their effect on tourism using:

- Hypotheses on emissions regulation. These hypotheses were developed with regard to recent studies by IPCC researchers, international commitments and the post-Kyoto negotiation process (especially in the aviation field).
- Hypotheses on mechanisms specific to the tourism sector in each of the regions concerned.

Results for each territory were compared against those for other territories and metropolitan France (Table 9.1).

TABLE 9.1 Tourism eco-efficiency by destination

	CO_2-e/Euro spent (kg)
Towards metropolitan France – all international markets	2.10
Towards New Caledonia	3.61
Towards French Polynesia	4.24
Towards Reunion Island	6.52
Towards Guadeloupe	6.87
Towards Martinique	7.33

Source: Ceron, Dubois and De Torcy (2010).
Note: CO_2-e/Euro spent – CO_2 equivalent per euro of tourism expenses

Strategies were identified for tourism development in French overseas territories and considered in the light of international developments in the field of climate change and GHG restrictions. They include:

- reducing air travel (developing closer markets, reducing flight distances, developing the local tourism market)
- improving passenger load factors
- increasing the length of stay
- increasing tourist expenditure per night.

The eco-efficiency results were used to build strategies: first to optimize the use of a limited carbon budget within the tourism sector, and further to deal with the issue of the share of tourism within the global carbon budget of each territory. The scenarios concluded that for all the destinations studied, a drop in emissions means a drop in arrivals (average -14 per cent). The extent of this decrease and the consequences on revenues depend on the viability of substitute markets and the ability to adopt revenue rather than volume strategies. The scenarios endeavour to combine economic development with decreased environmental damage. However, they necessarily involve important societal shifts. Populations are currently unprepared for such radical changes. Examples include:

- A decrease in tourism mobility. This is in direct contrast to the current trend, established over the last ten years, which involves frequent short stays. While this may be acceptable for pleasure tourists, the same cannot be said for visiting friends and relatives (VFR) traffic. In the scenarios developed, VFR traffic has been maintained, although it generates lower revenues. This seems to be an important priority for the populations of French overseas departments and territories. Theoretically, other choices are possible.

- A decrease in tourist arrivals. While the scenarios indicate an increase in revenues, the changing carbon constraint will undoubtedly affect the structure of the tourism sector and will lower the expected growth (see Table 9.2, for the Reunion island case). Increased competition, shifts in demand, changes in seasonality, and fewer facilities (closed because of fewer arrivals) are likely to be some consequences.

TABLE 9.2 Scenarios for arrivals in La Reunion island: 2003, 2020 official strategy, and alternative vision for 2025

	2003	2020 (regional strategy)	2020 (alternative vision)
Tourist arrivals	30,000	1,000,000	272,000
Average length of stay (days)	16.2	10 to 12	14.7
Turnover (× 1000 euros)	365,000	950,000	455,000
GHG emissions (tons CO_2-e)	1,678,000	4,125,000	1,014,000
Eco-efficiency (kg CO_2-e/euro)	5.2	4.3	2.2

The Mediterranean

The Blue plan study (the technical regional centre of the UNEP Mediterranean action plan, not published yet) deals with the Mediterranean countries. Its goal is to assess the possibilities of reduction of GHG emissions from tourism in the medium and long term (2020s to 2050s), the effects on arrivals and the capacity of adaptation of tourism to this new context. It encompasses both international and domestic tourism, market and non-market measures. It elaborates on several scenarios considering various hypotheses (which feed a sophisticated model of system dynamics) for:

- carbon prices
- technological progress
- infrastructure development
- regulation measures for tourism transport, including the use of a specific carbon market for the sector.

The overall conclusion is that none of the scenarios, even the most extreme ones, result in reductions in line with what scientists show are necessary to avoid dangerous climate change (a 65 to 80 per cent reduction in GHG emissions). Only an extreme price of $1000 per ton of CO_2 would make it possible to start curbing emissions significantly in 2050 (S4) compared with 2005, though not to an extent that enables tourism to take a fair share of the reduction of GHG in the economy. Furthermore the reduction also depends on the background scenario assumed for global population and GDP growth (A1 or A2, see IMAGE-team 2006, IPCC 2000). The growing economy of the Mediterranean, with several emerging and

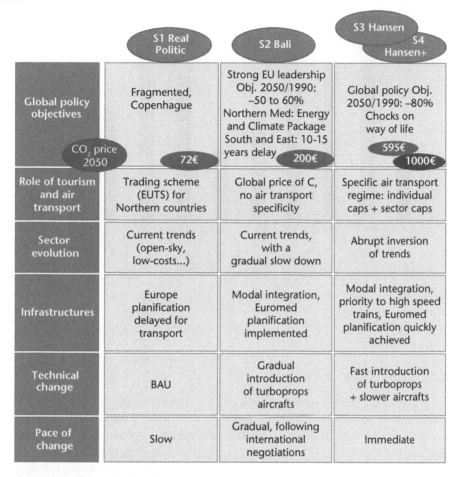

	S1 Real Politic	S2 Bali	S3 Hansen / S4 Hansen+
Global policy objectives	Fragmented, Copenhague	Strong EU leadership Obj. 2050/1990: −50 to 60% Northern Med: Energy and Climate Package South and East: 10-15 years delay	Global policy Obj. 2050/1990: −80% Chocks on way of life
CO_2 price 2050	72€	200€	595€ 1000€
Role of tourism and air transport	Trading scheme (EUTS) for Northern countries	Global price of C, no air transport specificity	Specific air transport regime: individual caps + sector caps
Sector evolution	Current trends (open-sky, low-costs...)	Current trends, with a gradual slow down	Abrupt inversion of trends
Infrastructures	Europe planification delayed for transport	Modal integration, Euromed planification implemented	Modal integration, priority to high speed trains, Euromed planification quickly achieved
Technical change	BAU	Gradual introduction of turboprops aircrafts	Fast introduction of turboprops + slower aircrafts
Pace of change	Slow	Gradual, following international negotiations	Immediate

FIGURE 9.2 Climate policy scenarios

developing economies that are tourism destinations, hinders the effect of climate policies.

A conclusion is that whereas a price attached to carbon is not by itself an efficient tool to curb emissions, it easily generates an amount of funds quite sufficient to structurally modify transport infrastructure (specifically extending high-speed rail), to foster a large modal shift, and thus to shape a new tourist demand less dependent on long-haul air transport, which finally may contribute to a change in lifestyles. The scope of this study is much wider than the previous ones, in the number of parameters taken into account, the time horizon (2050), and the boundaries (international and domestic tourism). It also goes further (like Ceron et al. 2009) in analysing adaptation strategies to a lower emissions context: for instance, promoting domestic tourism and changing lifestyles, reshaping infrastructures and showing that if market measures can contribute to reaching the goals, non-market measures are indispensable to fulfil them.

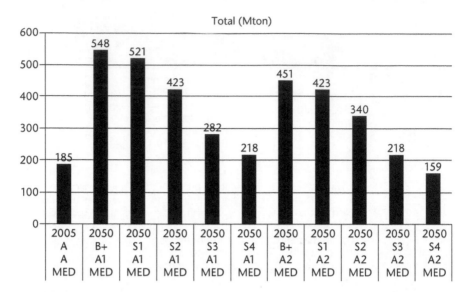

FIGURE 9.3 Evolution of emissions according to scenarios and economic context (overall Mediterranean basin)

B+: Baseline, A1 and A2: GDP per capita growths of respective IPCC SRES scenarios, MED: all Mediterranean basin.

Conclusions and discussion

The lessons learned from the sample of cases presented can be split between methodological recommendations and policy insights, even though both are closely interrelated. Indeed, modelling or elaborating scenarios is seldom neutral, but reflects some orientations (a trust/faith in technology for example) and sometimes some more philosophical options that predate the modelling exercise (such as the optimism or pessimism of the researcher) (Dahan-Dalmedico 2007).

In methodological terms, the ways research projects and instruments (models) are conceived are influenced by a dominant view on tourism: they take an excessive perspective on international tourism and international operators, and give insufficient consideration to domestic and proximity markets. A majority of studies limit their scope geographically, regarding the time frame, tourism markets, transport modes and tourism motives. This generally causes a bias towards the disadvantages of existing or envisaged measures within tourism. For example, limiting a study to international tourism ignores the opportunity to preserve a large share of the tourism sector by shifting from international outbound to domestic tourism, which could avoid part or all of the economic impact on the local tourism industry. A study dedicated to air transport only (like Veryard 2009) will always conclude there are large damages to the aviation sector, but will not acknowledge the opportunities for the rail and automotive industries. A study just investigating remote least developed islands will not show that some large less remote least-developed countries would actually benefit from less air transport as it will develop their (generally large) potential short-haul markets.

Therefore, more comprehensive modelling is required, as well as more transparency in choice of parameters. For instance elasticities are only constant for very small changes and in the short term, therefore elasticity-based studies should consider evolving elasticities. Furthermore an economic model based on elasticities will not be able to capture second-order impacts caused by structural changes in the tourism system, like a shift in infrastructure investments away from air transport towards rail transport and the impacts of increased patronage of high-speed rail connections on their medium-term quality (an increase as the frequency of the services will increase, reducing travel time and increasing opportunities to use the service).

Regarding climate policies, a few lessons can be derived from this sample of long-term surveys:

• Relying on carbon pricing only will probably not be sufficient to curb emissions, given the potential for growth of world tourism and the low substitutability of long-haul air transport.
• Open carbon trading schemes point to deadlocks: since air transport can afford to pay high prices for a ton of carbon and would have such a large amount of emissions to offset, aviation would likely buy most of the emission permits, and therefore prevent some flexibility in other sectors. A closed trading scheme could force aviation to reach some more ambitious goals.
• Scenarios leave the door open for alternative visions: a combination of technological improvement, but also behavioural changes and adaptation of the tourism and transport supply (infrastructure, products) would allow destinations to keep some tourism revenues, even if the growth will be lower than expected.
• Therefore, even if market instruments are useful, notwithstanding their undesired potential effects such as inequality, alternative policy options should be more frequently discussed. Given the specificity of air transport, banning some short-haul flights, capacity restraints in airport development, and introducing individual carbon budgets (Fawcett 2005; Fleming 1998; Lane, Harris and Roberts 2008, Starkey and Anderson 2005) are potential policy measures.
• Contrary to the situation observed in the past decades, under ambitious climate policies, air transport might become a rare service, the allocation of which would have to be optimized to maximize well-being and economic revenues. This clearly requires a change in mentality towards an activity that has recently been more and more deregulated.

Climate change mitigation, if taken seriously, could become a growing constraint and driving force for future tourism policies. Therefore it is more and more important to integrate this issue into discussions on the sustainability of the tourism sector, which often focus on local aspects (cultural impacts, effects on nature conservation and landscapes for instance), neglecting the effect of origin/destination transport on the environment and destination choices.

References

Aall, C. and Hille, J. (2009) 'Consumption – a missing dimension in climate policy.' In Bhaskar, R., Frank, C., Høyer, K. G., Naess, P. and Parker, J. (eds), *Interdisciplinarity and Climate Change*. London: Routledge.

British Airline Pilots Association (BALPA) (nd) 'Aviation and the environment: the pilot's perspective.' Available at: http://www.aerohabitat.eu/uploads/media/BALPA_REPORT-_Aviation_and_the_Environment.pdf (accessed 1 June 2012)

Bastianoni, S. and Pulselli, F. M. (2004) 'The problem of assigning responsibility for greenhouse gas emissions.' *Ecological Economics,* (49), 253–57.

Bows, A., Anderson, K. and Peeters, P. (2007) 'Technologies, scenarios and uncertainties.' Paper for the E-CLAT technical seminar 'Policy Dialogue on Tourism, Transport and Climate Change: Stakeholders meet researchers', 15 March. UNESCO, Paris.

Brons, M., Pels, E., Nijkamp, P. and Rietveld, P. (2002) 'Price elasticities of demand for air travel: a meta-analysis.' *Journal of Air Transport Management*, 8(3), 165–75.

Ceron, J.-P., Dubois, G. and De Torcy, L. (2009) *Développement touristique de l'outre-mer et dépendance au carbone*. Marseilles: TEC.

Commissariat Général au Développement Durable (CGDD) (France) (2010) *CO2 et activités économiques de la France. Tendances 1990–2007 et facteurs d'évolution*. 27 Paris: CGDD.

Dahan-Dalmedico, A. (2007) *Les modèles du futur. Changement climatique et scénarios économiques: enjeux scientifiques et politiques* (Coll. Recherches). Paris: La Découverte.

Department of Environmental Affairs and Tourism (DEAT) (South Africa) (2009) *Feasibility Study for a Carbon Neutral 2010 FIFA World Cup in South Africa*. Pretoria: Econ Pöyry AB.

Dings, J., Peeters, P. M., Heijden, J. R. v. d. and Wijnen, R. A. A. (2000) *ESCAPE: Economic screening of aircraft preventing emissions; background report*. Publ. code: 00.4404.17. Delft: Centrum voor Energiebesparing en Schone Technologie.

Dubois, G., Ceron, J. P., Peeters, P. and Gössling, S. (2011) 'The future tourism mobility of the world population: emission growth versus climate policy.' *Transportation Research – A*, 45(10), 1031-1042.

Edgar, G., Hertwitch, E.G. and Peters, G. (2009) 'Carbon footprint of nations: a global, trade-linked analysis.' *Environmental Science and Technology*, 43(16), 6414–20.

European Commission (EC) (2001) *Nameas for air emissions. Results of pilot studies*. Luxemburg: EC.

Fawcett, T. (2005) 'Personal carbon allowances.' Background document for the 40 per cent House report. Oxford: Environmental Change Institute.

Fleming, D. (1998) 'Domestic tradable quotas as an instrument to reduce carbon dioxide emissions.' Paper for EC workshop, 1–2 July, Brussels.

Gössling, S., Hall, C. M., Peeters, P. and Scott, D. (2010) 'The future of tourism: can tourism growth and climate policy be reconciled? A climate change mitigation perspective.' *Tourism Recreation Research*, 35(2), 119–30.

Gössling, S. and Peeters, P. (2005) '"It does not harm the environment": an analysis of discourses on tourism, ait travel and the environment.' *Mobility and Local-Global Connections*, Eastbourne.

Gössling, S., Peeters, P. M., Ceron, J. P., Dubois, G., Patterson, T. and Richardson, R. B. (2005) 'The eco-efficiency of tourism.' *Ecological Economics*, 54(4), 417–34.

Gössling, S., Peeters, P. and Scott, D. (2008) 'Consequences of climate policy for international tourist arrivals in developing countries.' *Third World Quarterly*, 29(5), 873–901.

Hamilton, J., Maddison, D. and Tol, R. (2005) 'Climate change and international tourism: a simulation study.' *Global Environmental Change*, 15(3), 253–66.

Helm, D. and Smale, R. (2007) *Too Good To Be True? The UK's climate change record.* Oxford: New College.

Hileman, J. I., Ortiz, D. S., Bartis, J. T., Wong, H. M., Donohoo, P. E., Weiss, M. A. and Waitz, I. A. (2009) *Near-Term Feasibility of Alternative Jet Fuels.* Santa Monica, Calif.: Rand.

International Air Transport Association (IATA) (2009) *Aviation and Climate Change: Pathway to carbon-neutral growth in 2020.* Switzerland: IATA.

Institut français de l'Environnement (IFEN) (2006) *NAMEA, un outil pour relier activités économiques et pressions environnementales.* Orléans, France: IFEN.

IMAGE-team (2006) *The IMAGE 2.2 Implementation of the SRES Scenarios. A comprehensive analysis of emissions, climate change and impacts in the 21st century.* CD-ROM 500110001 (former 481508018) Bilthoven, Netherlands: National Institute for Public Health and the Environment.

Intergovernmental Panel on Climate Change (IPCC) (1996) *Revised 1996 IPCC Guidelines for National Greenhouse Gas Inventories.* Geneva: IPCC.

IPCC (2000) *Special Report on Emission Scenarios.* Geneva: IPCC.

IPCC (2001) *Climate Change 2001: Synthesis report.* Cambridge: Cambridge University Press.

IPCC (2009) 'Chapter outline of the working group III contribution to the IPCC Fifth Assessment Report (AR5).' Geneva: IPCC Secretariat.

Lane, C., Harris, B. and Roberts, S. (2008) 'An analysis of the technical feasibility and potential cost of a personal carbon trading scheme.' London: Accenture and Centre for Sustainable Energy/DEFRA.

Lenglart, F., Lesieur, C. and Pasquier, J. L. (2010) *Les émissions de CO_2 du circuit économique en France.* Paris: Service de l'observation et des statistiques (SOeS), Commissariat général au développement durable.

Mayor, K. and Tol, R. S. J. (2010) 'Scenarios of carbon dioxide emissions from aviation.' *Global Environmental Change*, 20(1), 65–73.

Munasinghe, M. and Dasgupta, P. (2009) *Consumers, Business and Climate Change.* Manchester: University of Manchester Sustainable Consumption Institute.

Munksgaard, J. and Pedersen, K. (2001) 'CO_2 accounts for open economies: producer or consumer responsibility?' *Energy Policy*, 29, 327–34.

Pasquier, J. L. (2010) 'Les comptes physiques de l'environnement, une base pour de nouveaux indicateurs sur l'interface économie environnement. Le cas des émissions de CO2 de la France.' *La Revue du Service de l'observation et des statistiques (SOeS) du Commissariat général au développement durable (CGDD).*

Peeters, P. (2010) *Gestion de l'énergie transport aérien et tourisme en Méditerranée. Modélisation: méthodologie et sources de données.* Marseilles: TEC.

Peeters, P. M. and Dubois, G. (2010) 'Tourism travel under climate change mitigation constraints.' *Journal of Transport Geography*, 18, 447–57.

Pentelowe, L. and Scott, D. (2009) 'The implications of climate change mitigation policy and oil price volatility for tourism arrivals to the Caribbean Conference: "Travel and tourism in the age of climate change. Beyond numbers."' Paper for the 6th International Symposium on Tourism and Sustainability. Eastbourne: Centre for Tourism Policy Studies, University of Brighton.

Peters, G. P. and Hertwich, E. G. (2006) 'Pollution embodied in trade: the Norwegian case.' *Global Environmental Change*, (16), 379–87.

Scott, D., Peeters, P. and Gössling, S. (2010) 'Can tourism deliver its "aspirational" greenhouse gas emission reduction targets?' *Journal of Sustainable Tourism*, 18(3), 393–408.

Seetaram, N. (2010) 'Computing airfare elasticities or opening Pandora's box.' *Research in Transportation Economics*, 26(1), 27–36.

Starkey, R. and Anderson, K. (2005) 'Domestic tradable quotas: a policy instrument for reducing greenhouse gas emissions from energy use.' Tyndall Technical Report no. 39, Tyndall Centre.

Tol, R. S. J. (2007) 'The impact of a carbon tax on international tourism.' *Transportation Research Part D: Transport and Environment*, 12(2), 129–42.

United Nations (2003) *Handbook of National Accounting: Integrated environmental and economic accounting 2003*. United Nations, European Commission, International Monetary Fund, OECD and World Bank.

UN World Tourism Organization (UNWTO) (2004) *Tourism and Poverty Alleviation Recommendations for Action*. Madrid: UNWTO.

UNWTO (2009) *Discussion Paper on Climate Change Mitigation Measures for International Air Transport*. Madrid: UNWTO.

UNWTO, UN Environment Programme (UNEP) and World Meteorological Organization (WMO) (2007) 'Davos declaration: climate change and tourism: responding to global challenges.' *Second International Conference on Climate Change and Tourism*, 4. Davos, Switzerland.

UNWTO, UNEP and WMO (2008) *Climate Change and Tourism: Responding to global challenges*. Madrid: UNWTO.

Uyarra, M. C., Cote, I. M., Gill, J. A., Tinch, R. R. T., Viner, D. and Watkinson, A. R. (2005) 'Island-specific preferences of tourists for environmental features: implications of climate change for tourism-dependent states.' *Environmental Conservation*, 32(1), 11–19.

Veryard, D. (2009) *Study of International Visitor Flows and Greenhouse Gas Emissions for a Template to Examine the Impact on APEC Economies of Future Market-based Measures Applying to International Transport*. Canberra: GHD Meyrick.

Wilbanks, T. J., Romero Lankao, P., Bao, M., Berkhout, F., Cairncross, S., Ceron, J. P., Kapshe, M., Muir-Wood, R. and Zapata-Marti, R. (2007) 'Industry, settlement and society.' In Parry, M. L., O. F. C., Palutikof, J. P., van der Linden, P. J. and Hanson, C. E. (eds), *Climate Change 2007: Impacts, adaptation and vulnerability. Contribution of Working Group II to the Fourth Assessment Report of the Intergovernmental Panel on Climate Change*, 357–90. Cambridge: Cambridge University Press.

10

THE IMPORTANCE OF VISITOR PERCEPTIONS IN ESTIMATING HOW CLIMATE CHANGE WILL AFFECT FUTURE TOURIST FLOWS TO THE GREAT BARRIER REEF

Marine Ramis and Bruce Prideaux

A growing chorus of scientists (Hoegh-Guldberg, Mumby and Hooten 2007, IPCC 2007) are predicting the demise of coral reef systems as a direct consequence of climate change. In many tropical nations coral reefs are important tourism drawcards, and any decline in quality is likely to have serious implications for communities that benefit from this form of tourism activity. In Australia for example the Great Barrier Reef (GBR) is a major national icon that is estimated to generate upwards of A\$5.1 billion in direct and indirect tourism income each year (GBRMPA 2009). Given the importance of this asset there is an urgent need to investigate the extent of the impact that climate change is likely to have on the GBR, particularly its future ability to attract domestic and international tourists. The aim of the research reported in this chapter is to examine how tourists may respond to the impacts of climate change on the Great Barrier Reef in the future. Understanding of this nature provides important data for marine tourism operators who will need to adjust their marketing message as climate change begins to have an impact on the GBR, and for the Great Barrier Reef Marine Park Authority (GBRMPA), the authority that administers the GBR.

In a recent paper Prideaux, Coghlan and McNamara (2010: 187) observed that 'climate change will force a revision of the way we view the world, or in the language of Urry (1990), the way we gaze on the landscapes that constitute the tourist experience'. The way contemporary tourists gaze on and even consume the landscapes of our time is in part an outcome of what they are told by the media and marketers is good, bad and even ugly. Views and opinions change over time as new events occur, tastes change and new destinations are promoted. Thus what contemporary tourists regard as a desirable experience or destination may have been seen in a very different light by earlier generations of visitors. For example, mountains were once seen as forbidding isolated places inhabited by trolls, dragons and uncivilized mountain men (Bernbaum 1997), but today mountains are generally viewed as friendly inviting places, the location for adventure and a place to enjoy a vacation. Similar changes in outlook will continue into the future. Understanding the process that lies behind the shaping of visitor perceptions, how they change over time and how they are influenced by marketers and the media is an important first step in developing strategies that allow destinations under threat from forces such as climate change to revise and adapt their marketing message and continually renew and refresh their image over time.

The role and power of visitor perceptions was demonstrated by an experiment designed to measure visitors' views of the quality of a rainforest that had suffered severe damage in a cyclone event in northern Australia in 2006. Prideaux, Coghlan and Falco-Mammone (2007) tested visitor views of the cyclone-affected rainforest three months and fifteen months after the cyclone. Three months after the cyclone almost every person surveyed agreed that the rainforest looked seriously damaged, with many trees having lost most if not all large branches. Twelve months later tourists who had never previously visited the rainforest were asked to comment on the condition of the same forest. Most failed to observe any damage, which by that time was effectively camouflaged by new branches and regrowth of leaves. The damage was however still apparent to the trained observer. The point is that perceptions of what is good, bad and ugly are heavily influenced by marketers and the media. Positive images produce positive perceptions and negative images produce negative perceptions. Thus if visitors are not subjected to negative influences they are more inclined to have positive perceptions.

Some members of the scientific community have been very vocal in their views on how climate change will adversely affect the quality of the GBR (Hoegh-Guldberg et al. 2007), and as a consequence have generated strong negative media messages. Continued reporting of negative views is likely to have a significant impact on how tourists view the reef, and will influence their choice about whether they select the region or look for alternatives. Reef-dependent communities and operators are confronted with several choices in the manner in which they respond to adverse media and the reality that the reef will suffer from climate change. They might write the reef off and look for other opportunities, or develop strategies to respond to changes in the quality of the reef. If the latter course is adopted, strategies must emphasize positive rather than negative images and statements, but at the same time must be truthful. In responding to the reef's decline it is vital that destinations and operators consider that tomorrow's tourists and their expectations will be very different from today's tourists. As with the previously cited case of visitor response to climate-affected rainforests, visitors respond favourably to positive messages. Recent research into the health of all reefs indicates that the GBR remains one of the world's best-managed reef systems (GBRMPA 2009), and even as it undergoes change it will continue to offer visitors a world-best experience. If a positive message is given that the GBR remains the best reef in the world, visitors are more likely to be reassured that they will be able to participate in a quality experience. This proposition was tested in the research that is reported upon in this chapter.

Another issue related to climate change but largely ignored by tourism academics and many protected area managers is the assumption that sustainability of natural areas can be maintained if protective borders, in this case in the form of a park boundary, are erected and the quality of the ecosystem within the protected area border is maintained. This belief assumes that ecosystems are stable and that stability can be maintained over the long term. In reality ecosystems are rarely stable over the long term, and are generally in a constant state of flux, although on human timescales changes of this nature are usually barely noticeable (Prideaux 2010). Climate change has accelerated the rate of change and reduced the level of stability of many ecosystems including the GBR. For this reason pervious notions of sustainability based on long-term stability are no longer valid, and in the future the whole issue of sustainability will need to be revaluated and redefined.

GBR tourism

The Great Barrier Reef was inscribed on the UNSESCO World Heritage list in 1981 and is managed by the Great Barrier Reef Marine Park Authority (GRBMPA). The reef is one of Australia's best known attractions and is visited by 2.2 million tourists each year (GBRMPA 2009). About 770 tourism operators and 1700 tourism vessels are permitted to operate in and around the GBR, and offer a range of experiences including day trip diving, snorkelling and sightseeing tours, overnight diving trips, recreational fishing charters and visits by international cruise ships. An estimated 14.6 million recreational visits are made annually to the GBR for fishing, snorkelling, diving, sightseeing, adventure sport and sailing (GBRMPA 2009). Strict zoning and management by the GBRMPA of commercial activity including tourism operations and commercial and recreational fishing has minimized the impact of these activities. Management strategies used to protect the GBR include zoning plans, management plans, permits that define the type and extent of commercial activity, ongoing research into the reef ecosystem, water-quality strategies and codes of practice. Collectively these measures give the GBR a high level of protection from human abuse and overuse. However, despite a high level of protection the GBR will suffer as the effects of climate change increase in coming decades, forcing the tourism industry to adopt a range of adaptive strategies.

Literature review

There is a growing body of work on the possible impacts of climate change on the global tourism industry (Becken 2004, Becken and Hay 2007, Dubois and Ceron 2006, Gössling and Scott 2008, Gössling and Svensson 2006, Hall and Farge 2003, Hall and Higham 2005), but it is not the intent of this chapter to review this body of literature. Instead this chapter will briefly review the literature on climate-change issues specific to the GBR, and how changes of this nature might affect tourism activity. Coral reefs will be affected by a number of climate-change-generated forces including an increase in sea surface temperature, acidification, increased severity of tropical wind storms (hurricanes, cyclones and typhoons), rising sea levels and changes in the hydrological cycle that will affect terrestrial runoff into the ocean. The factors most likely to have the greatest impact on reef quality and long-term survival are temperature increase and acidification. Predicted increases in sea temperature pose a huge threat to the GBR because of its effect on coral health (IPCC 2007, Stern 2006). Increasing sea temperature causes coral bleaching, which occurs when heat-stressed corals expel the single-celled alga (zooxanthellae) with which they have formed a symbiotic relationship. The resulting loss of colour produces a bleached appearance. If heat stress continues, corals are unable to regain algae and die. A number of coral-bleaching events have occurred on the GBR, with the most severe occurring in 1998 when nearly half the reef was affected and 5 percent suffered long-term damage. If average global temperatures rise by more than 2 °C (IPCC 2007), bleaching is likely to be an annual event, with most reefs affected (GBRMPA 2009). Mortality of corals leads to a rapid decline in reef ecosystems as corals are replaced by algae. Coral-dependent fish will suffer the greatest decline in abundance, followed by high-order predators. This decline will eventually affect all trophic linkages, leading to a decline in abundance of marine mammals, turtles and other large fish (Munday et al. 2007).

Other impacts of an increase in temperature include the effect on marine turtles, which depend on sand temperature of between 25 and 33 °C during incubation of their eggs. If the air temperature reaches the upper end of this thermal band window, there will be a lower proportion of males hatching, which in the long term will alter the sex ratio of turtle species and affect the long-term viability of turtle populations (Hamann, Limpus and Read 2007).

Acidification is likely to have a major impact on coral health, and on a wider scale on the health of all ocean flora and fauna. Oceans absorb atmospheric carbon dioxide (CO_2), and in the last 200 years are estimated to have absorbed about half of the CO_2 released by human activity over that period. Carbon is either taken up by phytoplankton during photosynthesis and enters the food chain or is converted into carbonic acid (Lough 2007). The absorption of CO_2 and its conversion into carbonic acid have resulted in a probable decrease in oceanic pH of 0.1. As a consequence of this process oceans are becoming more acidic (GBRMPA 2009). Ocean acidification reduces the concentration of carbonate ions and increases the concentration of bicarbonate ions, affecting the ability of marine organisms such as coral and molluscs to develop skeletons or shells. Recent research (GBRMPA 2009, Wei et al. 2009) indicates that ocean acidification has already affected one coral species, *Porites* spp, which has suffered a decline in calcification of up to 14.2 percent since 1900. Continuing emissions of CO_2 are projected to decrease oceanic pH by 0.4 to 0.5 units by 2100 (from pH 8.2 to about pH 7.8). This level of ocean acidity not been experienced for several hundred thousand of years (Lough 2007), and will have long-term adverse impacts on all reef ecosystems.

While a great deal is known about the impact of climate change on reef ecosystems, little is known about how either tourists or members of local communities will be affected by the decline of the GBR. If tourists become concerned to the extent that they seek alternative destinations, local tourism-dependent communities will suffer significant stress as tourism-generated income falls, producing large-scale unemployment. A recent paper (Prideaux et al. 2010) examined how climate change may affect visitation to the wet tropics rainforests of North Queensland, the region's second most significant tourism icon after the GBR. The paper also demonstrated how scientific and social science research can be integrated to develop a model that may be used to ascertain the impact of climate change on tourism activity including reefs. The Climate Change Impact Model (see Figure 10.1) identified the current boundaries between science and social science research, and suggested how each can assist the other. The underlying hypothesis of the model is that climate change will generate ecosystem changes that will in turn impact on the patterns of human settlement, the health of local economies and the opportunities available for tourism in climate-modified landscapes.

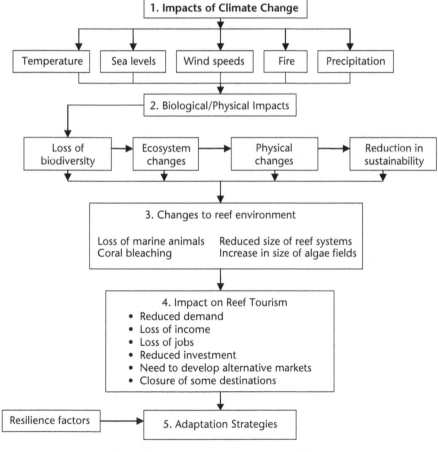

FIGURE 10.1 Climate change impact model applied to the GBR

Adapted from Prideaux, Coghlan and McNamara (2010).

Stage 1 of the model identifies temperature, sea levels, wind speeds, fire and precipitation as the major climate-change elements that will collectively produce a range of biological/physical impacts, identified in stage 2 as loss of biodiversity, ecosystem changes, physical changes and changes in sustainability. These impacts produce changes to landscapes (marine in this case) and species richness and abundance. The changes identified in stage 3 will have an impact on the tourism potential of an ecosystem, in this case the GBR, and are identified in stage 4. Changes may be either negative or positive. In the case of the GBR almost all results will be negative for the tourism industry. To combat negative impacts the tourism industry will need to adopt adaptive strategies as illustrated in stage 5.

As argued earlier in this chapter, positive perceptions of reef quality are essential for the continued welfare of GBR-dependent tourism destinations. The manner in which the impacts identified in stage 3 are presented to prospective visitors to the region will therefore be critical. If the strongest voice is that of the group highlighting negative impacts there is a strong possibility that tourists will substitute other destinations, believing that the GBR might be degraded to the extent that they would waste their time visiting it. If on the other hand a positive message is generated that the GBR remains the best reef in the world despite the effects of climate change, there is a strong chance that visitor interest will be able to be maintained for many years.

Methodology

The aim of this research was to examine how tourists may respond to the impacts of climate change on the Great Barrier Reef in the future. The specific objectives were to identify:

- factors that constitute a good reef experience
- the extent to which a decline in coral quality will affect overall visitor satisfaction in the future.

To assess the impact of climate change on visitor satisfaction, surveys were undertaken on three reefs, two of which had good-quality hard coral reef cover (Paradise Reef and Moore Reef) and one which a had a low level of hard coral cover (Michaelmas Cay). A four-page self-completed survey instrument which took approximate fifteen minutes to complete was used to gather a range of data on topics that included visitor demographics, perceptions of the reef and satisfaction with their reef trip. Three versions of the survey were used, one for Michaelmas Cay, a second that asked visitors to compare Paradise Reef and Michaelmas Cay, and a third for visitors to Moore Reef. The basic questions asked in each survey were identical. A convenience sampling method was used. The survey instrument was piloted and several adjustments were made based on feedback. The surveys were administered aboard two reef tour boats. On the boat that visited Michaelmas

Cay and Paradise Reef two survey periods were organized every day, the first for respondents who had visited Michaelmas Cay and the second for respondents who had visited both Michaelmas Cay and Paradise reefs. On the second boat that only visited Moore Reef, surveys were administered on the return voyage to Cairns. A total of 459 surveys were collected, 203 from respondents at Michaelmas Cay morning, 198 from respondents who had visited Michaelmas Cay and Paradise Reef, and 48 from respondents who had visited Moore Reef.

A number of limitations were encountered and should be considered before generalizing the results. First, the survey was conducted at the beginning of the peak tourism season and results may not reflect variations in seasonality over a twelve-month period. Weather factors should also be considered as a limitation because poor weather may generate negative views of the reef experience. The distribution of the survey instrument in English only should also be considered a limitation as the views of non-English speakers were not recorded. Finally, the survey was distributed by only two reef tour boat operators, thus the results may not reflect the views of all visitor segments visiting the GBR.

Study sites

Reef images used in marketing of the destination usually emphasise hard corals, vivant colours, clear water and an abundance of fish. The diversity of colour and coral shapes are central to this image. As the impact of climate change intensifies the reef will gradually lose its hard corals and the colours and shapes that currently define a good-quality reef experience. Two reefs that reflect the current images of a healthy reef were selected as the benchmark against which to measure perceptions of reef quality. Paradise Reef was selected because it currently conforms to the popular image of a healthy reef. One tour operator describes Paradise Reef as 'a hard coral reef where fractured coral form a ribbon of small reefs. With depths of up to 25 meters along the edge, water clarity is good and the area is host to many exciting fish species' (Passion of Paradise 2010). Moore Reef also conforms to current images of the GBR, and is described by a reef tour operator as 'The Marine World site has been handpicked for its superior water clarity, biological diversity and overall quality of marine life. It is without doubt one of the most beautiful reef locations available anywhere in Australia and perfect for snorkelers' (Reef Magic 2010).

One of the impacts of climate change will be a reduction in the extent of hard coral cover and a loss of colour. Michaelmas Cay matches this description, and is not able to offer a comparable level of experience to the image of the Great Barrier Reef that is commonly used in marketing. Michaelmas Cay can therefore be regarded as a proxy for a future where the amount of hard coral has been reduced by climate change. The cay does however offer opportunities to view migratory birds and a large variety of fish and marine animal life. The selection of reefs for this study was made on advice from reef tour operators and the Association of Marine Park Tour Operators (AMPTO).

Results

Just under a third of respondents (30 percent) were Australians. The second largest group of respondents were from the United Kingdom and Ireland (23 percent), followed by Europe excluding the UK and Ireland (20 percent), North America (17 percent), New Zealand (5 percent) and Asia (3 percent). These results cannot be generalized to all GBR visitors, particularly the result for the Asian market, as many Asian groups use other tour boat operators to visit the reef.

Almost three-quarters (74 percent) of the respondents were less than 30 years old, reflecting the market share targeted by the operators of the tour boats where the surveys were collected. Most respondents were travelling with friends (34 percent) or as couples (20 percent) rather than alone (14 percent). Students (43 percent) comprised the largest group of respondents, followed by professionals (25 percent) and office workers (7 percent). The most popular activities undertaken by respondents were snorkelling (94 percent), swimming (44 percent), an introductory dive (27 percent) and glass-bottomed boat viewing (19 percent).

Respondents were asked about their previous reef experiences and how these compared with the reefs they visited on the day that they were surveyed (see Figure 10.2). Just over a quarter (26 percent) of respondents had previously visited the Great Barrier Reef, while 11 percent had previously visited Caribbean reefs and 11 percent had previously visited reefs in South East Asia. A small number of respondents had visited other reefs such as Hawaii (7 percent), the South Pacific (7 percent), the Indian Ocean (4 percent) and the Red Sea (4 percent). Of the ninety respondents who had previously visited the GBR, 60 percent thought that the quality of the reef they saw during the day they were surveyed was the same as the reef on the GBR they have previously visited. Nearly half (48 percent) of the respondents who have been to Caribbean (n=44) thought that the GBR was better, 21 percent thought it was the same and 31 percent thought that the Caribbean was better.

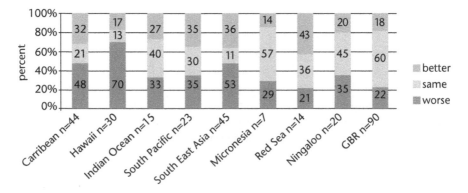

FIGURE 10.2 Respondents' comparison between the GBR and previously visited reefs

Comparison of the three GBR reefs

Visitors were asked to rate their satisfaction with a range of reef activities and attractions on a 1 to 5 Likert scale (where 1 was not at all satisfied and 5 was very satisfied). A 'not seen' option was also available.

Table 10.1 presents the parameters analysed in the following discussion and how they were grouped. For example the parameter labelled 'coral represents' is the mean calculated from visitors' satisfaction of coral cover, colour and diversity. It should be noted that respondents who answered 'not seen' or did not answer were not included in the calculation of the mean.

Comparison of Michaelmas Cay and Paradise Reef results

Figure 10.3 shows the comparison between respondents (203) who were surveyed after visiting Michaelmas Cay in the morning and respondents (189) surveyed in the afternoon after visiting both Michaelmas Cay and Paradise Reef. A Mann Whitney U test was used to compare these non-parametric data. The means for the

TABLE 10.1 Analysed parameters

Parameters	Means	Means
Coral cover	Coral	Reef total
Coral colour		
Coral diversity		
Reef fish number	Reef fish	
Reef fish diversity		
Reef fish size		
Open water fish number	Open water fish	
Open water fish diversity		
Open water fish size		
Shark		
Turtle		
Ray		
Giant clam		
Starfish		
Algae		

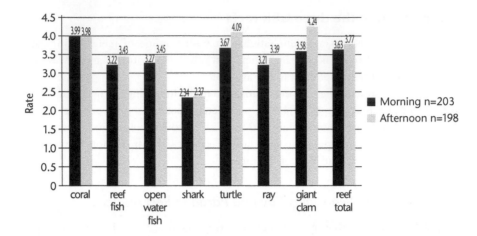

FIGURE 10.3 Comparison of satisfaction with Michaelmas Cay in the morning and afternoon surveys

'reef total' (3.63 for Michaelmas Cay and 3.77 for Michaelmas Cay and Paradise Reef) are not significantly different (p=0.08>0.05). Respondents who visited both sites enjoyed Michaelmas Cay as much as respondents who at the time of the morning survey had only visited Michaelmas Cay. One interesting result was that visiting Paradise Reef after first visiting Michaelmas Cay did not impact on Michaelmas Cay visitors' level of satisfaction in the afternoon survey. The satisfaction rates for the number of turtles and giant clams were the only factors that were significantly different. The results indicate that when visitors are told they are going to great sites, they expect them to be great even if they are different from the image of the GRB that appears in marketing material.

Michaelmas Cay/Paradise Reef/Moore Reef

Figure 10.4 shows comparisons of results from all three reef surveys: 198 respondents for Paradise Reef (end of the day), 203 respondents for Michaelmas Cay (morning), and 47 respondents for Moore Reef (end of the day). A Mann Whitney U test (using SPSS v.18) was conducted to compare all the parameters between these reefs.

Coral

There was no significant difference for all coral parameters between Michaelmas Cay and Moore Reef and between Paradise Reef and Moore Reef (p>0.05). All the parameters (coral cover, colour, diversity) were significantly different between Paradise Reef and Michaelmas Cay. The mean for coral on Paradise Reef was 4.20 whereas the mean for Michaelmas Cay was 3.98. Respondents had a preference for the coral on Paradise Reef, although the difference was small.

Reef fish

No significant difference between Paradise Reef and Moore Reef were observed in relation to reef fish parameters. Michaelmas Cay and Moore Reef are significantly different for reef fish number (MR=4.48, MC=4.13) and reef fish mean (MR=4.30, MC=3.98). Respondents gave a slightly higher mean for the fish at Moore Reef than for Paradise Reef. Michaelmas Cay and Paradise Reef differed significantly for all the parameters (reef fish number, diversity, size and mean). Respondents rated reef fish as 3.98 for Michaelmas Cay and 4.29 for Paradise Reef.

Open water fish

There was no significant difference for all parameters between Michaelmas Cay and Moore Reef and between Paradise Reef and Moore Reef. Once again, all the parameters were significantly different between Michaelmas Cay and Paradise Reef, with respondents preferring open water fish in Paradise Reef (Michaelmas Cay 3.45 and Paradise Reef 3.72). However, these results need to be taken with care because the term 'open water fish' appeared to be confusing to some respondents.

Sharks

Moore Reef had the highest mean of all reefs for sharks (3.35), and was significantly higher than Michaelmas Cay (2.37) and Paradise Reef (2.03). However, there is no significant difference between Michaelmas Cay and Paradise Reef.

Turtles

Michaelmas Cay was the best reef for turtle seeing, with a mean of 4.09 compared with 3.25 for Paradise Reef and 2.33 for Moore Reef. There were also significantly different results between Moore Reef and Paradise Reef.

Rays

Michaelmas Cay scored significantly better for rays (3.39) than Paradise Reef (2.65) and Moore Reef (2.50). However, the rates between Moore Reef and Paradise Reef were not significantly different.

Giant clams

Respondents preferred Michaelmas Cay for its giant clams (4.24) over Paradise Reef (3.77) and Moore Reef (3.67) (significantly different). However the difference between these two last reefs was not significant.

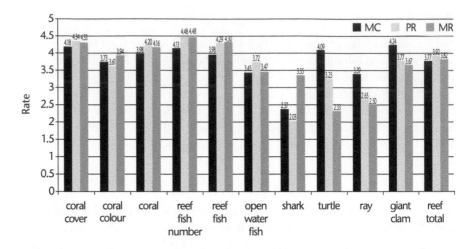

FIGURE 10.4 Comparison between three reefs

Starfish and algae

There was no significant difference between the three reefs for these parameters.

Reef total

Only the means of Paradise Reef (3.92) and Michaelmas Cay (3.77) are significantly different; other comparisons are not.

The comparison of reefs leads to a number of interesting results. First, results for Paradise reef and Moore Reef were fairly similar, with only the results for sharks and turtles being significantly different. Satisfaction with coral and fish was slightly higher for Paradise Reef and Moore Reef than for Michaelmas Cay. Results also indicate that satisfaction for viewing turtles, sharks, rays and giant clams was rated significantly better for Michaelmas Cay and Moore Reef (shark) than for Paradise Reef. The differences are higher than the result for just coral and fish. This result suggests that as long as coral is present in addition to marine animals and fish, visitors are satisfied, even if the coral quality is not optimal. Marine animals appear to act as a compensator for the lack of colour or hard coral, and lead to almost the same global rate at the end.

Satisfaction

Respondents to the afternoon survey on the boat that visits Michaelmas Cay and Paradise Reef were asked which reef they preferred and why. Just over half (55 percent) preferred Paradise Reef and 45 percent preferred Michaelmas Cay. Respondents who preferred Michaelmas Cay cited marine animals, clear calm water condition and activities (glass-bottomed boat, first introductory dive) as the factors that influenced their selection over Paradise Cay. Respondents who

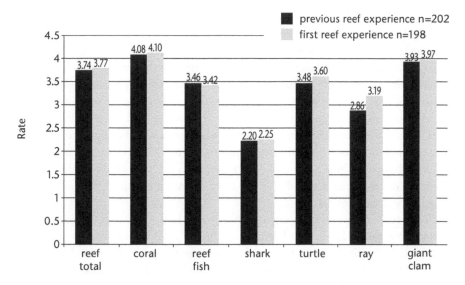

FIGURE 10.5 Comparison between respondents with previous reef experience and first-time reef visitors

preferred Paradise Reef cited fish (number and colour), coral cover and colour as their reason for selecting the reef. These results leads to the conclusion that a reef that does not conform to the ideal of what a good reef should be like may still be found attractive providing other forms of marine life such as fish are present.

Two questions were included about aspects of satisfaction. The first question looked at satisfaction with various elements of the reef experience, and used a 1 to 5 Likert scale where 1 was low and 5 was high. The second question asked respondents to give an overall satisfaction rating on their trip, using a 1 to 10 Likert scale where 10 represented the highest level of satisfaction.

Figure 10.5 shows the comparison of satisfaction between respondents who had previously visited a coral reef before this trip and respondents for whom this trip was their first to a coral reef. The analysis of data did not reveal any significant difference in reef satisfaction between the two groups. This result suggests that visitors' enjoyment of the GBR is not significantly affected by previous visits to coral reefs. Overall satisfaction is quite high, with a mean of 8.1; respondents mainly enjoy their trip to the GBR a lot.

Discussion and conclusion

There is growing evidence that climate change will have a serious impact on many ecosystems including coral reef systems. There is evidence that reefs have begun to suffer the effects of climate change (Hoegh-Guldberg et al. 2007), but to date this has not been to the extent that reefs have lost their appeal to visitors. The actual rate of decline will depend on actions taken by the world community to combat the factors that have caused climate change (IPPC 2007). Most of the damage currently suffered by reefs has been from poor management and abuse by human users. However as sea temperatures increase, bleaching events will become more frequent, and in the long term if mitigation strategies fail to slow global warming, the GBR and other coral reefs will continue to deteriorate, leading to reduction of biodiversity and even the extinction of species. Reefs will also be adversely affected by acidification. Impacts of this nature have serious implications for reef-dependent tourism destinations. While this situation is serious it should not be assumed that reef systems are necessarily doomed, nor should it be assumed that just because reef systems will suffer some form of decline in coming decades, tourism interest in visiting these magnificent places will disappear. For the perspective of the tourism industry the major concern should be how to maintain tourist interest in reefs during the process of decline.

The results of this research indicate that at least in the first stages of reef decline when the extent of hard corals begins to decline, visitors are not likely to be overly concerned. Results indicate that while respondents are sensitive to the level of coral cover, they show greater sensitivity to the availability of marine animals. For example in Figure 10.3 it is apparent that Paradise Reef was preferred by a small majority of people based on the reef's coral cover. Michaelmas Cay was less popular primarily because it had less coral. In both reefs and at Moore Reef, visitors responded positively to the presence of marine animals. In this study, the 'climate-change-impacted' reef was also the best reef for viewing marine animals, leading to its popularity. When the mean rates for the three reefs were calculated by coral, fish and marine animals, the differences between the 'control group' reef and 'climate-change-impacted' reef were very small. These results suggest that as long as fish and marine animals are present, visitors are likely to have reasonable levels of satisfaction. One impact of climate change will be the replacement of corals with algae, and parallel to this process a replacement of coral-feeding fish with algae-feeding fish, at least in the short term.

Visitor satisfaction is in part based on meeting pre-trip expectations. Results indicate that the mean for satisfaction was 8.1, with 55 percent of visitors ranking this trip as a 5 on the five-point Likert scale. To avoid disappointment in the future it will be necessary to ensure that the image of the reef projected by marketers accurately reflects the actual condition of the GBR. As the majority of future tourists are likely to have no or little previous reef experience they are likely to be heavily influenced by the messages used in destination marketing and received from the media. Thus, if the management of the GBR is directed to ensuring that it remains the best-managed reef in the world, despite the impacts of climate change, and the tourism industry continues to present the GBR as the best-managed reef in the world, visitors will be inclined to believe this message and be satisfied by the experience.

From the tourism industry perspective there is an ongoing and urgent need for the impacts of climate change identified in stage 3 of the Climate Change Impact Model (Figure 10.1) to be used as a baseline for developing responses to climate change. If mitigation efforts fail to stabilize global temperature increases at 2 °C, many of the negative outcomes identified in stage 4 will occur, but in the interim, strategies to present the reef in a positive rather than negative light will almost certainly encourage tourists to visit the reef even if the quality of the experience in the future is different from that of today. The adaptation strategies that should be considered include continually adapting the image of the GBR to always truthfully reflect its current state, maintain management at a level that ensures that the GBR is the best-managed reef system in the world, and promote strategies that encourage fish and marine animals to live in and around the GBR.

The findings of this chapter also highlight the need to further explore the nexus between sustainability and climate change. The assumption that protected area boundaries can be erected to provide long-term stability is not defendable when climate change begins to impact on ecosystems, causing impacts such as local extinction and in-migration and out- migration of species. Climate change will have a significant impact on sustainability, and this will need to be recognized by protected area managers as well as the tourism industry which relies on the quality of protected ecosystems for its viability.

Acknowledgements

This research would not have been possible without the assistance of Col McKenzie of the Association of Marine Tour Operators and Alan Wallish, proprietor of Passions of Paradise, a marine tour boat that operators out of Cairns Australia. Our thanks to AMPTO and Passions of Paradise.

References

Becken, S. (2004) 'How tourists and tourism experts perceive climate change and forest carbon sinks', *Journal of Sustainable Tourism*, vol. 12, pp. 332–345.
Becken, S. and Hay, J. (2007) *Tourism and Climate Change: risks and opportunities*. Channel View Publications, Bristol.
Bernbaum, E. (1997) *Sacred Mountains of the World*, University of California Press, London.
Cabrini, L. (2009) 'From Davos to Copenhagen and beyond: advancing tourism's response to climate change', UN World Tourism Organization (UNWTO) background paper.
Dubois, G. and Ceron, J.-P. (2006) 'Tourism and climate change: proposals for a research agenda,' *Journal of Sustainable Tourism*, vol. 14, no. 4, pp. 399–415.
Gössling, S. and Scott, D. (2008) 'Climate change and tourism: exploring destination vulnerability', *Tourism Review International*, vol. 12, pp. 1–3.
Gössling, S. and Svensson, P. (2006) 'Tourist perceptions of climate change: a study of international tourists in Zanzibar', *Current Issues in Tourism*, vol. 9, no. 4–5, pp. 419–35.
Great Barrier Reef Marine Park Authority (GBRMPA) (2009) *Outlook Report 2009*, Townsville, GBRMPA.
Hall, M. and Farge, D. (2003) 'Modeled climate-induced glacial change in Glacier National Park, 1850–2100. *Biological Science*, vol. 53, pp. 131–40.
Hall, M. and Higham, J. (2005) *Tourism, Recreation and Climate Change*. Channel View, Bristol.
Hamann, M., Limpus, C. and Read, M. (2007) 'Vulnerability of marine reptiles in the Great Barrier Reef to climate change'. In Johnson, J. E. and Marshall, P. A. (eds), *Climate*

Change and the Great Barrier Reef, Great Barrier Reef Marine Park Authority and Australian Greenhouse Office, Australia, pp. 465–96.

Hoegh-Guldberg, O., Mumby, P. and Hooten, A. (2007) 'Coral reefs under rapid climate change and ocean acidification', *Science,* vol. 318, no. 1737, pp. 1757–1742, DOI:10.1126/science.115209.

Intergovernmental Panel on Climate Change (IPCC) (2007) 'Summary for policy makers', in Solomon, S., Qin, M., Manning, Z. Chen, M., Marquia, K., Averyt, M., Tignor, M. and Miller, H. (eds), *Climate Change 2007: The physical science basis. Contribution of Working Group 1 to the Fourth Assessment Report of the Intergovernmental Panel on Climate Change.* Cambridge University Press, Cambridge and New York.

Lough, J. (2007) 'Climate and climate change on the Great Barrier Reef', In Johnson, J. E. and Marshall, P. A. (eds), *Climate Change and the Great Barrier Reef,* Great Barrier Reef Marine Park Authority and Australian Greenhouse Office, Australia, pp.15–50.

McKinnon, A. D., Richardson, A. J., Burford, M. A. and Furnas, M. J. (2007) 'Vulnerability of Great Barrier Reef plankton to climate change'. In Johnson, J. E. and Marshall, P. A. (eds), *Climate Change and the Great Barrier Reef,* Great Barrier Reef Marine Park Authority and Australian Greenhouse Office, Australia, pp. 121–52.

Munday, P., Jones, G., Sheaves, M and Willliams, A. (2007) 'Vulnerability of fishes of the Great Barrier Reef to climate change'. In Johnson, J. E. and Marshall, P. A. (eds), *Climate Change and the Great Barrier Reef,* Great Barrier Reef Marine Park Authority and Australian Greenhouse Office, Australia, pp. 357–92.

Passion of Paradise, (2010) 'Day trip boat Passion of Paradise.' Available at: www.passions.com.au/paradise.php (accessed 26 August 2010).

Prideaux, B. (2010) *Sustainability in a Period of Climate Change,* University of Dar es Salaam, August.

Prideaux, B., Coghlan, A. and Falco-Mammone, F. (2007) 'Post crisis recovery: the case of after Cyclone Larry', *Journal of Tourism and Travel Marketing,* vol. 23, no. 2/3/4, pp. 163–74.

Prideaux, B., Coghlan, A. and McNamara, K. E. (2010) 'Assessing the impacts of climate change on mountain tourism destination using the climate change impact model', *Tourism Recreation Research,* vol. 35, pp. 187–200.

Reef Magic (2010) 'Snorkelling in marine world.' Available at: www.reefmagiccruises.com/your-day/snorkeling/ (accessed 1 September 2010).

Stern (2006) ref to follow.

Wachenfeld, D., Johnson, J., Skeat, A., Kenchington, R., Marshall, P. and Innes, J. (2007) 'Introduction to the Great Barrier Reef and climate change', in Johnson, J. E. and Marshall, P. A. (eds), *Climate Change and the Great Barrier Reef,* Great Barrier Reef Marine Park Authority and Australian Greenhouse Office, Australia, pp. 1–14.

Wei, G., McCulloch, M., Mortimer, G., Deng, W. and Xie, L. (2009) 'Evidence for ocean acidification in the Great Barrier Reef of Australia', *Geochimica et Cosmochimica Acta,* vol. 73, no. 8, pp. 2332–46.

11

TOURISM ADAPTATION TO CLIMATE CHANGE IN THE SOUTH PACIFIC

Min Jiang, Terry DeLacy, Louise Munk Klint and Emma Wong

Introduction

Tourism in small island developing states (SIDS), including those in the South Pacific, is crucial to the social and economic development of their communities. It is the largest export sector, a key contributor of gross domestic product (GDP), and a major employer for most SIDS in the Pacific (South Pacific Tourism Organization – SPTO 2007). With its potential to lift people out of poverty through the employment and entrepreneurial opportunities it provides, the tourism sector also embraces, and has the potential to make a substantial contribution to, the achievement of the United Nations' Millennium Development Goals (MDGs) (UNWTO, UNEP and WMO 2008). At the same time the tourism sector is highly vulnerable to climate change impacts (UNWTO 2005). As a climate-dependent industry, tourism is highly sensitive to climate change as the physical and ecological attributes of destinations are altered, compromising the levels of enjoyment, safety and comfort of tourists (Becken and Hay 2007), and consequently influencing the levels and patterns of travel.

Climate change is arguably the most important long-term threat to Pacific island tourism. SIDS in the Pacific are highly vulnerable to sea level rise and increased storm intensity owing partly to their small land masses surrounded by ocean, and their location in regions prone to natural disasters (SPREP 2008). While climate change affects all people globally in different countries, Pacific people are on the front line as the catastrophe is currently unfolding for them, slowing progress towards MDGs and deepening inequalities within and across countries (UNDP 2007).

In order to assist the Pacific island tourism sector to adapt to climate change impacts, a research project, funded by Australia's International Development Agency (AusAID) as one of its annual Australian International Development Research Awards (ADRA), Pacific Tourism-Climate Adaptation Project

(PT-CAP), seeks to develop a vulnerability/resilience framework suitable for the tourism sector in the Pacific. The project will aid in developing an understanding of how tourism-related policies in place contribute to the resilience of Pacific island tourism to climate change, and based on this, make recommendations on tourism adaptation policies and strategies in Pacific SIDS.

This chapter discusses the policy analysis of the PT-CAP research, which aims to examine the conduciveness of policies in six Pacific SIDS (Fiji Islands, Samoa, Vanuatu, Papua New Guinea (PNG), Solomon Islands and Tonga) for the tourism sector to adapt to climate change. This research activity enables a comprehensive understanding of the existing policy environment in the Pacific SIDS, identifies adaptation issues that still remain as policy gaps, and helps assess the vulnerability of destinations to climate change impacts. The knowledge obtained from the research will inform the future directions of climate change adaptation policies and strategies for the tourism sector in the Pacific region.

Following the introduction, the second section describes Pacific island tourism, its importance to human and social development of the communities in the region, and the challenges that confront it through climate change. The third section reviews the policy analysis frameworks and approaches that have been applied in the PT-CAP research. In section four, research findings are presented including an overview of key regional climate change and tourism related policies and policy environments in the six Pacific destinations. The chapter concludes with implications identified in the policy analysis and recommendations on how Pacific policies can further develop to assist the tourism sector adapt to climate change.

Pacific tourism and climate change

Tourism in the Pacific

Tourism is a major economic sector in the Pacific. It is the largest export sector for most Pacific SIDS and offers great opportunity for economic growth, employment and sustainable development (DeLacy 2008). While a decade ago tourism in the region was dominated by Fiji and the two French territories, Tahiti and New Caledonia, the sector is now truly widespread in its economic impact, and has led growth in most Pacific Island countries (PICs) (Everitt 2009). Tourism is a main contributor to GDP (Becken and Hay 2007) and is the fastest-growing sector in the Pacific (Crocombe 2008). In 2005 for instance, tourism exports as a percentage of GDP accounted for approximately 15–20 percent in Samoa, 20–25 percent in Fiji, 25–30 percent in Vanuatu, 50 percent in the Cook Islands and 65–70 percent in Palau (AusAID 2009, Harrison 2010). Despite the global economic downturn, tourists to the South Pacific continued to grow at about 3–4 percent in 2007 and 2008. Some destinations in the region were in double-digit growth in 2008, such as the Cook Islands, Vanuatu, Samoa, Solomon Islands and PNG (Everitt 2009).

As a major economic sector in the Pacific, tourism is important in achieving the MDGs for Pacific communities (UNDP 2006). In Pacific SIDS the sector is a major employer, providing 31 percent of total employment in Fiji and 42.4 percent in Vanuatu (ESCAP 2008). Two-thirds of tourism expenditure stays in the country, and these tourism export receipts benefit the poor due to the sector's labour intensity, use of low-skilled workers and the opportunities for small and informal business (AusAID 2009). Many governments in the Pacific have identified the importance of the tourism sector to alleviate poverty and achieve the MDGs (Jiang, DeLacy and Noakes 2009).

Climate change impacts on Pacific tourism

Pacific small island states are highly vulnerable to climate change. Phenomena consistent with the adverse consequences of climate change on natural and human systems for small island states anticipated by the Intergovernmental Panel on Climate Change (IPCC) 2007 climate change assessment report are already an unfortunate reality for Pacific Islanders (SPREP 2008). These impacts include inundation of low-lying areas, extensive coastal erosion, coral bleaching, salinization of groundwater, persistent alternation of regional weather patterns, decreased productivity in fisheries and agriculture, and increases in the distribution and frequency of mosquito-borne disease. The potential magnitude of the climate change impacts threatens the achievement of sustainable development and MDGs and the very existence of some PICs (SPREP 2008). An Australian Commonwealth Scientific and Industrial Research Organization (CSIRO) study projects the following impacts of climate change in the Pacific region (Preston et al. 2006):

- Temperature increase of 0.5–2 °C by 2030 and 1–7 °C by 2070.
- Increased rainfall during summer monsoon season in decades ahead (although some uncertainty related to the regional distribution of this).
- Regional sea variability will occur, but on a global scale the following sea level rises have been predicted: 3–16 cm by 2030 and 7–50 cm by 207.
- More intense tropical cyclones.
- Changes to the El Niño-Southern Oscillation (ENSO), a coupled ocean–atmosphere phenomenon and an important mode of climate variability (IPCC 2007).

With close connections to the environment and climate itself, tourism is highly sensitive to climate-change risks, something in which it is similar to agriculture, insurance, energy and transportation (IPCC 2007, Simpson et al. 2008). Pacific tourism will continue to face challenges due to the specific characteristics of SIDS and their vulnerability to climate change impacts (Sem and Moore 2009). Based on the climate change projections mentioned earlier, Pacific tourism is likely to be affected in the following ways:

- Infrastructure – With the majority of the Pacific islands' infrastructure being coastal-based, Pacific tourism will be extremely vulnerable to sea level rise and more intense tropical cyclones (ESCAP 2000, Pelling and Uitto 2002).
- Tourist destination values and attractiveness – Coastal deterioration in the form of beach erosion and coral bleaching caused by climate change will expectedly cause a decrease in tourism destination values (NIWA Research 2007).
- Marine environments – Coral reefs and mangroves play a significant role as a resource in Pacific island communities (MacLellan et al. 2009). Climate change is already putting, and will continue to put a lot of stress on coral and mangrove environments (Garrod and Gössling 2008, MacLellan et al. 2009). This will impact on dive tourism conditions (Garrod and Gössling 2008). It will also reduce an important barrier to tsunami waves and storm surges (UNEP-WCMC 2006).
- Tourism flows and demands – The Pacific islands are remote, requiring international visitors to travel large distances to reach them (Weaver and Oppermann 2000). Existing and prospective climate change mitigation policies which increase the cost of long-haul travel will reduce Pacific island destinations' competitiveness, and green ethical impacts on consumers may also effect long-haul air travel differentially (DeLacy and Lipman 2010).

Pacific tourism suffers from a range of specific difficulties, including isolation from major markets, small populations, inadequate transportation links, lack of local appropriate skills and inadequate amounts of local capital, which lead to a lower resistance to external shocks (Scheyvens and Momsen 2008). Concerted efforts are required to strengthen the resilience of the tourism sector against the various challenges and risks resulting from climate change.

Policy analysis frameworks and approaches

One aim of PT-CAP was to undertake a policy analysis to examine the conduciveness of the policy environment in six PICs (Fiji, PNG, Samoa, Solomon Islands, Tonga and Vanuatu) for the South Pacific island tourism sector to adapt to climate change.

Key objectives of the policy analysis

The key objectives of the policy analysis were to:

- create an inventory of policies pertinent to Pacific tourism climate adaptation
- examine the policy-making environment that provides the context for future policy recommendations
- examine the policy-making mechanisms that would inform how future policy recommendations can be implemented

- identify policy gaps – adaptation issues that are yet to be addressed – by studying how existing policies contribute to (or hinder) the climate change adaptation of the tourism sector
- provide input into the evaluation of the adaptive capacity of the tourism sector.

Types of policy or policy area

The definition of a policy applied in this policy analysis refers to a course of action, inaction, decisions and non-decisions of public authorities to address a given problem, interrelated sets of problems, concerns or opportunities (Hall and Jenkins 1995). The types of policy or policy area that were analysed included climate change, environment, tourism development and risk and disaster management policies at supranational, national, regional or local levels. In terms of timelines of policies, the analysis included policies that are currently in effect, policies that are being conceptualized or formulated, and policies that are no longer in effect but have significant impact on current practice.

Frameworks

The research began with the construction of a policy analysis framework (Table 11.1) which sets out in detail the type of data required to create an inventory of policies and to examine the policy environment and mechanisms.

The framework has eight key components. Components 1 to 3 – name, purpose and geographical scope of policy – prompt for basic information about the policy. Policies that were wholly or partly formulated with the intention to address climate change are categorized as explicit policies. Usually, the term 'climate change' would be mentioned in the title and/or certain components of the policies. Policies that were formulated with the intention to address issues other than climate change, but have components that are pertinent to climate change, are categorized as implicit policies.

Components 4 to 6 are stages in the policy-making process – conceptualization, decision, and implementation and coordination. For each stage, details such as time period, trigger and agencies involved (items in the left column) are identified. Such information is crucial to the understanding of the policy-making environment and mechanisms of the destination in question, which in turn informs future policy recommendation.

Finally, Component 7, which records the outcome of the policy, and Component 8, which asks about implications for climate change adaptation for the tourism sector, help identify how existing policies contribute to adaptation and issues yet to be addressed. The PT-CAP policy analysis looked at five types of climate change adaptation that are relevant to the tourism sector, as identified by Scott, De Freitas and Matzarakis (2008):

TABLE 11.1 A snapshot of the policy analysis framework

Date:	Time:	Venue:
Interviewee's name:	Designation:	Organization:

1. Name of policy (if any)/policy area

2. Purpose of the policy: on paper and in reality (e.g. to plan, regulate, control...?)

3. Geographical scope (supranational, national, or local?)

4. Conceptualization

5. Decision

6. Implementation & Coordination

a) Time period

b) If it is a climate change specific policy, which climate scenario projection was the policy based on?

c) Trigger (e.g. factors in the macro environment: decision of an individual; result of another policy etc.)

d) Issues to be resolved

e) Agencies involved (governmental or non-governmental)

   i) *Name of agency*

   ii) *National, regional or local?*

   iii) *Influential individuals*

   iv) *Nature of involvement/role*

v) *Relationship with other agencies*
   (e.g. issues of territoriality, competition, power
   arrangement etc.)

vi) *Relationship with other policies*
    (e.g. complementarity, contradiction,
    improvement etc.)

f) Key events/cornerstones

g) Resources required/deployed

h) Commitment demonstrated

i) Policy instruments employed

7. Outcome

a) Time period

b) Intended outcome

c) Unintended outcome

d) Stakeholders' response

8. Implications for climate change adaptation for the tourism sector

a) Does the policy facilitate or hinder climate
   change adaptation for the tourism sector?
   How?

b) Adaptation issues to be addressed

c) Agencies/individuals to be involved

d) Policy instruments/resources required

• technical – changes made to physical infrastructure or provisions

- business management – changes made by the private sector in their businesses
- behavioural – behavioural changes made by tourists or communities
- policy – changes in government plans or strategies
- research and education – initiatives to strengthen the understanding of adaptation, explore adaptation options, and educate communities.

Policies are also examined against characteristics of SIDS that make them especially vulnerable to climate-change risks. These have been highlighted by Sem and Moore (2009) as limited size, limited natural resources, natural hazards, water, low economic resilience, population growth and density, infrastructure, and limited funds and human resource skills. Climate change adaptations addressing these characteristics will help make the SIDS less vulnerable.

Table 11.2 illustrates how the policy analysis was undertaken by integrating the elements of policy process, adaptation types and SIDS characteristics. The table allows each policy to be judged as to whether its objectives have been met, are in progress or delayed, or are not met.

Method

Data was collected from both secondary and primary sources. The use of multiple sources helps assure the conformability (or objectivity) and credibility of findings (Lincoln and Guba 1985).

Secondary resources included official policy documents as well as background information about the geography, history, politics, institutional structure, economy and climate-change-related hazards of the countries in the Pacific. Due to the time and resource limit, policy analyses for PNG, Solomon Islands and Tonga were conducted from extensive literature reviews of existing policy documents, academic literature, news reports and other relevant sources. Consequently, as these are based on secondary data only, not all of the policy analysis objectives could be addressed for these countries. This applied particularly to the ability to examine the different perspectives on policy issues, gaining an understanding of the power and interest dynamics involved, as well as examining the policy-making mechanisms in the country, as these often are not documented in the available literature. Nonetheless, desktop policy analyses provide an excellent understanding of important policies and their policy environment, which was vital for the PT-CAP research.

Fiji, Samoa and Vanuatu were chosen for extensive in-country primary data collection, which made it possible for data not available in secondary sources to be collected, and to examine policy issues from multiple perspectives. Semi-structured in-depth interviews (averaging forty minutes in length) were conducted face to face in the three Pacific countries between September 2009 and June 2010.

Interviewees included individuals who have been highly involved in the formulation and/or implementation of the policies identified, and those who are

TABLE 11.2 The PT-CAP pacific tourism and climate change policy analysis framework

Adaptation Process (Hall and Higham, 2005)		Policy	Objectives Met?				Types of Adaptation (Scott et al., 2008)										SIDS Characteristics that highlight Vulnerability as identified by Sem and Moore (2009)							
			Met	In Progress	Delay	Not met	Technical		Business Management		Behavioural		Policy		Research & Education		a) limited size	b) limited natural resources	c) natural hazards	d) water	e) low economic resilience	f) population growth and density	g) infrastructure	h) limited funds and human resource skills
							General	Tourism	General	Tourism	General	Tourism	General	Tourism	General	Tourism								
	Explicit																							
	Implicit																							

highly knowledgeable about those policies. They were identified based on publicly accessible information on the Internet, and the research team's professional network. A snowball sampling technique was also used, where interviewees recommended other individuals to be interviewed.

Table 11.3 shows the sample of primary data collected in Fiji, Samoa and Vanuatu. Interviewing stopped when the data saturation point was reached, that is, when the themes that emerged from the interviews started to be repeated. A total of twenty-six, thirty-four and twenty-seven interviews were conducted in Fiji, Samoa and Vanuatu respectively, across seven stakeholder groups: government, intergovernmental organizations, supranational organizations, tourism industry, donor-development organizations, non-government organizations (NGO) and research institutes/universities.

TABLE 11.3 Sample of primary data collection in Fiji, Samoa and Vanuatu

Stakeholder group	Number of interviews		
	Fiji	*Samoa*	*Vanuatu*
Government	6	18	7
Intergovernmental organization	1	0	0
Supranational organization	4	3	0
Tourism industry	2	6	14
Donor/development organization	4	4	1
NGO	6	2	4
Research institute/university	3	1	1
Total number of interviews	26	34	27

Policy analysis findings

Key regional policies in the Pacific

A number of regional policies can be considered to be highly relevant to climate change adaptation in the South Pacific. In this section, four are highlighted: the Disaster Risk Reduction and Disaster Management Framework for Action (DRRDMFA) 2005–2015, the Pacific Islands Framework for Action on Climate Change (PIFACC) 2006–2015, the 2005 Pacific Plan and the Pacific Adaptation to Climate Change (PACC) Project (see Table 11.4).

Among these four regional policies, the PACC project can be considered the best funded, and, therefore the best orchestrated, adaptation-focused project in the region. PACC strategies are based on country-driven priorities identified in the National Communications to the United Nations Framework Convention on Climate Change (UNFCCC), and are consistent with National Adaptation Programmes for Action (NAPAs) and the regionally endorsed PIFACC 2006–2015. These regional policies collectively provide a conducive policy environment to climate-change adaptation in the South Pacific region. They show that country leaders are aware of the challenges climate change brings, and are willing to address these challenges. PACC, for example, has set out specific adaptation strategies that are or will be adequately funded. Achieving all targeted outcomes takes time, money and commitment from all stakeholders. But as the policy documents commonly point out, an important priority for the governments is to improve the adaptive capacity of the public sector, the communities and infrastructure.

Policy environment in Fiji, Samoa and Vanuatu

The policy analysis identified the following number of policies pertinent to climate change adaptation of the tourism sector: twenty-three in Fiji, twenty in Samoa and twenty-six in Vanuatu.

Of the three Pacific SIDS, Samoa is leading in terms of explicit policies, with thirteen out of twenty explicit policies wholly or partly formulated with the intention to address climate change. One of the most important policies related to tourism adaptation to climate change is the launch of NAPA in 2005 with the assistance of the UN Development Programme (UNDP) and Global Environment Facility (GEF). NAPA laid important groundwork for the existing climate-change policies for Samoa, as it provided a detailed account of the current risks and vulnerabilities, and identified nine priority projects, one of which was for tourism. This project aimed to 'establish a National Sustainable Tourism Policy so that other sectors involved and communities have a constructive knowledge on procedures and protocols relative to the industry taking into account climate change and climate variability'(NTT 200: 55). The other eight projects relate to water, forest protection, climate health, climate early warning system, food security, zoning, coastal infrastructure and ecological conservation. In 2009, formulation of plans to implement the tourism project began. At the time of writing, details of those plans are still being finalized. One of the proposed plans is called ADAPT, which involves building a carbon-neutral village or resort using new green technologies (Wong et al. 2010).

Fiji has eight explicit climate change policies out of its twenty-three policies identified by the policy analysis, which indicates that the Fijian government intends to integrate climate change into sectoral policies including the tourism sector. The Fiji tourism master plan, *Tourism Development Plan 2007–2016*, identified climate change as a risk and the need to understand climate change impacts on the tourism sector (STDC 2007). A GEF-funded tourism adaptation project was developed in 2006 but unfortunately remains inactive with a four-year funding approval delay since the initial stakeholder workshop. The summary report of the workshop, however, identifies a wide range of possible adaptation measures for tourism, as well as adaptation barriers that exist in the current policy setting of Fiji (Fiji Ministry of Tourism, UNWTO and GEF 2006).

Compared with Samoa and Fiji, climate change adaptation (especially for the tourism sector) in Vanuatu was less explicitly considered in policy development. Among three explicit climate-change policies, only one addressed both tourism and climate change. This policy, titled NAPA 2007, included a sustainable tourism development project as one of the main project concepts (Republic of Vanuatu et al. 2007).

Apart from the explicit climate-change policies, the implicit policies in tourism development, disaster management and the environment in the three countries also play instrumental roles in climate-change adaptation and help address the SIDS characteristics that make them vulnerable to climate change risks. Generally

TABLE 11.4 Key regional climate-change policies in the Pacific

Name of policy	Disaster Risk Reduction and Disaster Management Framework for Action (DRRDMFA) 2005–2015 (2005)	The Pacific Islands Framework for Action on Climate Change (PIFACC) 2006–2015 (2005)
Implementing organization	Applied Geoscience and Technology Division (SOPAC) of the Secretariat of the Pacific Community (SPC)	South Pacific Regional Environment Programme (SPREP)
Objectives	To build disaster risk management capacity of Pacific Island communities through (SOPAC, 2005, p.6): a) Development and strengthening of disaster risk reduction and disaster management, including mitigation, preparedness, response and relief/recovery systems; b) Integration of disaster risk reduction and disaster management into national sustainable development planning and decision-making processes at all levels; and c) Strengthening partnerships between all stakeholders in disaster risk reduction and disaster management.	To ensure Pacific peoples and communities build their capacity to be resilient to the risks and impacts of climate change (SPREP, 2005). It entails six elements: a) implementing adaptation measures; b) governance and decision making; c) improving the region's understanding of climate change; d) education, training and awareness; e) contributing to global greenhouse gas reduction; and f) partnerships and cooperation.
Potential contribution to tourism adaptation	Particularly relevant to tourism or accommodation operators located along the coastline, which face the risks of storm surge associated to cyclones.	Provides a framework for improving various aspects of adaptive capacity. While it does not address the tourism sector directly, it shows the governments' commitment to fight climate change and their readiness to support sector-specific adaptation initiatives.

The Pacific Plan (2005)	Pacific Adaptation to Climate Change (PACC) (2008)
Pacific Islands Forum (PIF)	United Nations Development Programme (UNDP) in partnership with SPREP
To provide a wide development agenda including economic growth, sustainable development, governance and security. The challenges brought about by climate change was acknowledged and addressed in the Plan. The commitment of implementing both PIFACC and DRRDMFA was re-emphasized.	To address adaptation issues in the Pacific on three fronts (SPREP, 2008): a) Improving government capacity to mainstream climate change adaptation into government policies and plans; b) Addressing the urgent need for adaptation measures through systematic guidelines for adaptation and pilot demonstration in the coastal management, food security and water resources sectors; and c) Laying the foundation for a comprehensive approach to address adaptation over the medium–long term at the regional level.
Gives the rationale for the tourism sector, an important economic driver in the region, to strengthen its adaptive capacity.	Tourism-specific adaptation strategies are included in some countries' PACC plan (e.g. Samoa). Funding and resources would be made available for tourism to adapt.

speaking, these explicit and implicit policies in Fiji, Samoa and Vanuatu do provide a reasonably conducive policy environment for their tourism sectors to adapt to climate change. Tables 11.5 and 11.6 indicate how the policies have addressed adaptation types and SIDS characteristics in Fiji, Samoa and Vanuatu.

TABLE 11.5 Policies and the corresponding adaptation types addressed in Fiji, Samoa and Vanuatu

| *Type of policies* / *Adaptation types* | *Number of policies* | | | | | |
| | *Fiji* | | *Samoa* | | *Vanuatu* | |
	Explicit (8)	*Implicit (15)*	*Explicit (13)*	*Implicit (7)*	*Explicit (3)*	*Implicit (23)*
Technical	3	2	5	2	2	11
Business management	1	2	4	2	1	5
Behavioural	1	0	2	0	1	3
Policy	8	15	11	5	3	22
Research and education	3	8	7	1	2	19

TABLE 11.6 Policies and the corresponding SIDS characteristics addressed in Fiji, Samoa and Vanuatu

| *Type of policies* / *SIDS characteristics* | *Number of policies* | | | | | |
| | *Fiji* | | *Samoa* | | *Vanuatu* | |
	Explicit (8)	*Implicit (15)*	*Explicit (13)*	*Implicit (7)*	*Explicit (3)*	*Implicit (23)*
Limited size	1	3	0	0	0	2
Limited natural resources	2	7	3	0	3	19
Natural hazards	2	5	8	4	2	6
Water	2	3	3	1	1	4
Economic resilience	2	4	6	3	3	10
Population growth and density	1	0	1	0	0	6
Infrastructure	3	2	6	3	2	10
Funds and human resources	6	11	10	1	3	20

The policy analysis also identified policy gaps that are yet to be addressed for climate change adaptation in the three Pacific countries. As Table 11.4 shows, most of the climate change initiatives are policy-level adaptations, and research and education is the second adaptation type that is relatively well addressed. While these provide a good foundation for further actions, other aspects of adaptation including technical, business management, and behavioural need to be more comprehensively addressed. With respect to SIDS characteristics, Table 11.5 shows that the issues of limited funds and human resources are more addressed than other SIDS characteristics in all three countries. While Fiji and Vanuatu pay more attention to protecting their limited natural resources, Samoa tends to care more about natural hazards. Among other SIDS characteristics, the limited size and population growth and density are the two that seem neglected and less addressed by the existing policies in the three countries.

Policy environment in PNG, Solomon Islands and Tonga

The desktop policy analysis identified eleven policies in PNG, ten in the Solomon Islands and twelve in Tonga pertinent to tourism adaptation to climate change (Table 11.7). The findings show that the policy environments in PNG and Solomon Islands are not highly conducive for the tourism sector to adapt to climate change despite some positive signs. In PNG, none of the six explicit policies include climate-change adaptation specifically for the tourism sector. It is not a least developing country (LDC) under the UN Framework Convention on Climate Change (UNFCCC), and therefore does not implement NAPA. Climate change is yet to be mainstreamed into tourism development as its *Tourism Sector Development Review and Master Plan 2007–2017* does not include climate-change-specific adaptation plans (ICCC and PNGTPA 2006). However, the tourism plan indirectly allows for adaptation through several non–climate-specific plans such as a diversification of the market as well as improvement of infrastructure and institutional capacity.

Similarly in Solomon Islands, the *2010 Workplan Tourism* by the Ministry of Culture and Tourism does not address climate change adaptation, although it makes allowances through measures such as product diversification and environmental protection. Unlike PNG not implementing NAPA, tourism adaptation to climate change in Solomon Islands is predominantly driven by the NAPA process, which contains tourism as one of the priority adaptation areas (Law et al. 2011). But there are also challenges and concerns particularly in regards to the very limited awareness of NAPA and other adaptation policies in place among both the government and the tourism industry.

Slightly different to the situations in PNG and Solomon Islands, Tonga has been making great efforts to address climate change issues, although it has not had an updated tourism plan in place since 1990. Its recently established Ministry of Environment and Climate Change indicates the current high awareness of climate change in Tonga and serious political commitment to addressing this issue. Tonga has also made significant progress in the mainstreaming of climate change into sectoral

TABLE 11.7 Policies identified in PNG, Solomon Islands and Tonga

Number of policies	Type of policies		
	PNG	Solomon Islands	Tonga
Explicit	6	8	7
Implicit	5	2	5
Total	11	10	12

policies. The 2008 *Forestry Policy* recognized the forestry sector's role in mitigation and also included a section focusing on tourism and forestry-based recreation (GOT 2008). More recently in July 2010, Tonga submitted its Second National Communication under the UNFCCC, which is also known as the *Joint National Action Plan on Climate Change Adaptation and Disaster Risk Management*. The Communication included tourism adaptations to increase its resilience to climate change impacts. Within a reasonably conducive policy environment, Tonga's tourism sector can move forward to develop its policies and strategies to adapt to climate change.

Tables 11.8 and 11.9, indicate how the policies have addressed adaptation types and SIDS characteristics in PNG, Solomon Islands and Tonga.

The findings are quite similar to what has been found in Fiji, Samoa and Vanuatu. Policy level adaptation and research and education are the two best addressed adaptation types, but technical, business management and behavioural adaptations mostly remain as policy gaps. With respect to SIDS characteristics, the issues of limited funds and human resources are better addressed than other issues, followed by the issue of limited natural resources and natural hazards. Among other SIDS characteristics, limited size and population growth and density seem neglected and less addressed by the existing policies in all three countries.

TABLE 11.8 Policies and the corresponding adaptation types addressed in PNG, Solomon Islands and Tonga

Adaptation types \ Type of policies	Number of policies					
	PNG		Solomon Islands		Tonga	
	Explicit (6)	Implicit (5)	Explicit (8)	Implicit (2)	Explicit (7)	Implicit (5)
Technical	2	2	2	0	5	2
Business management	0	1	1	0	2	2
Behavioural	0	0	1	0	0	0
Policy	6	4	8	2	7	5
Research and education	5	4	7	2	6	3

TABLE 11.9 Policies and the corresponding SIDS characteristics addressed in PNG, Solomon Islands and Tonga

Type of policies / SIDS characteristics	Number of policies					
	PNG		Solomon Islands		Tonga	
	Explicit (6)	Implicit (5)	Explicit (8)	Implicit (2)	Explicit (7)	Implicit (5)
Limited size	0	0	2	0	4	0
Limited natural resources	4	2	6	1	6	3
Natural hazards	3	1	5	1	5	3
Water	1	2	2	1	3	1
Low economic resilience	1	3	1	1	1	1
Population growth and density	0	0	1	0	1	0
Infrastructure	0	2	1	0	3	1
Funds and human resources	6	5	8	2	3	2

Implications and recommendations

Pacific island people are faced with more severe challenges from climate change than most others. Climate change is currently having significant impacts on Pacific island countries. As a highly climate-sensitive sector, tourism in the Pacific has been witnessing real climate-change impacts on both the supply and demand side of the sector, which challenges the protection and growth of livelihoods of Pacific communities (Jiang et al. 2009).

The policy analysis allowed a comprehensive understanding of the existing policies related to climate change and the policy environment for the tourism sector to adapt to climate-change impacts. Generally speaking, positive signs have been observed from the regional to the individual country level that policies and initiatives have been developed and implemented to cope with climate change in the Pacific region. A number of PICs have identified the tourism sector as a priority area for their sustainable development. The significance of climate change and sustainable development through tourism has been recognized increasingly by the governments, although individual countries have shown different paces and levels of addressing tourism adaptation to climate change. Research is encouraged and funded to strengthen the understanding of adaptation and explore adaptation options, and awareness programs are undertaken to educate government representatives and communities.

Despite these positive developments, Pacific tourism still has a long way to go in its climate-change-adaptation journey. Indeed, climate change is yet to be mainstreamed into the sector. Due to its close relationship with natural resources and the environment, the tourism sector does benefit from adaptations of other sectors such as water, environmental protection and disaster risk management. Nevertheless, the risks brought about by climate change are threatening the sustainable growth of the tourism industry, and therefore, tourism-specific adaptation strategies need to be developed to assist the sector to protect and grow local livelihoods in the Pacific. Governments in the Pacific will need to collaborate with the private sector, communities and other stakeholders to address those adaptation gaps identified through the policy analysis.

Based on the policy analysis findings, we made these key recommendations:

- At the regional level, develop collaboration between the environment and disaster-focused organizations such as the South Pacific Regional Environment Programme (SPREP) and Pacific Islands Applied Geoscience Commission (SOPAC) and tourism organizations such as the SPTO, and investigate the possibility of joint tourism adaptation initiatives.
- At the individual country level, improve coordination of climate change adaptation between different sectors and government agencies, incorporate climate change into the tourism sector planning and take further measures to deal with weakly addressed SIDS characteristics in the existing policy environment such as limited size, water, low economic resilience, population growth and density, and limited funds and human resources skills.
- At the tourism sector level, strengthen the public private partnership in climate change adaptation for the tourism sector, and explore more tourism adaptation options in technical, business management and behavioural aspects that are weakly addressed in the existing policy environment.

References

AusAID (2009) *09 Pacific Economic Survey: Engaging with the world,* AusAID, Canberra.

Becken, S. and Hay, J. E. (2007) *Tourism and Climate Change: Risks and opportunities,* Channel View, Bristol, Buffalo and Toronto.

Crocombe, R. (2008) *The South Pacific,* IPS Publications, University of the South Pacific, Suva.

DeLacy, T. (2008) 'Pacific tourism adaptation to climate change risks', Paper for SPREP Conference on Climate Change in the South Pacific, October 2008, Apia, Samoa.

DeLacy, T. and Lipman, G. (2010) 'GreenEarth. Travel: Moving to carbon clean destinations', in C. Scott (ed.), *Tourism and the Implications of Climate Change: Issues and actions,* Emerald, Bingley, UK.

United Nations Economic and Social Commission for Asia and the Pacific (ESCAP) (2008) *2008 Statistical Yearbook for Asia and the Pacific,* ESCAP, Bangkok.

ESCAP (2000) 'Climate change and the Pacific Islands.' Fourth ministerial conference on environment and development in Asia and the Pacific, September, ESCAP, Kitakyushu City.

Everitt, T. (2009) 'Tourism's role in the South Pacific economy', presentation at the PT-CAP kick-off workshop, June, Suva, Fiji.

Fiji Ministry of Tourism, UNWTO and Global Environmental Facility (GEF) (2006) *Adaptation to Climate Change in the Tourism Sector in the Fiji Islands: Summary report of the initial stakeholder workshop,* Fiji Ministry of Tourism, Suva.

Garrod, B. and Gössling, S. (eds) (2008) *New Frontiers in Marine Tourism: Diving experiences, sustainability, management,* Elsevier, Amsterdam.

Government of Tonga (GOT) (2008) *National Forest Policy for Tonga,* GOT, Nuku'alofa.

Hall, C. M. and Jenkins, J. M. (1995) *Tourism and Public Policy,* Thomson, London.

Harrison, D. (2010) 'Tourism challenges for Pacific island states: the case of Fiji', Paper for Fiji Economy Update, July, University of South Pacific, Suva.

Independent Consumer and Competition Commission PNG (ICCC) and PNG Tourism Promotion Authority (PNGTPA) (2006) *Papua New Guinea Tourism Sector Review and Master Plan (2007–2017): Growing PNG tourism as a sustainable industry,* ICCC and PNGTPA, Port Moresby.

Intergovernmental Panel on Climate Change (IPCC) (2007) *Climate Change 2007: Impacts, adaptation and vulnerability. Contribution of Working Group II to the Fourth Assessment Report of the IPCC,* IPCC, New York.

Jiang, M., DeLacy, T. and Noakes, S. (2009) 'Tourism, the millennium development goals and climate change in the South Pacific islands', paper at the International Conference on 'Meeting the Millennium Development Goals: Old Problems, New Challenges', December, Melbourne.

Law, A., Jiang, M., Dan, C., Wong, E., Klint, L. and DeLacy, T. (2011) *Policy Analysis for Papua New Guinea, Solomon Islands, and Tonga,* Centre for Tourism and Services Research, Victoria University, PT-CAP technical report no 5, Melbourne.

Lincoln, Y. S. and Guba, E. G. (1985) *Naturalistic Inquiry,* Sage, Beverly Hills, Calif.

MacLellan, N., Keough, L., Richards, J. A., Pride, J., Ensor, J., Dent, K., Coates, B., Elliot, M. and Garman, J. (2009) 'The future is here: climate change in the Pacific', in N. Field (ed.), *Oxfam Briefing Paper 2009,* Oxfam, Carlton.

National Adaptation Programme of Action Task Team (NTT) (2005) *National Adaptation Programme of Action, Samoa,* Ministry of Natural Resources, Environment and Meteorology, Apia.

National Institute of Water and Atmospheric (NIWA) Research (2007) *Pacific Islands Suffer Signs of Climate Change,* NIWA Science, Auckland.

Pelling, M. and Uitto, J. I. (2002) 'Small island developing states: natural disaster vulnerability and global change', *Environmental Hazards,* vol. 3, pp. 49–62.

Preston, B. L., Suppiah, R., MacAdam, I. and Bathols, J. (2006) *Climate Change in the Asia/ Pacific Region,* consultancy report for the Climate Change and Development Roundtable, Commonwealth Scientific and Industrial Research Organization, Canberra.

Republic of Vanuatu, GEF, UN Development Programme (UNDP) and UN Framework Convention on Climate Change (UNFCCC) (2007) *National Adaptation Programme for Action (NAPA),* Port Vila, Republic of Vanuatu.

Scheyvens, R. and Momsen, J. (2008) 'Tourism in small island states: from vulnerability to strengths', *Journal of Sustainable Tourism,* vol. 16, no. 5, pp. 491–510.

Scott, D., De Freitas, C. and Matzarakis, A. (2008) 'Adaptation in the tourism and recreation sector', in K. L. Ebi and I. Burton (eds), *Biometeorology for Adaptation to Climate Variability and Change,* Kluwer Academic, Dordrecht.

Secretariat of the Pacific Community (SOPAC) (2005) *An Investment for Sustainable Development in the Pacific Island Countries – Disaster risk reduction and disaster management framework for action 2005–2015,* SOPAC, Suva.

Sem, G. and Moore. R. (2009) *The Impact of Climate Change on the Development Prospects of the Least Developed Countries and Small Island Developing States*, UN Office of the High Representative for the Least Developed Countries, Landlocked Developing Countries and Small Island Developing States, New York.

Simpson, M. C., Gössling, S., Scott, D., Hall, C. M. and Gladin, E. (2008) *Climate Change Adaptation and Mitigation in the Tourism Sector: Frameworks, tools and practices.* UNEP, University of Oxford, UN World Tourism Organization (WTO) and World Meteorological Organization (WMO), Paris.

South Pacific Regional Environment Programme (SPREP) (2005) *Pacific Islands Framework for Action on Climate Change 2006–2015*, SPREP, Apia.

SPREP (2008) *Pacific Adaptation to Climate Change Project Description*, SPREP, Apia.

South Pacific Tourism Organization (SPTO) (2007) *South Pacific Action Strategy for Green Tourism*, prepared by TRIP Consultants, Suva.

Sustainable Tourism Development Consortium (2007) *Fiji Tourism Development Plan 2007–2016*, Department of Tourism, Suva.

UNDP (2006) *Trade on human Terms: Transforming trade for human development in Asia and the Pacific, Asia-Pacific human development report 2006*, UNDP, New York.

UNDP (2007) *Fighting Climate Change: Human solidarity in a divided world, Human development report 2007/2008*, UNDP, New York.

UN Environment Programme (UNEP)-World Conservation Monitoring Centre (WCMC) (2006) *In the Front Line: Shoreline protection and other ecosystem services from mangroves and coral reefs*, UNEP-WCMC, Cambridge, UK.

UNWTO, UNEP and WMO (2008) Climate Change and Tourism – Responding to global challenges, *UNWTO, Madrid.*

UNWTO (2005) *Tourism Market Trends: Asia and the Pacific*, UNWTO, Madrid.

Weaver, D. and Oppermann, M. (2000) *Tourism Management*, John Wiley & Sons Australia, Milton.

Wong, E., Jiang, M., Klint, L. and DeLacy, T. (2010) *Policy Analysis for Samoa*, Centre for Tourism and Services Research, Victoria University, PT-CAP technical report No. 3, Melbourne.

12

SCENARIOS OF CLIMATE CHANGE AND IMPACTS ON BRAZILIAN TOURISM

A case study of the Brazilian north coast tourism region

Gilson Zehetmeyer Borda, Elimar Pinheiro do Nascimento, Helena Araújo Costa, João Paulo Faria Tasso and Leticia Ramos

Introduction

Research on climate change and tourism is recent in Brazil. Although Rio-92 stimulated sustainable-development-related investigation (Sachs, Wilheim, and Sérgio 2001), it is only recently that the impact of these changes has been studied consistently. Brazil has been structuring its research on climate change through two networks: Climate Net, launched in 2008, with ten thematic sub-nets uniting more than forty universities and research institutes throughout the country, and INCT for Climate Change, launched in 2009, involving over ninety research groups from sixty-five different Brazilian and international institutions, with more than 400 participants and twenty-six ongoing projects (INCT 2010: 5). These are the biggest research nets on climate change in Brazil; nevertheless, they have not undertaken specific research on climate change and tourism development. There are few national studies on this topic (Borda and Brasileiro 2010).

The UN World Tourism Organization (UNWTO) (2008: 2) reflects: 'given tourism's importance in the global challenges of climate change and poverty reduction, there is a need to urgently adopt a range of policies which encourages truly sustainable tourism that reflects a "quadruple bottom line" of environmental, social, economic and climate responsiveness'. In the same spirit, as the objectives of this book state, sustainability and climate change 'have to be tackled as similar problems' by all the actors of the tourism industry – as 'common challenges'. So the importance of research regarding climate change and sustainability for the tourism industry, the search to create social value in trying to achieve poverty reduction (Borda and Nascimento 2011) as well as the lack of research about the Brazilian reality were the main reasons for the authors to reflect about the subject.

This chapter aims to analyse the positive and negative future impacts of climate change on tourism along the north coast of Brazil. This reflection might help responsible tourism planning worldwide (Felix and Borda 2009). The north coast was chosen as a case study for its integrated itinerary under the Brazilian Tourism Development Regionalization Programme (MTUR 2005) with major social and environmental sensitivities. The itinerary comprises the coastline of three states, Maranhao, Piaui and Ceara, extending for about 300 km, and includes twelve counties organized in three tourism regions. It is an area of exotic natural beauty where tourism has been growing rapidly, and brings the possibility and hope of reducing social and economic isolation, poverty and social inequality.

This chapter is divided in three parts. The first part examines climate change impact forecasts in Brazil. It focuses on the north-east region and is based on literature and on the tourism characteristics of the country. The second part presents the biotic and abiotic characteristics of the north coast, and includes development scenarios for the itinerary mentioned above. The third part analyses the probable impacts of climate change on north coast tourism, keeping the focus on the two main tourism destinations: Jericoacoara (Ceara) and Lencois Maranhenses (Maranhao).

Climate change in Brazil and tourism development

Climate change represents a major challenge for sustainability, a dynamic process of balancing social, environmental and economic issues. The challenges become more obvious when it is considered that sustainability claims for long-term development strategies are based not on a predatory use of natural resources (Cavalcanti 1999), but on intergenerational solidarity, democracy and care in the use of natural resources (Hardi and Zdan 1997, Sharpley 2000, Lenzi 2006).

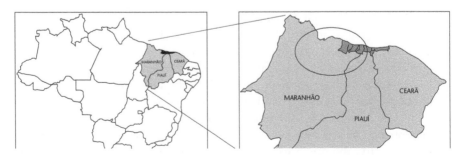

FIGURE 12.1 Map of Northeast Brazil

Source: Screenshot by the authors

Therefore, it is not possible to consider the existence of a sustainable future if the risks and impacts associated with the tremendous changes in the climate worldwide are ignored. The *Fourth Report* published by IPCC (2007) about climate change pointed out that human beings are an important vector of these changes. The report presented thirty-five different scenarios for the twenty-first century, based on data about anthropogenic greenhouse gas emissions. Six scenarios were considered the most important: B1, A1T, B2, A1B, A2 and A1F1, with results for respective gas emissions in 2100: 600, 700, 800, 850, 1250 and 1550 parts per million, which suggests an increase of global superficial temperature between 1.1 °C and 6.4 °C and a rise in coastal sea levels of between 0.18 m and 0.59 m.

In general, the environmental system response to an increase of temperature is gradual. However, research has shown that it can quickly be accelerated. Scheffer et al. (2001: 591) suggested that the ecosystem resilience is one of the aspects that promote its sudden reorganization to an alternative state of dynamic equilibrium.

Aceituno et al. (2007) and Marengo (2007b) estimate that Latin America will show a significant reduction of biodiversity and water availability because of changes on precipitation rates and glacier retreat. The sea-level rise will cause greater risk of floods in coastal areas. The temperature rise associated with the decrease of groundwater will gradually tend to change the distribution of rainforest, replacing rainforest with savannah vegetation in the eastern part of the Amazon region. Semi-arid agricultural areas will experience increased salinization and desertification. Productivity will decline and the stock of resources will decrease, leading to drastic consequences regarding food security, except soya beans, from the temperate zones. Estimates concerning climate change in Brazil are no less severe. They are summarized in Table 12.1.

Studies suggest that the frequency of intense droughts during the hottest periods of the year will increase in the north and north-east, while droughts and floods will become more frequent in the south and south-east of Brazil. Before the end of this century there will be an additional temperature rise during summer in most of the country to around 2 °C to 3 °C above pre-industrial levels, associated with major biodiversity losses. The loss will probably be more significant in the Amazon region and in the vegetation of the Brazilian interior (*cerrado*). A rise in sea level will occur along all Brazilian's coastline – the worst impacts being experienced by low-lying areas.

The impacts of climate change in the north-east of Brazil

The economy of the north-east of Brazil (an area of 1,558,196 sq km with 52 million inhabitants) is based on agriculture, cattle breeding, industry and services including tourism. Sugar cane is the major product while other important products include cotton, tobacco, beans, soya beans, castor beans, fruits and nuts like grape, melon, cashew nut, mango and West Indian cherry (acerola). These products are cultivated for export or for internal consumption. Cattle breeding is the most important livestock activity, but in arid areas more drought-resistant animals, like

TABLE 12.1 Estimates on climate change impacts by geographic region in Brazil

Region	Probable impact	Source
North	Big part of the east side of the Amazon biome will be overlapped by the savannah	Cramer et al. (2004) Nobre, Sampaio and Salazar (2007)
	Drought during the hottest periods of the year	Wara, Ravelo and Delaney (2005) Marengo (2007b)
	More forest fires	Nepstad et al. (2001)
	Loss of forest areas on the north side of the Amazon	Jones et al. (2003) Cox et al. (2004)
	Floods and erosion in the lower areas close to the coastline	IPCC (2001)
	More cases of malaria and dengue	Moreira (1986) Lieshout et al. (2004)
	Seasonality of rainfall rate will affect the variance and amount of water flow in the Amazon watershed and distribution of the aquatic species	Carpenter et al. (1992) Lake et al. (2000)
	Loss of biodiversity	Higgins (2007) Miles, Grainger and Phillips (2004) Latini and Petrere (2004)
	Rainfall deficiency or rainfall growth depending on the situation	Marengo (2009) Nobre et al. (2009)
Northeast	Semi-arid and arid areas will have less water and the semi-arid vegetation will probably be substituted by typical arid area vegetation	IPCC (2007) Marengo (2009) Nobre et al. (2008)
	Loss of coastline to the sea	Marengo (2007b)
	The rise in air temperature will cause more evaporation in the region, which will reduce the amount of groundwater. As a result, there will be a hydrological imbalance.	Araujo, Doll and Guntner (2006) WWF (2006)
	Less subsistence agriculture and irrigation capacity	Marengo (2007b) Krol and Bronstert (2007)
	Climate change extreme events more frequent, groundwater and rainfall reduction, agriculture productivity reduction	Lima et al. (2010)

Region	Probable impact	Source
Central West	Rainfall rate will triple and river flows will raise; as a result, there will be more floods	Hulme and Sheard (1999)
	Biodiversity reduction	Marengo (2007b)
	Loss of agricultural areas	Magrin (2007)
	More malaria cases	Lieshout et al. (2004)
Southeast	The intensity and frequency of floods in big cities will increase because of growing rainfall mainly on the south of the region	IPCC (2007)
	Floods and erosion of big proportion in Jequitinhonha Valley/SP	Dominguez; Martin; Bittencourt (2006)
	Loss of agricultural areas	Magrin (2007)
	More intense temperature peaks will have an impact on agriculture, population health and electricity generation	Marengo (2007b)
South	The rise in sea level will cause flooding and erosion on the coastline	Esteves, Williams and Dillenburg (2006)
	Severe loss of grain production	Siqueira et al. (2000)
	The rise in rainfall will cause floods and erosion	Mendonça (2007)
	Loss of araucaria forests	Marengo (2007b)
	Increase in cases of leishmaniasis	Peterson and Shaw (2003)

Source: adapted from Mota, Graozione and Góes (2009: 11).

pigs, goats, sheep and domestic birds, are raised as well. Heavy industry is concentrated in the main metropolitan regions (Recife, Salvador and Fortaleza). The region produces iron, electronic goods and petrochemical products. The petroleum industry spreads along the coastline and the continental platform. Shoes, fabrics and sea salt are also relevant products.

Tourism is an important economic activity, and the area attracts many tourists attracted by the beautiful beaches. Tourism also has a major impact on direct and indirect employment.

It is estimated (see Figure 12.2) that the semi-arid areas will suffer water resource reduction and part of their vegetation will be replaced by vegetation typical of arid regions (IPCC 2007). The estimated replenishment of the aquifers will dramatically diminish by more than 70 percent until the mid-twenty-first century. According to Worldwide Fund for Nature (WWF) (2006) studies, 38 percent to 45 percent of the *cerrado* flora will be in danger of extinction if the temperature rises by 1 °C.

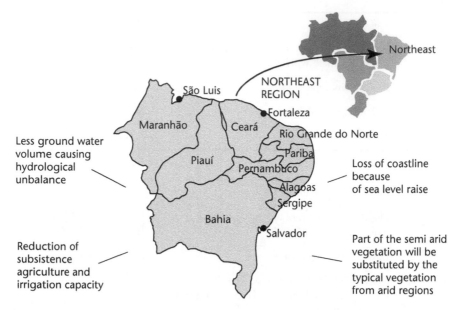

FIGURE 12.2 The impacts of climate change in the north-east of Brazil

Source: adapted from Mota et al. (2009: 14).

In the short term the increased evaporation will reduce the volume of groundwater, which will cause water shortages, a reduction in subsistence agriculture and a loss of irrigation capacity (Araújo et al. 2006). These factors may contribute to the growth of poverty and migration, which will aggravate the social problems in this most socially challenged region of Brazil (Araújo 1995).

Besides these impacts, Marengo (2007b) calls attention to the significant loss of coastline territory because of the sea level rise. In Recife the coastline has already receded approximately 25 m between 1985 and 1995.

Tourism in Brazil and in the north-east region

In addition, the world economic crisis, bird flu, climate change and natural disasters caused a 4 percent decrease in global international arrivals in 2009 (UNWTO 2010), but there was a rise of 6.7 percent in 2010. There was a 10 percent rise in tourism flow in South America between 2009 and 2010, which represented a great recovery. Future growth is estimated to be around 4.1 percent per year (UNWTO 2011). There were a record number of domestic flights in Brazil, with 56 million arrivals in 2009 – an increase of 14.6 percent over 2008 and more than 11.7 percent over 2007, the best year in recent times (MTUR 2010c). In 2010 there were 67 million domestic arrivals with an increase of 20.8 percent over 2009. Likewise, during the same period, there was a rise of 20.9 percent (from 6.5 million to 7.8 million) in international arrivals (MTUR 2011a). In 2011, 9 million international arrivals and 70 million domestic arrivals were expected (MTUR 2011b). In 2014, because of the World Cup – FIFA 2014 – 500,000 tourists might arrive in Brazil. It is hoped 2 million formal and informal jobs might be created and foreign exchange reserves grow by 55 percent, an increase from US$3.95 billion to US$5.56 billion between 2010 and 2014 (MTUR 2010a).

The main tourism segment in the north-east is 'sun and beach'. Bahia's capital city, Salvador, is the main destination. Ecotourism does not have a significant impact in the region at present but is growing. There is, for instance, the Archaeological Park in Piaui known as the Capivara Mountain Range. Cultural tourism is a consolidated segment due to cultural manifestations such as the carnival, São Joao party and New Year's Eve. Moreover, Olinda, São Luis and Pelourinho – in Salvador – are UNESCO World Heritage sites (MTUR 2011a).

The north coast and the tourism development scenarios

North coast tourism is mainly based on leisure, relaxation and outdoor adventure sports. It includes twelve counties throughout the states of Maranhao, Piaui and Ceara. The main attractions of the region are the national parks of Lencois Maranhenses and Jericoacoara. There are other federally protected areas such as the Parnaiba and Jericoacoara deltas, and eleven beaches distributed among twelve counties (LIMA/COPPE/UFRJ 2007a).

The reality of tourism in the places that were investigated is remarkably varied (Costa and Nascimento 2010). Destinations have different lifecycle moments and big differences regarding number of tourists, quality of the services offered, income achieved by tourism activities and dependency on tourism as the main economic activity (Costa 2009). Jericoacoara is the most visited for its attractiveness and reputation. Barreirinhas is the anchor county for those who intend to visit Lencois Maranhenses. Jericoacoara and Lencois Maranhenses are considered the most important tourism destinations in the region because the first one is considered one of the ten most beautiful beaches in the world (Jeri.com 2011) and the second is the only destination on the planet that combines a large expanse of freshwater ponds with amazing white sand dunes that are close to the coast (M&C Lifestyle

FIGURE 12.3 Federal conservation unities and the main attractions of the north coast

Source: Screenshot by the authors.

2009). For the reasons mentioned above, the focus of the chapter is on these two national parks.

North coast tourism is seasonal, and each destination has its particular dynamic. It is usually related to Brazilian and European school holidays and also the amount of rain, which is irregularly distributed throughout the year. Normally the precipitation rates are highest in January and April. From May until November there is less rain, but from November rainfall is on an ascending cycle (LIMA/COPPE/UFRJ 2007a). This oscillation has a great impact on the seasonality of the tourism in the region, because it affects the destination's attractiveness as shown in Figure 12.4.

The season has peaks from December until March (during the Brazilian summer until the carnival) and from July until September. In August, because of European holidays, there are more foreigners in the region, representing more profitability to tourism entrepreneurs. The rainy season decreases tourist flows because sea bathing is less attractive and access to smaller places is difficult. However, intensive rain is essential to sustain water ponds, the biggest attractions of Lencois Maranhenses. May is considered the most interesting period of the year to visit Lencois Maranhenses, since there is less rain and the freshwater ponds are full.

The following tourism statistics refer only to Barreirinhas (Lencois Maranhenses) and Jericoacoara, which are the focus of this discussion. Approximately 160,000 tourists visited in 2004 – 80,754 coming to Barreirinhas and 74,725 to Jericoacoara (SEBRAE/SENAC/MTUR 2006). Most visitors were Brazilian, especially in Barreirinhas (95 percent of the visitors), and 24 percent originated from the state of São Paulo. In Jericoacoara 66.1 percent of the tourists were Brazilian and about 30 percent came from the state of São Paulo. In decreasing

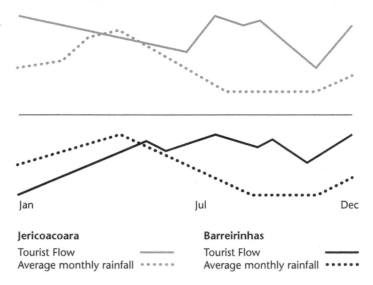

FIGURE 12.4 Average monthly rainfall and approximate tourism seasonality

Source: Screenshot by the authors.

order, the Netherlands, France, Argentina and Switzerland were the main foreign tourist-generating countries (SEBRAE/SENAC/MTUR 2006). Most tourists are aged between 26 and 50, with a level of schooling ranging between secondary level and university degree level. Average tourist monthly income is around U$1,875 for both locations. In Jericoacoara tourists spend less than U$37.50 per day and in Barreirinhas $64.51 per day. Tourists stay much longer in Jericoacoara, an average of eight days compared with three days in Barreirinhas (SEBRAE/SENAC/ MTUR 2006).

In summary, the region has a population of approximately 458,000 of whom 16,880 live in Jericoacoara and 50,354 in Barreirinhas (Lencois Maranhenses) (MI 2009, IBGE 2010). The north coast is extremely poor, with low human development indexes (HDI) all below the Brazilian average (0.766) (PNUD 2006). In addition, there has been a loss of cultural identity and there are very limited economic alternatives (Nascimento, Costa and Boucas 2010). In some counties the main productive sector is tourism, such as in Jericoacoara where tourism accounts for 82.4 percent of the county's domestic internal product (GDP) (SEBRAE/ SENAC/MTUR 2006). The main economic activities in other counties are fishing and agriculture, which includes fruits like mango, banana, cashew nut and coconut. There are almost no manufacturing industries in the region (SEBRAE/ SENAC/MTUR 2006).

The region is characterized by a tropical climate with rainfall from summer until autumn. The average temperature ranges between 35 °C and 22 °C. The dry season varies from five to six months and the annual rainfall rate is 1364 mm (BRAZTOA/SEBRAE/MTUR 2006). There is great environmental diversity in the territory with cliffs, fixed and mobile sand dunes, temporary and permanent ponds, mangroves, woodlands, beaches, islands, carnauba palm fields, savannas and vegetation from the Brazilian interior (*cerrado*). The coastal biome consists of herbaceous plants and grass. The fauna is mainly represented by avifauna (38 bird species – some rare and/or in danger of extinction), fish fauna and cetaceans. However, there is evidence of small and medium-sized mammals (Fonteles 2004, Portal do Mar 2006).

There are three critical characteristics of these ecosystems: fragility, biodiversity and their importance to aquatic productivity (LIMA/COPPE/UFRJ 2007a). On the north coast the main environmental problems are water and soil contamination by sewage and shrimp production waste, overfishing of shellfish, crustaceans and fish, monoculture cropping, particularly soya beans, pressure from extensive cattle raising (MI 2009), and the deforestation and occupation of fragile areas. Serious institutional management problems affect conservation along the coast, mainly because of a lack of resources and labour (LIMA/COPPE/UFRJ 2007a).

Tourism development scenarios on the north coast

The 2007 Environmental Strategic Assessment (LIMA/COPPE/URFJ 2007b) of the north coast defined three scenarios related to the development of tourism until

2021: one for reference and two others based on the performance of public policies. The reference scenario is based on the spontaneous growth of tourism where there is no strategy to give structure to the growth of the sector and training opportunities are limited and unplanned. Supply chain and workforce problems inhibit tourism development, and there is a tendency to structure the tourism industry around large developments, with the result that benefits and revenue leak out to other regions. Lack of articulation with the public sector and other sectors that could give support, misuse of natural attractions, and badly structured and poorly diversified tourism products tend to deteriorate the quality of the tourist experience and gradually reduce the attractiveness of the north coast region in the short, medium and long term.

The second scenario considers the impact of ineffective federal, state and municipal policies for tourism. However, they are capable of promoting associations, involving local people in developing the tourism product, organizing tourism products and controlling tourist numbers. Nevertheless, the lack of diversity regarding tourism products keeps the pressure and focus on the two dominant regions (Jericoacoara – CE and Lencois Maranhenses/ Barreirinhas – MA). Consequently the attractiveness of the tourism product is maintained in the short term, but with a reduction over the medium and long term.

The third scenario is based on more consistent and effective public policies. The strategy is to integrate the three governmental levels and the tourism sector in order to make tourism the main vector of regional development. The aim is to promote enhanced workforce training, to stimulate cooperation within and the organization of the private sector, to encourage social environmental awareness and to train entrepreneurs to develop local supply chains. The result would be a diversified, qualified and adequate tourism service, appropriate to the conservation needs of the natural attractiveness of the region. The objective is to generate the activity in the short term and maintain it over the medium and long term (LIMA/ COPPE/UFRJ 2007b). These alternative scenarios will support the development of next discussion.

Direct and indirect impacts of climate change on north coast tourism

Using the literature on climate change in Brazil (see Table 12.1), and the scenarios mentioned above (LIMA/COPPE/UFRJ 2007a), it is possible to apply a robust strategy methodology. This methodology uses the most common elements and the ones with greater chances of occurring from the different scenarios (Nascimento et al. 2010b, Godet and Durance 2011) to define the variables for the analysis that follows:

- object of the scenarios variables: rainfall (downfall), biodiversity (loss), temperature and sea level on costal zones (elevation)

- north coast tourism variables: attractiveness (degree), tourist flows (volume), tourist flows type (nature), competition (competing destinations), tourism seasonality in the region (change)
- north coast economic characteristics variables: fishing and aquaculture, vegetable extraction, agriculture, livestock and handicrafts.

The exchange rate, political instability and social security, among other factors, will be excluded from this analysis because the object of the research is climate-change impacts on tourism development. Increasing, uniform and continuous effects were considered until 2100, when they are forecast to achieve their peaks – although it is known that climate-change-critical events can both rapidly modify the situation in different places and generate big immediate impacts. As mentioned above, Lencois Maranhenses (Barreirinhas) and Jericoacoara were the destinations chosen because together they represent the main forms of tourism in the analysed region (MI 2009). Each destination has its own characteristics; therefore two different analyses have been done.

Climate change and the direct impacts on tourism development in Jericoacoara

Besides the natural beauty of its beaches, the region of Jericoacoara attracts tourists who enjoy wind sports like surfing, kite-surfing and wind-surfing (M&C Lifestyle 2009), traditional community life, the charm of a village and freshwater ponds (Briley 2010). A temperature rise or precipitation reduction will cause negative impacts on the attractiveness of the tourism product. The critical events that are expected to happen in the Caribbean and in the south and south-east of Brazil will reduce competition to local attractiveness. The north coast is relatively free of tsunamis, hurricanes, tornados, earthquakes and storms. The decrease of precipitation could increase inbound and domestic tourist flows because during the rainy season the tourist flows are reduced. Also, the decrease of floods will enable tourists to have access to certain tourist attractions like visits to seahorse sites or villages in the area to which access is difficult during the rainy season (Santos/ ICMBio, 2011). On the other hand, the rise in sea level might be an obstacle to local attractiveness because of the extreme vulnerability of the coastline (BRAZTOA/SEBRAE/MTUR 2006).

Biodiversity loss might occur and epidemics increase locally in the north-east region, but these will not directly affect tourism. A hot and dry climate is not propitious for these types of events. In Jericoacoara, most beaches are known as being windy most of the time (average of 4.8m/s and regular peaks above 10m/s). The wind is a counterpoint to the high temperatures (Carvalho and Santos 2010). Thus, the climate change shown in most scenarios will have different impacts on the development of this tourism destination. Positive factors will predominate, like the rise in tourist flows and increase of attractiveness in this area.

Climate change and direct impacts on the development of tourism in Lencois Maranhenses

Climate change may define the positioning and survival of Lencois Maranhenses It is strongly dependent on ecosystem services and its main attraction is landscape and informal recreation activities (MMA 2010). A reduction in rainfall and a probable temperature rise might have a direct impact on the formation of Lencois Maranhenses National Park's freshwater ponds. The ponds and the dunes are the main attraction for this tourist destination (BRAZTOA/SEBRAE/MTUR 2006). If they disappeared or shrank, the tourism destination would lose most of its attractiveness and its uniqueness. A rise in sea level could also flood the small isthmus on which the park is located, enabling the ocean to invade the area.

Thus, in the long term the attractiveness of Lencois Maranhenses will tend to drop. The consequences would be loss of tourist flows and investment, which would compromise the destination.

Climate change and indirect impacts on north coast tourism

The climate variations in Lencois Maranhenses and Jericoacoara can, throughout the years, generate impacts on the primary productive sectors like fishing, aquaculture, livestock and handicrafts, which will have direct implications for the tourism sector. The fishing and aquaculture sectors – headed by shrimp (MMA 2010) – can have their dynamics affected by water temperature change. This can directly harm the fish productivity for various reasons: less availability of food from the tropical chain basis, inappropriate reproduction conditions, increased mollusc death and decreased fish catches. The energy absorption and the rise of the sea level can bring risks (waves and cyclones) to navigation and insecurity to local residents (Marengo et al. 2009). In Maranhao the mangroves – cradles of biodiversity – could be directly affected and species reproductive rates could be reduced.

The agriculture sector consists mainly of subsistence activity. Rural and arable land could suffer a decrease in productivity because of the increase in periods of drought. Specifically, Ceara could lose between 70 percent and 80 percent of its productive areas between 2010 and 2050 (Marengo et al, 2009). Production could decrease because of the lack of water. Irrigation may not be advisable given the emergence of competition between domestic and agricultural consumption (Marengo et al. 2009). Heatwaves could lead directly to the premature death of animals, mainly because of difficulty in accessing water supplies. Traditional handicraft production, using natural materials found locally, could decrease because the droughts will affect production, with a direct impact on the revenue of local craftspeople. All of these possible impacts could directly cause damage to local productive sectors of the economy and indirectly affect the tourism sector. The consequences could be:

- growing demand for work, job and revenue opportunities in tourism industry especially in Jericoacoara
- reduced tourist flows because of reduced attractiveness, owing to factors such as the lack of typical products, polluted beaches in Jericoacoara or dry ponds in Lencois Maranhenses, among others.

Final considerations

The prospective analysis of the six climate change scenarios from the IPCC (Mota et al. 2009) and three scenarios for regional tourism (LIMA/COPPE/ UFRJ 2007a) suggests there will be limited impact in the short term, but that the impact will increase over time, with the possibility of greatly reducing tourist flows. The long-term impacts might happen mainly in Lencois Maranhenses, because as noted above, the changes are likely to reduce its attractiveness for tourism. Impacts in Jericoacoara will be caused by changes in the sea level, which will lead to a reduction of river flows, loss of coastline and increased salinization of fresh water. Furthermore, the local population that is directly or indirectly dependent on tourism face a worsening in their socioeconomic situation. The projections based on tourism planning for the north coast region show the importance of the robust strategy over the short, medium and long term, with consistent public policies (Costa and Nascimento 2010) aimed at environmental, sociocultural, economic and political-institutional sustainability (Sachs, 2009) and also taking into account the unmistakable connection between climate change and sustainability.

In summary, a reduction in greenhouse gas emissions might help prevent or mitigate a future temperature rise and its consequences, which have been extensively presented in this chapter, although this is not the only aspect that should be taken into consideration. It is also essential that the Brazilian government adopt more consistent social inclusion policies and encourage community effort to generate more tourist attractions, for instance immersion in traditional communities, sport fishing and luau parties.

It is important to consider the tourism industry as a complex system of sectors with integrated activities that need a systematic approach (Budeanu 2004). From this perspective the impacts of climate change on tourism might have negative implications, not only for natural and cultural heritage, tourist attractions and the typical activities of the industry, but also for related activities such as agriculture, fishing and handicrafts. For all that, the promotion of multi-sector strategic plans for mitigation and adaptation to these impacts should focus on the interactive relations of the diverse agents and sectors involved in building a governance model of sustainable tourism development. Furthermore, community-based sustainable tourism development (Reddy, Shaw and Williams 2006) can reduce poverty and encourage social and economic inclusion, and it can also generate perceived social value by enhancing the quality of life of local people (Borda and Nascimento 2011).

A new tourism development scenario can only be introduced if the effectiveness of these integrated and participative policies is taken into consideration. Likewise, the implementation of strategic tourism planning must take mitigation measures into account, and suggest adaptation actions regarding the possible climate change impacts in the region. Only then can another development scenario be added, one that allow the perpetuation of tourist activity in the north coast region – a natural, cultural and landscape heritage for Brazil and the whole planet – for future generations.

References

Aceituno, P., Rosenbluth, B., Boiser, J. P., Quintana, J. and Villarroel, C. (2007) 'Recent climate changes on the west coast extra tropical region of South America', in Dias, P. L. S., Ribeiro, W. C. and, Nunes, L. H. (eds), *A Contribution to Understanding the Regional Impacts of Global Change in South America*, Instituto de Estudos Avançados da Universidade de São Paulo, São Paulo, pp. 63–71.

Araújo, T. B. (1995) 'Nordeste, Nordestes: que Nordeste?' in Affonso, R. B. A. and Silva, P. L. B. (eds), *Federalismo no Brasil, desigualdades regionais and desenvolvimento*, FUNDAP/ UNESP, São Paulo.

Araújo, J. C., Doll, D. and Guntner, A. (2006) 'Water scarcity under scenarios for global climate change and regional development in semiarid northeastern Brazil', *Water International*, vol. 29, no. 2, pp. 209–20.

Borda, G. Z. and Brasileiro, I. (2010) 'Mudanças Climáticas and Turismo no Brasil: um estudo prospectivo de suas relações', *XI ENTBL – Encontro Nacional de Turismo com Base Local*, Niterói – RJ, 12–14 April, vol. 5, pp. 940–56.

Borda, G. Z. and Nascimento, E. P. (2011) 'Capital Social Organizacional: Confiança and Valor Social', *Polêmica*, vol. 10, pp. 103–14.

BRAZTOA/SEBRAE/MTUR (2006) 'Roteiro integrado Jericoacoara – Delta do Parnaíba – Lençóis Maranhenses – Caderno de Subsídios', available at: www.turismo.gov.br/ export/sites/default/turismo/programas_acoes/regionalizacao_turismo/downloads_ regionalizacao/cadsubsidios_CEPIMA.pdf (accessed 8 May 2011).

Briley, J. (2010) 'On Brazil's northeast coast an oasis beckons', *Washington Post*, available at: www.washingtonpost.com/wp-dyn/content/story/2010/10/08/ST2010100804022. html?sid=ST2010100804022 (accessed 3 May 2011).

Budeanu, A. (2004) 'Introduction and overview of the *Journal of Cleaner Production*: special issue on sustainable tourism,' *Journal of Cleaner Production*, vol. 13, no. 2, pp. 79–81.

Carpenter, S. R., Fisher, S. G., Grimm, N. B. and Kitchell, J. F. (1992) 'Global change and freshwater ecosystems', *Annual Reviews of Ecology and Systematics*, vol. 23, pp. 119–39.

Carvalho, I. V. and Santos, J. S. (2010) 'Análise da velocidade do vento em dois municípios da Costa do Estado do Ceará – Jericoacoara and Beberibe', available at: http://connepi. ifal.edu.br/ocs/index.php/connepi/CONNEPI2010/paper/view/665/386 (accessed 8 May 2011).

Cavalcanti, C. (1999) 'Políticas de Governo para o Desenvolvimento Sustentável' in Cavalcanti, C. (ed.), *Meio Ambiente, Desenvolvimento Sustentável and Políticas Públicas*, Cortez, São Paulo, pp. 21–40.

Costa, H. A. (2009) 'Mosaico da sustentabilidade em destinos turísticos: cooperação and conflito de micro and pequenas empresas no roteiro integrado Jericoacoara – Delta do Parnaíba – Lençóis Maranhenses', PhD thesis, University of Brasília, Brazil.

Costa, H. A. and Nascimento, E. P. (2010) 'Relações de cooperação de micro and pequenas empresas (MPE) do turismo: um estudo em Jericoacoara, Delta do Parnaíba and Lençóis Maranhenses (Brasil)', *Revista Turismo & Desenvolvimento/Journal of Tourism and Development*, vol. 13/14, pp. 64–75.

Cox, P. M., Betts, R. A., Collins, M., Harris, P. P., Huntingford, C. and Jones, C. D. (2004) 'Amazonian forest dieback under climate-carbon cycle projections for the 21st Century', *Theoretical and Applied Climatology*, vol. 78, pp. 137–56.

Cox, P. M. and Stephenson, D. A. (2007) 'Changing climate for prediction', *Science*, vol. 317, pp. 207–8.

Cramer W., Bondeau, A., Schaphoff, S., Lucht, W., Smith, B. and Sitch, S. (2004) 'Tropical forests and the global carbon cycle: impacts of atmospheric carbon dioxide, climate change and rate of deforestation', *Biological Sciences*, vol. 359 no. 1443, pp. 331–43.

Dominguez, J. M. L., Martin, L. and Bittencourt, A. C. S. P. (2006) 'Climate change and episodes of severe erosion at the Jequitinhonha strand plain SE Bahia, Brazil', *Journal of Coastal Research*, vol. 3, pp. 1894–7.

Esteves, L. S., Williams, J. J. and Dillenburg, S. R. (2006) 'Seasonal and interannual influences on the patterns of shoreline changes in Rio Grande do Sul, Southern Brazil', *Journal of Coastal Research*, vol. 22, no. 5, pp. 1076–93.

Félix, J. and Borda, G. Z. (eds) (2009) *Gestão da Comunicação and Responsabilidade Socioambiental*, Atlas, São Paulo.

Fonteles, J. O. (2004) *Turismo and Impactos Sócio-Ambientais*, Aleph, São Paulo.

Godet, M. and Durance, P. (2011) *La prospective stratégique: Pour les enterprises et les territoires*, UNESCO – Dunod, Paris.

Hardi, P. and Zdan, T. (1997) *Assessing Sustainable Development: Principles in practice*, IISD, Winnipeg.

Higgins, P. A. T. (2007) 'Biodiversity loss under existing land use and climate change: an illustration using northern South America', *Global Ecology and Biogeography*, vol. 16, no. 2, pp. 197–204.

Hulme, M. and Sheard, N. (1999) *Climate Change: Scenarios for Brazil*, Climatic Research Unit, Norwich, UK.

Instituto Brasileiro de Geografia and Estatística (IBGE) (2010) 'Perfil Municipal', available at: www.ibge.gov.br (accessed 3 May 2011).

National Institute of Science and Technology for Climate Change (INCT) (2010) 'INCT for Climate Change 2009–2010 Activity Report', available at: www.ccst.inpe.br/inct/INCT_report percent20v2312.pdf (accessed 1 March 2011).

Intergovernmental Panel on Climate Change (IPCC) (2001) *Climate Change 2001: Impacts, Adaptation and Vulnerability – Summary for Policymakers and Technical Summary of the Working Group II Report*, Cambridge University Press, Cambridge.

IPCC (2007) *Climate Change 2007: Synthesis Report – Summary for Policymakers, Fourth Assessment Report*, Cambridge University Press, Cambridge.

Jeri.com (2011) 'The official website of paradise – History.' Available at: www.jericoacoara.com/j1/pages/english/place/history.php (accessed 2 May 2011).

Jones, C. D., Cox, P. M., Essery, R. L. H., Roberts, D. L. and Woodage, M. J. (2003) 'Strong carbon cycle feedbacks in a climate model with interactive CO_2 and sulphate aerosols', *Geophysical Research Letters*, vol. 30, no. 9, p. 1479.

Krol, M. S. and Bronstert, A. (2007) 'Regional integrated modelling of climate change impacts on natural resources and resource usage in semi-arid Northeast Brazil', *Environmental Modelling and Software*, vol. 22, no. 2, pp. 259–68.

Lake, P. S., Palmer, M. A., Biro, P., Cole, J., Covich, A. P., Dahm, C., Gibert, J., Goedkoop, W., Martens, K. and Verhoeven, J. (2000) 'Global change and the biodiversity of freshwater ecosystems: impacts on linkages between above-sediment and sediment biota', *Bio Science*, vol. 50, no. 12, pp. 1099–107.

Latini, O. A. and Petrere, M. Jr. (2004) 'Reduction of a native fish fauna by alien species: an example from Brazilian fresh-water tropical lakes', *Fish Management Ecology*, vol. 11, no. 2, pp. 71–9.

Lenzi, C. L. (2006) *Sociologia Ambiental: risco and sustentabilidade na modernidade*, EDUSC, São Paulo.

Lieshout, M. V., Kovats, R. S., Livermore, M. T. J. and Martens, P. (2004) 'Climate change and malaria: analysis of the SRES climate and socio-economic scenarios', *Global Environmental Change*, vol. 14, no. 1, pp. 87–99.

LIMA/COPPE/UFRJ (2007a) 'Avaliação Ambiental Estratégica: linha de base aspectos do turismo na Costa Norte', available at: www.lima.coppe.ufrj.br/lima/files/aaeturismocostanorte/06_LB_Turismo_01.pdf (accessed 10 March 2011).

LIMA/COPPE/UFRJ (2007b) 'Avaliação Ambiental Estratégica: Região Costa Norte – Cenários do Turismo na Costa Norte', available at: www.lima.coppe.ufrj.br/lima/files/aaeturismocostanorte/08_LB_CenariosTurismo_01.pdf (accessed 10 March 2011).

Lima, J. R., Alencar, J. S., Barbosa, M., Souza, E. F., Valadares, L., Fontes, C., Freire, L. L. R. and Magalhães, A. R. (2010) *Mudanças Climáticas and suas Implicações para o Nordeste*, MMA, Brasília.

M&C Lifestyle (2009) 'Dunes and lagoons beckon in Brazil's Northwest', available at: www.monstersandcritics.com/lifestyle/travel/features/article_1508213.php/Dunes-and-lagoons-beckon-in-Brazil-s-wild-north-east (accessed 29 April 2011), pp. 1–2.

Magrin, G. O. (2007) 'Climatic change and the agricultural sector in south east South America' in Dias, P. L. S., Ribeiro, W. C. and Nunes, L. H. (eds), *A Contribution to Understanding the Regional Impacts of Global Change in South America*, Instituto de Estudos Avançados da Universidade de São Paulo, São Paulo, pp. 151–62.

Marengo, J. A. (2007a) 'Use of regional climate models in impacts assessments and adaptation studies from continental to regional and local scales: the CREAS (Cenários Climáticos Regionalizados de Mudanças de Clima para a América do Sul) initiative in South América' in Dias, P. L. S., Ribeiro, W. C. and Nunes, L. H. (eds), *A Contribution to Understanding the Regional Impacts of Global Change in South America*, Instituto de Estudos Avançados da Universidade de São Paulo, São Paulo, pp. 9–19.

Marengo, J. A. (2007b) *Mudanças Climáticas Globais and seus Efeitos sobre a Biodiversidade – caracterização do clima atual and definição das alterações climáticas para o território brasileiro ao longo do Século XXI,* Ministério do Meio Ambiente/Secretaria de Biodiversidade and Florestas, Brasília

Marengo, J. A. (2009) 'Vulnerabilidade, impacts and adaptação à mudança do clima no semi-árido do Brasil', *Parcerias Estratégicas Annals,* Brasília, 27 December, pp. 149–76.

Marengo, J. A., Schaeffer, R., Zee, D. M. W. and Pinto, H. S. (2009) 'Mudanças Climáticas and Eventos Extremos no Brasil', available at: www.fbds.org.br/cop15/FBDS_MudancasClimaticas.pdf (accessed 2 May 2011).

Mendonça, F. (2007) 'Aquecimento global and suas manifestações regionais and locais', *Revista Brasileira de Climatologia*, no. 2, pp. 71–86.

Miles, L., Grainger, A. and Phillips, O. (2004) 'The impact of global climate change on tropical biodiversity in Amazonia', *Global Ecology and Biogeography*, vol. 13, pp. 553–65.

Ministério da Integração Nacional – Brasil (MI) (2009) Plano de Desenvolvimento Sustentável da Região Turística do Meio-Norte, MI/MTUR, Brasília.

Ministério do Meio Ambiente – Brasil (MMA) (2010) *Panorama da Conservação dos Ecossistemas Costeiros and Marinhos no Brasil*, MMA/SBF/GBA, Brasília.

Moreira, C. J. E. (1986) 'Rainfall and flooding in the Guayas river basin and its effects on the incidence of malaria 1982–1985', *Disasters*, vol. 10, no. 2, pp. 107–11.

Mota, J. A., Grazione, J. and Góes, G. S. (2009) *Economia das Mudanças Climáticas*, IPEA, Brasília.

Ministério do Turismo – Brasil (MTUR) (2005) *Programa de Regionalização do Turismo: diretrizes operacionais*, MTUR, Brasília.

MTUR (2010a) 'Brasil 2014: Uma visão a partir do marketing and do turismo', available at: www.copa2014.turismo.gov.br/copa/copa_cabeca/detalhe/artigo_Josep-Chias_20100108.html (accessed 18 April 2011).

MTUR (2010b) 'Turismo no Brasil 2011 – 2014', available at: /www.turismo.gov.br/ export/sites/default/turismo/noticias/todas_noticias/Noticias_download/Turismo_no_ Brasil_2011_-_2014.pdf (accessed 19 March 2010).

MTUR (2010c) 'Turismo and a dimensão social,' in *Estudos da Competitividade do Turismo Brasileiro*, available at: www.turismo.gov.br/export/sites/default/turismo/o_ministerio/ publicacoes/downloads_publicacoes/TURISMO_E_A_DIMENSÃO_SOCIAL.pdf (accessed 24 December 2010).

MTUR (2011a) 'Desembarques batem recorde histórico, em 2010,' available at: http://200.143.12.93/dadosefatos/geral_interna/noticias/detalhe/20110120.html (accessed 11 January 2011).

MTUR (2011b) 'Mais recordes no turismo', available at: www.turismo.gov.br/turismo/ noticias/todas_noticias/20110428.html (accessed 19 April 2011).

Nascimento, E. P., Costa, H. A. and Boucas, D. (2010) 'Dificuldades de inclusão social pela cultura: o caso do Pólo Costa Norte (Maranhão, Piauí and Ceará)', *Participação (UnB)*, vol. 15, pp. 33–9.

Nascimento, E. P., Neves, M. J. M. and Cristofhidis, D. (2010a) 'Prospecção no mundo das águas: a experiência de construção do plano nacional de recursos', *Geosul*, vol. 25, pp. 27–62.

Nascimento, J. L. and Campos, I. B. (eds) (2010) *Atlas da Fauna Brasileira Ameaçada de Extinção em Unidades de Conservação Federais*, ICMBio/MMA, Brasília.

Nepstad, D., Carvalho, G., Barros, A. C., Alencar, A., Capobianco, J. P., Bishop, J., Moutinho, P., Lefebvre, P., Lopes Silva Jr., U. and Prins, E. (2001) 'Road paving, fire regime feedbacks, and the future of Amazon forests', *Forest Ecology and Management*, vol. 154, no. 3, pp. 395–407.

Nobre, C. A., Lapola, D., Sampaio, G., Salazar, L. F., Cardoso, M. and Oyama, M. (2007) *Mudanças climáticas and possíveis alterações nos biomas da América do Sul*, INPE/CTA, São Paulo.

Nobre, C. A., Sampaio, G. and Salazar, L. (2008) 'Mudanças Climáticas and Amazônia', *Ciência and Cultura*, vol. 59, no. 3, pp. 22–7.

Nobre, C. A., Sampaio, G. and Salazar, L. (2009) 'Cenários de mudança climática para a América do Sul para o final do século 21', *Parcerias Estratégicas Annals*, Brasília, 27 December 2008, pp. 19–42.

Peterson, A. T. and Shaw, P. (2003) 'Lutzomyia vectors for cutaneous leishmaniasis in Southern Brazil: ecological niche models, predicted geographic distributions, and climate change effects,' *International Journal for Parasitology*, vol. 33, no. 9, pp. 919–31.

PNUD (2006) *Atlas do Desenvolvimento Humano no Brasil*, PNUD, Brasília.

Portal do Mar (2006). 'A Zona Costeira Cearense', available at: www.portaldomar.org.br (accessed 28 April 2011).

Reddy. M. V., Shaw. G. and Williams, A. M. (2006) 'Impact of the tsunami on tourism industry and ecosystem: the Andaman and Nicobar Islands, India', pp. 1–60 in *South-South Cooperation Series*, UNESCO, Paris.

Sachs, I. (2009) *A Terceira Margem: em busca do ecodesenvolvimento*, Companhia das Letras, São Paulo.

Sachs, I., Wilheim, J. and Sérgio, P. (eds) (2001) *Brasil: um século de transformações*, Companhia das Letras, São Paulo.

Santos/ICMBio (2011) 'Parna de Jericoacoara autoriza pesquisa and promove curso sobre cavalos marinhos', available at: www.icmbio.gov.br/comunicacao/noticias/20-geral/821-parna-de-jericoacoara-autoriza-pesquisa-e-promove-curso-sobre-cavalos-marinhos (accessed 8 May 2011).

Scheffer, M. and Carpenter, S. R. (2001) 'Catastrophic shifts in ecosystems', *Nature*, vol. 413, pp. 591–6.

SEBRAE/SENAC/MTUR (2006) *Planejamento Roteiro Turístico Integrado: Jericoacoara, Delta do Parnaíba, Lençóis Maranhenses*.

Sharpley, R (2000) 'Tourism and sustainable development: exploring the theoretical divide', *Journal of Sustainable Tourism*, vol. 8, no. 1.

Sharpley, R. (2009) *Tourism Development and the Environment: Beyond sustainability?* Earthscan, London.

Siqueira, O. J. H, Steinmetz, S., Ferreira, M. F., Costa, A. C. and Wozniak, M. A. (2000) 'Mudanças climáticas projetadas através dos modelos GISS and reflexos na produção agrícola brasileira', *Revista Brasileira de Agrometeorologia*, vol. 8, no. 2, pp. 311–20.

UN World Tourism Organization (UNWTO) (2008) 'From Davos to Bali: a tourism contribution to the challenge of climate change', available at: www.climalptour.eu/content/sites/default/files/CC_Broch_DavBal_memb_bg.pdf (accessed 4 October 2011).

UNWTO (2010) 'Tourism 2020 Vision', available at: www.unwto.org/facts/eng/vision.htm (accessed 12 February 2011).

UNWTO (2011) 'International tourism 2010: Multi-speed recovery', available at: http://85.62.13.114/media/news/en/press_det.php?id=7331&idioma=E (accessed 20 March 2011).

Wara, M. W., Ravelo, A. C. and Delaney, M. L. (2005) 'Permanent El Niño-Like conditions during the Pliocene Warm Period', *Science*, vol. 309, pp. 758–61.

World Wildlife Fund for Nature (WWF) (2006) 'O planeta reage ao homem', available at: www.wwf.org.br/natureza_brasileira/meio_ambiente_brasil/clima/index.cfm (accessed 22 December 2010).

13

THE ROLE OF CLIMATE CHANGE IN TOURISM DEVELOPMENT STRATEGIES

A sustainability perspective in tourism strategies in the Nordic countries

Kaarina Tervo-Kankare and Jarkko Saarinen

Introduction

During the 1990s, the idea of sustainable development emerged as a paradigm in tourism research and development policies. The academic and public demand for more environmentally sensitive practices in tourism grew much earlier (see Hall and Lew 1998, Mathieson and Wall 1982), though, but during the 1990s, the issue of sustainability as a policy perspective began to guide and control the economic and political structures and processes of the tourism development (Bramwell and Lane 1993, Mowforth and Munt 1998, Bianchi 2004, Saarinen 2006). The growing need for sustainability in tourism was obviously a result of sustainable development discussions in general public and political agendas (see WCED 1987). However, in tourism studies it also related to increased knowledge and concern regarding the actual and potential future impacts of the global development of the industry to the environment (see Holden 2003, Macbeth 2005).

Although the idea of sustainability and the increased concern with the limits to growth in tourism development were global, the scale of analyses mainly focused on tourist destinations (such as resorts, resort complexes and tourism towns) and their better management (see Gössling and Hall 2006). According to Inskeep (1991: xviii), for example, 'the sustainable development approach can be applied to any scale of tourism development, from larger resorts to limited size special interest tourism' (see also Clarke 1997, UNWTO 2004). Thus, while tourism has evolved into a global–scale economy and sociocultural activity, the focus of sustainability in tourism has nevertheless been mainly on tourist destinations and tourism practices on local scales (Saarinen 2006).

Recently, there has been an increase in concern about the contribution of tourism to global-scale changes, especially climate change (Higham and Hall 2005, Bramwell and Lane 2008, Simpson et al. 2008, UNWTO-UNEP-WMO 2008).

Despite the global scale of this relatively new concern, it has often been approached as the idea of sustainability in tourism – locally. Another feature relating to the concern about climate change is its duality: on the other hand, tourism is seen as a contributor to climate change, and on the other hand it is considered to be affected by that very same change. Tourism as a contributor can be seen as operating in a global–local nexus, while impacts on tourism are often considered to be mainly local by nature (see Saarinen 2006). This duality has been reflected in tourism research, and despite the global nature of climate change and its impacts, the research on tourism, sustainability and climate change often focuses on destination-scale issues, such as changes in travel patterns, seasonality, environmental conditions and tourists' preferences. Simpson et al. (2008: 12–13), for example, divide the impacts on tourism destinations into four categories: direct climatic impacts, indirect environmental impacts, impacts of mitigation policies on tourist mobility, and indirect societal change impacts.

The focus on localized and destination-scale issues in research is quite understandable as, perhaps, local changes cover the most visible or concrete processes and impacts related to global tourism, climate change and sustainability (but as indicated by Gössling 2000, only a fragment of the total!). Moreover, the impacts and suitable adaptation methods often are local by nature and vary by geographic region and market segment (Wall 2007, UNWTO-UNEP-WMO 2008). Thus, destination-scale studies are needed in practice to avoid false generalizing of the implications of climate change.

Nevertheless, destination-scale studies are not the only way to approach climate change and sustainability. Related to the policy elements and societal context, one potential approach to go beyond a single destination focus is an examination of tourism strategies and the roles given to the dimensions of sustainability and climate change in these strategies. On one hand these tourism development strategies can be seen as spatially limited plans covering local, regional, national or supranational scales at the best. Thus, they do not reach a multi-level or global-scale analysis. On the other hand, they can be seen as intermediates in a local–global nexus (Hall 2000), manifesting 'local' responses to global change and how globalization from below (Giddens 1999) operates at various regional policy levels.

This chapter approaches the sustainability of tourism development from a climate change perspective according to which the consideration of climate change at a practical level for tourism development may become an essential requisite for viable tourism in the future (Simpson et al. 2008). Many forms of tourism rely heavily on natural resources such as water, sun and snow, and the whole industry is highly dependent on aviation as a means of transport, which leads to tourism being vulnerable to the impacts of climate change and the policies which aim to mitigate the change. Moreover, the growing environmental and climate-change awareness of tourists may bring along new challenges for tourism entrepreneurs. Finally, the climate-change-related actions in tourism may also determine the future sustainability of the whole tourism industry (UNWTO-UNEP-WMO 2008).

The purpose of this study is to examine the infiltration of climate change awareness into practical-level tourism development and its relation to sustainable principles. The foundations of the chapter are with the assumption that national and international policy processes create structures that guide, promote and also aim to limit certain types of tourism development and tourism consumption, while local policy governance networks and tourism developers and entrepreneurs are in a major position regarding the implementation of these structures and guidelines (McKercher et al. 2010, UNWTO-UNEP-WMO 2008). This kind of interpretation and the implementation of the relations of structure and agency (see Giddens 1979) is examined in a Finnish context by analysing the occurrence and content of climate change references in national, regional (Lapland and Central Finland) and local (two municipalities – Kittilä and Jämsä – with skiing destinations, one in each region) scale tourism development strategies and reports. Moreover, the references are compared with the findings of an interview study realized in two tourism destinations located in the above-mentioned regions and municipalities (Tervo-Kankare 2011). The comparison aims at examining whether and how the recognition of climate change in strategy papers also becomes visible in practice.

The data used in this study consists of two sets of material. First, we utilize a set of development papers and reports: national and regional tourism development strategies and local (city or tourism destination level) development plans and project reports. Second, another set of data was collected in 2009 and 2010 by interviewing tourism stakeholders (altogether nineteen interviewees representing tourism entrepreneurs (thirteen), tourism development officials (three interviews, five interviewees) and related industry (one)) in two tourism destinations that have been built on the surroundings of successful downhill skiing centres and where skiing continues to be a very important attraction for tourists (see Tervo-Kankare 2011).

The first set of data included documents that were published some years before the interviews took place. The reason for this was to make sure that the principles described in them had had some time to be implemented. While the interviews were realized, updates on several national strategies were made, but they were not included in the study for the abovementioned reason. The interview data was collected from tourism stakeholders who have linkages with the destinations' development plans. The selection of the interviewees was done using the snowball method. First, each destination's potential opinion leaders and implementing forces – the development authorities and representatives of the destinations' focal tourism enterprises (ski resorts) – were contacted to invite them to share thoughts on climate-change-related issues in the context of the destination. They were also asked to suggest tourism entrepreneurs or other stakeholders whose participation for the realization of the destinations' development plans they considered significant. Additionally, these new contacts were able to recommend interviewees they considered to possess climate-change-relevant information and to hold an important role in the destinations' tourism development. The main aim was to reach at least one representative for each of the most popular tourism forms (skiing, safari (snow mobile) operator, dog sledging, and reindeer activities) and development agencies.

The main themes covered in the interviews included awareness of climate change and local projects related with it, collaboration and networks in the region, and future plans.

All data were analysed using content analysis in the NVivo computer program. Analysis was realized by classifying and coding sustainability and climate-change-related information acquired from documents and interviewees into nodes and examining potential relationships between them. To enable the anonymity of the participants, interviewees' identities or references to exact locations are not mentioned in the text.

Sustainable tourism and climate change: growing climate change awareness in tourism

The quest for sustainability in tourism has lately been challenged by criticism which is based on climate change and the increasing trend of greenhouse gases, originating in particular from tourism transportation (Peeters, Gössling and Becken 2006). From the criticism perspective, tourism is seen as a geographical system that includes not only destinations, but also tourist-sending areas and the routes and transit areas integrating them (see Leiper 1979). Thus, the whole system should be the focus when its sustainability is to be considered. Although, for example, the current share of tourism transport emissions can be considered to be relatively small in the global scale (~5 per cent of all direct emissions), the future possibilities to limit and stabilize the impact of especially aviation-based transportation may be problematic for an industry that claims to be one of the largest and fastest-growing economic sectors in the world (Simpson et al. 2008, UNWTO-UNEP-WMO 2008). In other words, the growing aviation mobility in tourism and the increasing demand to limit overall emissions in future create a challenging equation. This becomes especially problematic if and when other major industries manage to decrease their emissions and, thus, the relative share of aviation-based emissions grows remarkably. In addition, even though transportation generates three-quarters of the total contribution of greenhouse gases from tourism (UNWTO-UNEP-WMO 2008), the contribution of tourism activities and facilities that generate emissions should also be examined carefully (Peeters et al. 2006). All this makes the relationship between climate change and sustainability critical to the tourism industry and its future.

Simultaneously with the growing international attention towards climate change, the number of climate-change-related tourism research publications has increased (see Scott, Wall and McBoyle 2005; Bramwell and Lane 2008). The growing number of research and development projects that focus on assessing the potential impacts of climate change and/or the adaptation and mitigation capacity of tourism destinations also indicates an increasing consideration of climate change in tourism (Becken 2008, UNWTO-UNEP-WMO 2008). In tourism development, the increasing general awareness has brought about the appearance of concerns over a changing climate in tourism development strategies and papers such as the national tourism strategies of Norway and Finland (Table 13.1).

TABLE 13.1 The consideration of climate change in the national tourism strategies of Finland, Norway and Sweden

Country and the name of the document (year of publication)	Description of the impacts	Proposal for action/other remarks
Finland		
Tourism Strategy to 2020 and Action Plan for 2007–2013 (2006)	Changing season lengths	• The lengths of the seasons must be taken into consideration in the construction of tourist destinations and product development • The development of supplementary products, especially required in southern Finland • Strengthening anticipation, provision and adaptation • Increasing international cooperation
Norway		
The Government's Tourism Strategy. Valuable Experiences – National Strategy for the Tourism Industry (2008)	The climate becomes more unstable	• The sustainable tourism policy must support Norway's climate policy in reducing (transport) emissions • The general awareness of climate change will increase
Sweden		
A Policy for Long Term Competitive Swedish Tourism (2005)	Climate change is not mentioned	• None

Often, these strategies address the role of tourism as a 'victim' of climate change, and focus on estimating the potential impacts on a country's tourism industry, while the contribution of tourism to climate change receives less attention. Moreover, climate-change-related issues are discussed on an abstract and advisory level, and hardly any practical guidance is given on how the industry could take climate change into consideration (see Table 13.1). Another approach is to disregard the whole issue: in the Swedish tourism strategy from the year 2005, for example, climate change is not mentioned. The absence of climate change in the Swedish strategy can probably be explained by the earlier publication of the strategy document than those for Finland and Norway: before 2005 there was hardly any information available on climate change in relation to tourism in the Nordic countries.

The analysis of tourism strategies provides one way to assess the role and level of sustainable development in tourism (see Ruhanen 2004). In the Nordic countries, for example, the pursuit of sustainability becomes evident in national tourism strategies that emphasize the importance of following sustainable tourism principles and creating images of sustainable destinations. Sweden, Norway and Finland, for example, all consider themselves to have a great potential to become well-known sustainable destinations (see Ministry of Trade and Industry 2006, Norwegian Ministry of Trade and Industry 2008, Svensk Turism AB 2010). According to the Norwegian Ministry of Trade and Industry (2008), for example, one of the three main objectives of Norwegian tourism is to develop the country as a sustainable destination, which the Ministry defines as follows:

> Sustainable tourism means that the development of the industry must promote sustainable local communities, good, stable workplaces and economically viable tourism companies, whilst keeping a firm focus on the environmental perspective. Tourism must also aspire to ensure low emissions of greenhouse gases and waste and protect our natural and cultural landscape. The Government's definition of the concept of sustainable tourism also includes social responsibilities.
>
> *(Norwegian Ministry of Trade and Industry 2008: 10)*

Even though the above-mentioned strategies partly indicate that climate change, at least as a concept, is penetrating the tourism industry (see also McEvoy et al. 2008), it remains unclear whether tourism stakeholders understand the role of climate change in sustainable tourism development, and the complex relationships between tourism, sustainability and climate change. Moreover, it remains unknown whether the appearance of climate change in tourism strategies leads to actions such as joint and multi-level efforts towards mitigation at the tourism destination scale (see Turton et al. 2010). Becken (2005), for example, examined climate-change-related actions in Fiji and noticed that no strategies to address the interactions between climate change and tourism had been developed in the destination's resorts and that there was no association promoting climate-change-related activities. In order to shed light on this matter in the Nordic context, we now examine the consideration of climate change at the tourism destination scale in Finland.

The consideration of climate change and sustainability in Finnish tourism development strategies

Following the publication in 2006 of Finland's national tourism strategy, which aimed to respond to international and EU-driven policy needs, climate change has featured in regional-level tourism strategies. The presence of climate change has been recognized in *Lapland's Tourism Strategy 2007–2010* (Regional Council of Lapland 2008) and in *Central Finland's Tourism Strategy 2015* (Regional Council of Central Finland, 2008), for example, both of which were published in 2008. In these strategies, climate change is regarded as a threat and a possibility, but the justification for the varying view is missing. In general, the impacts of the changing climate are considered to be positive in the short run and become more negative over the course of time. The estimations concerning the impacts focus on winter (snow-dependent) and summer tourism, which are the main seasons in both of the regions (even though summer tourism in Lapland continues to be less significant than the revenues received from the winter season) (see also Saarinen and Tervo 2006) (Table 13.2).

In both regions, the proposals for actions to avoid the negative impacts of a changing climate are presented on a general level, suggesting that 'something' should be done and tourism products should be developed towards climate-independence. Other remarks state that climate change should lead to an increase in collaboration or to the formation of collaborative networks where the participation of political decision makers and representatives of other industries becomes more common (at both national and international levels). In total, the amount of the climate-change-related information delivered by these documents is limited and the few paragraphs that refer to climate change are almost identical, despite the major differences between the tourism industries, products and seasonality of the two regions. Certain paragraphs are even copied onto several documents, which may be due to the fact that the same consultant agencies have participated in the strategy processes in different policy levels and regions.

In the local-level strategies, such as 'Levi 3 Kehittämissuunnitelman loppuraportti' (Suunnittelukeskus 2004) for the town of Kittilä in Lapland and 'Jämsän seudun matkailun master plan' (Suunnittelukeskus 2005) for the town of Jämsä in Central Finland, the indicated references to climate change are lower than in regional strategies. They do not provide actual information on climate change, its nature or

TABLE 13.2 The consideration of climate change in regional tourism strategies in Finland

Document	Description of the impacts	Proposal for action
Central Finland's Strategy for the Tourism Industry 2015	• Not possible to assess yet • A new rise in ecotourism? • The (cool) Finnish summer may lure more tourists • Warming, a challenge for winter tourism	• Actions should be planned • The shortening of the winter season should be taken into consideration in product development
Lapland's Tourism Strategy 2007–2010	• Gives Lapland a competitive advantage due to snow deficiency elsewhere and since the winters are becoming milder • Problems due to early seasons with no snow • More summer tourists to Lapland • Tourists become more aware of environmental matters • The future of aviation?	• Solving the question requires extensive collaboration • Proposed actions: product development (snow-independent products) and market communication (the focus on other factors than just the snow)

the potential impacts on the local tourism industry. This may indicate that the global-scale processes of climate change are not yet seen concretely enough in local-scale tourism policy making. This is somewhat surprising as the majority of tourism-related climate change studies have been focusing on the destination: that is, on local-scale issues. The minor references to climate change in local-scale tourism strategies are probably due to the early publication of the latest destination-level plans (before or just after the preparation and publication of the national strategy in 2006). The general goals of the local plans in both destinations are somewhat similar, and follow the principles that are presented in national and regional-level strategies: growth in tourism revenues and the number of tourists visiting the region, the establishment of the regions' image and brand, the enhancement of (service) quality, improving collaboration, increasing all-year and international tourism and the implementation of sustainable tourism principles.

It is noteworthy that, together with all-year tourism, sustainability and sustainable tourism have an important role in all of the documentation under scrutiny. They are mentioned in several contexts and, contrary to climate change, discussed widely in relation to national, regional and local-level tourism. Thus, in contrast to climate change, sustainability is actually scaled to various policy documents in different levels. The missing role of climate change on the local scale is surprising as the role of seasonality in general is much emphasized. Strong seasonality has traditionally hindered tourism in Finland (see Saarinen 2003), which may be an explanation for the frequent occurrence of the pursuit of all-year tourism in all of the planning. The need for sustainable tourism in tourism strategies is often justified by growing environmental awareness among tourists, the maintenance of natural resources and the high quality of Finnish tourism.

Local-scale views and responses to climate change

Despite the small amount of information delivered by official documents, some development projects which have been realized in Finnish winter tourism destinations have taken climate change into consideration. For example, the CLIM-atic project (Järviluoma and Suopajärvi 2009), the aim of which is to ease the adaptation of northern peripheral communities to climate change, is being carried out in three Lappish tourism destinations located in Kittilä, Kolari and Rovaniemi. Another example referring to climate change has been implemented in Jämsä, in Central Finland (Pelkonen 2008). In order to assess the infiltration of climate change awareness to grassroots-level tourism stakeholders, the stakeholders' awareness and participation in these projects was examined via an interview study realized in the tourism resorts of Kittilä and Jämsä. The tourism stakeholders' (tourism development officials, tourism entrepreneurs) conceptions and opinions on climate change and on general tourism development at the destinations are summarized in Table 13.3.

The participants in the interview study assessed that the contradictory perceptions of climate change among them were due to a lack of knowledge and a poor level

TABLE 13.3 A summary of climate-change-related opinions among tourism stakeholders in Kittilä and Jämsä

Climate change
Regarded as an important issue to tourism at the destination (and in the whole country)
Considered to be both a threat and a possibility (mainly in regard to the changing seasons)
No actions implemented
The importance of snow-making facilities for future tourism considered high
Climate change is a minor factor affecting the tourism development of the destinations, contradictory perceptions on its importance and role
It is trendy to refer to climate change
No information delivered from official (state, municipality etc) sources
Other remarks on local tourism development
Overall development goals are well-known
Sustainability and all-year tourism is gaining most of the attention
The knowledge of individual projects is poor among tourism entrepreneurs

Source: Tervo-Kankare (2011).

of information. Despite the scarcity of information, a number of individuals had a good understanding about the causes and effects of the change. The main source for climate change information seemed to be the media, but some stakeholders had also discussed climate-change-related issues in the meetings of some tourism organizations such as the Finnish Ski Area Association (Suomen Hiihtokeskusyhdistys). When asked if or what kind of climate change information the interviewees had received, they mentioned either the great attention the topic has attracted in the media or their personal observations on seasonal and weather changes (for instance, permanent snow arrives at a later date), as in this comment:

> Well, yes, we have received surprisingly well it (information) so that, like last winter also quite many noticed that ... there hasn't been so cold weather as for example in last winter for ages ... so that you can see it there and also in autumn you can see it from what time the snow arrives and that really shows it well so.

The representatives of local development agencies in Lapland regarded climate change, with its complex cause and effect relationship, to be too broad, scary and too paralyzing an issue to handle. In contrast to climate change, the pursuit of sustainability was regarded to be easier for tourism entrepreneurs to understand and to process:

> And it [climate change] feels such a huge change to know what it means considering the whole world and then you notice how small you are and feel that I can't do this, I just let it be.

> And that when you talk about friendliness to the environment and about those methods how to act to save the environment, they make the issue much more concrete to those stakeholders than to talk about climate change, which may be remoter as a term ... so that I have greater possibility to influence to this saving of the environment than to that climate, that's the way people probably think. ... Those kind of cause and effect relationships they have to be easily verified so that if you act his this way this will follow. So if you don't make it concrete enough then there is less possibility that people will commit to that action.

On the other hand, the representatives of local development agencies shared the opinion that many of the aspects of climate change, such as mitigation, were already included in the general discussions about sustainable tourism:

> Climate change ... as a word it may not be mentioned in these (i.e. the development documents) ... but that sustainable development is here already and related projects have been realized in here.

> Yes, more like sustainable development. But also climate change was mentioned there, but we started more from this sustainable development and how can you save energy in your firm and sustainably and so on.

Thus, there was no need to make specific references to climate change. This seemed to be the common view, and the interviewees often connected the ideas about sustainability and the pursuit of all-year tourism with climate change. According to tourism entrepreneurs, the demanded collaboration between the diverse groups of stakeholders primarily took place in order to develop and increase all-year tourism, that is, to reduce the problems of seasonality, not to benefit from or to avoid climate change impacts. On its own, climate change was not considered to be a very interesting (that is, important) topic. In general, the stakeholders usually connected climate change with observations on warming winters, belated winter season starts and the need to develop snow-independent activities:

> I don't know if the municipality has taken any stand in this, but on tourism side it is discussed constantly that the (winter) season is shortening from both ends.
>
> *(tourism entrepreneur)*

Discussion

The connections between sustainability and climate change are evident and obvious in tourism. However, based on the tourism strategy analysis, the nature and weight of their consideration and the implementation at various policy levels and in discussions differ. While sustainability is driven in all levels of policy making, the issue of climate change has, at least partly, remained theoretical, abstract and left aside from the local-scale strategies and actions. This is somewhat unexpected as past research interest has tended to favour a destination-level analysis. Thus, based on the findings and material used in this paper, the theoretical idea of local and regional-scale policy documents and strategies working as intermediates between local and global scales is not fully manifested – at least, not yet.

With climate change being such a high-level international concern, it is surprising that the tourism strategies give such little advice on concrete planning and preparing for climate change. One reason for this may be the small amount of research that has been conducted – or there are enough research publications and volumes, but policy makers do not have access, knowledge or a perceived need to search them. In spite of the reason, there does not seem to be enough useful and usable information available for the policy-making purposes and practical uses of the tourism industry. Several research-driven participatory development projects which are taking place may be of assistance in this matter, but active collaboration between the researchers and tourism stakeholders and the 'marketing' of study results may be more widely required in the future if the indicated awareness gap between sustainability and climate change is attempted to be bridged.

In relation to the concerns of the tourism authorities and policy makers on climate change, Dodds and Graci (2009: 49) have reported that 'although concern is high among stakeholders, there is little being done'. Another study by Hall (2006) in New Zealand concluded with similar attitudes: climate change was considered to be a low-level concern for small and medium-sized enterprises (SMEs) (see also Saarinen and Tervo 2006). If it is looked at critically, a similar situation – high rhetoric, low action – may be the case with sustainability in tourism. However, as said, sustainability has been transformed more clearly towards goals and actions at all of the policy levels, while climate change remains abstract and does not feature in local-scale strategies and actions. Thus, climate change awareness has not found its way to the practical level yet.

The key findings of Turton et al.'s (2010) adaptation study in Australia support this conclusion. Instead of an adaptation to climate change, the themes identified by tourism stakeholders, such as adaptation, can be better linked to the general idea of sustainable development in tourism. Nevertheless, as Ruhanen (2004) concludes in her study on the integration of sustainable development principles at the tourism destination level, even the application of general sustainable guidelines in practice is not yet obvious in some destinations. Hence, the implementation of specific climate change principles at the destination level may be an increasingly far-fetched idea.

The analysis of tourism strategies offered a fruitful way to assess the nature of sustainability in tourism and its connection to the issues referring to climate change. With sustainability dominating the strategy papers and discussions, the connections to climate change adaptation and mitigation need an 'interpretative capacity' as they are often 'written between the lines': that is, it is indirectly implied and considered in the strategy documents. A pursuit of all-year tourism, for example, can be understood as lessening the risk of losses during climatically bad winters, by making destinations less dependent on snow-based winter activities and leading to the development of new non-snow activities. Moreover, sustainable tourism serves a mitigation purpose since many of the sustainability goals, such as energy efficiency and the development of environmentally friendly ways to reach destinations, support efforts to fight climate change. Thus, the climate-change-related actions in tourism development will also determine the future sustainability of the whole tourism industry, as the decisions made and directions selected now will have long term impacts to the environment.

Considering this, it can be asked whether it is important to emphasize climate change independently or whether more efforts should be directed to the overall pursuit of sustainability in tourism and related development policies and activities, In the latter case, however, the focus of sustainability in tourism should be rescaled to cover not only the destination-level issues but also the wider scales of the tourism system and related mobilities, including transportation between tourists' home regions and destinations. Indeed, stronger integration between climate change discussions and sustainability is urgently needed.

Acknowledgements

This chapter is based on research funded by the Academy of Finland under the auspices of the FiDiPro programme 'Human–Environment Relations in the North: resource development, climate change and resilience' at the Thule Institute, University of Oulu, and the Ficca Programme. The research has been realized in close collaboration with the Vaccia and KeMMI projects that have been funded by the European Union.

References

Beaumont, N. and Dredge, D. (2010) 'Local tourism governance: a comparison of three network approaches', *Journal of Sustainable Tourism*, vol. 18, no. 1, pp. 7–28.

Becken, S. (2005) 'Harmonizing climate change adaptation and mitigation: the case of tourist resorts in Fiji', *Global Environmental Change*, vol. 15, no. 4, pp. 381–93.

Becken, S. (2008) 'Report: The UN Climate Change Conference, Bali: what it means for tourism?' *Journal of Sustainable Tourism*, vol. 16, no. 2, pp. 246–8.

Becken, S. and Hay, J. E. (2007) *Tourism and Climate Change: Risks and opportunities*, Channel View, Bristol.

Bianchi, R. (2004) 'Tourism restructuring and the politics of sustainability: a critical view from the European periphery (the Canary Islands)', *Journal of Sustainable Tourism*, vol. 12, no. 6, pp. 495–529.

Bramwell, B. and Lane, B. (1993) 'Sustaining tourism: an evolving global approach', *Journal of Sustainable Tourism*, vol. 1, no. 1, pp. 1–5.

Bramwell, B. and Lane, B. (2008) 'Priorities in sustainable tourism research', *Journal of Sustainable Tourism*, vol. 16, no. 1, pp. 1–4.

Browne, S. and Hunt, L. (2007) 'Climate change and nature-based tourism, outdoor recreation, and forestry in Ontario: potential effects and adaptation strategies', Thunder Bay: Ontario Ministry of Natural Resources, available at: www.mnr.gov.on.ca/ stdprodconsume/groups/lr/@mnr/@climatechange/documents/document/276926. pdf, (accessed 25 March 2011).

Clarke, J. (1997) 'A framework of approaches to sustainable tourism', *Journal of Sustainable Tourism*, vol. 5, no. 3, pp. 224–33.

Dodds, R. and Graci, S. (2009) 'Canada's tourism industry – mitigating the effect of climate change: a lot of concern but little action', *Tourism and Hospitality Planning and Development*, vol. 6, no. 1, pp. 39–51.

Giddens, A. (1979) *Central Problems in Social Theory: Action, structure and contradiction in social analyses,* Macmillan, London.

Giddens, A. (1999) *Runaway World: How globalization is reshaping our lives,* Profile Books, London.

Gössling, S. (2000) 'Sustainable tourism development in developing countries: some aspects of energy use', *Journal of Sustainable Tourism*, vol. 8, no. 5, pp. 410–25.

Gössling, S. and Hall, C. M. (eds) (2006) *Tourism and Global Environmental Change: Ecological, social, economic and politic interrelationships*, Routledge, London.

Gössling, S. and Hall, C. M. (2008) 'Swedish tourism and climate change mitigation: an emerging conflict?' *Scandinavian Journal of Hospitality and Tourism*, vol. 8, no. 2, pp. 141–58.

Gössling, S., Haglund, L., Kallgren, H., Revahl, M. and Hultman, J. (2009) 'Swedish air travellers and voluntary carbon offsets: towards the co-creation of environmental value?' *Current Issues in Tourism*, vol. 12, no1, pp. 1–19.

Gössling, S. and Hall, C. M. (2009) 'Climate change responses of Swedish tourism actors: an analysis of actor websites', in C. M. Hall, D. K. Müller and J. Saarinen (eds), Nordic Tourism: Issues and cases, Channel View, Bristol.

Grenier, A. A. (2007) 'The diversity of polar tourism: some challenges facing the industry in Rovaniemi, Finland', *Polar Geography*, vol. 30, no. 1, pp. 55–72.

Hall, C. M. (2000) *Tourism Planning*, Prentice Hall, Harlow.

Hall, C. M. (2006) 'New Zealand tourism entrepreneur attitudes and behaviours with respect to climate change adaptation and mitigation', *International Journal of Innovation and Sustainable Development*, vol. 1, no. 3, pp. 229–37.

Hall, C. M. and Lew, A. A. (1998) 'The geography of sustainable tourism: lessons and prospects', in C. M. Hall and A. A. Lew (eds), *Sustainable Tourism: A geographical perspective*, Longman, New York.

Hall, C. M. and Williams, A. M. (2008) *Tourism and Innovation*, Routledge, London and New York.

Higham, J. and Hall, C. M. (2005) 'Making tourism sustainable: the real challenge of climate change?' in C. M. Hall and J. Higham (eds), *Tourism, Recreation and Climate Change*, Channel View, Bristol.

Holden, A. (2003) 'In need of new environmental ethics for tourism', *Annals of Tourism Research*, vol. 30, no. 1, pp. 94–108.

Inskeep, E. (1991) *Tourism Planning: An integrated and sustainable development approach*, Van Nostrand Reinhold, New York.

Järviluoma, J. and Suopajärvi, L. (2009) *Ilmastonmuutoksen ennakoituihin vaikutuksiin sopeutuminen Rovaniemellä. Clim-Atic-hankkeen raportti,* Lapin yliopisto, Rovaniemi.

Jylhä, K., Fronzek, S., Tuomenvirta, H., Carter T. R. and Ruosteenoja, K. (2008) 'Changes in frost, snow and Baltic Sea Ice by the end of the twenty-first century based on climate model projections for Europe', *Climatic Change,* vol. 86, no. 3–4, pp. 441–62.

Jylhä, K., Tuomenvirta, H. and Ruosteenoja, K. (2004) 'Climate change projections for Finland during the 21st century', *Boreal Environment Research,* vol. 9, no. 2, pp. 127–52.

Kaltenborn, B. P., Haaland, H. and Sandell, K. (2001) 'The public right of access – some challenges to sustainable tourism development in Scandinavia', *Journal of Sustainable Tourism,* vol. 9, no. 5, pp. 417–33.

Leiper, N. (1979) 'The framework of tourism', *Annals of Tourism Research,* vol. 6, no. 4, pp. 390–407.

Mathieson, A. and Wall, G. (1982) *Tourism: Economic, physical and social impacts,* Longman, New York.

Macbeth, J. (2005) 'Towards an ethics platform for tourism', *Annals of Tourism Research,* vol. 32, no. 4, pp. 962–84.

McEvoy, D., Cavan, G., Handley, J., McMorrow, J. and Lindley, S. (2008) 'Changes to climate and visitor behaviour: implications for vulnerable landscapes in the North West region of England', *Journal of Sustainable Tourism,* vol. 16, no. 1, pp. 101–21.

McKercher, B., Prideaux, B., Cheung, C. and Law, R. (2010) 'Achieving voluntary reductions in the carbon footprint of tourism and climate change', *Journal of Sustainable Tourism,* vol. 18, no. 3, pp. 297–317.

Ministry of Trade and Industry (2006) 'Suomen matkailustrategia vuoteen 2020 & Toimenpideohjelma vuosille 2007–2013' (Finland's Tourism Strategy 2020 and Action Plan 2007–2013), available at: http://ktm.elinar.fi/ktm_jur/ktmjur.nsf/all/3D61DB118 241A034C22571800022FEC4/$file/jul21elo_2006_netti.pdf (accessed 4 May 2010).

Mowforth, M. and Munt, I. (1998) *Tourism and Sustainability: A new tourism in the third world,* Routledge, London and New York.

Norwegian Ministry of Trade and Industry (2008) 'The Government's Tourism Strategy. Valuable Experiences: National Strategy for the Tourism Industry', available at: www.regjeringen.no/upload/NHD/Vedlegg/strategier2007/engelsk%20utgave%20 -%20hele.pdf (accessed 15 December 2010).

Peeters, P. (ed.) (2007) *Tourism and Climate Change Mitigation: Methods, greenhouse gas reductions and policies,* NHTV Academic Studies No. 6, Breda, Netherlands.

Peeters, P., Gössling, S. and Becken, S. (2006) 'Innovation towards tourism sustainability: climate change and aviation', *International Journal of Innovation and Sustainable Development,* vol. 1, no. 3, pp. 184–200.

Pelkonen, H. (2008) 'Himoskylä 2015 – visiosta käytäntöön vaihe II', available at: www.jamsek.fi/@Bin/27678/Himoskyla2015IIloppuraportti.pdf (accessed 15 September 2010).

Pollock, A. (2008) 'The climate change challenge implications for the tourism industry: a discussion paper', Icarus Foundation, available at: www.theicarusfoundation.com/pdf/ Icarus_Discussion_Paper%20MAR_08.pdf (accessed 20 July 2010).

Regional Council of Central Finland (2008) *Keski-Suomen matkailuelinkeinon strategia 2015 (Central Finland's Tourism Strategy 2015),* available at: www.keskisuomi.fi/ filebank/10343-KSMatkailustrategia2015.pdf (accessed 26 May 2010).

Regional Council of Lapland (2008) *Lapin matkailustrategia 2007–2010 (Lapland's Tourism Strategy 2007–2010),* available at: www.lapinliitto.fi/matkailu/matstra20072010.pdf (accessed 7 May 2010).

Ruhanen, L. (2004) 'Strategic planning for local tourism destinations: an analysis of tourism plans', *Tourism and Hospitality Planning*, vol. 1, no. 3, pp. 239–53.

Saarinen, J. (2003) 'The regional economics of tourism in northern Finland: the socio-economic implications of recent tourism development and future possibilities for regional development', *Scandinavian Journal of Hospitality and Tourism*, vol. 3, no. 2, pp. 91–113.

Saarinen, J. (2006) 'Traditions of sustainability in tourism studies', *Annals of Tourism Research*, vol. 33, no. 4, pp. 121–1240.

Saarinen, J. and Tervo, K. (2006) 'Perceptions and adaptation strategies of the tourism industry to climate change: the case of Finnish nature-based tourism entrepreneurs', *International Journal of Innovation and Sustainable Development*, vol. 1, no. 3, pp. 214–28.

Saarinen, J. and Tervo, K. (2010) 'Sustainability and emerging awareness to changing climate: tourism industry's knowledge and perceptions of the future of nature-based winter tourism in Finland', in C. M. Hall and J. Saarinen (eds), *Tourism and Change in Polar Regions: Climate, environment and experiences*, Routledge, London and New York.

Scott, D. and Becken, S. (2010) 'Adapting to climate change and climate policy: progress, problems and potentials', *Journal of Sustainable Tourism*, vol. 18, no. 3, pp. 283–95.

Scott, D., de Freitas, C. and Matzarakis, A. (2009) 'Adaptation in the tourism and recreation sector', in K. L. Ebi, I. Burton and G. McGregor (eds), *Biometeorology for Adaptation to Climate Variability and Change*, Springer Science + Business Media.

Scott, D., McBoyle, G., Minogue, A. and Mills, B. (2006) 'Climate change and the sustainability of ski-based tourism in eastern North America: a reassessment', *Journal of Sustainable Tourism*, vol. 14, no. 4, pp. 376–98.

Scott, D., Wall, G. and McBoyle, G. (2005) 'The evolution of the climate change issue in the tourism sector', in C. M. Hall and J. Higham (eds), *Tourism, Recreation and Climate Change*, Channel View, Bristol, Buffalo, N.Y. and Toronto.

Simpson, M. C., Gössling, S., Scott, D., Hall, C. M. and Gladin, E. (2008) *Climate Change Adaptation and Mitigation in the Tourism Sector: Frameworks, tools and practices*, UN Environment Programme (UNEP), University of Oxford, UN World Tourism Organization (UNWTO) and World Meteorological Organization (WMO), Paris.

Suunnittelukeskus Oy (2004) *Levi 3. Kehittämissuunnitelman loppuraportti*, Kittilän kunta, Kittilä.

Suunnittelukeskus Oy (2005) *Jämsän seudun matkailun master plan*, Jämsek, Jämsä.

Svensk Turism AB (2010) 'Nationell strategi for svensk besöksnäring' (Swedish national tourism strategy), available at: www.strategi2020.se/upload_dokuments/SHR_Strategidokument.pdf, (accessed 15 December 2010).

Tervo-Kankare, K. (2011) 'The consideration of climate change at the tourism destination level in Finland: coordinated collaboration or talk about weather?' *Tourism Planning and Development*, vol. 8, no. 4, pp. 1–16.

Turton, S., Dickson, T., Hadwen, W., Jorgensen, B., Pham, T., Simmons, D., Trembley, P. and Wilson, R. (2010) 'Developing an approach for tourism climate change assessment: evidence from four contrasting Australian case studies', *Journal of Sustainable Tourism*, vol. 18, no. 3, pp. 429–47.

UNWTO (2004) 'Sustainable development of tourism conceptual definition', available at: www.world-tourism.org/frameset/frame_sustainable.html (accessed 10 February 2011).

UNWTO, UNEP and WMO (2008) 'Climate change and tourism – responding to global challenges', UNWTO, UNEP and WMO, Madrid, available at: www.unep.fr/shared/publications/pdf/WEBx0142xPA-ClimateChangeandTourismGlobalChallenges.pdf (accessed 20 July 2010).

Wall, G. (2007) 'The tourism industry and its adaptability and vulnerability to climate change', in B. Amelung, K. Blazejczyk and A. Matzarakis (eds), *Climate Change and Tourism – Assessment and coping strategies*? Maastricht, Warsaw and Freiburg.

Wolfsegger, C. (2005) 'Perception and adaptation to climate change in low altitude ski resorts in Austria', Master's Thesis, Lund University Master's Programme in International Environmental Science, Sweden.

World Commission on Environment and Development (WCED) (1987) *Our Common Future*, Oxford University Press, Oxford.

14

TOURISM AND CLIMATE CHANGE IN SOUTHERN AFRICA
Sustainability and perceived impacts and adaptation strategies of the tourism industry to changing climate and environment in Botswana

Jarkko Saarinen, Wame Hambira, Julius Atlhopheng and Haretsebe Manwa

Introduction

The connections between tourism, climate change and sustainability have been emphasized in recent tourism literature and policy documents (see Gössling and Hall 2006, Bramwell and Lane 1993, UNWTO and UNEP 2008, UNWTO 2009, Scott 2011). In many respects, however, the discussions on sustainability and climate change issues in tourism development and research have been operating in separate fields and on separate scales (see Holden 2003, Macbeth 2005, Saarinen 2006), and there are even contradictory views between the objectives of sustainable tourism development and adaption needs to climate change in tourism (see Weaver 2011). However, as indicated by Bramwell and Lane (2008), climate change can also be seen as a priority area for the sustainable tourism research agenda and a new and timely issue in the study of tourism–environment relations (see also Peeters 2009, Scott 2011).

Tourism, sustainability and climate change are deeply intertwined issues. On the one hand, tourism industry and related activities can be seen as major contributors to climate change (Wall 1998), which has an effect on the sustainability of the industry. On the other hand, the tourism industry is regarded as a highly climate-sensitive economic sector,: that is, the future of the tourism industry is seen to be greatly dependent on global climate change and its local outcomes as climate forms a major basis for attracting tourists to visit certain kinds of environments. All these will have implications on the sustainability of tourism in certain destinations, but in addition to direct impacts on destinations, changes in source markets' environments and their climatic conditions will affect future travel patterns, for example. According to the UN World Tourist Organization (UNWTO) (2009), the impacts of climate on the tourism system can be direct climatic or/and indirect environmental changes; they can be focused on mitigation policies on tourism mobilities or they can be indirect societal changes. From the industry's perspective all these call for a development of adaptation mechanisms and strategies.

The development of adaptive capacity is one of the most urgent issues in the context of developing countries, where the impacts of climate change may be very severe in the relatively near future (see Gössling 2000, Mirza 2003, Ramos and Kahla 2009). This is because the necessary capital and technologies are mainly missing and the nature of the tourism system makes it most vulnerable. Regions like southern Africa and especially countries such as Botswana, where the industry and its activities and attractiveness are mainly based on the natural environment and wildlife, are seen as highly vulnerable (Saarinen et al. 2011). Climate change will also have a variety of non-tourism-related impacts on local communities and their traditional livelihoods, which will create further challenges to poverty alleviation and sustainable use of the environment, for example. In addition, the current emphasis on using the tourism industry as a tool to diversify national economies in the region (see UNWTO 2008) makes the development of adaptive capacity even more crucial, as tourism will be introduced to new places and communities in future, increasing the list and numbers of those dependent on the industry.

Therefore, it is somewhat surprising that the impacts of climate change on the tourism sector in the region have so far received minimal attention. Tourism and other development policies portray the industry as one of the key economic sectors in the region, and one which has huge potential for wealth creation for nations and the local communities (Republic of Botswana 2003, Boko et al. 2007, UNWTO 2008). According to the World Tourism and Travel Council (WTTC) (2007), tourism's direct contribution to Botswana's gross domestic product (GDP) is about 9.5 per cent of overall GDP and it has a direct employment effect of over 23,000 jobs. The direct and indirect employment impact, however, is almost 60,000 jobs, representing 10.6 per cent of total employment in Botswana. This makes tourism the second most important sector of the national economy, and over the next decade Botswana's tourism growth is expected to be 5 per cent per year.

Previous studies on tourism and climate change have mainly focused on the north and snow-based winter tourism activities (see e.g. Scott 2006, Moen and Fredman 2007, Tervo 2008, Saarinen and Tervo 2006, 2010). In general, Boko et al. (2007: 450) have noted that very few assessments of estimated impacts 'on tourism and climate change are available' in African contexts. In response to this relative gap, the purpose of this chapter is to discuss the impacts of climate change on the tourism industry in southern Africa, especially in Botswana. The specific aim is to provide an overview of the potential impacts of climate change on the industry (and its operational environment) and to examine the local tourism operators' perceptions and intended adaptation strategies to the impending impacts and processes. The operators' role, views and level of knowledge are important for the present and future innovation potential of the industry, its sustainability and the construction of an adaptive capacity towards climate change in tourism. The case study aims to summarize the perceptions and adaptation strategies of tourism operators on climate change in the arid Kgalagadi (Kalahari) and Okavango Delta wetland environments.

Impacts of climate change on tourism and sustainability in southern Africa

Tourism is a complex system which depends directly and indirectly on many other processes, including natural systems and their changes. These systems and changes have direct and indirect links to sustainability, and there is an increasing need to know how these changes may affect tourism attractions and patterns, and how they affect some of the tourism industry values and goals such as sustainable development and pro-poor tourism (Boko et al. 2007, Bührs 2008, Tao and Wall 2009), for example. Therefore, several attempts have been made in research to assess the impacts of climate change on various natural resources and scales. In mapping out climate change impacts on tourism, the study may involve several parameters such as the expected impacts (ecological, economic, and sociocultural: Holt and Hattam 2009), the extent and severity of the impacts, as well as indicators of the impacts (Prato 2008).

As research on climate change intensifies, so does the awareness of possible impacts on the tourism sector (see Velarde et al. 2005; Biggs et al. 2008; Hein, Metzger and Moreno 2009; Hall and Saarinen 2010). The Intergovernmental Panel on Climate Change (IPCC) (2007) has estimated that average temperatures are likely to rise globally by about 3 °C by the end of the century. Several regional estimations (see Hulme et al. 2001, Vogel 2005, 2009) imply that climatic changes will be significant in southern Africa, and especially in the central parts of the region where Botswana is located. For example, Hulme's (1996) scenario for 2050 indicates an increase in temperature by 2 °C in the central parts of southern Africa and about 1.5 °C along the coastal regions. Although rainfall may increase during the wet season, it will probably be offset by a decrease in the remaining months of the year, resulting in increased aridity in most of the region (Preston-Whyte and Watson 2005). For the Western Cape, for example, the warming may coincide with decreasing evaporation as the wind run decreases, hence there are less evaporative conditions. The net effect could be more moisture in the region, which coupled with higher carbon dioxide levels, would lead to more woody biomass growth (Brown 2009).

Further, Midgley and Guo (2009) have used the probability of certain events occurring in relation with calibrated climate simulation data and found that the rainfall for drier events is likely to decrease by up to 30 mm/month, with the wetter events increasing by 10–50 mm/month in Namibia, for example. Similar findings were made by Chamaillé-James, Fritz and Murindagomo (2007) when they used quantile regressions on rainfall analysis in Hwange National Park, Zimbabwe. These have implications for certain wildlife species, especially those dependent on the lush green grazing, which will most probably negatively affect the tourism attractiveness of the region.

Some of the major challenges of assessing the impacts of climate change involve the patching together of results of simulation models with varying scales and research study objectives to understand not only the impact on biodiversity but also socio-ecological interactions at local and regional scales. Tourism, being multi-layered (as it depends on interactions with other systems), thus poses such challenges, as some of the research findings are not applicable to other sites (Hein et al. 2009). This is quite problematic. In addition, the climatic future estimations do not include a view on the future societal context, which obviously plays a major role in determining how the impacts of climate change will actually affect social and economic systems such as tourism.

In southern Africa the mentioned trends and processes in climate change may cause shifting rainfall patterns, health hazards, increasing droughts, decreasing biodiversity and wildlife extinctions, general declines in ecosystem services (see Hulme 1996, Mirza 2003, van Jaarsveld et al. 2005, Bates et al. 2008, Allen et al. 2010) and mobilization of the current stable sand dunes (Thomas, Knight and Wiggs 2005). These kinds of changes could probably compromise Botswana's economic diversification processes (see Saarinen et al. 2012), in which the tourism industry plays a major role. It is already the second largest economic sector after mining (Republic of Botswana 2003, UNWTO 2008). Although global climate change will have an impact on the whole tourism sector, nature-based and wildlife tourism will face significant changes, mainly because of their profound dependency on the characteristics of the natural environment and climate (weather) conditions (Agnew and Viner 2001, Tervo-Kankare and Saarinen 2011).

Since the role of nature-based tourism is crucial in Botswana, the effects of changing climate may have serious consequences for the industry, its sustainability and the society (see Preston-Whyte and Watson 2005, Eriksen and Watson 2009). In climate-change-related discussions it is crucial to acknowledge the connections between tourism, societies and sustainability, as tourism is highly dependent on the general socio-economic and environmental contexts in which it operates.

In general, sustainability has been noted as being problematic in tourism development (see Sharpley 2000, 2009, Saarinen 2006). With reference to climate change adaptation processes, sustainability is challenging in 'high-end' tourism products (such as safari operations in the Okavango Delta) as international clients may expect luxury and comfort as a priority, 'often over environmental concerns' (Smerecnik and Andersen 2011: 190). However, climate change adaptation to ensure the comfort of customers should not compromise the long-term sustainability of the industry (see Scott 2011). That would be problematic not only to the environment but also to the socio-economic and political legitimatization of an industry that aims to provide an increasing number of employment and business opportunities for local communities and people in the future (see UNWTO 2008, Saarinen et al. 2012).

Case study: perceived impacts, practices and adaptation strategies of the tourism industry to climate change in the Kgalagadi and Okavango Delta, Botswana

Study areas: land use issues and research material

Botswana's tourism industry is based on nature due to its abundant natural resources. The resource endowment is linked to among other things, the prevailing climatic conditions and geological attributes pertaining to the area (NCSA 2000). This study is based on two ecologically distinct study sites: Tshabong, situated in south-western Botswana in Kgalagadi South District, and Maun, located in Ngamiland District in northern Botswana (Figure 14.1). The physical environments of Tshabong and Maun can be classified as dry sand veldt and wet sand veldt respectively (see NCSA 2000). The rainfall in Botswana is seasonal and highly erratic. The northern part of the country where Maun is located normally receives the highest rainfall in the country, while the Kgalagadi district where Tshabong is situated normally records the lowest rainfall amounts in the country.

Consequently the main livelihood source in Tshabong is pastoral farming, while arable farming is carried out on a lesser scale. Formal employment is provided mainly by central and local government since Tshabong is the administrative centre of the district. However employment opportunities are not adequate, as evidenced by informal employment such as vending, 'piece jobs', handicraft and hide turning (see Hambira et al. 2010). None the less, tourism activity is still relatively low in this area, and according to Moswete et al. (2000a), this is attributable to low tourism awareness, poor infrastructure development, low literacy rates and inadequate marketing of the region. This however does not negate the area's tourism potential.

The natural resources in the area are commensurate with its physical environment, ranging from diverse plant and animal life to topographical features that include palaeo channels, fossil valleys, sand-dunes and pan depressions. This refutes the perception of desert as a barren, valueless land, and the unending space and isolation are the principal attractions, making the Kgalagadi 'the ultimate wilderness destination' (BTB 2009). Tshabong is located relatively close to the Kgalagadi Transfrontier Park (KTP) which is made up of the South Africa's Kalahari Gemsbok National Park and Botswana's Gemsbok National Park. KTP is a so-called peace park jointly managed and developed by the two countries (three-quarters of it fall in Botswana). It was the first peace park to be established in Africa (BTB 2009).

Maun, in contrast, can be dubbed the mainstay of the tourism industry not only in the Ngamiland District but in Botswana as a whole. While Tshabong is the administrative centre of the Kgalagadi South District, Maun plays the same role in the Ngamiland District, with intensive services for tourists who are mainly international (see Mbaiwa 2005, Moswete et al. 2000b). Maun is the gateway to the much-acclaimed Okavango Delta, which is one of the largest inland deltas in the world (see Ramsar 2011). While many cultures have learned to exploit their

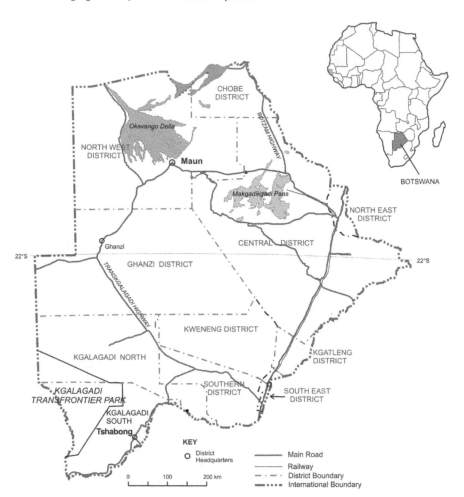

FIGURE 14.1 The case study places in Botswana. The study sites are located in two ecologically distinct places: Tshabong, situated in southwestern Botswana in Kgalagadi South District, and Maun, located in Ngamiland District in northern Botswana

Map courtesy of G. Koorutwe.

wetlands for economic benefit and others have quickly drained their landscape (Magole and Magole 2009), the Okavango Delta has thus far maintained its integrity (DEA 2008), and is a key tourist destination in Botswana due to its rich wilderness diversity and scenic beauty. The main livelihood sources include tourism, livestock rearing, hand crafts and small to medium-scale industries (Mbaiwa and Stronza 2010). Despite the proliferation of tourism, the community's livelihood is still largely dependent on agriculture coupled with formal and informal employment (see Hambira et al. 2010). The tourism demand and growth has brought with it infrastructure development for transportation, accommodation, telecommunications and banking services (Mbaiwa 2005). These have added to the employment base in the town. Other tourist attractions in the area include the Moremi game reserve, the Chobe National Park and the Tsodilo Hills.

The research material is based on pilot thematic interviews in Tshabong and Maun (Hambira et al. 2010, Saarinen et al. 2012). The interviewees were working in management positions in tourism businesses or tourism-service-providing organizations: businesses providing accommodation (hotels, motels, campsites) and nature-based tourism activities (wildlife safaris). In addition, the research material from Tshabong involves one development trust offering guiding and hunting safari services. The interviews were conducted in August 2009 in the Tshabong area and in November 2009 in Maun. Compared with Maun the number of tourism operations in the Tshabong area is relatively small (seven). The practical aim of this pilot study was to collect about the same amount of interview material from both sites, thus the study involves seven operations from Tshabong and eight from Maun, which allows us to discuss some of the similarities and possible differences in the perceptions and adaptation strategies among the interviewed tourism operators in the two study sites, which represent different kinds of tourism products.

Perceived impacts and adaptation strategies

Most of the interviewees in Tshabong and Maun were of the opinion that climate change is happening, and they had observed some changes in the environment in the past five years (Hambira et al. 2010, Saarinen et al. 2012). In both places these observations were related to changes in ambient temperatures (warmer than before) and rainfall patterns (seasons have shifted and have become more erratic). Only very few interviewed operators expressed some doubts about the process, arguing that the changes in the rainfall patterns and ambient temperature are mainly normal periodical cycles.

In Maun it was also noted that the quality of vegetation has declined owing to a rise in temperatures. Consequently, most of the interviewed operators in Tshabong and Maun maintained the perception that climate is changing, and they indicated that there were economic implications of the climate change: a decline in agricultural produce was especially stressed. In addition sociocultural and socio-economic aspects were mentioned, in relation to the availability of traditional medicinal plants, for example. An accommodation operator in Maun commented, 'Our culture is very much attached to nature, for example traditional medicine.'

In spite of the different type of (tourism) environment, the interviewees in Tshabong and Maun had rather similar views on the impact of climate change on business operations in general and on their specific activities and attractions. In Tshabong, none of the interviewees considered there were any impacts on their own operations and activities from climate change, although a clear majority of them perceived general environmental impacts. Thus, the current situation was seen rather positively for tourism. Surprisingly, however, the future implications of changing climate were seen rather negatively: the majority of interviewed operators in Tshabong perceived the impacts on future business growth and Botswana's competitiveness in tourism pessimistically. This was mainly based on the assumed decline of visitor numbers because of the expected extreme temperatures. In addition, decreasing wildlife numbers in the Kgalagadi Transfrontier Park were seen to have a negative influence on the competitiveness of the tourism business in future.

Similarly, in Maun the rise in temperatures was seen negatively as it was assumed to be likely to reduce the number of visitors in future or turn them to more passive pursuits. This was liable to mean lower consumption levels in nature-based tourism activities and programmes as a result of the warming temperatures. As in Tshabong, most interviewees perceived the negative impacts of climate change as likely to occur in the future, rather than this being their current experience. Also in Maun the high temperatures were seen as problematic for the wildlife, as the effect of heat on vegetation was seen to be leading to the (out) migration of wildlife. In addition, because of the increasing periods of extreme heat, the visibility in the scenic flights over the Okavango Delta was perceived to be likely to be poorer in future, which might have a negative effect on the tourist demand.

In Maun there was also a fear of declining water resources capacity because of the rise in temperatures. Contrasted with Tshabong, most operators of accommodation services in Maun had not experienced any impacts from climate change and did not anticipate any in future. Thus, most of the accommodation businesses that were interviewed in the study sites did not see a connection between a lower environmental attractiveness, decreasing number of tourists in the region and the future success of their own business. In Tshabong this view may be based on the currently dominant clientele structure, which depends heavily on government personnel visiting the town for workshops and other meetings: 'Visitors come mostly on business travel, not leisure', an accommodation operator in Tshabong said.

With respect to adaptation strategies, there was a clear difference between the tourism operations in Tshabong and Maun. In Tshabong the businesses interviewed did not really have any specific adaptation measures or strategies in place (see Saarinen et al. 2012). Contrasting with that, most of the interviewed establishments in Maun had adaptation strategies in place or under 'active' planning (Hambira et al. 2010). Those few interviewees who did not have any climate change adaptation strategies in place were the same ones who had not realized there were any impacts of climate change on their business operations. Those businesses that mentioned adaptation mechanisms and strategies included tree planting, use of natural air flow open structures, swimming pools, air conditioners, shade-nets, use of renewable energy and development of an environmental management plan focusing on environmental stewardship, for example. However, in Tshabong too the operators had views on how to adapt to the impacts of climate change if needed in future. The mentioned strategies and mechanisms were rather similar to those in Maun, such as constructing swimming pools and using air conditioners. In addition, creating shade and planting trees, raising awareness in the community (to save water, for example), borehole water for the wildlife and increasing collaboration between businesses and between the private and public sectors were mentioned.

Discussion and conclusions

As indicated by Tervo-Kankare and Saarinen (2011), the changing climate is leading – or should lead – to a more climate-conscious phase of development and planning in the tourism industry. Indeed, the impacts of climate change and related adaptation strategies have become major issues in contemporary tourism policy discussions. Based on the empirical case study the operators in Tshabong and Maun were relatively aware of the general impacts of climate change, but the majority of them did not perceive any critical impacts to the current tourist activities or tourism industry in their operational environment. This may explain why there were almost no adaptation strategies in place among the tourism businesses (Saarinen et al. 2012).

Related to the challenging issues of the impacts of climate change, adaptation and sustainability in tourism, Weaver (2011) argues that adaptation to climate change is not directly or necessarily related to environmental or social sustainability in tourism. Rather, it represents a rational business response to the changing operational environment. Although this line of thinking may be problematic in respect to the broader ideas, principles and goals of sustainable development in tourism (see Scott 2011), it is somewhat supported by the presented case study. Based on the research material the connections of climate change and adaptation to sustainable development in tourism are still not fully emphasized or realized at a practical level. Most of the interviewed businesses had responded or were aiming to respond to the changing climate, if needed, by using mechanisms which actually aim to maintain or increase customer comfort (Hambira et al. 2010), but which would also contribute negatively to climate change mitigation. Such adaptation strategies included swimming pools and air conditioners, for example. On the other hand, there were also adaptation strategies that involve mitigation aspects such as planting trees, raising awareness in the community, use of renewable energy and development of environmental management procedures, which are positively addressed in recent climate change and tourism discussions (see Weaver 2011: 13).

From the industry's perspective there is an urgent need to develop adaptation mechanisms and strategies. This requires sufficient knowledge on the estimated impacts of climate change at global and local scales, capacity building, collaboration, and financial and other support (see Saarinen et al. 2012). From the environmental and sociocultural perspectives, however, stronger connection between climate change impacts, adaptation and sustainability is needed (see Scott 2011). As noted by Scott, de Freitas and Matzarakis (2009) and Scott (2011), adaptation can have major implications for different economies and societies and their sustainability. This is especially the case in developing countries where tourism is highly vulnerable to external changes, and the general and societal capacity to respond to external or internal pressures is often relatively low. In addition, the connections between the tourism industry, local communities, sustainable use of resources and poverty reduction are often very concrete in the context of developing countries. Although Botswana is a middle-income country, the macroeconomic indicators hide the issue that over 40 per cent of the households live in poverty (see Conteh 2008).

Therefore, from the community perspective too the obvious links between climate change impacts, adaptation and sustainability in tourism need to be seen and firmly established. This need involves integrated policies, development strategies and operations (see Burns 1999, Hall 1994, 2000), but also research, and possible disconnections in the practices between climate change adaptation and sustainability should not be legitimized easily.

As noted, tourism in Botswana is fundamentally based on nature and wildlife viewing opportunities. This alone makes the industry highly vulnerable to climate change and its local outcomes. Therefore, in order to achieve the economic but also environmental and social sustainability of tourism in Botswana, there is an urgent need for adaptation strategies that also aim to mitigate the climate change and its impacts in future. Although tourism development and planning may operate in a short time frame, especially at an individual business level, there is a need for long-term perspectives that support the widely accepted and agreed goals of sustainable development in tourism (see Lew 2010). It is important to realize that the currently emerging tourism development paths, practices and decisions made will have long-term implications, not only to the tourism industry and its success but also to the environment and people. At policy level in Botswana, tourism is increasingly seen as a tool for the diversification of the economy and distribution of net benefits to communities in the peripheral parts of the country, as outlined in the new *Botswana Tourism Policy* (UNWTO 2008). This aim should also involve the protection of the main attraction elements of tourism when responding to the challenge of climate change impacts and adaptation.

Acknowledgements

This chapter is based on research funded by the Office of Research and Development, University of Botswana, and Academy of Finland project Tourism for Development. The authors acknowledge the financial support received, and also wish to thank the tourism operators in Tshabong and Maun areas and the Ministry of Environment, Wildlife and Tourism for their warm support.

References

Agnew, M. D. and Viner, D. (2001) 'Potential impacts of climate change on international tourism', *Tourism and Hospitality Research*, vol. 3, no. 1, pp. 37–60.
Allen, C. D., Macalady, A. K., Chenchouni, H., Bachelet, D., McDowell, N., Vennetier, M., Kitznerger, T., Rigling, A., Breshears, D. D., Hogg, E. H., Gonzalez, P., Fensham, R., Zhang, Z., Castro, J., Demidova, N., Lim, J-H., Allard, G., Running, S.W., Semerci, A. and Cobb, N. (2010) 'A global overview of drought and heat-induced tree mortality reveals emerging climate change risks for forests', *Forest Ecology and Management*, vol. 259, no. 4, pp. 660–84.
Bates, B. C., Kundzewicz, Z. W., Wu, S. and Palutikof, J. P. (2008) 'Climate change and water.' Technical Paper of the Intergovernmental Panel on Climate Change (IPCC) Secretariat, Geneva.

Biggs, R., Simons, H., Bakkenes, M., Scholes, R. J., Eickhout, B., van Vuuren, D. and Alkemade, R. (2008) 'Scenarios for biodiversity loss in southern Africa in the 21st century', *Global Environmental Change*, vol. 18, pp. 296–309.

Boko, M., Niang, I., Nyong, A., Vogel, C., Githego, A., Medany, M., Osaman-Elasha, B., Tabo. R. and Yanda, P. (2007) 'Africa', in Parry, M. L., Canziani, O. F., Palutikof, J. P., van der Linden, P. J. and Hanson, C. E. (eds), *Climate Change 2007: Impacts, adaptation and vulnerability,* Cambridge University Press, Cambridge.

Botswana Tourism Board (BTB) (2009) *Travel Companion: Kgalagadi/Central.* Gaborone: BTB Headquarters.

Bramwell, B. and Lane, B. (1993) 'Sustaining tourism: An evolving global approach.' *Journal of Sustainable Tourism,* vol. 1, no. 1, pp. 1–5.

Bramwell, B. and Lane, B. (2008) 'Priorities in sustainable tourism research', *Journal of Sustainable Tourism,* vol. 16, no. 1, pp. 1–4.

Brown, R. (2009) 'Observing the present and considering the past to ponder the future', *South African Journal of Science,* vol. 105 (Jan. /Feb.), pp. 13–14.

Burns, P. (1999) 'Paradoxes in planning: tourism elitism or brutalism?' *Annals of Tourism Research,* vol. 26, no. 1, pp. 329–48.

Bührs, T. (2008) 'Climate change policy and New Zealand's "national interest": the need for embedding climate change policy into a sustainable development agenda', *Political Science,* vol. 60, no. 1, pp. 61–72.

Chamaillé-James, S., Fritz, H. and Murindagomo, F. (2007) 'Detecting climate changes of concern in highly variable environments: quantile regressions reveal that droughts worsen in Hwange National Park, Zimbabwe', *Journal of Arid Environments,* vol. 71, pp. 321–6.

Conteh, C. (2008) 'Rethinking Botswana's economic diversification policy: dysfunctional site-market partnership', *Commonwealth and Comparative Politics,* vol. 46, no. 4, pp. 540–54.

Department of Environmental Affairs (2008) *Okavango Delta Management Plan (ODMP),* ODMP Secretariat, Maun, Botswana.

Eriksen, S. E. H. and Watson, H. K. (2009) 'The dynamic context of southern African savannas: investigating emerging threats and opportunities to sustainability', *Environmental Science and Policy,* vol. 12, pp. 5–22.

Gössling, S. (2000) 'Sustainable tourism development in developing countries: some aspects of energy use', *Journal of Sustainable Tourism,* vol. 8, no. 5, pp. 410–25.

Gössling, S. and Hall, C. M. (eds) (2006) *Tourism and Global Environmental Change,* Routledge, London.

Hall, C. M. (1994) *Tourism and Politics,* Chichester, John Wiley.

Hall, C. M. (2000) *Tourism Planning: Policies, processes and relationships,* Prentice Hall, Harlow.

Hall, C. M. and Saarinen, J. (2010) 'Geotourism and climate change: paradoxes and promises of geotourism in Polar regions', *Teóros,* vol. 29, no. 2, pp. 77–86.

Hambira, W. Atlhopheng, J. Manwa, H. and Saarinen J. (2010) 'Planned and used climate change adaptation strategies and practices in nature based tourism in the Okavango region, Botswana' (manuscript).

Hein, L., Metzger, M. J. and Moreno, A. (2009) 'Potential impacts of climate change on tourism, a case study for Spain', *Current Opinion in Environmental Sustainability,* vol. 1, pp. 170–8.

Holden, A. (2003) 'In need of new environmental ethics for tourism', *Annals of Tourism Research,* vol. 30, no. 1, pp. 94–108.

Holt, R. and Hattam, C. (2009) 'Capitalizing on nature: how to implement an ecosystem approach', *Biology Letters,* vol. 5, pp. 580–2.

Hulme, M. (1996) *Climate change and southern Africa: an explanation of some potential impacts and implications in the SADC region.* Climate Research Unit, University of East Anglia, Norwich, UK and WWF International. Breckland Print, Switzerland.

Hulme, M., Doherty, R., Ngara, T., New, M. and Lister, D. (2001) 'African climate change: 1900–2100', *Climate Research*, vol. 17, no. 2, pp. 145–68.

Intergovernmental Panel on Climate Change (IPCC) (2007) *Climate Change 2007: Synthesis Report – Summary for Policymakers, Fourth Assessment Report*, Cambridge University Press, Cambridge.

Lew, A. (2010) 'Time as a major barrier to sustainable development', *Tourism Geographies*, vol. 12, no. 3, pp. 481–3.

Macbeth, J. (2005) 'Towards an ethics platform for tourism', *Annals of Tourism Research*, vol. 32, no. 4, pp. 962–84.

Magole L. and Magole L. I. (2009) 'The Okavango: whose delta is it?' *Physics and Chemistry of the Earth*, vol. 34, pp. 874–80.

Mbaiwa J. E. (2005) 'Enclave tourism and its socio economic impacts in the Okavango delta, Botswana', *Tourism Management*, vol. 26, no. 1, pp. 157–72.

Mbaiwa, J. E. and Stronza, A. L. (2010) 'The effects of tourism development on rural livelihoods in the Okavango Delta, Botswana', *Journal of Sustainable Tourism*, vol. 18, no. 5, pp. 635–56.

Midgley, G. F. and Guo, D. (2009) *Potential Impacts of Climate Change on Namibia*, SANBI, Cape Town, South Africa.

Mirza, M. (2003) 'Climate change and extreme weather events: can developing countries adapt?' *Climate Policy*, vol. 3, pp. 233–248.

Moen, J. and Fredman, P. (2007) 'Effects of climate change on Alpine skiing in Sweden', *Journal of Sustainable Tourism*, vol. 15, no. 4, pp. 418–37.

Moswete, N., Thapa, B. and Lacey, G. (2000a) 'Village based tourism and community participation: a case study of the Matsheng villages in Southwest Botswana', in J. Saarinen, F. Becker, H. Manwa and D. Wilson (eds), *Sustainable Tourism in Southern Africa: Local communities and natural resources in transition*, Channel View, Bristol.

Moswete N., Thapa B., Toteng, E. and Mbaiwa, J. (2000b) 'Resident involvement and participation in urban tourism development: a comparative study in Maun and Gaborone, Botswana', *Urban Forum*, vol. 19, no. 4, pp. 381–94.

National Conservation Strategy (NCSA) (2000) *State of the Environment Report.* NCSA, Gaborone.

Peeters, P. (2009) 'Pro-poor tourism, climate change and sustainable development', *Tourism Recreation Research*, vol. 34, no. 2, pp. 203–5.

Prato, T. (2008) 'Conceptual framework for assessment and management of ecosystem impacts of climate change', *Ecological Complexity*, vol. 5, pp. 329–38.

Preston-White, R. A. and Watson, H. K. (2005) 'Nature tourism and climatic change in Southern Africa', in C. R. Hall and J. Higham (eds), *Tourism, Recreation and Climate Change*, Cromwell Press, Great Britain.

Ramos, M. and Kahla, V. (2009) 'Climate change: opportunities for Africa', *Global Journal of Emerging Market Economies*, vol. 1, no. 2, pp. 259–71.

Ramsar (2011) 'Okavango Delta system', available at: www.ramsar.wetlands.org/GISMaps/WebGIS/tabid/809/Default.aspx (accessed 17 February 2011).

Republic of Botswana (2003) 'National Development Plan 9', Gaborone: Ministry of Finance and Development Planning.

Saarinen, J. (2006) 'Traditions of sustainability in tourism studies', *Annals of Tourism Research*, vol. 33, no. 4, pp. 1121–40.

Saarinen, J. and Tervo, K. (2006) 'Perceptions and adaptation strategies of the tourism industry to climate change: the case of Finnish nature-based tourism entrepreneurs', *International Journal of Innovation and Sustainable Development*, vol. 1,no. 3, pp. 214–28.

Saarinen, J., Hambira, W., Atlhopheng, J. and Manwa, H. (2011) 'Perceived impacts and adaptation strategies of the tourism industry to climate change in Kgalagadi South District, Botswana', *Development Southern Africa*, vol. 28, no. 2.

Saarinen, J. and Tervo, K. (2010) 'Sustainability and emerging awareness to changing climate: tourism industry's knowledge and perceptions of the future of nature-based winter tourism in Finland', in C. M. Hall and J. Saarinen (eds), *Tourism and Change in Polar Regions: Climate, environment and experiences*, Routledge, London and New York.

Saarinen, J., W. Hambira, J. Althopheng and H. Manwa (2012) Perceived impacts and adaptation strategies of the tourism industry to climate change in Kgalagadi South District, Botswana. Development Southern Africa 29: 2, 273–285.

Scott, D. (2006) 'US ski industry adaptation to climate change', in S. Gössling and C. M. Hall (eds), *Tourism and Global Environmental Change: Ecological social, economic and political interrelationships*, Routledge, London.

Scott, D. (2011) 'Why sustainable tourism must address climate change', *Journal of Sustainable Tourism*, vol. 19, no. 1, pp. 17–34.

Scott, D., Amelung, B., Becken, S., Ceron, J. P., Dubois, G., Gossling, S., Peeters, P. and Simpson, M. C. (2008) *Climate Change and Tourism – Responding to global challenges*. United Nations World Tourism Organization (UNWTO), Madrid.

Scott, D., de Freitas, C. and Matzarakis, A. (2009) 'Adaptation in the tourism and recreation sector', in K. Ebi, I. Burton and G. McGregor (eds), *Biometeorology for Adaptation to Climate Variability and Change*, Springer, Dordrecht.

Sharpley, R. (2000) 'Tourism and sustainable development: exploring the theoretical divide', *Journal of Sustainable Tourism*, vol. 8, no. 1, pp. 1–19.

Sharpley, R. (2009) *Tourism Development and the Environment: Beyond sustainability?* Earthscan, London.

Smerecnik, K. R. and Andersen, P. A. (2011) 'The diffusion of the environmental sustainability innovation in North American hotels and ski resorts', *Journal of Sustainable Tourism*, vol. 19, no. 2, pp. 171–96.

Tao, T. C. H. and Wall, G. (2009) 'Tourism as a sustainable livelihood strategy', *Tourism Management*, vol. 30, pp. 90–8.

Tervo, K. (2008) 'The operational and regional vulnerability of winter tourism to climate variability and change: the case of the nature-based tourism entrepreneurs in Finland', *Scandinavian Journal of Hospitality and Tourism*, vol. 8, no. 2, pp. 317–32.

Tervo-Kankare, K. and Saarinen J. (2011) 'Climate change and adaptation strategies of tourism industry in Northern Europe', in P. Maher, E. Stewart and M. Lück (eds), *Polar Tourism: Human, environmental and governance dimensions*, Cognizant Communications, Elmsford.

Thomas, D. S. G., Knight, M. and Wiggs, G. F. S. (2005) 'Remobilization of southern African desert dune systems by twenty-first century global warming', *Nature*, vol. 435, 30 June, pp. 1218–21.

UNWTO (2008) *Policy for the Growth and Development of Tourism in Botswana*. UNWTO/Government of Botswana Project for the Formulation of a Tourism Policy for Botswana, July 2008. UNWTO and Department of Tourism.

UNWTO (2009) *From Davos to Copenhagen and Beyond: Advancing tourism response to climate change*. UNWTO, Madrid.

UNWTO and UN Environment Programme (UNEP) (2008) *Climate Change and Tourism: Responding to global challenges*. UNWTO and UNEP, Madrid.

Van Jaarsveld, A. S., Biggs, R., Scholes, R. J., Bohensky, E., Reyers, B., Lynam, T., Musvoto, C. and Fabricius, C. (2005) 'Philosophical Transactions of the Royal Society', *Biological Sciences,* vol. 360, pp. 425–41.

Velarde, S. J., Malhi, Y., Moran, D., Wright, J. and Hussain, S. (2005) 'Valuing the impacts of climate change on protected areas in Africa', *Ecological Economics,* vol. 53, pp. 21–33.

Vogel, C. (2005) 'Seven fat years and seven lean years: climate change and agriculture in Africa', *IDS Bulletin,* vol. 36, no. 2, pp. 30–5.

Vogel, C, (2009) 'Business and climate change: initial explorations in South Africa', *Climate and Development,* vol. 1, no. 1, pp. 82–97.

Wall, G, (1998) 'Implications of global change for tourism and recreation in wetland areas', *Climatic Change,* vol. 40, no. 2, pp. 371–89.

Weaver, D. (2011) 'Can sustainable tourism survive climate change?' *Journal of Sustainable Tourism,* vol. 19, no. 1, pp. 5–15.

World Tourism and Travel Council (WTTC) (2007) *Botswana: The impact of travel and tourism on jobs and the economy.* WTTC, London.

15

CONTRADICTIONS IN CLIMATE CONCERN
Performances at home and away

Scott A. Cohen and James E. S. Higham

Introduction

There is a burgeoning body of academic literature (e.g. Becken 2007; Gössling et al. 2006; Hares, Dickinson and Wilkes 2010) that examines if and how consumer concern about climate change manifests itself in tourist behavioural practices. These works build on a wealth of previous studies that consider how consumer concern over issues of sustainable development may also affect tourist behaviour. Indeed, while tourism's climate impacts have lately been a hot topic, there is no doubt that issues of climate change are within the remit of, and need to be considered alongside, wider discourses of sustainable development (Weaver 2011).

Recent research focused explicitly on the climate impacts of tourism and associated tourism transport reflects the realization in the academy that the tourism industry, characterized by energy-intensive consumption, is a significant contributor to accelerating global climate change. Despite the claim, however, that tourism is increasingly blended into the fabric of everyday life (Edensor 2007), the mass of tourism still largely occurs as a bounded experience outside the rhythms of the day to day, which is both extraordinary and often involving conspicuous consumption. With tourism often experienced as an event set apart from the day to day, it is unsurprising that few studies, with the notable exception of Barr et al. (2010), have sought to understand tourist environmental concern in relation to a wider scope of everyday lives and daily decision making.

The present chapter seeks to further understandings of how tourism consumption, and its consequent carbon emissions, are made sense of and justified by consumers in relation to everyday life decisions. Based on thirty open-ended, semi-structured interviews carried out in the United Kingdom and Norway in 2009, the chapter illustrates consistencies and inconsistencies in the climate sensitivities of UK and Norwegian consumers in relation to both everyday domestic (home) and tourism (away) practices. Modern theory on tourism as liminoid space (Turner 1982) and postmodern theory that suggests personal identity (and consequently behaviour) is inconsistent and performed differently across varying contexts (Bell 2008, Edensor 2001) are used as complementary explanatory devices for understanding some of the participants' seemingly contradictory consumption decisions. The research consequently reveals significant paradoxes in consumer climate sensitivities between the everyday and holidays. These findings hold important implications for the viability of climate change mitigation strategies and sustainable development goals that rely, at least in part, on nudging individual lifestyles towards less carbon-intensive consumption choices.

Consumer climate concern and tourism

There is increasing pressure on the tourism industry to move to a sustainable emissions path (Gössling 2009). It is widely acknowledged that the tourism industry is implicated in climate change in terms of both cause and effect. Tourism is an energy-intensive industry (Becken 2007) that is currently directly accountable for 4.4 per cent of global carbon dioxide (CO_2) emissions (Peeters and Dubois 2010). Of this amount, 40 per cent can be conservatively attributed to tourist air travel (Gössling 2009). In comparison with tourism transport alternatives such as rail, road and sea-based passenger modes, air travel is the most harmful for the climate system (Gössling and Peeters 2007) and presents one of the tourism industry's largest challenges if it seeks to sustain contemporary aeromobility-dependent tourism practices (Burns and Bibbings 2009).

Correspondingly, much of the recent academic concern over tourism's climate-change impacts has centred upon issues surrounding tourist air travel (Gössling and Upham 2009). Scholarship has engaged with a range of issues in this area, including the effectiveness of voluntary carbon offsets for aviation-based emissions (Smith and Rodger 2009), land-based alternatives to air travel that may qualify as modes of 'slow travel' (Dickinson, Lumsdon and Robbins 2011), the multifarious ways in which tourist air travel is embedded within contemporary social life (Randles and Mander, 2009a), the notion of excessive tourist air travel, or 'binge flying', as a site of behavioural addiction (Cohen, Higham and Cavaliere 2011) and consumer climate concern towards extreme long-haul air travel (Higham and Cohen 2011). Literature that focuses on consumer sensitivities towards tourism's climate-change impacts, as manifest in modifications in attitudes and behaviours towards and within tourism practices, notes that 'such changes may include choice of destination and timing of visits, perhaps extending to the abandonment of some destinations, and the discontinuation of some forms of tourism' (de Freitas 2005, Higham and Cohen 2011: 99). Whether these latter changes will actually materialize is still largely an open empirical question.

Consumer attitudes towards, and perceptions of, tourism's climate-change impacts are both more widely explored than behavioural adaptations, and to date a source of conflicting evidence. For instance, whereas Miller et al. (2010) find public reluctance in the United Kingdom to engage in sustainable tourism through taking fewer holidays, Cohen and Higham (2011) report a growing movement of UK consumers who are approaching tourism-related air travel decisions with a 'carbon conscience'. Furthermore, while Gössling, Peeters and Scott (2008: 875) observe that 'pro-environmental concerns are clearly emerging among consumers, and may play a significant role in travel decisions in the future', Hares et al. (2010) note, at least for UK consumers, a lack of consideration of climate change in decision making when planning holidays. Reinforcing this latter finding, Caletrío (2011) suggests that few UK tourists are willing to sacrifice aspects of their annual holidays based on environmental grounds.

Explanations for these contradictions in consumer climate concern in recent literature can be abstracted in a number of ways. First, seemingly conflictive findings in Caletrío (2011), and Cohen and Higham (2011) arguably represent voices from different cross-sections within UK society, with the former reflecting individuals who self-profess being financially constrained to a one-week annual holiday and the latter (upon whom the present chapter is also based) being comprised of relatively affluent, highly educated (and consequently hypermobile) individuals. Hence, individuals may express a higher willingness to sacrifice holidays when in the relatively privileged economic position of being able to afford multiple holidays per year. This highlights a need for future empirical research that analyses consumer concern over tourism's climate-change impacts in relation to demographic variables such as income and education level.

Second, pro-environmental attitudes offered by consumers can represent a filtered reluctance to present socially undesirable accounts of continued hyperconsumption in the face of accelerating climate change (Cohen et al. 2011). Lastly, there may be a dissonance between self-professed environmental attitudes and subsequent steps to modify behaviours. In particular, and most important for the aim of the present chapter, is the possibility of a tension between the contexts of everyday domestic life decisions and consumption choices made while away on holiday.

Liminoid space and contextualized performances

Tourism practices, for most individuals, exist in contexts largely set apart from everyday life. Both a modern perspective that positions tourism experiences as an escape from the everyday self (Cohen and Taylor 1992, Cohen 2010a), and a postmodern perspective that views selves, and in turn behaviours, as performed and contextually dependent (Bell 2008), suggest that just because individuals perform one way in a situation, does not mean that behaviours transfer consistently across contexts. This has implications for understanding the transferability of pro-environmental attitudes and behaviours across differing life contexts, as each of these worldviews suggest that behaviour is contextually, or situationally, dependent.

Within modern literature on tourist motivation, the need to escape has long been posited as a key motivator for individuals to go on holiday (Crompton 1979,

Dann 1977). Crompton (1979: 416) notes that the desire to 'escape from a perceived mundane environment', or in other words the tedium of routine, forms one of the major motives driving tourist behaviour. Breaking from everyday routine is linked to Turner's (1982) description of the 'liminoid', characterized as a departure from the structure of everyday life (Lett 1983). Sharpley (2003: 5–21) applies the liminoid to tourism experiences, noting that while away on holiday, tourists may feel 'temporarily freed from … household chores, social commitments and, generally, the behavioural norms and values of their society.' Furthermore, Kim and Jamal (2007: 184) suggest that within 'liminal touristic space, conventional social norms and regulations are often temporarily suspended as tourists take advantage of the relative anonymity and freedom from community scrutiny'. Indeed, the notion of tourism occurring in liminoid space melds well with more recent academic literature that holds tourism is a furtive ground for extraordinary experiences (see Morgan, Lugosi and Ritchie 2010; Tung and Ritchie 2011). These twofold discourses, of escape and in turn extraordinary experience, attempt to map out tourism space as fundamentally different from the everyday, effectively dichotomizing 'home' and 'away'.

In accordance with this modernist position, a postmodernist approach also draws into question the degree to which performances of identity, and hence behaviour, are likely to consistently transcend contexts. A performance perspective (Bell 2008, Edensor 2001), rising out of Goffman's (1959) work on selves, in which individuals perform different 'faces' depending on the situation, suggests that personal identities are too fragmented, contextually dependent and relational (Finnegan 1997, Vaughan and Hogg 2002) for it to be reasonable to expect behavioural consistency (for a more exhaustive review of self-identities as multiple and fluid see Cohen 2010b). Within this perspective, dissonance between attitudes and behaviours and inconsistencies in patterns of behaviour across contexts are each easily reconciled because consistency is not presumed from the start.

These modernist and postmodernist worldviews, with behaviour dichotomized between 'here' and 'there' in the former, and performances of identity fragmented and unstable across contexts in the latter, may seem of distant relation when returning to the focus of consumer climate concern and the prospect of sustainable tourism. However, these issues are paramount if we seek to mitigate tourism's climate-change impacts through strategies that attempt to nudge tourists towards pro-environmental behaviour. With identities, and in turn attitudes and behaviours, largely contingent on social context, there can be no certain expectation that consumer climate concern in daily life practices will necessarily transfer across to tourism practices.

Method

The empirical material presented in this chapter is part of a wider study on consumer climate concern and tourist practices in European markets. The qualitative materials consist of thirty semi-structured open-ended interviews conducted in Norway and the United Kingdom in 2009. Our interest in Norway and the United Kingdom arises from tensions between the conspicuous aeromobility of sections of their respective populations and government initiatives aimed at mitigating climate change (Gössling 2009, Hares et al. 2010, Høyer 2000). The interview programme sought to explore consumer opinions on climate change and engage participants in a discussion of potential climate change concerns and actual behaviours as they relate to both day-to-day domestic and tourism practices.

Interviews were carried out first in Stavanger, Norway (fifteen participants) and immediately after in Bournemouth, UK (fifteen participants), when the lead author was based as a visiting researcher at both the University of Stavanger and Bournemouth University. Participants in both locations were recruited using a snowball sampling technique relying initially on key informants in each location, from both within and outside the universities. The only selection criteria were that participants self-identify as Norwegian or British nationals, and be willing to be interviewed face-to-face in English. The interview participants were fifteen females and fifteen males with ages that ranged from 18 to 67 (Table 15.1). Their occupations were twelve industry professionals, six university academics, five university administrators, four postgraduate students, two undergraduate students and one retiree.

The majority of the participants were highly educated and moderately affluent, representing the research sample being driven out of a university context, but also reflecting a particularly relevant group to consider when addressing the conspicuous consumption of tourism. It is this subset of the total population in Europe who have the economic resources that give them the option of consuming tourist products on a frequent basis. The findings do confirm the participants were highly aeromobile for tourism purposes, with several flights per year not being uncommon. Participants in both countries expressed a common need for regular holidays in warm destinations outside of their country of origin.

Consistencies between home and away

The study found significant inconsistencies in the participants' climate sensitivities and related behaviours between domestic day-to-day and tourism contexts. However, a minority of the participants suggested there was no difference between the environmental sustainability of their practices in domestic decisions and those made while away on holiday. As Oliver (British, 30) maintained:

> Exactly the same principles would apply. If I'm staying in a hotel, I wouldn't dream of leaving the room with the lights on, for example. If I'm in a hotel, I'm not going to boil more water than I need. I'm not going to stand under the shower for ten minutes longer than is necessary.

TABLE 15.1 Summary profile of interview programme participants

Pseudonym	Gender	Age	Nationality	Occupation	Highest qualification
Frode	M	37	Norwegian	Industry professional	Masters
Rita	F	34	Norwegian	Industry professional	Masters
Bjørn	M	41	Norwegian	Industry professional	PhD
Silje	F	45	Norwegian	Industry professional	Masters
Svein	M	35	Norwegian	Industry professional	High school
Tone	F	58	Norwegian	Postgraduate student	Masters
Ida	F	52	Norwegian	University administrator	Masters
Grete	F	27	Norwegian	Postgraduate student	Undergraduate
Lars	M	53	Norwegian	Academic	PhD
Pål	M	34	Norwegian	Industry professional	Masters
Hilda	F	67	Norwegian	Retiree	Masters
Håkon	M	48	Norwegian	Industry professional	Undergraduate
Johannes	M	57	Norwegian	Academic	PhD
Anette	F	35	Norwegian	Industry professional	Masters
Grethe	F	27	Norwegian	Postgraduate student	Masters
Cindy	F	42	British	University administrator	High school
Jack	M	35	British	Industry professional	Undergraduate
Grace	F	36	British	University administrator	Masters
Jessica	F	48	British	University administrator	High school
Ruby	F	41	British	Industry professional	High school
Amy	F	30	British	Academic	PhD
Hannah	F	48	British	Postgraduate student	Masters
Oliver	M	30	British	Academic	Masters
Thomas	M	38	British	Academic	Masters
Harry	M	40	British	Industry professional	Undergraduate
Daniel	M	18	British	Undergraduate student	High school
Mia	F	21	British	Undergraduate student	High school
James	M	63	British	Academic	PhD
William	M	42	British	Industry professional	Undergraduate
Lewis	M	39	British	Industry professional	Undergraduate

This type of statement was typically used to discount the notion that economic motives underpinned some pro-environmental behaviour. William (British, 42) put this issue in a stark light. When we go to Florida, I wouldn't just leave the air-conditioning on all day and all night because I'm not paying for it. I would be responsible about it.

Furthermore, Svein (Norwegian, 35), when asked how important money was in his attitudes towards the environment whilst on holiday, replied:

For me, economics is not a big issue. I'm not above average in Norway. We're so rich and comfortable here and what I want more of in my life is other qualities than monies and luxury and that kind of wealth. So it's not motivated by money.

Svein gave primacy to consuming ethically across the different facets of his life. As he recognizes, however, this is a position of privilege made available through his citizenship in an affluent nation.

In each of these cases, tourism practices were viewed holistically as part of a broader lifestyle in which consistency was sought in values, attitudes and behaviours across different facets of life. Barr et al. (2010: 475) describe this notion of a 'sustainable lifestyle' as implying 'individuals would demonstrate a series of commitments across lifestyle practices, not merely as part of their routine, but also in tourism contexts'. Svein further elaborated a view that the everyday and holidays as inextricably interlinked, with the carbon savings accumulated through practices such as cycling to work seen as nonsensical when positioned alongside the prospect of flippant tourist air travel: 'So you can't ride your bike to your job and use a plane everywhere without thinking about it – it would be stupid.' This type of consistent 'rational actor' approach, however, was relatively rare in the participants.

Inconsistencies between home and away

Instead of achieving alignment between approaches to environmental sustainability in everyday practices and those while on holiday, participants evidenced that tourism spaces are often the stage for performances of less stringent climate concern and more environmentally destructive consumption practices. Supporting the work of Barr et al. (2010), these individuals, who may be committed to environmental practices at home (such as reducing waste and energy use, buying organic and 'ethical' purchasing), are often unwilling to reduce holiday air travel. For instance, Harry (British, 40), whose undergraduate degree was in environmental management, undertook a range of practices in everyday life to mitigate his climate impact, but was unwilling to transfer sustainable practices to the realm of tourism-related air travel, where he privileged speed and convenience over sustainability:

> I have a small car with a small engine and that is purely from a global warming point of view, from a pollution point of view. I do see the impact [of air travel] and I would get on an airplane and go on a long-haul flight because I want to travel, I want to get to this place, and I can't think of another way to do it reasonably quickly, reasonably safely, minimum of fuss. It's the convenience, it boils down to that.

Supporting this type of behavioural inconsistency between home and away, Frode (Norwegian, 37) took great interest in reducing waste in his everyday life, but chose not to buy voluntary carbon offsets or reduce his frequent air travel:

> I'm not buying CO_2 quota on the planes when I'm flying, I'm not buying that. What I'm doing – I'm recycling quite a bit. I think that's the most important thing that I'm doing – I'm quite concerned about how I distribute my garbage. So good with garbage, not that good with travel – travel like always.

Frode's concern about garbage, but not air travel, may reflect the deep social embeddedness of environmental practices such as recycling within his society, which may have become habit. Quite oppositely, Randles and Mander (2009b) argue that tourist air travel itself has become a habit for some sections of society, and that there are only 'flickerings' of evidence of consumer environmental concern over aviation. Bjørn (Norwegian, 41), however, argued that decisions, rather than being habit, are often consciously weighed, but typically cannot be attributed to a singular motivation, such as climate concern. In his case, as a father, climate concern needed to be balanced against a range of other considerations, such as cost, time and comfort:

> These values are a little bit related to how much does it cost for me also, I must admit. I feel like a bit schizophrenic in terms of climate, because on one end I want to contribute and at the same time I have all these requirements during every day with small kids, going to shopping, all this practical stuff you have to do. There is a set of motivating factors, and environmental is one aspect of many. And the importance of that aspect is partly related your situation in life at the present moment.

Bjørn's words suggest that the primacy given to environmental values may vary through the lifecourse, as other demands, such as family, compete in consumption decisions. He also reminds us that motivations are often multidimensional and contextual (Ryan 1997). Contexts become infused with meaning, and it is the meanings individuals attribute to, and derive from, certain spaces and places that structure behaviour.

Liminoid tourism spaces

Several of the participants perceived tourism practices as existing relatively outside of the social norms that they used to structure their behaviour in everyday life. In this sense, tourism space was seen as liminoid (Kim and Jamal 2007), and hence freer from the behavioural norms and values of the day to day. As such, Pål, (Norwegian, 34), when asked if he saw a difference in energy consumption decisions he might take in daily life versus on a holiday, responded:

> I think so – because when you're on holiday you're in a different mode. You are somewhere else and you want to get the most out of it and go home and be filled with impressions and experiences.

Pål viewed the spaces of tourism as extraordinary, wherein climate-change sensitivity took backseat to securing memorable experiences, theoretically on offer through tourist practices (Morgan et al. 2010, Tung and Ritchie 2011). As Ida (Norwegian, 52) said of making the most of her holidays, rather than stopping to take time to consider their climate impacts – 'I'm not stopping and thinking, no. I'm there and I want to see much and do what I want to do.' Participants who attached too high an importance to their holidays to consider adapting them because of climate change mirrored the findings of Hares et al. (2010), in which there is reluctance to forgo the perceived positive benefits made accessible by tourist air travel in order to reduce personal emissions.

For Rita (Norwegian, 34), both the importance of escaping to an attractive overseas destination to relax and the trip's corresponding economic cost outweighed concern over the climate impacts of her holidays. She attributed this to the relative infrequency of her holidaying:

> Holiday trips are maybe once a year and other issues would be more important – where to go and economic questions – would be more important on my annual travels. The things I can do every day are easier to be conscious about and to make a decision about than what you do once a year. Because then it's more important to me to go to a nice place and relax for two weeks.

This issue of the difference in frequency between tourism and domestic decisions was also cited as an important factor by Tone (Norwegian, 58):

> Daily life is more important. I'm more concerned about daily life because we don't travel all the time. It's [flying is] kind of abstract, because you are not doing this every day and it is a little bit away from you when you have landed and then you go home.

Hence, the infrequency of tourism practices, combined with their typical occurrence in spaces outside of everyday life, provided justification for sustainable practices to be temporarily suspended. A temporary suspension of environmental norms when on holidays lends support to Barr et al.'s (2010: 475) observation that a sustainable lifestyle will only exist once 'individuals are able to transfer their behaviours between contexts, as part of an embedded set of lifestyle practices'.

Contextualized performances of consumer concern

Rather than consistent performances of identity aligned with an embedded set of lifestyle practices, through a commitment to reducing climate impacts across all life contexts, many of the participants narrated performances of consumer concern that were contingent upon context. In some cases, the contradiction between striving for sustainable practices in everyday life, only for a single long-haul flight taken to exceed annual per capita sustainable emission levels (Gössling et al. 2009), was duly acknowledged:

> I think it's a contradiction. I think a lot of people do it. But you kind of, you kind of try to put it back of your mind and try not to worry about it. Well, you think, I'm seeing the world and it's great for the kids to see the world. So you try to put it to one side. Silly really.
>
> *(Ruby, British, 41)*

In another instance, a participant who regularly stayed in the United Kingdom and went camping for her holidays, because of both lower costs and pro-environmental attitudes, recognized that if her economic circumstances were to change, that she would probably not be able to resist taking tourism trips via long-haul air travel:

> Say I won a load of money tomorrow – I'd probably go [to New Zealand]. It's awful, isn't it? You feel guilty but you justify it to yourself in some respect.
>
> *(Grace, British, 36)*

Thus, for Grace, her travel behaviour was contingent on the social and economic context in which she might be positioned, rather than an enduring set of core values.

For another participant, different performances were offered between home and away, which while inconsistent, were not recognized as conflictive with the participants' environmental values:

> I probably don't think about it actually. You know what, I went to Turkey last year, and it was 40 degrees and we had air conditioning and we left it on. We went out and left the air conditioning on. And I don't think that I, for one moment, thought about the effects on the environment. And I've even done an environmental degree.
>
> *(Harry, British, 40)*

For Harry, who closely monitored his domestic energy consumption at home and even studied for an environmental degree at university, both air travel and energy usage once in the destination were subject to a lower level of climate concern than in daily life practices.

The inconsistency between these different 'faces' offered depending on context, which constitute what we term 'multiple environmental identities', were not experienced by the participants as a source of concern that needed any mediation or reconciliation. Multiple identities, with climate-change sensitivities adapted to suit the participant's needs in each situation, were narrated to make sense of and justify what may be externally perceived as behavioural contradictions. As Lewis (British, 39) revealed of his recent holiday in Florida, after attesting to a grave personal concern about climate change and its potential implications in the future for his two young children:

> For example, we've been to Florida, there were four families with four cars and we drove everywhere every single day to a different location to do something. And even when you're in those locations chances are you're using amenities that are extremely wasteful on electricity and emissions as well. So you think a lot less about the environmental impacts then. You're in an apartment, you pay for it, it's not yours, whether you go out and leave the lights on – chances are you're a lot less environmentally aware when you're on holiday than when you're not.

Indeed, these contradictions in climate concern and environmental behaviour across contexts of home and away serve to further destabilize the notion of sustainable lifestyles.

Conclusion

This chapter has sought to further understandings of how tourism consumption, a source of significant CO_2 contributions, is made sense of and justified by consumers in relation to everyday life decisions. Based on empirical evidence from an aeromobile subsection of Norwegian and British society, exploratory findings suggest it is not uncommon for tourism spaces to be subject to lower levels of environmental concern than day-to-day contexts. For our participants, while there were some consistencies between the environmental sustainability of their practices in domestic decisions and those made while away on holiday, there were also many cases in which their environmentally destructive tourism consumption practices were subject to less stringent, or even exempt from, climate concern.

Whether these behavioural inconsistencies and contradictions are taken as a modern expression of tourism practices occurring in liminoid space, or from a postmodern perspective in which identities have become fragmented and contextually dependent, and hence multiple (Finnegan 1997, Vaughan and Hogg 2002), has little bearing upon the phenomenon's practical management implications. The outcome of both ways of looking at these contradictions in practice between 'home' and 'away' is that behavioural adaptations motivated by environmental concern do not necessarily, and often do not, transfer across contexts, especially in the case of tourism practices. These findings highlight a significant challenge for both the governance of climate change and agendas for sustainable development. Consequently, strategies that seek to tackle these issues, whether through education or media, by aiming to nudge individual lifestyles towards less carbon-intensive consumption choices, need to be tempered with an awareness that environmental identities, like other aspects of personal identities, cannot be relied upon to lead to consistent behaviour. This indicates that national and international agencies that seek carbon mitigation and sustainable development through even a partial reliance on individual behavioural adaptations, alongside collective political and technological innovations, must recognize the barriers and limits to achieving consistent sustainable lifestyles.

References

Barr, S., Shaw, G., Coles, T. and Prillwitz, J. (2010) '"A holiday is a holiday": Practicing sustainability, home and away', *Journal of Transport Geography*, vol. 18, no. 3, pp. 474–81.

Becken, S. (2007) 'Tourists' perception of international air travel's impact on the global climate and potential climate change policies', *Journal of Sustainable Tourism*, vol. 15, no. 4, pp. 351–68.

Bell, E. (2008) *Theories of Performance*, Sage, Los Angeles.

Burns, P., and Bibbings, L. (2009) 'The end of tourism? Climate change and societal challenges', *21st Century Society*, vol. 4, no. 1, pp. 31–51.

Caletrío, J. (2011) 'Simple living and tourism in times of "austerity"', *Current Issues in Tourism*, doi: 10.1080/13683500.2011.556246.

Cohen, S.A. (2010a) 'Searching for escape, authenticity and identity: Experiences of "lifestyle travellers"', in M. Morgan, P. Lugosi and J. R. B. Ritchie (eds), *The Tourism and Leisure Experience: Consumer and managerial perspectives*, Channel View, Bristol.

Cohen, S.A. (2010b) 'Chasing a myth? Searching for "self" through lifestyle travel', *Tourist Studies*, vol. 10, no. 2, pp. 117–33.

Cohen, S. A. and Higham, J. E. S. (2011) 'Eyes wide shut? UK consumer perceptions on aviation climate impacts and travel decisions to New Zealand', *Current Issues in Tourism*, vol. 14, no. 4, pp. 323–35.

Cohen, S.A., Higham, J. E. S. and Cavaliere, C. T. (2011) 'Binge flying: behavioural addiction and climate change', *Annals of Tourism Research*, vol. 38, no. 3, pp. 1070–89.

Cohen, S. and Taylor, L. (1992) *Escape Attempts: The theory and practice of resistance to everyday life*, Routledge, London.

Crompton, J. (1979) 'Motivations for pleasure vacation', *Annals of Tourism Research*, vol. 6, no. 4, pp. 408–24.

Dann, G. (1977) 'Anomie, ego-enhancement and tourism', *Annals of Tourism Research*, vol. 4, no. 4, 184–94.

De Freitas, C. (2005) 'The climate–tourism relationship and its relevance to climate change impact assessment', in C. M. Hall and J. E. S. Higham (eds), *Tourism, Recreation and Climate Change,* Channel View, Bristol.

Dickinson, J. E., Lumsdon, L.M. and Robbins, D. (2011) 'Slow travel: Issues for tourism and climate change', *Journal of Sustainable Tourism*, vol. 19, no. 3, pp. 281–300.

Edensor, T. (2001) 'Performing tourism, staging tourism', *Tourist Studies*, vol. 1, no. 1, pp. 59–81.

Edensor, T. (2007) 'Mundane mobilities, performances and spaces of tourism', *Social and Cultural Geography*, vol. 8, no. 2, pp. 199–215.

Finnegan, R. (1997) '"Storying the self": Personal narratives and identity', in H. Mackay (ed.), *Consumption and Everyday Life*, Sage, London.

Goffman, E. (1959) *The Presentation of Self in Everyday Life*, Penguin, Middlesex.

Gössling, S. (2009) 'Carbon neutral destinations: a conceptual analysis', *Journal of Sustainable Tourism*, vol. 17, no. 1, pp. 17–37.

Gössling, S., Bredberg, M., Randow, A., Sandström, E. and Svensson, P. (2006) 'Tourist perceptions of climate change: a study of international tourists in Zanzibar', *Current Issues in Tourism*, vol. 9, nos 4&5, pp. 419–35.

Gössling, S., Haglund, L., Kallgren, H., Revahl, M. and Hultman, J. (2009) 'Swedish air travellers and voluntary carbon offsets: Towards the co-creation of environmental value', *Current Issues in Tourism*, vol. 12, no. 1, pp. 1–19.

Gössling, S., and Peeters, P. (2007) '"It does not harm the environment!" An analysis of industry discourses on tourism, air travel and the environment', *Journal of Sustainable Tourism*, vol. 15, no. 4, pp. 402–17.

Gössling, S., Peeters, P., and Scott, D. (2008) 'Consequences of climate policy for international tourist arrivals in developing countries', *Third World Quarterly*, vol. 29, no. 5, pp. 873–901.

Gössling, S., and Upham, P. (2009) *Climate Change and Aviation: Issues, challenges and solutions*, Earthscan, London.

Hares, A., Dickinson, J. and Wilkes, K. (2010) 'Climate change and the air travel decisions of UK tourists', *Journal of Transport Geography*, vol. 18, no. 3, pp. 66–473.

Higham, J.E.S. and Cohen, S.A. (2011) 'Canary in the coalmine: Norwegian attitudes towards climate change and extreme long-haul air travel to Aotearoa/New Zealand', *Tourism Management*, vol. 32, no. 1, pp. 98–105.

Høyer, K. (2000) 'Sustainable tourism or sustainable mobility? The Norwegian case', *Journal of Sustainable Tourism*, vol. 8, no. 2, pp. 147–60.

Kim, H. and Jamal, T. (2007) 'Touristic quest for existential authenticity', *Annals of Tourism Research*, vol. 34, no. 1, pp. 181–201.

Lett, J. W. (1983) 'Ludic and liminoid aspects of charter yacht tourism in the Caribbean', *Annals of Tourism Research*, vol. 10, no. 1, pp. 35–56.

Miller, G., Rathouse, K., Scarles, C., Holmes, K. and Tribe, J. (2010) 'Public understanding of sustainable tourism', *Annals of Tourism Research*, vol. 37, no. 3, pp. 627–45.

Morgan, M., Lugosi, P. and Ritchie, J. R. B. (2010) *The Tourism and Leisure Experience: Consumer and managerial perspectives*, Channel View, Bristol.

Peeters, P., and Dubois, G. (2010) 'Tourism travel under climate change mitigation constraints', *Journal of Transport Geography*, vol. 18, no. 3, pp. 447–57.

Randles, S., and Mander, S. (2009a) 'Aviation, consumption and the climate change debate: "Are you going to tell me off for flying?"', *Technology Analysis and Strategic Management*, vol. 21, no. 1, pp. 93–113.

Randles, S. and Mander, S. (2009b) 'Practice(s) and ratchet(s): a sociological examination of frequent flying', in S. Gössling and P. Upham (eds), *Climate Change and Aviation: Issues, challenges and solutions*, Earthscan, London.

Ryan, C. (1997) *The Tourist Experience: A new introduction*, Cassell, London.

Sharpley, R. (2003) *Tourism, Tourists and Society*, Elm, Huntingdon.

Smith, I. J. and Rodger, C. J. (2009) 'Carbon offsets for aviation-generated emissions due to international travel to and from New Zealand', *Energy Policy*, vol. 37, no. 9, pp. 3438–47.

Tung, V. W. S. and Ritchie, J. R. B. (2011) 'Exploring the essence of memorable tourism experiences', *Annals of Tourism Research*, vol. 38, no. 3, doi: 10.1016/j.annals.2011.03.009.

Turner, V. (1982) *From Ritual to Theatre: The human seriousness of play*, PAJ, New York.

Vaughan, G. M. and Hogg, M. A. (2002) *Introduction to Social Psychology*, 3rd edn, Pearson Education, Frenchs Forest, NSW.

Weaver, D. (2011) 'Can sustainable tourism survive climate change?', *Journal of Sustainable Tourism*, vol. 19, no. 1, pp. 5–15.

INDEX

Note: page references in *italics* indicate tables or figures

accommodation sector: and cost saving 73; uptake of environmental management systems 51; *see also* hotels
accreditation schemes 47–56, 134–5, 138, 139
acidification, ocean 176, 186
adaptation strategies 29, 60; Australia 124, 128–30, 187, 237; Brazil 221–2; developing countries 244, 251; Mediterranean region 167; negative 251; New Zealand 128–30; Pacific region 198, 199, 200, 203, 204–6; southern Africa/Botswana 244–5, 246, 249–50, 251–2; by tourism industry (Hawaii) 74–6; UK 114; Weaver on 251
Africa, southern: adaptation strategies 244, 246; impacts of climate change 245–6; vulnerability to climate change 244; *see also* Botswana
agriculture 13–14; Botswana 247, 248, 249, 250; Brazil 211, 213, 214, 217, 220
aid budgets 11
air conditioning 250, 251, 266
air travel 82–3, 228, 230, 258–9, 261; capacity restraints 169; costs 113; fuel consumption 88; long-haul 159, 160, 163, 192, 258; mitigation policies and 155, 156, 157–70, 192;

reluctance to reduce 128, 263–4, 265, 266; short-haul 158–9, 160, 169; tax on 158–9
Ali, Imam 54
Amazon region 211, 212
anchoring 26, 35
Anguilla 162
AP6 *see* Asia Pacific Partnership on Clean Development and Climate
APEC *see* Asia Pacific Economic Cooperation
arrivals 12, 67, 88, 89, 157–9, 160, 161, 162–4, 165, 166, 214–15
Asia Pacific Economic Cooperation (APEC): 162; conference (2007) 124
Asia Pacific Partnership on Clean Development and Climate (AP6) 122
Asia Pacific region: mitigation policies 162–4
associations, professional: discussions in 235; effectiveness 148; as information source 65; membership of 139; suitably placed to support environmental schemes 52, 54
auditing, environmental 136
AusAID 189
Australia: adaptation strategies 124, 128–30, 187, 237; attitude to Kyoto Protocol 120–1, 127; CCIA Gumnut Awards

43–6, 52, 53, 54; climate change
policy 117–24, 127–33; educational
tourism 92; and emissions 119, 120,
121, 123, 124; impacts of climate
change 118; industry attitudes to
environmental regulation 61;
political system 118–19; possible
benefits of mitigation policies 163–4;
SeaChange for Sustainable Tourism
46–9, 52; Symmetry project 49–51,
52; tourist economy 117; uptake of
sustainability schemes by SMEs
51–6; *see also* Great Barrier Reef
Australian Climate Change Science Program
– Strategic Research Agenda 122
Australian Greenhouse Office (AGO) 121,
123
Australian Industry Group 51
Australian International Development
Research Awards (ADRA) 189–90
Australian National Climate Change
Adaptation Programme 122
Australia's Climate Change Policy 124
awareness, environmental: of hoteliers 144;
of managers 141, 142, 148; of staff
147; of tourists 36–8; *see also*
perceptions

Bali Road Map (2007) 6, 13
Ban Ki-Moon 10, 83
Barbados Programme of Action 13
Barr, S. 37, 257, 263, 265
Barreirinhas, Brazil 215, 216, 217, 218
Basher, R. E. 125
Beach Climate Index (BCI) 98, 99–100,
105, 107–8, 111, 112
Becken, S. 60, 62, 128, 232
Beeton, R. J. S. 4–5
behaviour, inconsistencies in 259–60, 261,
263–8
Bellagio Conference (1996) 7
Bennett, J. 61, 71
biodiversity 5, 66, 85, 89, 118, 122, 136,
186, 211, 219, 220, 246
biosphere regions 87
biosphere reserves 81, 83–7, 89–95; buffer
zones 86; Jiuzhaigou Valley 89–90;
Lanzarote 86, *87*; Madrid Action
Plan 87, 89; Mata Atlantica 93;

Seville Strategy and Statutary
Framework 84–5, 89; Shouf 93;
Sierra Gorda 91; Wuyishan 88
Blanco, E. 54–5
Boko, M. 244
Bolger, Jim 124, 125
Bonaire 162
borders, protective 175
Boston, J. 129
Botswana: adaptation strategies 244–5, 246,
249–50, 251–2; case study 247–52;
economic returns of tourism 244;
estimated temperature rise 245;
impacts of climate change 246; map
248; vulnerability to climate change
244
Botswana Tourism Policy 252
Bournemouth, UK: climate projections
100, 101, 102–4, 107, 108, 109,
110, 112, 113–14; interviews on
climate concern 261
Bournemouth University 3, 261
Boykoff, M. T. 35
Bramwell, B. 8, 243
branding 50, 90
Brazil 87, 88, 209–26; agriculture 211, 213,
214, 217, 220; central/west 213;
climate change 210–14, 218–21;
environmental diversity 217; industry
213; Mata Atlantica reserve 93;
methodology of study 218–19; north
212; north-east/north coast *210*, 211,
212, 213, *214*, 214–22; policy 218,
221; seasons 216, 217, 219; south
213; south-east 213; tourism
development 214–18, 219–22; tourist
statistics 214–15, 216–17
Brazilian Tourism Development
Regionalization Programme 210
British Airways Environment Awards 142
Brundtland Commission: *Our Common
Future* (1987) 5, 6, 27
buffer zones 86
buildings: in biosphere reserves 86; effect of
sea level rise on 67
Business Environment Network 142

Caletrío, J. 259
Canary Islands 86

Cancun Agreements (COP16; 2010) 6, 13
Capivara Mountain Range, Brazil 215
Caravan and Camping Industry Association (CCIA) of NSW 51; Gumnut Awards 43–6, 52, 53, 54; Travelling Green program 53
carbon budgets 165, 169
carbon dioxide (CO₂) emissions: green economy approach to 13, 14; produced by tourism 42; scenarios of mitigation potential in 2035 *12*; tourism and 258; UNWTO projections *10*; *see also* greenhouse gas emissions
carbon dioxide (CO₂) levels: and acidification of oceans 176; in southern Africa 245
carbon footprints 88, 138
carbon offsets: biosphere reserves and 91, 93
carbon price 162–3, 166–7, 169
carbon tax 125, 127–8, 134, 159
carbon trading schemes *see* emissions trading schemes
Carbon Trust Award 138
Caribbean 219; Anguilla 162; Bonaire 162; coral reefs 180; Guadeloupe 165; Jamaica 160; Martinique 165; mitigation policies and 160–1
Carson, Rachel: *Silent Spring* 27
CCIA *see* Caravan and Camping Industry Association
Ceara, Brazil *210*, 215, 220
Central Finland's Tourism Strategy 2015 232–3, *233*
Ceron, J. -P. 164
Chamaillé-James, S. 245
chambers of commerce 52, 54, 140
Chan, E. 51, 52
Chapman, R. 129
'Charter for sustainable tourism' (1995) 7
China: biosphere reserves 88, 89–90; economic role of diaspora 88; poverty and emissions 82
Chobe National Park, Botswana 249
CIT *see* Climate Index for Tourism
Clancy, M. 122
climate change: awareness of (in tourism) 58, 60, 230–2; constraints

preventing responses to 59–61; definitions 25, 34; denial of human role in 64; dichotomy of approaches to tourism and 28–9; impact on tourism 42, 96–7; increased focus on 3, 27–8, 134; information sources 63–5; media coverage of 35; planning for 74; public perceptions of 34–5; relationship with sustainability 9–11, 24, 27–9, 34–6, 83, 187; role in tourism development strategies 227–42; social representations of 32–5; societal context 246; as too large an issue 235–6, 237; *see also* adaptation strategies; mitigation strategies; sustainability
Climate Change Adaptation Actions for Local Government, Australia 124
Climate Change Impact Model *177*, *178*, 186
Climate Change Office, New Zealand 128
Climate Impacts Programme, UK 97; *see also* UKCP09
Climate Index for Tourism (CIT) 112
Climate Net, Brazil 209
climate projections: data and methods 98–101; results of study 102–8; and South-West England 96–116; value of probabilistic projections 111
Climate South West, UK 114
CLIM-atic project, Finland 234
Club of Rome 5
COAG *see* Council of Australian Governments
coastlines: changing 114, 192, 212, 213, 214, 221; development 118, 129; erosion 113, 114, 191, 192, 212, 213; flooding 113, 114, 118, 191, 211, 212, 213
Coccossis, Harry N. 8
Coghlan, A. 173, 174, 177
Cohen, S. A. 259
Commonwealth Scientific and Industrial Research Organization (CSIRO) 123, 191
communities, local 43, 150, 176–7, 190, 191, 200, 205, 220, 221, 244; biosphere reserves and 85, 87, 93;

dependence on tourism 177, 178, 189; involvement of owners/managers in schemes 141; raising awareness of 251
companies: and environmental management 136, 138; *see also* corporate social responsibility; small enterprises; SMEs
competition 69, 144
consumer concern 55, 257–70; contextualized performances of 266–7; contradictions in 258–9, 260, 261, 263–5, 267–8; effect on demand 67; influence of 70, 144, 145; motivations for tourism 259–60; profile of programme participants *262*; study 260–8
consumption: approaches based on 128; energy 149; by households 155; negative consequences 28
Cook Islands 190
COP16 *see* Cancun Agreements
Copenhagen Summit and Accord (United Nations Climate Change Conference, 2009; COP15) 10, 14
coral reefs 173, 175–6, 185–6, 192; acidification 176, 186; bleaching 176, 186, 191; visitor experiences 180; *see also* Great Barrier Reef
core indicators 8
corporate social responsibility (CSR) 25, 27, 33, 47, 70, 72–3, 138–9, 143–4, 146–7
costs: to businesses 69, 72; fuel/energy 67, 73, 134, 135; saving 144, 145, 146; transport 68, 113
Council of Australian Governments (COAG) 123, 124
Creswell, J. 62
CSIRO *see* Commonwealth Scientific and Industrial Research Organization
CSR *see* corporate social responsibility
cyclones 118, 174, 191, 192, 200

Davos *see* Second International Conference on Climate Change and Tourism
demand, customer: affected by climate concern 67; low influence of 144, 145; *see also* consumer concern

Department for Environmental, Food and Rural Affairs (DEFRA), UK 97; *see also* UKCP09
desertification 211
developing countries: adaptation strategies 244, 251; agriculture 13–14; aid to 11; concerns of 82; economic development theory and 4–5; and green economy approach 14; mitigation policies 161–2, 168–9; *see also* small island developing states
diasporas, role of 88
Disaster Risk Reduction and Disaster Management Framework for Action (DRRDMFA) 198, 200
disasters: experience of 66; preparedness for 66, 73, 74
diving 175, 180, 192
Djerba *see* First International Conference on Climate Change and Tourism
Dodds, R. 237
Doha Declaration (2008) 11
domestic tourism 113, 158–9, 160, 161, 162, 163, 168, 214, 216
drought 118, 211, 212, 220, 246
Dunphy, D. 61, 65

Earth Summits *see* United Nations Conference on the Environment and Development (Rio, 1992); World Summit on Sustainable Development (Johannesburg, 2002)
Ebeling, S. 138
eco-development concept 82
Eco–Management and Audit Scheme (EMAS), UK 136
economic development theory 4–5
economic downturn 10–11, 82, 146
ecotourism 11, 38, 215
education: environmental 14; US land grant colleges 93
educational travel 92
El Niño – Southern Oscillation (ENSO) 191
elasticities, limitations of 157–8, 169
emissions *see* carbon dioxide emissions; greenhouse gas emissions
emissions trading schemes (ETS) 123, 124, 126, 127, 134, 160, 161, 169

employment: Botswana 247, 248–9;
provided by tourism 177, 189, 191,
213, 215, 221, 244; unemployment
82, 177; *see also* staff
energy: costs 67, 73, 134, 135; demand for
134; need for legislation on
consumption 149; renewable 122,
123, 250, 251
Energy Research and Development
Program (ERDP), Australia 120
Energy White Paper (Australia, 2004) 122
environmental management (EM) 135,
137–40, 142, 143, 144
environmental management plan (EMP) 48
environmental management systems (EMS)
135, 136, 137–9; barriers to 148–50;
certification schemes 145; enterprises
with a written policy 138; factors
influencing introduction of 144–7;
perceptions and attitudes of
managers 139–42; progress towards
146, 147, 148; social responsibility
and 143–4
environmental performance (EP) 134–5;
auditing 136; study of tourism
enterprises 136–52
environmentalism, development of 4, 27
ethics, environmental 68
ETS *see* emissions trading schemes
European Union (EU): carbon reduction
objectives 161–2; influence 144, 232
European Union Emissions Trading
Scheme (EUETS) 161–2
experience, past 66

fair trade 12, 25, 33
Falco-Mammone, F. 174
FAO *see* Food and Agriculture
Organization
ferries 158
Fiji 190, 191 196, 197–8, 199, 202–3, 232
Finland: consideration of climate change
and sustainability in tourism
development strategies *231*, 232–4;
interview study 229–30, 234–6;
local level strategies 233–4, 237–8;
local/regional/national policy 229;
regional strategies 232–3, *233*,
237–8; seasonality 234

Finnish Ski Area Association 235
First International Conference on Climate
Change and Tourism (Djerba,
2003) 9
First International Forum on 'Sustainability,
Climate Change and Tourism'
(Bournemouth, 2009) 3
fish: Brazil 220; Great Barrier Reef 183
Flick, U. 29
flood risk: Brazil 211, 213; coastal 113,
114, 118, 191, 211, 212, 213
Food and Agriculture Organization (FAO)
10–11
Forestry Policy (Tonga) 204
Foster, J. 29
French overseas territories 164–6
French Polynesia 165
Fritz, H. 245
fuel: airline consumption 88, 159; carbon-
neutral 156; costs 67

Galapagos Islands 87
GGE *see* greenhouse gas emissions
Glasgow Caledonian University 137
Global Environment Facility (GEF) 199
Global Tourism and Transport
(GTTMadv) model 163
global warming 9, 34, 58, 123; target limit
155; *see also* heatwaves; temperature
rise
globalization 228
Goffman, E. 260
Gossling, S. 11, 60, 128, 161–2, 228, 259
governments: ineffective policies 69, 71;
intervention of 60–1, 67, 71, 135,
144, 149–50, 221; lack of trust in
71; responsibilities expected of 72; as
sources of information 64–5; *see also*
policy
Graci, S. 237
grants 52, 53, 54
Great Barrier Reef (GBR) 118, 173–88;
climate change impact model *177*,
178, 186; fish and marine animals
183–4, 186; literature on impacts of
climate change 175–8; Michaelmas
Cay 178–9, 181–5, 186; Moore
Reef 178, 179, 182–5, 186; need for
positive message about 174; Paradise

Reef 178–9, 181–5, 186; survey of tourist response to climate change impacts 178–87; tourism activities and safeguards 175

Great Barrier Reef Marine Park Authority (GBRMPA) 173, 175

Green Economy approach 13–15, 19–20

Green Tourism Business Scheme (GTBS), UK 136, 138, 139

Greenbiz 147

Greenhouse Gas Abatement Program (GGAP), Australia 121

greenhouse gas (GHG) emissions (GGE): accommodation sector and 73; agriculture's contribution to 13–14; air travel and 82–3, 158–9; anthropogenic 64, 118, 119, 127, 211; AP6 and 122; Australia and 119, 120, 121, 123, 124; emissions trading schemes (ETS) 123, 124, 126, 127, 134, 160, 161, 169; green economy approach to 13, 14; Kyoto Protocol and 82, 119–20; mitigation policies 155–70; New Zealand and 126–7; and ocean acidification 176; projections 155; Scottish policy 136; sinks 120, 127; tourism's contribution to 3, 9–10, 42–3, 118, 155–6, 230; *see also* carbon dioxide emissions

greening markets 68, 72

Grindlinger, Brooke 92

Guadeloupe 165

Guo, D. 245

Hall, C. M. 8, 11, 60, 128, 129, 237

Hamburg tourism model 159–60

Hardy, A. L. 4–5

Hares, A. 259, 265

Hart, P. 60, 62, 128

Hawaii 60, 62–78; constraints and influences on action 68–70; coral reefs 180; environmental concern 66–8; findings of qualitative study into tourism industry responses to climate change 63–75; methodology of study 59, 62–3; question of responsibility 70–3; strategy formulation and implementation 73–5

Hawaii Tourism Strategic Plan 74

heatwaves: Brazil 220; effect on tourism 113–14; projecting 101, 109, 110, 112

Hendriks, C. 122

Hewson, John 127

Higham, J. E. S. 60, 259

Historic Scotland 138

HIV-AIDS 11

Holden, A. 8

Hong Kong: hotels 51

hotels: in biosphere reserves 90, 91; centralized ownership and management 70; initiatives by 73; managers' perceptions of demand for 'green' hotels 145; and oil prices 160; poor progress towards environmental management 147; uptake of environmental management schemes 51

Howard, John 118, 119, 121, 123, 124, 127, 129

humidity, relative 100

Hunter, C. 8

hurricanes 66, 74, 176

Huybers, T. 61, 71

Hwange National Park, Zimbabwe 245

identities: multiple 267; personal 260, 268

INCT *see* National Institute of Science and Technology for Climate Change

Independent, The 86

India 82, 87, 88

indirect tourism income multiplier 163

industrialized nations 82

information *see* knowledge

infrastructure: biosphere reserves and 86–7, 90–1; Botswana 248–9; Pacific Islands 192; South-West England 113-14

Inskeep, E. 227

Institute for Responsible Tourism, Spain 91

Institute of Hospitality, UK 139, 140

Intergovernmental Panel on Climate Change (IPCC) 9, 221, 245; on Australia and New Zealand 118, 128–9; on emissions 127; reports 60, 63, 96, 128, 156, 191, 211;

supported in New Zealand 124, 125, 127

International Hotels Environment Initiative 142

International Union for the Conservation of Nature (IUCN) 5, 6

internet 35, 64

IPCC *see* Intergovernmental Panel on Climate Change

ISO 14001 (international standard) 136, 142

IUCN *see* International Union for the Conservation of Nature

Jamaica 160

Jamal, T. 260

Jämsä, Finland 229, 233–5

Jansen, B. J. 35

Jericoacoara National Park, Brazil *215*, 215–17, 218, 219, 220, 221

Jiuzhaigou Valley Biosphere Reserve (JVBR), China 89–90

Journal of Sustainable Tourism 7

Kgalagadi (Kalahari), Botswana 247, *248*, 249–50

Kgalagadi Transfrontier Park (KTP) 247, 250

Kim, H. 260

Kittilä, Finland 229, 233–5

knowledge: availability of information 60, 74; gaps 11, 46, 50, 52, 55, 65, 75; indigenous 14; receptivity to 46; role of media 35; sources of 63–6, 75

Kolari, Finland 234

Kyoto Protocol (1997) 6, 9, 13, 119–20, 155; AP6 and 122; Australia's and New Zealand's attitudes to 120–1, 126, 127; definition of climate change 25, 34

Lake District National Park, UK 136–7, 140, 146

Lane, B. 243

Lanzarote Biosphere Reserve 86, *87*

Lanzarote Conference (1995) 7

Lapland: local development agencies 235–6

Lapland's Tourism Strategy 2007–2010 232–3, *233*

Latin America 211, 214; *see also* Brazil

leadership, need for 70, 76, 149

Lençóis Maranhenses National Park, Brazil *215*, 215–17, 218, 219, 220, 221

Liberal Party, Australian 127

liminoid space 259–60, 264–5, 267

Limits to Growth (report) 5

local produce and products 143–4, 146, 149, 220

long-haul tourism 159, 160, 163, 192, 258

Macarthur Business Enterprise Centre (MBEC) 49, 50

Macarthur Centre for Sustainable Living (MCSL) 49

Macarthur region, Australia 49–51

Macarthur Regional Organization of Councils (MACROC) 49

McNamara, K. E. 173, 177

Madagascar 162

Madrid Action Plan for Biosphere Reserves 87, 89

Malaysia 163, 164

Malthus, Thomas 27

Man and the Biosphere (MAB) Programme 83, 93

Management of the Environmental Effects Associated with the Tourism Sector (New Zealand report, 1997) 125

managers: barriers to action by 148–50; factors influencing 144–7; membership of organizations 139, *140*, 142; perceptions and attitudes 139–42, 249–50; social representations (SRs) of 30–5; and social responsibility 143–4

Mandated Renewable Energy Targets (MRET), Australia 121, 122

Mander, S. 264

mangroves 192, 220

Manly, Australia 46–9

Mansfield, M. 35

Maranhao, Brazil *210*, 215, 220

Marengo, J. A. 211, 214

marketing: of accreditation schemes 50, 53, 55; advantages of being 'green' 46, 70, 72; being 'green' used as a ploy 140, 141; branding and logos 50; positive *vs.* negative 174

Marrakech Process 13
Marshall, J. 53
Martinique 165
Masero, S. 135
Mata Atlantica Biosphere Reserve,
    Brazil 93
Mather, S. 65, 70
Maun, Botswana 247–8, *248*, 249, 250,
    251
Mauritius Declaration (2005) 13
MDGs *see* Millennium Development Goals
MEA *see* Millennium Ecosystem
    Assessment
Measures for a Better Environment,
    Australia 121
media: coverage of climate change 35;
    influence on tourists 186; positivity
    vs. negativity 174; as source of
    information 64, 75, 235;
    trustworthiness 64
Mediterranean region 96, 113, 166–8
metaphor 26
Michel Batisse Award 93
micro-businesses 135, 136, 138
Midgley, G. F. 245
Mieczkowski, Z. 98–9, 104
Millennium Development Goals (MDGs)
    8, 10, 11, 12, 189, 191
Millennium Ecosystem Assessment (MEA;
    2005) 11, 13, 92
Miller, G. 258–9
mind maps 30, 33–4
mining 27, 38, 49, 246
mitigation strategies 29, 42–3, 60; Australia
    and 124, 128, 129; Brazil 221–2;
    case studies 159–70; customers'
    influence on 70; industry action 73,
    75–6; methodological options for
    assessing and modelling 157–9,
    168–9; New Zealand 126–7, 128,
    129; tourism sensitivity to 155–72
modelling 157–9, 168–9
modernist theory 259–60
Monterrey Consensus (2002) 11
Moore, R. 196
Moremi game reserve, Botswana 249
Morgan, R. 98, 99
Morill Land-Grant Act (USA, 1862) 93
Moscovici, Serge 26

mosquito-borne diseases 191, 212, 213
Murindagomo, F. 245

Namibia 245
National Adaptation Programmes for
    Action (NAPA) 198, 199, 203
National Climate Change Adaptation
    Framework, Australia 123, 124
National Energy Efficiency Program,
    Australia 120
National Greenhouse Strategy,
    Australia 121
National Institute of Science and
    Technology for Climate Change
    (INCT), Brazil 209
National Science Strategy Committee on
    Climate Change (NSSCCC), New
    Zealand 124, 127–8
National Trust, UK 114, 138, 140
National Weather Service, UK 97
New Caledonia 165, 190
New South Wales, Australia: assistance
    programs 52; caravanning and
    camping 43–6, 51; Macarthur region
    49–51; Manly (resort) 46–9;
    Sustainable Development
    Conference 51; tourist
    accommodation 51
New Zealand: attitude to Kyoto Protocol
    120, 127; Becken and Hart study of
    stakeholders 62; climate change
    policy 117–20, 124–33, 237;
    emissions 121; impacts of climate
    change 118; lack of adaptation
    strategy 128–30; political system
    118–19; possible benefits of
    mitigation policies 163–4; tourism
    expenditure 117
New Zealand Climate Change Office
    (NZCCO) 125–6
New Zealand Climate Change Program
    124
New Zealand Emissions Trading Scheme
    (NZETS) 126
*New Zealand Tourism and Climate Change
    Plan* 128
New Zealand Tourism Strategy 2010 125
New Zealand Tourism Strategy 2015 126
New Zealand Transport Strategy 125

Ngamiland District, Botswana 247–8, *248*
Nianyong, H. 90
Nordic countries 227–42; sustainable
    tourism strategies 231–2; *see also*
    Finland; Norway; Sweden
Norway: consideration of climate change
    in tourism strategies *231*; consumer
    concern 257–8, 261–7; and
    sustainability 232

objectification 26
oceans: acidification 176, 186; *see also* sea
    level rise
oil: availability 67; prices 160, 162
Okavango Delta, Botswana 246, 247–9,
    248, 250

Pacific Adaptation to Climate Change
    (PACC) project 198, 201
Pacific Islands Framework for Action on
    Climate Change (PIFACC) 198, 200
Pacific Plan (2005) 198, 201
Pacific region: adaptation policies 198, 199,
    200, 203, 204–6; key regional
    climate-change policies *200–1*;
    mitigation policies 162–4; tourism
    190–2; *see also* Hawaii; South Pacific
    SIDS
Pacific Tourism-Climate Adaptation
    Project (PT-CAP) 189–90, 192–
    206; findings 198–205; frameworks
    and approaches 192–8; implications
    and recommendations 205–6
Palau 190
Palmer, Geoffrey 124
Papua New Guinea (PNG) 164, 190, 196,
    203–5
Parnaiba delta, Brazil 215, *215*
Parpairis, Apostolos 8
peace parks 247
Peacock, Andrew 127
Pearman, Graeme 123
Peeters, Paul 128, 161, 164, 259
Pentelowe, L. 160, *161*
Penzance, UK 100, 101, 104, 107, 108,
    109, 110, 111, 112
perceptions: management 139–42, 249–50;
    public 34–8; visitor 173–4, 178, 187;
    see also awareness

personal beliefs, role of 50
Piaui, Brazil *210*, 215
PICs (Pacific Island Countries) *see* Pacific
    region; South Pacific
pilgrimages 92
Pittock, Barrie 123
planning 74, 112–15
PNG *see* Papua New Guinea
policy: Australia and New Zealand 117–33;
    Botswana 252; Brazil 218, 221;
    local/regional/national 229; policy
    makers' lack of access to information
    237; scenarios *167*; South Pacific
    SIDS 192–206; UK 135–6; *see also*
    adaptation strategies; governments;
    mitigation strategies
Policy Research Contract Scheme, New
    Zealand 124
pollution: cost of control measures 54–5;
    produced by tourist traffic 114
Poole, UK 102, 113–14
population growth 8, 13, 118, 203, 204
postmodernist theory 259, 260, 267
poverty 14, 155, 161; Botswana 251; Brazil
    217; China and India 82; reduction
    through tourism 12, 88, 156, 189,
    191, 244
Preigo, M. J. B. 138
prices: carbon 162–3, 166–7, 169;
    competitiveness 69; effect of carbon
    tax on 159; energy 135; increases 42,
    134; oil 160, 162
Prideaux, Bruce 173, 174, 177
profitability 72, 145–6
psychoanalysis 26
PT-CAP *see* Pacific Tourism-Climate
    Adaptation Project
public private partnership 206

Queensland, Australia 118, 177
Quesnay, Francoise 27

railways 167, 168, 169
rainfall: Australia and New Zealand 118;
    Botswana 247, 249; Brazil 213, 216,
    217, 219; Pacific region 191;
    projecting 101, 109, 110, 112;
    southern Africa 245; vulnerability of
    South-West England 113

rainforests 174, 177, 211
Randles, S. 264
Rayleigh distribution: of wind speeds 100
reactive culture 69
Recife, Brazil 214
recycling 138, 264
REDD+ (reducing emissions from
    deforestation and forest degradation)
    14
Reddy, Shaw and Williams 221
regulation: compliance with 61; need for
    149–50; self- 60–1, 71, 72;
    unawareness of 144; *see also*
    governments; policy
Resource Management Act (New Zealand,
    1991) 124, 125, 128
'responsible': use of term 25
responsibility 70–3, 75; social 143–4; *see
    also* corporate social responsibility
Reunion Island 165, 166
Rio conferences *see* United Nations
    Conference on the Environment and
    Development, Rio, 1992; United
    Nations Conference on Sustainable
    Development (Rio+20), 2012
risk management 74
Rovaniemi, Finland 234
Ruhanen, L. 237

Saarinen, J. 251
safaris 246
Safeguarding the Future, Australia 120–1
salinization 191, 211, 221
Salvador, Brazil 215
Samoa 190, 196, 197–8, 199, 202–3
sand dunes 215, 217, 220, 246
Saudi Arabia 88
Scandinavia 227–42; sustainable tourism
    strategies 231–2; *see also* Finland;
    Norway; Sweden
Scheffer, M. 211
science: Australian government's attitude to
    123; everyday interpretation of 26;
    as information source 63, 64; New
    Zealand and 124–5
Scotland 135, 137, 138, 140
Scott, D. 3, 11, 128, 160, 161, 251, 259
sea level rise: Brazil and 211, 213, 214,
    219, 220, 221; coral reefs and 176;

Hawaii and 66; Pacific 189, 191,
    192; South-West England and 96,
    111, 113
sea temperature rise 176, 186
Seachange for Sustainable Tourism,
    Australia 46–9, 52
Second International Conference on
    Climate Change and Tourism
    (Davos, 2007) 9
self-regulation, industry 60–1, 71, 72
Sem, G. 196
Seville Strategy 84–5, 89
Seychelles 161, 162
shareholders 70
sharks 183
shellfish 183, 220
Shipley, Jenny 124, 125
shipping 156; cruises 68; ferries 158
short-haul tourism 158–9, 160, 169
Shouf Biosphere Reserve, Lebanon 93
SIDS *see* small island developing states
Sierra Gorda Biosphere Reserve,
    Mexico 91
sightseeing 99, 112
Simmons, B. 52, 54
Simpson, M. C. 228
Singapore 163, 164
skiing destinations 229, 234–6, 238
slow travel concept 158, 258
small enterprises: and environmental
    performance and management 135,
    136, 138, 141; need for regulation
    149–50; and social responsibility
    143; *see also* SMEs
small island developing states (SIDS) 9, 14,
    82–3, 161; Mauritius Declaration
    13; mitigation policies 161–2; South
    Pacific 189–208; vulnerable
    characteristics 196
SMEs (small to medium businesses):
    Australian environmental tourism
    schemes for 42–57; barriers to
    adoption of schemes for 52–6;
    climate change as low-level concern
    237; lack of engagement by 51–2;
    see also small enterprises
Smith, Adam 27
snowball sampling technique 230, 261
social change 14, 15

social constructionist approach 62
social democracy 8
social psychology 26
social representations (SRs) 26, 29; of managers 30–5; public 35–8
social representations theory (SRT) 24, 26, 29–41; visual images and mind maps 26, 30–5
social responsibility 143–4; *see also* corporate social responsibility
sociocultural issues 58–9, 249, 251
socio-ecological interactions 246, 249
sociology 26
soil contamination 217
solar panels 14
Solomon Islands 190, 196, 203–5
SOPAC (Applied Geoscience and Technology Division of the Secretariat of the Pacific Community) 200, 206
South Pacific Regional Environment Programme (SPREP) 200, 201, 206
South Pacific SIDS 60, 189–208; policy analysis approaches and frameworks 192–8; policy analysis findings 198–205; recommendations 205–6; tourism 190–2
South Pacific Tourism Organisation (SPTO) 206
South-West England, interpreting climate projections for 96–116; data and methods of study 98–101; discussion on projections 111–12; incidence of extreme weather 101, 109–11; results of study 102–8; risks to coastline 113, 114; tourism planning 112–15; value of tourism economy 112–13; vulnerability to weather events 113
South West Tourism Alliance, UK 97, 112
Spink, A. 35
Sri Lanka 162
SRs *see* social representations
SRT *see* social representations theory
staff: retention of 146–7; role of 72
stakeholders: environmental performance of enterprises (UK) 134–52; level of understanding of climate change and sustainability (Finnish study) 232,

234–6, 237; New Zealand studies of 128; social representations (SRs) of 29–37; *see also* hotels; managers; SMEs; tourists
Starkey, R. 135
Stavanger, Norway 261
Stewart, J. 122
Stockholm Conference (UN Conference on Human Environment, 1972) 5, 6, 8, 81, 82
storm surges 43, 66, 113
storms 67, 118; *see also* cyclones; hurricanes
Strasdas, W. 42, 55
subsidization 50; *see also* grants
Surinam 161
sustainability: and behaviour of tourists 261, 263; categories of businesses' responses to 61; definition 25; five dimensions of 25; focus on 3, 28; growing awareness in tourism 230–2; history of 27–8; local and global relevance to tourism 227–8; relationship with climate change 9–11, 24, 27–9, 34–6, 83, 187; sociocultural issues 58–9, 249, 251; three pillars of 5; tourism industry's attitude to 60; visual images and mind maps 26, 30–5; *see also* climate change; sustainable development
sustainable development: application to tourism 4, 7; Ban Ki-Moon on 83; and climate change and tourism 87–9; emergence as paradigm 227; key events 6; origins of concept 82; shifts in focus 4–11, 27
sustainable living: twelve most frequently mentioned guidelines for 36
Sustainable Restaurant Association, UK 143
sustainable tourism: four forms of 8; scholars on 8–9
'Sustainable tourism plan of action' (1995) 7
Sweden 231, 232
swimming pools 250, 251
Sydney, Australia 46–7, 49
Symmetry Sustainable Business Project, Australia 49–51, 42

Tahiti 190
taxation 67; on air travel 158–9; carbon tax 125, 127–8, 134, 159; incentives 72, 144
TCI *see* Tourism Climate Index
temperature rise: Brazil 211, 212, 213, 220; Pacific 191; seas 176, 186; southern Africa/Botswana 245, 249, 250; *see also* global warming
Tervo-Kankare, K. 251
Thailand 163, 164
Tol, R. S. J. 159
Tonga 196, 203–5
tourism: all-year 238; cultural 215; domestic 113, 158–9, 160, 161, 162, 163, 168, 214, 216; ecotourism 11, 38, 215; educational 92; 'high-end' 246; inbound 92, 162, 163, 219; long-haul 159, 160, 163, 192, 258; nature-based 42, 49, 246, 247, 250, 252; recreational 93, 175, 219, 220; short-haul 158–9, 160, 169; visiting friends and relatives (VFR) traffic 165; *see also* tourism industry; tourists
Tourism and Climate Change Taskforce, Australia 123
'Tourism, Climate Change and Sustainability' (2012 conference) 15
Tourism Climatic Index (TCI) 98–9, 100–1, 102–7, 111, 112
Tourism Council of Australia 61
tourism industry: action by 73–6; application of sustainable development to 4, 7; arrivals 12, 67, 88–9, 157–9, 160, 161, 162–4, 165, 166, 214–15; awareness and understanding of climate change 60, 230–2; concerns of 66–8, 75; Brazil statistics 214–15; community dependence on 177, 178, 179; constraints and influences on 68–70, 75; contribution to emissions 3, 9–10, 42–3, 118, 155–6, 230; development strategies 227–42; dichotomy of approaches to climate change and 28–9; duality of relationship with climate change 228, 231, 243; economic

contribution of 12, 82, 88–9, 90, 93, 117, 189, 190–1, 213, 215, 217, 244; as employer 177, 189, 191, 213, 215, 221, 244; environmental performance of enterprises 134–52; green economy approach to 14–15; growth statistics 12; Hawaiian survey of 62–78; history of sustainability in 28–9; impact of climate change 42, 96–7; increasing role of 11–12, 83; as information source 65; knowledge sources 63–6, 75; lack of planning 74; local *vs.* global focus on 227–8; need for leadership 70, 76; Pacific 190–2; responses to environmental regulation 60–1; responsibility of 71–3, 75; role of diasporas 88–9; self-regulation 60–1, 71; sensitivity to climate change 189, 191, 205, 206; sensitivity to mitigation policies 155–72; as social system 246; SRT approach to 26; *see also* stakeholders; tourism; tourists
Tourism Minister's Council, Australia 123
Tourism Northern Territory, Australia 42
Tourism Society, UK 139, 140
Tourism Task Force, UK 136
Tourism White Paper (Australia, 2004) 122, 128
tourists: awareness and behaviour 36–8; changing perceptions of 173–4; importance of weather to 113; motivations of 92, 259–60, 263–5; positive and negative perceptions by 174, 178, 187; pre-trip expectations 186; sustainable behaviour of 261, 263, 265; *see also* consumer concern; demand, customer; tourism
transport: costs 68, 113; and emissions 118, 127, 128, 230; infrastructure modification 167, 169; as low priority 36; pollution from 114; slow travel concept 158, 258; *see also* air travel; railways
tree planting 250, 251
Tshabong, Botswana 247, 249–50, 251
Tsodilo Hills, Botswana 249
Turner, V. 260

turtles, marine 176, 183
Turton, S. 237

UKCP09 97–116; data and methods
    98–101; discussion 111–12;
    incidence of extreme weather 101,
    109–11; relevance for tourism
    planning 112–15; results 102–8;
    Threshold Detector (TD) 101,
    109–11, 112; Weather Generator
    (WG) 101, 111
Umbrella Group 120
unemployment 82, 177
United Kingdom (UK): consumer concern
    257–9, 261–7; lack of adaptation
    policy 114; surveys of tourism
    enterprises 136–50; tourism policy
    135–6; *see also* Scotland; South-West
    England; UKCP09
United Nations Climate Change
    Conference (Copenhagen, 2009) 10,
    14
United Nations Conference on Human
    Environment *see* Stockholm
    Conference
United Nations Conference on Sustainable
    Development (Rio+20), 2012
    6, 13–15, 81, 82, 83
United Nations Conference on the
    Environment and Development
    (UNCED), Rio de Janeiro, 1992 6,
    7, 81, 119, 209; 'Agenda 21' 7, 134;
    assessment of progress 8; criticisms of
    15
United Nations Convention on Biological
    Diversity (1997) 7
United Nations Development Programme
    (UNDP) 13, 199, 201
United Nations Educational, Scientific and
    Cultural Organization (UNESCO)
    13; biosphere reserves 81, 83–95;
    Madrid Action Plan 87, 89; Seville
    Strategy 84–5, 89; World Heritage
    sites 86, 89–90, 175, 215
United Nations Environment Programme
    (UNEP) 13, 27, 82, 166; Marrakech
    Process 13; Mediterranean action
    plan 166–8; *Towards a Green
    Economy* 13, 14–15

United Nations Framework Convention
    on Climate Change (UNFCCC),
    1992 7, 9, 119, 198, 204;
    Conference of Parties 82; definition
    of climate change 25, 34
United Nations Geneva Preparatory
    Conference (2011) 14
United Nations International Conference
    on Financing for Development
    (Doha, 2008) 11
United Nations Research Institute for Social
    Development (UNRISD) 13, 14
United Nations World Tourism
    Organization (UNWTO) 209,
    243–4; 'core indicators' 8; on
    emissions 10, 156; reports 9, 12
Upton, Simon 124–5, 127

Vanuatu 190, 191, 196, 197–8, 199, 202–3
Vietnam 87, 164
visiting friends and relatives (VFR) traffic
    165
VisitScotland 136, 140
visual images 26, 30–2

Wain, Fiona 121–2
water resources: Australia and New
    Zealand 118; Botswana 250; Brazil
    211, 212, 213, 214, 220;
    contamination 217; salinization 191
weather patterns, extreme: Australia and
    New Zealand 118; Brazil 212;
    forecasting 67; Hawaii 66, 67;
    South-West England 96, 101,
    109–11, 114; unpredictable 113
Weaver, D. 7, 8, 11–12, 251
Weber, E. U. 27
Welford, R. 135
Western Cape 245
Western Sydney, University of (UWS) 43,
    47, 49
Whitbread plc 138
Wilkins, R.: *Strategic Review of Australian
    Government Climate Change Progams*
    121
wind: counterpoint to high temperatures
    219; effect of decrease in 245;
    measuring values of 100, 104, 112;
    sports 219

winter sports destinations 229, 234–6, 238, 244

World Commission on Environment and Development *see* Brundtland Commission

World Congresses of Biosphere Reserves 83, 84–5

World Conservation Strategy (IUCN, 1982) 5, 6

World Economic Impact Report (WTTC, 2012) 12

World Heritage sites 86, 89–90, 175, 215

World Network of Biosphere Reserves (WNBR) 81, 83–7, 89–90, 93; Seville Strategy 84–5, 89

World Summit on Sustainable Development (Johannesburg, 2002) 6, 7–8, 81; three pillars 82, 83

World Tourism Organization *see* United Nations World Tourism Organization

World Travel and Tourism Council (WTTC) 12, 244

World Wide Fund for Nature 140, 213

Worldwide serious climate policy (WSCP) 161–2

Wuyishan Biosphere Reserve, China 88

Zimbabwe 245